CURRICULUM

CURRICULUM
A Comprehensive Introduction

THIRD EDITION

John D. McNeil
University of California, Los Angeles

LITTLE, BROWN AND COMPANY
Boston   Toronto

Library of Congress Cataloging in Publication Data

McNeil, John D.
    Curriculum: a comprehensive introduction.

    Includes bibliographical references and index.
    1. Curriculum planning.   I. Title.
LB1570.M3178   1984   375'.001   84-21298
ISBN 0-316-56321-8

Library of Congress Catalog Card Number 84-21298

ISBN 0-316-56321-8

9 8 7 6 5 4 3 2 1

MV

Published simultaneously in Canada
by Little, Brown & Company (Canada) Limited

Printed in the United States of America

Acknowledgments

    Excerpt, p. 34: From Schools in Search of Meaning, ASCD Yearbook, 1975. Reprinted by permission of the publisher.
    Excerpt, p. 103: From Michael W. Kirst and Decker F. Walker, "An Analysis of Curriculum Policy Making," Review of Educational Research 41, no. 5 (December 1971): 485. Copyright 1971 by American Educational Research Association, Washington, D.C. Reprinted by permission.
    Excerpt, p. 149: From Collected Poems by Edna St. Vincent Millay. Copyright 1939, 1967 by Edna St. Vincent Millay and Norma Millay Ellis. Reprinted by permission of Norma Millay Ellis.
    Excerpt, p. 169: From Michael Kirst, "Policy Implications of Individual Differences and the Common Curriculum," Individual Differences and the Common Curriculum, NSSE Yearbook, 1983, published by University of Chicago Press. Reprinted by permission of the National Society for Study of Education.

Excerpt, pp. 209–210: Adapted from David Nevo, "The Conceptualization of Educational Evaluation," *Review of Educational Research* 53, no. 11 (Spring 1983). Reprinted by permission of the American Education Research Association.

Table 10.1: From R.E. Stake, "The Countenance of Educational Evaluation," in *Teachers College Record* 68 (1967). Reprinted by permission of Teachers College, Columbia University.

Excerpt, pp. 221–222: Drawn with permission from IOX *Illustrative Criterion-Referenced Test Specifications: Aesthetics K-12.* Los Angeles: Instructional Objectives Exchange, 1980.

Excerpt, p. 231: From Michael W. Kirst and Decker F. Walker, "An Analysis of Curriculum Policy Making," *Review of Educational Research* 41, no. 5 (1971). Copyright 1971 by American Educational Research Association, Washington, D.C. Reprinted by permission.

Preface

Educational reform is at the forefront. There is a common goal: to make excellence in the schools a reality. But how do we achieve that goal? That is where views diverge. What subject matter is most important for excellence? One group considers mathematics and science most important for all; another group gives priority to language; and another group emphasizes technology. There are still others who argue that academic achievement is less important than other goals, such as cognitive development, employment, self-worth, or the creation of a just society.

In addition to conflict about purpose and content, there are differences about many aspects of curriculum: how to improve textbooks, how to improve the education of minorities, how to organize programs and courses for effective learning, how to grant more students access to valued cultural resources, how to attain high standards without standardization. *Curriculum: A Comprehensive Introduction* is a tool for addressing the problems and issues of educational reform. It offers new procedures for answering the old questions of *what* and *how* to teach. The book is unique in spanning conflicting orientations to curriculum making: humanistic, academic, technological, and social reconstruction. Rather than presenting only one prescription or way of thinking, the analysis of various orientations will help all students of curriculum understand why some orientations are superior to others in achieving specific purposes. Stimulating the kinds of deliberation—the coalescing of aims, data, and judgments—that make creative planning possible is a pervading goal of this book.

Although this book is intended primarily for use in college and university courses in curriculum, it will prove useful to practicing teachers, administrators, parents, and concerned citizens who wish to engage in serious reflection about curriculum. The text provides realistic examples of curriculum drawn from elementary, secondary, and higher education, as well as from training programs and informal educational contexts so that the reader can connect generalizations to reality.

Readers are given an opportunity to acquire concepts from many fields of study in examining their curriculum problems.

Curriculum development at the local level is now on center stage. This is so, in part, because we now recognize that curriculum must be adapted to local interests and to the particular individuals to be served. At the same time, there should be a balance between the demands for programs reflecting world and national needs and the requirements of local communities. A further reason for the popularity of local curriculum development rests on the desire for effective schools. Effective schools are characterized by a strong sense of community and commonly shared goals and high expectations for student and staff performance. It is the interaction of administrators, teachers, and parents in planning, designing, evaluating, and preparing learning opportunities that enhances school efficacy. *Curriculum: A Comprehensive Introduction* offers practical suggestions for developing programs, courses, and materials to meet new demands. An innovative feature in this third edition is a focus upon the administrator's role in curriculum. Special attention is given to political influences and factors associated with successful programs. Concurrently, more emphasis has been given to the role of teachers in developing curriculum for their students. Attempts are made to help relate what you already know to the larger curriculum process. You are not expected, however, to have a knowledge of the technical skills needed in making curriculum. The necessary curriculum concepts and methods are explained and developed as required.

I have strived to articulate realistic notions of what constitutes curriculum and have suggested ways to do better the things that are necessary. Everything that ought to be known about curriculum has not been put into this book. Conversely, not all readers and instructors will want to give equal emphasis to each topic. For example, those preparing to be curriculum scholars will devote more attention to the chapters on curriculum theory, history, and research. Moreover, each topic has been given a certain degree of independence. The order in which the topics are sequenced may be changed. For example, some might choose to start with the last part of the book, preferring to have the curriculum field defined before embarking on its study.

Part I examines four prevailing conceptions of curriculum. The assumptions underlying these different orientations with respect to curriculum purpose, method, organization, and evaluation provide a framework for relating many subsequent topics. Part II features special knowledge of curriculum development. The chapters in this part help answer questions like "*What* should be taught," "*how* should it be taught," and "*how* can curriculum best be designed or organized." By examining various curriculum models, techniques, and practices, we can gain important insights into the task of making curriculum decisions. Part III continues with the art and techniques of curriculum making by focusing on the important problems of how to administer, implement, and evaluate the curriculum. This part also examines curriculum in a wider context and from a broader point of view, presenting a realistic picture of curriculum policy making.

Part IV deals with issues and trends of importance to citizens and curriculum specialists alike. Key issues such as bilingual education and the problem of giving all students access to prestigious knowledge are considered. In this third edition, more emphasis has been given to the importance of vocational education and how it can contribute to the learning of academic subjects. Trends in the teaching of the various subject matters are shown and criticized. Basic to the criticism is whether subject matter (a) should be used to develop an elite body of scholars in the field, (b) should be presented as an intellectual tool for helping all learners make wise judgments about society and its problems, or (c) should be regarded as a resource by which learners can construct personal meaning.

Finally, Part V is devoted to curriculum as field of study. One chapter creates a historical perspective of the field, and shows our inherited ways of thinking about curriculum problems. The last chapter describes the work of the scholars in the field of curriculum. The content of this chapter indicates the kinds of studies which will explain the nature of "the curriculum" and stakes out the domains and processes of curriculum inquiry.

This revised edition contains the major principles and concepts that were featured in the earlier editions. The content, however, is different in that it includes fresh descriptions of recent developments in curriculum practice, particularly those found in areas of rapid change— evaluation, current issues, directions in the subject fields, politics, and research. The text has been strengthened by adding material that clarifies basic ideas. For example, a more detailed differentiation between curriculum as social adaptation and social reconstruction has been made.

New sections have been added treating the influence of the computer upon curriculum; the management of curriculum; perspectives on the curriculum in effective schools; and controversial issues, such as curriculum competition with Japan and Western Europe and the hidden curriculum as a conspiracy. The sources used in preparing this revision represent the latest and most insightful work in curriculum.

I am greatly indebted to Mylan L. Jaixen who helped at every stage of the development of this book. His guidance and organizational abilities were essential to its fruition. I also wish to thank Reuben Hilde, Loma Linda University; Albert Lindia, Central Connecticut State College; John McClure, The University of Iowa; and James Walter, University of Nebraska, Lincoln for their suggestions and advice to improve the text. Terri Gitler, of Publication Services in Urbana, Illinois, has contributed to the text as well.

Finally, I wish to especially thank Mary Ellen McNeil for perceptive work in helping to clarify ideas and presenting them to you.

Contents

I / CONCEPTIONS OF CURRICULUM

Prevailing conceptions of the curriculum can be classified into four major categories: humanistic, social reconstructionist, technological, and academic. Proponents of each have different ideas about what should be taught, to whom, when, and how.

Those with a humanistic orientation hold that the curriculum should provide personally satisfying experiences for each individual. The new humanists are self-actualizers, who view curriculum as a liberating process that can meet the need for growth and personal integrity. They should not, however, be confused with those persons in the liberal arts tradition who regard the humanities as separate disciplines, such as art, music, or literature, and who attempt to deal with the human being solely through cultural creations.

Social reconstructionists stress societal needs over individual interests. They place primary responsibility on the curriculum to effect social reform and generate a better future for society. They emphasize the development of social values and their use in the critical thought process.

The technologists view curriculum making as a technological process for achieving whatever ends policymakers demand. They consider themselves agents of their clients and, accordingly, hold themselves accountable by producing evidence which indicates that their curriculum attains intended objectives. Theirs is not a neutral orientation, for the technologists espouse commitment to a method that in turn has consequences for curriculum goals and content.

Persons with an academic orientation see curriculum as the vehicle by which learners are introduced to subject matter disciplines and to organized fields of study. They view the organized content of sub-

1

jects as a curriculum to be pursued rather than as a source of information for dealing with local and personal problems. The persons
who fall into this category assume that an academic curriculum is the
best way to develop the mind—that mastery of the kind of knowledge commonly found in such a curriculum contributes to rational
thinking.

In the chapters that follow, each of the four categories will be described, analyzed, and evaluated. Students of curriculum who understand these four positions will be better able to formulate their own
ideas regarding purpose, content, method, organization, and evaluation of curriculum. The extent to which one or more of the conceptions applies at a given time and place is a unifying thread in the
organization of this text.

1 / THE HUMANISTIC CURRICULUM

The term *humanistic curriculum* may evoke a number of negative connotations—easy therapeutic gimmicks, antiscientific affinities, preoccupation with the esoteric rather than with everyday life, and the counter—cultural movement of the 1960s with its antinomian and drug-oriented features, to name a few. With the 1980s has come, however, a mighty wind of change away from a child-centered curriculum based on interests, natural mode of growth, and impulses for pupil action. In its place are strong pressures for a subject-oriented curriculum consisting in the high school of five basics—four years of English, three years of mathematics, three years of science, three years of social studies, and one-half year of computer science. Arguments for this shift away from the child-centered curriculum rest on the belief that our nation is at risk because foreign competitors are overtaking American preeminence in commerce, industry, science, and technological innovations. Charges are made that educational institutions have lost sight of the basic purposes of schooling; that the curriculum has been homogenized, diluted, and diffused; and that a curriculum smorgasbord exists which allows for extensive student choice and which has resulted in declining achievement scores in math, science, and "higher order" intellectual skills. A 1983 data bank of national curriculum studies lists thirty projects, most of which express concern about outdated curriculum—low standards, differential treatment of the sexes and minority students, and failure to equip students with the tools they need for employment.[1]

In view of the negative connotations and the imperatives for academic mastery, more rigorous standards, increased homework, and firm codes of discipline, can we simply write off a humanistic orientation to curriculum? Such a dismissal would be unfortunate, for there are strong arguments in favor of the humanistic approach.

The American people have a commitment to self-actualization. Repeatedly, parents express their interest in self-understanding, and in fostering the emotional and physical well-being of their children as well as the intellectual

[1] Alex Head, "National Studies Involving Curriculum," *Education Week,* 27 July 1983: 43–44.

3

skills necessary for independent judgment. The humanistic curriculum supports the American ideal of individualism, helping students discover who they are, not just shaping them into a form that has been designated in advance.

Americans place a premium on innovation and creativity. Thus it would be a mistake for educators in the United States to respond to competition from Japan by imitating the Japanese curriculum with its emphasis upon shaping a whole population to a high level of rigorous discipline and its focus upon the same basic academic subjects for all. Although in Japan the average amount of learning is higher, the range of knowledge is narrower. Japanese educators themselves are uneasy about Japan's emphasis on rote learning at the expense of critical thinking. One difference between education in the United States and Japan is that the Japanese cram more information into small children. What would be the curriculum for a fast track of college-bound students in the United States—including geometry and calculus—is routinely taught to most high school students in Japan.

In Japan, the intense pressure to achieve high scores on centrally imposed tests takes a significant psychological toll and places a higher premium on memorization than on creativity and understanding. The United States has maintained its competitive edge over Japan and other nations by the capacity of its citizens to create fresh ideas and new technology. Instead of adapting curriculum so that more pupils score higher on multiple-choice examinations, Americans should be concerned with maintaining their advantage in creativity, problem-solving skills, and innovation. The humanistic curriculum features activities which are exploratory, puzzling, playful, and spontaneous—all of which are vital for innovation and self-renewal. The best interests of Americans lie in providing students with a curriculum that is fixed on the future—on what is possible and potential, not on what is merely utilitarian or which will make the learner a helpless captive to what is already known.

The humanistic curriculum goes a long way toward solving a fundamental problem facing educators today: that much of what is taught is not learned and much of what is presented and tested for is not assimilated. Critics who think that greater learning results by pouring more facts into children's minds are mistaken. Earlier reformers who tried to raise standards in the curriculum with rigorous academic programs met with failure. What went wrong? The new programs were often too far removed from the backgrounds of the teachers and did not take into consideration how learners might construct meaning from the content. This should not be interpreted to mean that subject matter must be easy. Rather, it must be brought to life, taught in a way that demonstrates its relevance to daily living and to the learner. The humanistic curriculum offers an alternative to dull courses that do not relate to the learner.

Widespread dissatisfaction with much of the present curriculum is evidenced by high dropout rates, vandalism, and discipline problems among the bored, the unhappy, and the angry. The problem is not just one of motivating students to acquire academic content. A larger concern is determining the appropriate educational response to students who live desperate lives—students who lack a purpose for living, good personal relations, and self-regard. The humanistic curriculum addresses this concern.

When we consider the tools needed for employment, highest priority must be given to attitudes and human relations. The diminishing quality of job applicants is due more to their poor attitudes than to their lack of job skills. Wilms, for example, found that employers rate a positive attitude toward work the most important qualification for success on the job. Few employers, on the other hand, regard technical skills as most important to job success.[2] The humanistic curriculum aims at helping students live well, and this means, among other things, having desirable relations with others in the social community of work.

This chapter describes how humanists respond to the central questions of what and how to teach. Examples illustrate ways in which the humanistic curriculum promotes personal development, learning, and self-actualization. In the next few pages, we will examine humanistic methods of learning and opposition to the idea of subject matter as an end rather than as a source of personal development. We will discover, too, how the humanistic curriculum allows learners to consult themselves and to enjoy their capacity to discriminate and sense the world.

CHARACTERISTICS OF THE HUMANISTIC CURRICULUM

Purpose

Humanists believe that the function of the curriculum is to provide each learner with intrinsically rewarding experiences that contribute to personal liberation and development. To humanists, the goals of education are dynamic personal processes related to the ideals of personal growth, integrity, and autonomy. Healthier attitudes toward self, peers, and learning are among their expectations. The ideal of self-actualization is at the heart of the humanistic curriculum. A person who exhibits this quality is not only coolly cognitive, but is also developed in aesthetic and moral ways—i.e., one who does good works and has good character. The humanist views actualization growth as a basic need. Each learner has a self that is not necessarily conscious. This self must be uncovered, built up, taught.

Third force psychology is closely associated with the humanistic curriculum. This psychology is largely a reaction to what some psychologists found to be inadequacies in behaviorism and Freudian psychologies. The third

---

[2]W. W. Wilms, *Technology, Jobs, and Education,* Los Angeles Chamber of Commerce Report, UCLA Series, Graduate School of Education, 1983.

force psychologist believes that behaviorism is mechanistic and that behaviorists view the learner as a detached intellect, ignoring affective responses and higher order aspects of the personality such as altruism. Likewise, to the third force psychologist, Freudian psychologies appear overly cynical about the motives of persons and emphasize humankind's pathological and unconscious emotional forces.

The late Abraham Maslow was a key figure in the development of third force psychology. Maslow viewed self-actualization as having several dimensions. He saw it as a life achievement, a momentary state, and the normal process of growth when a person's deficiency motives are satisfied and his or her defenses are not mobilized by threat. Maslow assumed that the human being has a biological essence. Hence the search for self means attending to impulses from within that indicate that an individual is a part of nature as well as a unique being.[3]

If third force psychology is its foundation, it follows that the humanistic curriculum must encourage self-actualization, whereby learners are permitted to express, act out, experiment, make mistakes, be seen, get feedback, and discover who they are. Maslow thought we learn more about ourselves by examining responses to *peak experiences*—in other words, those experiences which give rise to love, hate, anxiety, depression, and joy. For Maslow, the peak experiences of awe, mystery, and wonder are both the end and the beginning of learning. Thus a humanistic curriculum should value and attempt to provide for such experiences as moments in which cognitive and personal growth take place simultaneously.

A reviewer of this book has pointed out that science teachers who feel attracted to humanistic views can reverse declining enrollments in their courses. A case in point is found in R. M. Ramette's peak experience which took place during a biology class. "The teacher was trying to teach us about sugars, and we yawned as he added glucose to some Fehling's solution. But when he heated the mixture and the blue solution turned into a red solid, I sat up straight and recognized the moment as a turning point in my life. Within a day I had bought a Gilbert chemistry set and began threatening my attic and the peace of mind of my parents."[4]

Role of the Teacher

A humanistic curriculum demands the context of an emotional relationship between students and teacher. The teacher must provide

[3]Abraham H. Maslow, "Some Educational Implications of the Humanistic Psychology," *Harvard Educational Review* 38: 685–96.

[4]R. M. Ramette, "Exocharmic Reactions," *Journal of Chemical Education* 57, no. 1 (Jan. 1980): 68-69.

warmth and nurture emotions while continuing to function as a resource center. He or she should present materials imaginatively and create challenging situations to facilitate learning. Humanistic teachers motivate their students through mutual trust. They encourage a positive student-teacher relationship by teaching out of their own interests and commitments while holding to the belief that each child can learn. Those who assume a leadership role in affective approaches to learning must get in touch with themselves; they must know how the teaching role affects both the teacher and the pupil. Manipulative methods are out; the humanistic teacher does not coerce students. Although numerous techniques are associated with humanistic teaching, not all who use these techniques can be called humanistic teachers. Only those who are committed to the ideas underlying the techniques are considered truly humanistic. Teachers who are kind and humane to students are not necessarily implementing a humanistic curriculum. Kindness may, in fact, be associated with any curriculum conception.

BASIS FOR SELECTING LEARNING OPPORTUNITIES

In the recent past, many resources offered exercises, techniques, and activities for advancing the humanistic goal of psychological growth. One way to select from among these resources was to identify a concern, theme, or topic, such as self-judgment, and then to select procedures or exercises that appeared to be related. Another way was to leave the content open-ended and to let themes and issues arise spontaneously from the teaching procedures and instructional materials. For the teacher who follows the latter mode, procedures and materials should match the learners' willingness to risk self-disclosure and give up privacy. Such willingness can, in turn, be increased when the procedures used create trust in the group situation, thus helping individuals view comfortably their own discomfort. The encounter group is one such approach used in business and education as a way to further human relations and personal functioning. In an encounter group there is very often little imposed structure. Group members decide upon the purposes. The teacher facilitates expression and clarifies the dynamics that are at work. After an initial warm-up period, members express themselves to each other. Facades give way, defenses are lowered, and hidden feelings and concerns are revealed. Group members give positive and negative reactions to these revelations. Usually the experience is valuable, resulting in better communication and self-understanding as well as increased understanding of others.

Self-awareness is believed best attained when one observes one's own feelings. Examination of one's own thoughts—sentences, dialogue, and fantasies—is a means to self-awareness. So, too, is the study of personal actions, movements, and physical expressions.

The humanistic curriculum increases self-awareness; it allows learners to seek typical personal patterns in their own responses to a series of activities. Acceptance rather than denial of one's own patterns is necessary in order to change an aspect of self. Under the humanistic approach, the learner is taught to distinguish ends from means. For example, an activity might provoke a silent member who wants to be viewed as intelligent to reveal that he or she thinks silence conveys such an impression. If he or she discovers, however, that silence is seen by others as reflecting intimidation rather than intelligence, the silent one may be willing to attempt a different approach to achieve the desired goal. The teacher should at this point provide activities that permit learners to experience alternative ways of behaving, and to evaluate these behaviors in terms of their consequences, such as the reactions of friends. These consequences, in turn, will enable learners to decide whether to keep all, some, or none of the new responses.

Humanistic curriculum is today characterized less by contrived and game-like activities aimed only at aspects of personal growth and more by examination of the inner life of students in the learning process—as in the context of acquiring subject-matter knowledge, vocational training, or basic skills. Whether providing instruction in typing, computer programming, or chemistry, the humanistic teacher creates opportunities for the learners to deal with their affective concerns—i.e., beliefs, values, goals, fears, and relationships. For example, a sixth grade teacher might give her pupils an opportunity at the end of each week to evaluate themselves and their work in terms of accuracy, what has been accomplished, and the usefulness of what they have learned. Students in this situation acquire new personal goals and form new attitudes about learning such as (a) the number of errors is not a sufficient criterion for determining failure or success, (b) errors can be useful in learning, and (c) consistently perfect scores may signal the need for more challenging tasks.

Organization

One great strength of the humanistic curriculum appears to lie in its stress on *integration*. Integration refers to the learner's increased unity of behavior. In helping learners integrate emotions, thoughts, and actions, humanists achieve an effective organization. Humanistic schemes do much to resolve the weakness of the traditional curriculum in which the logical organization of subject matter, as defined by an expert, fails to connect with the learners' psychological organization. The humanist's concerns for wholeness and Gestalt lead to a curriculum that encourages comprehensiveness of experience, thus counteracting the prevailing practice of fragmented curricula.

It is true, however, that at times humanistic curriculum has lacked sequence. Students may have had little chance to broaden and deepen a single aspect of their development. Glatthorn has written, for example, of schools that offered a smorgasbord curriculum of minicourses such as The Jazz Age, Sexism in America, Writing Poetry, and Zen and the Western World, in which the total program seemed to be just an unsystematic collection of bits and pieces.[5]

Sequence requires centering upon a single element—concern, value, concept, attitude, or problem—and then arranging activities so that the student becomes increasingly able to deal with or exhibit that element. In the case of Glatthorn's smorgasbord, had self-understanding been the focus or element, activities within each minicourse could have been cast so that they had a cumulative effect upon self-knowledge. Schemes for ordering activities so that the pupil derives the maximum benefit from each include providing opportunities for (a) dealing with preconceptual feeling before being asked to verbalize feelings and (b) taking action in a situation before trying to explain or understand the situation.

A particularly interesting scheme for sequencing dimensions of affective experiences has been proposed by Shiplett.[6] His strategy is to order experiences as follows: (1) Arrange activities to reveal concerns and blockages. Use experiences that help students deal with fears and unmet needs such as security and self-worth. (2) Introduce materials with orientation loadings; that is, arrange for activities that focus on topics, subject matter, and learning tasks likely to help make pupils want to learn. Activities that stimulate curiosity are cases in point. (3) Present engagement loadings (activities that are rewarding in and of themselves). The student should be given pleasurable experiences, such as movement and novelty. (4) Introduce accomplishment loadings (the effects of completing a learning task). Mastery and satisfaction are examples of accomplishment loadings.

[5]Allan A. Glatthorn, *Alternatives in Education Schools and Programs* (New York: Dodd, Mead, 1975).

[6]John M. Shiplett, "Beyond Vibration Teaching: Research and Curriculum Development in Confluent Education," in *The Live Classroom*, ed. George I. Brown (New York: Viking, 1975), pp. 121–31.

completing a learning task). Mastery and satisfaction are examples of accomplishment loadings.

Evaluation

Unlike the conventional curriculum, which is objectively defined and in which there are criteria for achievement, the humanistic curriculum stresses growth regardless of how it is measured or defined. The humanist as evaluator emphasizes process rather than product. Humanistic evaluators do, however, ask whether activities are helping students become more open, independent human beings. Humanists view activities as worthwhile in and of themselves and as a possible contribution to future values. They value classrooms that provide experiences to help pupils become more aware of themselves and others and develop their own unique potential. Humanistic teachers pride themselves on knowing how students are responding to activities, either by observing their actions or by seeking feedback once the activities are completed.

When asked to judge the effectiveness of their curriculum, humanists usually rely on subjective assessments by teachers and pupils. They also may present outcome measures, such as students' paintings or poems, or talk of marked improvement in pupil behavior and attitudes. Carl Rogers has summarized many of the research results showing positive association between affective classrooms and growth, interest, cognition, productivity, self-confidence, and trust. Rogers has documented evidence that students learn more, attend school more often, and are more creative and capable of problem solving when the humanistic curriculum is employed.[7] His evidence comes from studies in the military and other settings, in eight countries, at all levels of education and with students of different race, sex, and socio-economic status. By way of example, in a study on the effects of giving young children choices, pupils in an "educationally handicapped" third grade classroom were given the chance to design their own reading program. At first the pupils found it difficult to believe that they really could design their own program. Initially their responses were negative—"We don't want to do workbooks every day." But they also came up with constructive suggestions: "Could we have a quiet time when everybody just reads?" "Can we just read to you to hear, teacher?" "Can we read something else more than the reading book?" Students were also given the opportunity to tell the class anything important about themselves, and time was set aside so that students

---

[7]Carl Rogers, "Researching Person-Centered Issues in Education," in *Freedom to Learn* (Columbus: Merrill, 1983), pp. 197–221.

could come individually to the teacher to talk about anything they wanted her to know—something bothering them about school or themselves, or something exciting they wanted to share. At the end of a year, not one of these children, all of whom had been one or more years below grade level, made less than eleven months' progress in reading; some made three years' growth. Further, the fact that increased self-awareness was achieved is evidenced by their comments: "It's all right to be me." "Everyone has feelings and it's OK to express them." "Doing things that are important *to me* is worthwhile."

DIRECTIONS IN HUMANISTIC CURRICULUM

The 1970s saw two prevalent forms of humanistic curriculum—confluence and consciousness. In the 1980s humanists are planning curriculum with a focus on human development, while, at the same time, being responsive to public pressure for growth in subject-matter knowledge. These responses range from the fear that a concentration on subject matter may lead to depersonalization to the use of humanistic approaches in creating new meaning in the academic fields.

A Confluent Curriculum

Rationale for Confluence. The essence of confluent education is the integration of an affective domain (emotions, attitudes, values) with the cognitive domain (intellectual knowledge and abilities). It is an *add-on* curriculum, whereby emotional dimensions are added to conventional subject matter so that there is personal meaning to what is learned. Confluentists do not downplay objective knowledge, such as scientific information, in favor of subjective or intuitive (that is, direct and immediate) knowledge. The confluent teacher of English, for example, links affective exercises to paragraphing, organization, and argumentative and other discursive forms of writing. By beginning with the student's personal, imaginative, and emotional responses and working out from these, the confluentist helps learners both to acquire language skills and to discover themselves.

Confluentists do not believe that the curriculum should teach students what to feel or what attitudes to have. Their goal is to provide students with more alternatives to choose from in terms of their own lives, to take responsibility for appreciating the choices available, and to realize that they, the learners, can indeed make choices.

Shapiro and others have analyzed examples and nonexamples of confluence, concluding that a confluent curriculum is composed of the following elements:[8]

1. Participation. There is consent, power sharing, negotiation, and joint responsibility by coparticipants. It is essentially nonauthoritarian and not unilateral.
2. Integration. There is interaction, interpenetration, and integration of thinking, feelings, and action.
3. Relevance. The subject matter is closely related to the basic needs and lives of the participants and is significant to them, both emotionally and intellectually.
4. Self. The self is a legitimate object of learning.
5. Goal. The social goal or purpose is to develop the whole person within a human society.

Gestalt psychology is one of the bases for confluent education. The theory behind it is existentially based; that is, it focuses on what is happening here and now rather than interpreting one's history. With respect to the curriculum decision of what to teach, the Gestalt theory forces one to question goals, and to ask about our heritage such questions as: "Is it of value to us now? Does it make us more alive or does it deaden us and tend to keep us hung up on out-moded ways of thinking and perceiving? Does it tie us to old models and goals for ourselves and for our children that are . . . counterproductive to a [healthy] society?"

Activities Within the Confluent Curriculum. Confluent curricula have been prepared by teachers at various levels and in most fields. These curricula include goals, topics, materials, and texts. Confluent lessons, units, and course plans have been field-tested and are available for inspection.[9]

Many of these materials utilize *affective* techniques. George I. Brown has given us forty examples of such affective techniques including the following:

1. Dyads. As an exercise in communication, two persons—new friends—sit back to back and try to communicate without turning their heads. Next, they face each other and, without talking, try to communicate using only their eyes. They are to be aware of how

[8]Stewart B. Shapiro, "Developing Models by 'Unpacking' Confluent Education," Occasional Paper No. 12, *Development and Research in Confluent Education* (Santa Barbara: University of California, 1972).

[9]Ger. Metz, "Gestalt and Transformation," in *The Live Classroom,* ed. George Brown (New York: Viking, 1975), p. 21.

George I. Brown, "Examples of Lessons, Units, and Course Outlines in Confluent Education," *The Live Classroom,* ed. George Brown (New York: Viking, 1975), pp. 231–95.

they feel as they do this (for example, silly, embarrassed, fascinated). Later, they close their eyes and communicate by only touching hands; and, finally, they communicate any way they wish. The pedagogy of the exercise is to move participants from little risk to more. That is, one reveals more of oneself and becomes more vulnerable as the exercise proceeds.

2. Fantasy body trip. Members of a group are asked to close their eyes, be comfortable, move into themselves. Each person is asked to concentrate on different body parts, beginning with toes, moving up to the head, experiencing any sensations felt emanating from the separate parts of the body. After this fantasy trip, the group shares their experiences. Applications of this technique can be used in discussing such concepts as: "What is a person?" and "Who am I?" Students begin with rediscovering their bodies. Other exercises concentrate on other parts of the person or on the experience of being a whole.

3. Rituals. A large group is divided into five subgroups and asked to create a new ritual. A ritual is a custom or practice—such as shaking hands. The idea is to invent a ritual either to replace one we already have or for a situation in which no ritual at present exists.

4. Gestalt "I have available" technique. This technique is to help persons get in touch with their own strengths or resources. Each participant completes a sentence beginning with "I have available . . ." and gains understanding by being aware of whatever emerges. For example, one may recognize personal characteristics, other persons, and things that can help one cope with the world.[10]

Unlike most curriculum writers, the authors of confluent materials do not expect others to carry out the suggested plans exactly or even roughly as described. Whoever uses the confluent materials should make them a part of their own philosophy; they should not just regard them as techniques. Ideally, teachers will create new approaches for their own classrooms. To design such approaches, however, one should understand and accept the rationale underlying the techniques.

Weinstein and Fantini offer a "curriculum of concern," a type of confluent education in which students' basic concerns determine what concepts will be studied. They carefully distinguish between *interests* and *concerns*. Interests are the activities that attract students. Concerns are the basic physiological and sociological drives of students. Weinstein and Fantini point out, for instance, that a student might be *interested* in cars

---

[10]George I. Brown, *Human Teaching for Human Learning* (New York: Viking, 1971).

because he is *concerned* with feelings of powerlessness. Thus, the proper approach to the student is not necessarily *Hot Rod* magazine but some way to help the student explore an understanding of power.[11]

Application of the Weinstein-Fantini model illustrates a curriculum that features the major concerns of self-identity and allows students to explore the disparity between what they thought about in school, what they were concerned about in their own lives, and the way they acted. The curriculum outline consisted of a series of questions designed to lead the student to a personal sense of identity and finally to an examination of the actions that would express that sense of self. Some of the questions were: What is human about human? Who am I? How can we find actions to express our thoughts and feelings?

Such a curriculum can include a variety of activities, such as a trip to the zoo to contrast humans with animals, improvisational drama to imitate the movement of animals, discussion of animal metaphors in the characterization of humans, and debates about animal and human groups. Note that such activities can be undertaken without changing the orientation of the school in any major way. They can supplement the commitment to teaching reading, writing, and arithmetic.

Students draw generalizations as a result of these experiences. For example, students conclude that self-consciousness allows persons to use their own diversity for their own benefit. Thus, "If a consciousness of self is one of the major differences between animals and humans, then one of the most effective ways to make persons more human, or more humane, would be to help them explore the significance of their own diversity."[12]

Consciousness and Transcendency

Mysticism. Although humanistic psychologists typically emphasize the affective and cognitive domains, some humanists are interested in treating higher domains of consciousness as well. One of the means they use is *transcendental meditation* (TM). Transcendental meditation is concerned with altering states of consciousness, voluntary control of inner states, and growth beyond the ego. It has been tried as an adjunct to the high school curriculum partly because it is seen as a way to diminish drug abuse among students. Essentially, TM is a simple technique for turning attention "inwards toward the subtler levels of thought

[11]Gerald Weinstein and Mario Fantini, *Toward Humanistic Education: A Curriculum of Affect* (New York: Praeger, 1970).
[12]Terry Borton, "What Turns Kids On?" *Saturday Review,* 15 April 1967: 72–74.

until mind transcends the experience of the subtlest state of thought and arrives at the source of thought. This expands the conscious mind and at the same time brings it in contact with the creative intelligence that gives rise to every thought."[13] TM has been used to reach some very commonplace curriculum goals, such as reduction of social tension, increased learning ability, and improved athletic performance. It has also inspired more novel goals, such as growth in consciousness and in other ways of knowing.

The Mara Maharishi International University (MIU) at Fairfield, Iowa, offers degrees in a number of fields, such as physics, mathematics, biology, business, and education. However, as a university founded on a philosophy that employs transcendental meditation, it also offers opportunities for students to experience higher states of consciousness. Everyone—faculty, students, staff—at MIU practices a twice daily hour long routine of meditation. In addition, in all courses an effort is made to foster a principle of interdependence by which personal individuality is related to consciousness of whatever subject matter has been taught. As concepts are introduced in one course, students and teachers seek to recall corresponding concepts in other disciplines and how the concepts might be experienced in meditation. The likely consequence of this practice is a sense of personal relevance to knowledge and an integration of the different academic disciplines.[14]

One caution concerning transcendental meditation, practiced in such courses as The Science of Creative Intelligence, is that its inclusion in the curriculum may violate legal precedents opposed to sectarian indoctrination. The "science" of TM is held by some to be essentially a religious philosophy. Its presuppositions about the source of life and energy reflect monistic Hinduism with pantheistic consciousness.[15]

The religious idea of transcendence (that is, the experience of going beyond any state or realization of being) has implications for curriculum. It suggests that students should learn how a particular mode of investigation in a subject field relates to other specializations. A transcending consciousness also helps us recognize the incompleteness of any subject. To learn that no discipline provides the full and final disclosure of the nature of things may help learners discern new possibilities, new direc-

---

[13]Maharishi Mahesh Yogi, *Maharishi Mahesh Yogi on the Bhagavad-Gita, A New Translation and Commentary* (Baltimore: Penguin, 1969), p. 470.

[14]Robert Berrettini, "Pure Consciousness and Transdisciplinarity" (Paper delivered at American Educational Research Association [AERA] Annual Convention, Montreal, Canada, April 1983).

[15]David Haddon, "Transcendental Meditation—A K-8 Curriculum Option," *Learning* 4, no. 1 (August-September 1975): 71-72.

tions, and new questions. A curriculum of transcendence should foster a spirit of criticism toward existing practices and encourage undeveloped potential and hope in improving one's existence.

Other Transpersonal Techniques. Biofeedback for controlling brain waves, deep hypnosis, yoga, and the use of dreams are additional transpersonal techniques that have implications for curricula. In English, for example, dreams may be used as a basis for creative writing because they contain the emotional impact of messages from the unconscious. Physical education, too, may use aspects of the transpersonal in learning to control one's body for optimum health and physical fitness through biofeedback and yoga.

The use of such techniques as relaxation and imaginary journeys are sometimes used in academic courses. "A high school shop teacher relaxed his class and had them imagine they were electrons being pulled and pushed by the fields around induction coils. The next day the students read the chapter in the book dealing with induction coils. The students said they had no trouble visualizing the forces described in the book, and the quality of their lab work seemed to bear this out."[16]

Responses to Depersonalization

Self-Directed Learning. Self-directed learning is one response to the threat of depersonalization brought about by narrow focus on basic skills in reading, writing, and arithmetic. Humanists believe that the basics should include a sense of ability, clarity of values, positive self-concept, capacity for innovation, and openness—characteristics of the self-directed learner.

Key ideas to consider in planning a curriculum for self-directed learning are: *achievement motivation*—those persons who are motivated by hope of success have an incentive to learn when the task is not too easy and when there is an expectation of success. Persons motivated by fear of failure, on the other hand, tend to select tasks that are either so easy they cannot fail or so difficult that no embarrassment results when they do; *attributive theory*—achievement-oriented individuals are more likely to see themselves as a cause of their success; *children's interests*—when children find schoolwork distasteful and yet are driven to engage in more of the distasteful work, they acquire learned helplessness, having no interests related to learning. Freedom to undertake a self-directed study of some-

[16]Thomas Roberts, "Transpersonal: The New Educational Psychology," *Phi Delta Kappan* 56, no. 3 (November 1979): 191–92.

thing that concerns the learner seems to be an important condition for developing channeled effort; *locus of control*—locus of control is the extent to which persons feel they have control over their own destiny. Internal control is highly correlated with achievement.

A curriculum model for self-development has been proposed by Evan Keislar.[17] The goal of this curriculum is to optimize future growth and development of the individual. Learners are helped to mediate key decisions by reflecting on their level of cognitive development and by testing proposed courses of action. Resources are provided for helping learners deal with uncertainty, take risks, try out ideas, and profit from mistakes. The teacher's role is to make sure that the student faces situations that arouse questions and lead to exploration. Challenges are matched to the child's pattern of development. Although the teacher is available to help the pupils find needed resources, the teacher does not do so when information is readily available. Since growth proceeds through encounters with conflict and tension, this curriculum promotes an optimum level of uncertainty.

As with other humanistic curricula, the self-directed curriculum aims at development in several areas: *cognitive*—children respond to the requirements of problematic situations, not simply to external directions. By anticipating consequences, they learn to make wise choices about goals. Allowances are made for those children whose thinking is tied to immediate perceptions and for those who are ready for inferential thought; *affective*—children learn to deal, at an emotional level, with such uncertainties as social conflicts, evaluation, and challenge. They learn to view failure as a learning experience; *social*—assertiveness training, role training, experimenting with competitive and cooperative groups are among the activities provided; *moral*—moral development is fostered through consideration of moral conflicts that arise from the social activities of the class and the wider community; *ego development*—the development of self-respect and self-confidence occurs through a social climate in which a person's world does not depend on ability or level of maturity. Each individual has an opportunity to attain success for there is no scarcity of rewards.

In many ways, self-directed curriculum is consistent with what John Dewey suggested more than sixty years ago—a curriculum that poses problems rooted within the present experience and capacity of learners, problems that arouse an active quest for information and invite the production of new ideas.[18]

---

[17]Evan R. Keislar, "A Developmental Model for a Curriculum in the Primary Grades" (Unpublished paper, UCLA Graduate School of Education, Los Angeles, 1983).
[18]John Dewey, *Experience and Education* (New York: Macmillan, 1939).

Finding the Personal in the Academic. Philip Phenix believes that in concentrating on academic knowledge, the learner may be depersonalized. To counter this danger, he recommends two courses of action: (a) transcendency—recognizing the limitations of academic knowledge and acknowledging other forms of knowledge, and (b) finding personal meaning in subject matter.[19]

For Phenix, the optimally developed person is not one who has merely accumulated encyclopedic knowledge, but one who can live well, acting wisely in a wide range of circumstances and situations. The kind of knowledge that permits optimal development is not likely to be found in the conventional academic curriculum. More likely, it is found in personal knowledge—know-how achieved through active expression of one's existence and by interactive engagements with others and the natural environment. Walking and talking are illustrations of great achievements acquired by active expression. Good manners and the skills of mechanics, artisans, physicians, and engineers are examples of knowledge acquired by emulating master practitioners. In short, there are many other ways to gain knowledge than through the academic fields.

Although academic knowledge is not sufficient for personal development, under some circumstances, it can enhance personal knowledge, thus enabling a person to live better. What are these circumstances?

1. *The Arts.* There is personalization when the arts—music, art, dance—are taught with the idea of knowing how—how to produce patterns of the field and competencies in expressive movement—or at least, taught so that the learner is able to emphatically participate in the activity.

2. *Mathematics.* Unless the student is helped to become a participant in the process of mathematics, symbol-making, and manipulation according to the accepted canons of the mathematics community, the study of math is likely to be depersonalizing.

3. *Science and Social Science.* Personalization is enhanced through application and transcendency. Students see how knowledge of the material may be applied to the satisfaction of human need through technology and when they use knowledge of science in understanding self or seeing how the natural world supports personal life. Personalization exists when students are helped to see the mysteries yet unprobed by scientific undertaking as well as shifting perspectives and alternatives.

4. *History.* Personal development occurs in the study of history when

[19]Philip H. Phenix, "Promoting Personal Development Through Learning," *Teachers College Record* 84, no. 2 (Winter 1982): 301–17.

there is a dramatic re-creating of the past, making the past available for participation by persons now living, and when the students feel themselves personally involved in the historical happening. History as only chronicle is depersonalizing.

An outstanding example of teaching history as personal development is found in Arye Carmon's curriculum *Teaching The Holocaust*.[20] This curriculum helps the students formulate a set of moral rules for self through a confrontation with the Holocaust. The curriculum, which has been introduced in three countries—the United States, Germany, and Israel—places the adolescent at the focal point of the education process. The Holocaust serves as subject matter for responding to the needs of today's adolescents.

The theory of Erik Erikson underlies the construction of this curriculum.[21] Erikson felt that individuals are confirmed by their identities and societies regenerated by their life style. To enter history, students must be able to relate their childhood to the childhood experiences of former generations. They must be able to identify with the ideals conveyed in the history of their culture. According to Erikson, in youth, childhood dependence gives way; no longer is it the old teaching the young the meaning of life. It is the young who by their actions tell the old whether life as represented to them has some vital promise.

The major objective of this Holocaust curriculum is to heighten the student's awareness of the critical function of adult responsibility. This objective is achieved by fostering awareness of the human tendency toward stereotyping, prejudice, ethnocentrism, obeying authority, and thus escaping responsibilities.

The subject matter is organized into units—the socialization of a German adolescent in Nazi Germany, the socialization of a secret service man, the moral dilemmas of individuals and groups during the Holocaust, and the meaning of life in the post-Holocaust era. In each unit, students are given documents from the historical period. These documents provide historical background and serve as stimuli for discussion of the moral dilemma. The method of instruction is a combination of individual inquiry and group integration. Each person deals with a specific document; students split up into small groups to exchange feelings and opinions regarding the topics and their individual studies; and then the entire class completes the discussion of the topic at hand. The content is not alien to the students and they cannot remain apathetic

[20]Arye Carmon, "Problems in Coping with the Holocaust: Experiences with Students in a Multinational Program." AAPSS, *Annals*, 450 (July 1980).
[21]Erik Erikson, *Identity, Youth and Crisis*. (New York: W. W. Norton, 1968).

to it. Students face questions that are relevant to their own lives—Why sanctification of life rather than martyrdom? What are the dilemmas that confronted the individual and which confronted Jews as members of a community? Which of these dilemmas touch you personally? Why? What is the common denominator of the dilemmas? Discussion manifests a dialog between the student and his or her conscience, and between students and their peers.

During the first phase of the curriculum, reluctance toward the subject matter increases. Students tend to resist giving up their stereotypic attitudes and other protective mechanisms. Gradually this resistance fades, only to be replaced by a feeling of helplessness. At this point the study has opened students to the possibility of critical thinking and moral judgment. Students then begin to formulate the universal rule of confronting moral dilemmas—"How would I have behaved if I had been in this situation? How should I have behaved?"

CRITICISMS OF THE HUMANISTIC CURRICULUM

Four charges are commonly made against the humanists. (1) Critics charge that humanists prize their methods, techniques, and experiences instead of appraising them in terms of consequences for learners. The humanists, they say, have been lax in seeing the long-term effects of their programs. If they were to appraise their systems more thoroughly, the humanists might see that their use of emotionally charged practices such as sensitivity training and encounter groups can be psychologically or emotionally harmful to some students. The self-awareness they encourage is not always a happy experience, and a change in self-concept is not always a change for the better. (2) Critics maintain that the humanist is not concerned enough about the experience of the individual. Although humanists say that their curriculum is individualistic, every student in a given classroom is actually exposed to the same stimuli. For example, everyone may be expected to take part in group fantasy, hostility games, and awareness exercises. (3) On the other hand, critics also charge that humanists give undue emphasis to the individual. Critics would like humanists to be more responsible to the needs of society as a whole. (4) Critics charge that the theory on which humanistic curriculum rests is deficient. Instead of advancing unity and relatedness among the psychological principles from different schools of psychology, they say the theory increases the disconnectedness of scientific knowledge. Third force psychology does not bring together the collected knowledge of behaviorism and psychiatry.

Rebuttals to these attacks take varied forms. Humanists admit that their educational approach can be misused. However, as George I. Brown points out, teachers who would abuse their teaching role would do so whether or not they had affective techniques available. Further, because humanism helps teachers learn more about themselves, those teachers are likely to demonstrate fewer instances of negative and destructive behavior. Not all students should have to participate in the humanistic curriculum because it may not be appropriate for everyone at the curriculum's present stage of development. This curriculum promises a fuller realization of the democratic potential of our society. The goals of the humanistic curriculum call for students who can perceive clearly, act rationally, make choices, and take responsibility both for their private lives and for their social milieu.

The in-house differences of opinion regarding underlying theories of humanistic education attest to its intellectual vitality. Efforts to revise Maslow's writings are one indicator that the field is not moribund. Chiefly, these efforts center on difficulties with the concept of self-actualization on which the whole personal growth movement is based. Humanists must realize that vice and evil are as much in the range of human potentiality as virtue. Some humanists challenge the notion that our biology can carry our ethics and recognize that self-actualization may not always lead to the common good.[22]

F. Hanoch McCarty believes it is necessary to combat the perceptions of humanistic education as chaotic, lacking in purpose and a set of common goals. She would change the phrases of the '70s—"If it feels good, do it" and "Do your own thing"—by adding "as long as it does not rob others of their dignity and potential."[23] In other words, McCarty believes humanists must be involved with the welfare of others—one should not seek personal pleasure while others slave.

Shortly before his death, Maslow addressed the question of whether we can teach for personal growth and at the same time educate for competence in academic and professional fields.[24] He thought it was possible, although difficult, to integrate the two goals. (The teacher's role of judge and evaluator in competency education is often seen as incompatible with the humanistic role.) In his last article, Maslow

[22]Norman Leer, "On Self Actualization: A Transambivalent Examination of Focal Theme in Maslow's Psychology," *Journal of Humanistic Psychology* 19, no. 3 (Summer 1979): 13–27.

[23]F. Hanoch McCarty, "At the Edges of Perception: Humanistic Education in the '80s and Beyond" (Paper delivered at AERA Annual Meeting, Montreal, Canada, April, 1983).

[24]Abraham H. Maslow, "Humanistic Education," *Journal of Humanistic Psychology* 19, no. 3 (Summer 1979): 13–27.

expressed uneasiness over some practices in curricula of the ESALEN type, particularly trends toward anti-intellectualism and against science, discipline, and hard work. He worried about those who considered competence and training irrelevant. For Maslow, the learning of content need not be the denial of growth. He thought subject matter could be taught humanistically with a view to enlightenment of the person. Study in a subject field could be a help toward seeing the world as it really is, a training in sensory awareness, and a defense against despair. To believe that real knowledge is possible and that weak, foolish human beings can band together and move verified knowledge forward toward some small measure of certainty encourages us to count upon ourselves and our own powers.

There is a concern that many Americans view the humanistic approach negatively. Although most people would support increased human potential and self-worth as ends, they may be suspicious of what appear to be bizarre procedures, such as exploring the senses through touch/feel exercises and emphasizing the sensual, if not the sexual. If thought, feeling, and action cannot be separated, then neither should feelings be separated from injustices faced by one's fellows. Rather than *feel* the "joy" of a "blind walk," students might *feel* the "repulsion" and "outrage" of abused children.[25]

Critics of the humanistic curriculum reveal their own bias as social reconstructionists by demanding that the humanists do more than strengthen present courses. New teaching techniques that involve learners and their feelings in each lesson are not enough. They want to broaden the boundaries of the humanistic curriculum from self-study to political socialization; they would like it to include such problem areas as medicine, parental care, and journalism. These critics want humanistic curriculum to deal with the exposure of injustice so that the learner's growth would be less restricted. To do so, however, will require a blending of humanism and social reconstructionism.

CONCLUDING COMMENTS

Listening, self-evaluation, creativity, openness to new experiences, and goal setting are important curriculum goal areas. Learners have a real concern about the meaning of life, and curriculum developers should be responsive to that concern. Putting feelings and facts together

---

[25]Mario Fantini, "Humanizing the Humanism Movement," *Phi Delta Kappan* 15, no. 1 (February 1974): 400–2.

makes good sense. We should also help our learners acquire different ways of knowing. Still, few persons would want the humanistic curriculum to be the only one available or to be mandated for all. We have much to learn before we can develop curricula that will help pupils become self-directed.

Our best thinking today suggests that self-direction may follow from a climate of trust, student participation in decisions about what and how to learn, and efforts to foster confidence and self-esteem. The obstacles to be overcome are a desire by some institutions and persons to maintain power over others, a distrust of human nature, and a lack of pupil experience in taking responsibility for their own learning.

A fruitful approach to improving humanistic curriculum has begun. It includes focusing on the physical and emotional needs of learners and attempting to design learning experiences that will help fulfill these needs. The idea that curriculum objectives and activities should match emotional issues that are salient at particular stages of life is powerful. Curriculum developers should ask how particular subject matters might be structured in order to help pupils with developmental crises. Adolescents, for example, who are experiencing an identity crisis and trying to reconcile conflicts with parents might study history to illuminate the origins of parents' attitudes and beliefs, considering the present validity of these origins. They might use the sciences to reinterpret long-standing conflicts with parents. Or they might use the arts to express their feelings and their natural desire to be themselves.

QUESTIONS

1. Consider a subject matter of interest to you. How could this subject matter be taught to avoid depersonalizing learners?
2. What is your response to those who believe that schools should not undertake the complicated responsibilities that an affective curriculum implies and that such programs may infringe on the civil liberties of children?
3. What are the expected outcomes from a primary classroom in which there is a "sad corner"; an "I feel" wheel with an arrow that points to "fine," "tired," "sick," "scared"; and a plant that is ignored while another is loved so that pupils can see that "if we love it more, it will grow more, like people"?
4. Designers of affective programs have been accused of equating good mental health with conformity. They are said to promote compliance with school routines and instruction and to discourage the kind of initiative, individuality, and creativity that demands changes, "rocks the boat,"

and gives learners control over the institution in which they must exist. To what extent are these accusations true?

5. Reflect on some of the ideas, concerns, and activities associated with humanistic education. Which of these are likely to prove fruitful and have a continuing effect on what is taught in the curriculum? You may wish to consider (a) psychological assumptions about the importance of freedom, learning by doing, and risk taking; (b) views of knowledge such as those stressing subjective or intuitive knowledge and the idea that the subject that matters is one in which the learner finds self-fulfillment; and (c) instructional techniques (value clarification, cooperative games, use of dreams, etc.).

6. What is your stance on the nature of the individual? Do you believe evil is inherent in human nature or are persons essentially constructive? What are the curricular implications of your answer?

SELECTED REFERENCES

Berman, L. M. and Roderick, J. A., eds. *Feeling, Valuing and the Art of Growing: Insights into the Affective,* ASCO Yearbook. Washington, D.C.: ASCD, 1977.

Brown, George Isaac, ed. *The Live Classroom.* New York: Viking, 1975.

Della-Dora, Delmo and Blanchard, Lois Jerry, eds. *Moving Toward Self-Directed Learning: Highlights of Relevant Research and Promising Practices.* Alexandria, Va.: ASCD, 1979.

Journal of Humanistic Education and Development. Falls Chace, Va.: American Personnel and Guidance Association.

Journal of Humanistic Psychology. Association for Humanistic Psychology (current issues).

Levine, J. M. and Wang, M. C., eds. *Teacher and Student Perceptions: Implications of Learning.* Hillsdale, N.J.: Erlbaum, 1982.

Moustakas, Clark and Perry, Cereta. *Learning to be Free.* Englewood Cliffs, N.J.: Prentice-Hall, 1973.

Ornstein, Robert E. *The Psychology of Consciousness.* New York: Harcourt, Brace, Jovanovich, 1977.

Phenix, Philip H. "Promoting Personal Development Through Teaching." *Teachers College Record,* 84, no. 2 (Winter 1982).

Rogers, Carl K. *Freedom to Learn for the 80s.* Columbus: Merrill, 1983.

2 / THE SOCIAL RECONSTRUCTIONIST CURRICULUM

Social reconstructionists are interested in the relation between curriculum and the social, political, and economic development of society. Optimistic social reconstructionists are convinced that education can effect social change, citing, for example, literacy campaigns that have contributed to successful political revolutions. Pessimists, on the other hand, doubt the ability of the curriculum to change existing social structures. But both optimists and pessimists *want* a curriculum that challenges the social order. They consider the curriculum to be a vehicle for fostering social discontent. They want learners to understand how the curriculum is used to consolidate power and to define society.

Aspects of reconstructionism appeared in American curriculum thought in the 1920s and 1930s. Harold Rugg was concerned about the values for which the school should work. He tried to awaken his peers to the "lag" between the curriculum, a "lazy giant," and the culture, with its fast-paced change and its resultant staggering social dislocations. Rugg's textbooks, teaching, and professional leadership had one overriding quality—the spirit of social criticism. He wanted learners to use newly emerging concepts from the social sciences and aesthetics to identify and solve current social problems. Rugg and his colleague, George Counts, author of *Dare the School Build a New Social Order?*, were among the pioneer thinkers who called on the school to begin creating a "new" and "more equitable" society.[1]

In the early 1950s, Theodore Brameld outlined the distinctive features of social reconstructionism.[2] First, he believed in a commitment to building a new culture. Brameld was infused with the conviction that we are in the midst of a revolutionary period from which will emerge control by the

---

[1]George Counts, *Dare the School Build a New Social Order?* (Yonkers, N.Y.: World Book, 1932).

[2]Theodore Brameld, *Toward a Reconstructed Philosophy of Education* (New York: Dryden, 1956).

common people of the industrial system, of public services, and of cultural and natural resources. Second, Brameld felt that the working people should control all principal institutions and resources if the world is to become genuinely democratic. Teachers should ally with the organized working people. A way should be found to enlist the majority of people of all races and religions into a great democratic body with power to enforce its policies. The structure, goals, and policies of the new order must be approved at the bar of public opinion and enacted with popular support.

Third, Brameld believed that the school should help the individual, not only to develop socially, but to learn how to participate in social planning as well. The social reconstructionist wants no overstating of the case for individual freedom. Instead, the learners must see how society makes a people what they are and find ways to satisfy personal needs through social consensus. Fourth, said Brameld, learners must be convinced of the validity and urgency of change. But they must also have a regard for democratic procedures. Ideally, reconstructionists are opposed to the use of intimidation, fear, and distortion to force compromise in the attempt to achieve a "community of persuasion." However, the reconstructionists take sides and encourage all to acquire a common viewpoint about crucial problems, to make up their minds about the most promising situations, and then to act in concert to achieve those solutions. The social reconstructionists believe they are representing values that the majority, whether consciously or not, already cherish. Most people are not now able to act responsibly, they say, because they have been persuaded and stunted by a dominating minority—those who largely control the instruments of power. Hence most persons do not exercise their citizenship in behalf of their own interests—their cherished values—but in behalf of scarcity, frustration, and war.

This chapter presents the premises of social reconstruction and the different directions taken by different social reconstructionists—revolution, critical inquiry, futurism. A distinction is also made between a curriculum of reconstruction, which attempts to change the social order, and a curriculum of social adaptation, which helps students fit into a world they never made.

CHARACTERISTICS OF THE SOCIAL RECONSTRUCTIONISTIC CURRICULUM

Purpose

The primary purpose of the social reconstructionist curriculum is to confront the learner with the many severe problems that humankind faces. Social reconstructionists believe that these problems are not the exclusive concern of "social studies" but of every discipline, including economics, aesthetics, chemistry, and mathematics. We are now in a critical period, they claim. The crisis is universal, and the widespread nature of the crisis must be emphasized in the curriculum.

The social reconstructionist curriculum, however, has no universal objectives and content. For example, the first year of such a curriculum might be devoted to formulating goals for political and economic reconstruction. Activities related to this objective might include the following: (1) a critical survey of the community (for example, one might collect information on local patterns of savings and expenditures); (2) a study relating the local economy to national and worldwide situations; (3) a study treating the influence of historic causes and trends on the local economic situation; (4) an examination of political practices in relation to economic factors; (5) a consideration of proposals for change in political practices; (6) a determination of which proposal satisfies the needs of the most people.

Objectives in later years of the curriculum might include the identification of problems, methods, needs, and goals in science and art; the evaluation of the relationship between education and human relations; and the identification of aggressive strategies for effecting change.

Role of the Teacher

Because the faculty must help students discover their own interests, the curriculum maker must relate national and world purposes to the students' goals. Students thus use their interests to help find solutions to the social problems emphasized in their classes. If a community wants to encourage participation of different ethnic groups in public meetings, for example, a foreign language class could help facilitate this participation by interpreting. Such a program provides an opportunity for students to use their special skills and interests to promote community goals in discussion groups, general assemblies, and other local organizations.

The teacher stresses cooperation with the community and its resources. Students may, for example, spend time away from the school participating in community health projects (for science classes) or in community acting, writing, or dance programs (for arts and literature classes). Even the arts must be integrated with other concerns in the program. The interconnection between art and science and art and economics, for example, might be strengthened as the art student looks at art in home and city planning, contrasts unhealthy communities with "ideal garden cities," and attempts to see how the desire for business profits affects the quality of life.

In the primary school, the emphasis is on group experiences. Projects demand interdependence and social consensus. Children of different ages join in community surveys and other cooperative activities. The curriculum of an upper elementary school keeps the Utopian faith by providing generous exercises in social imagination. It might allow children to create rough models of future institutions, such as imaginary hospitals, television, or schools, and thus stimulate the children's awareness of grave contemporary problems.

BASIS FOR SELECTING LEARNING OPPORTUNITIES

For the social reconstructionist a learning opportunity must fulfill three criteria: it must be *real*; it must require *action*; and it must teach *values*. First, learners must focus on an aspect of the community which they believe they can change and to which they will devote their efforts. Passive study, simulations, and role playing do not meet this criterion. Further, the learners must have the opportunity to recognize the real importance of what they are to do. Second, they must act on an issue or problem, not just study it. Responsible action on a matter of public concern may include working with community groups, informing people about social problems, or taking a stand on controversial issues. Third, they must form a coherent system of values. A learning activity must offer an opportunity to employ a sense of what is right and wrong, desirable and undesirable; to supply the individual with a sense of purpose and a basis for both individual and collective effort.

Organization

A social reconstructionist organizes learning activities around such questions as these: Can the ordinary human being fulfill his or her own capabilities in the face of depersonalized forces? Can neighborhoods learn to work together to solve their own problems? Can the economic and political establishments be rebuilt so that people everywhere have access to environmental and cultural resources? Such questions are intended to invite explorations into learning, not only by means of books and laboratories, but by firsthand involvement in the experiences of people in communities.

At the secondary level, there may be an organizational pattern such as Theodore Brameld suggested. He likened his system to a wheel: the "hub" consists of a general assembly engaged in studying one of the central critical questions. The "spokes" are courses composed of discussion groups, content and skill studies, vocational training, and recreation. These courses support the topics treated in the hub. Less concrete but still clearly delineated in the curriculum plans is the "rim," or unifying theme for the enterprise. The theme might be a principle, predicament, or aspiration for all humankind. The rim synthesizes the questions treated in the general assemblies, binding the whole.

Evaluation

Students help to select, to administer, and to evaluate examinations. They examine tests critically for the bias and adequacy of their content and for their ability to reflect the goals of the social reconstructionists. Comprehensive examinations during the last year of school aid in the synthesis and evaluation of students' interpretation of prior work. But evaluation must deal with more than the students and their learning. A social reconstructionist is also interested in the effect of schooling on the community. Factors to be weighed include the growth of community consensus, increased political power of the working classes, and an improved quality of life.

SOCIAL RECONSTRUCTION IN PRACTICE

Changing the Community

Few schools have tried to develop a curriculum completely within the framework of social reconstructionism. Within the United States, such efforts have chiefly been in poor communities. Similarly, worldwide, the Peace Corps and the Third World countries have attended to the concept and have tried to apply it, primarily in rural areas. The recent trend of involving the community in establishing goals for their neighborhood schools and in participating in the conduct of learning opportunities in pursuit of these goals is consistent with social reconstructionism.

Some features of social reconstructionism can be found as early as the 1940s. For example, the school program at Holtville, Alabama, a consolidated rural high school located in a poor area, had as its ideal better living conditions in the community.[3] In Holtville, the students were challenged to study their local economy; they found many problems: heavy meat spoilage in the stores, purchase of canned fruits and vegetables from outside the community as opposed to purchase of the same fruits and vegetables grown in the community, and an overemphasis on the production of a single crop.

With the cooperation of local farmers, the students secured a loan from a governmental agency to construct a slaughterhouse and refrigeration plant. Guided by a teacher, the students began processing meat and renting lockers to the farmers. Soon, they had paid off the loan. Then they did more. They started a hatchery and arranged to sell chicks

[3] *The Story of Holtville: A Southern Association Study School* (Nashville: Cullum and Ghertner, 1944).

to the farmers and buy back eggs below the market price, making money on the enterprise. Subsequently, they undertook to manage a cannery at the school; installed a water supply; helped homes install modern facilities; restored homes; purchased modern machinery, which they rented or used in working for the farmers; planted over 65,000 trees to prevent erosion; planted, sprayed, and pruned 50,000 peach trees for farmers; and set up woodwork and machine shops, a beauty shop, a local newspaper, a movie theatre, a game library, a bowling alley, and a cooperative store in which many of their own products were sold, including toothpaste made in their chemistry department.

In a similar fashion, Myles Horton founded Highlander Folk School in Tennessee, a leading educational center for activists in labor, civil rights, and other social struggles.[4] Horton's curriculum guidelines call for starting with the people's problems. (They may not be able to state what they want in educational terms, but they know what they want in practical terms.) The program must be based on the people's perception of the problem, not the educator's. The curriculum maker must induce the people to use what they already know and to share it. The curriculum maker helps people diagnose their problem and helps learners supplement their knowledge. Limited use is made of the professional when the need for technical advice is obvious. At Highlander, participants are encouraged to take action—such as picketing the welfare office—and then analyze the action, to understand its importance and to internalize it.

Student activities conducted according to reconstructionist principles are also found in volunteer programs in which students attempt to solve local poverty problems, to organize community resources to aid consumers, to help foreign-born nursing home residents, to correct discriminatory employment practices, to determine community needs, to establish facilities for mental patients, or to reform state utility laws.

Paulo Freire's Practice of Social Reconstructionism

Today, the leading social reconstructionist in both theory and practice is Paulo Freire.[5] Although Freire has concentrated on the challenges facing Latin America and one African country in this time of change, he believes that other areas of the Third World differ only in small details and that they must follow his "cultural action for conscientization" if they are to be liberated from political and economic oppression.

---

[4]William B. Kennedy, "Highlander Praxis," *Teachers College Record* 83 (Fall 1981): 106–19.
[5]Paulo Freire, *Pedagogy of the Oppressed* (New York: Herder and Herder, 1970).

Conscientization. Conscientization is the process by which persons, not as recipients but as active learners, achieve a deep awareness both of the sociocultural reality that shapes their lives and of their ability to transform that reality.[6] It means enlightening people about the obstacles that prevent them from having a clear perception of reality. One of these obstacles is a standardized way of thinking—acting, for example, according to the prescriptions received daily from the communications media rather than recognizing one's own problems. Other obstacles are dehumanizing structures that control learning from the outside, educational systems whose schools are an instrument for maintaining the status quo, and political leaders who mediate between the masses and the elite while keeping the masses in a dependent state. Conscientization means helping persons apprehend the origins of facts and problems in their situations rather than attributing them to a superior power or to their own "natural" incapacity. Unless people see these facts objectively, they will accept the situation apathetically, believing themselves incapable of affecting their destiny.

Freire has put his philosophy into action. His plan and materials for teaching reading to adult illiterates show how to put the reconstructionist's theory into practice.[7] Table 1 shows the contrast between Freire's approach and the conventional approach to teaching reading in adult literacy campaigns.

Freire has put his philosophy into action. His plan and materials for teaching reading to adult illiterates show how to put the reconstructionist's theory into practice.[7] Table 2.1 shows the contrast between Freire's approach and the conventional approach to teaching reading in adult literacy campaigns.

to increase yields of their crops, for example, Freire assists them by examining the causes of their felt need for such instruction, thereby rediagnosing their need for the course. Probing into causes might lead the participants to conclude that a course in use of pesticides, as initially perceived, is not needed as much as a course on marketing practice.

The aim of education in Freire's approach is not to accommodate or adjust learners to the social system, but to free them from slavish adherence to it.

Eradicating Illiteracy. Despite attempts to cope with illiteracy, adult illiterates in the United States exceed 25 million. A recent report on the

[6]Paulo Freire, "Cultural Action and Conscientization," *Harvard Educational Review* 40, no. 3 (May 1970): 452–77.
[7]Paulo Freire, "The Adult Literary Process as Cultural Action for Freedom," *Harvard Educational Review* 40, no. 3 (May 1970): 205–25.

TABLE 2.1   Contrasting Approaches to the Teaching of Reading

Conventional Approach	Freire Approach
The teacher chooses words to read and proposes them to the learner.	Poor people create texts that express their own thought-language and their perceptions of the world.
Primers feature word selections that have little to do with the students' sociocultural reality. (For example, "The dog barks." "Mary likes the animals.")	Words are chosen for their (1) pragmatic value in communication with one's group. "Dangerous" words (i.e., *love* and *lust*, *lease* and *license*, *prison* and *power*), for example, the significant concepts that exist among the most broken of the poor; (2) connotations of indignation; (3) generative features, such as syllabic elements by which learners can compare and read new words of importance to themselves.
The teacher implies that there is a relationship between knowing how to read and getting a good job.	The teacher stresses that merely teaching persons to read and write does not work miracles. If there are not enough jobs, teaching reading will not create them.
Learning to read is viewed as a matter of memorizing and repeating given syllables, words, and phrases—following words across the page and understanding what is superficially there.	Learning to read is viewed as important to reflecting critically on the cultural milieu and to awakening students to the dehumanizing aspects of their lives.

efforts to eradicate illiteracy in the United States attests to the inadequacy of curricula that are not immediately relevant to people's lives. The report recommends that illiterates help design a literacy program based on their own needs.[8] Creating a network of community-based literacy programs in poor neighborhoods, the report contends, could potentially win the confidence of people who would otherwise be suspicious of solutions that they perceive as imposed on them from the outside.

[8]Carmen St. John Hunter and David Marman, "Adult Illiteracy in the United States," *A Report to the Ford Foundation* (New York: McGraw-Hill, 1979).

National literacy campaigns in Cuba, Nicaragua, and China using many of Freire's techniques—volunteer teachers and the participation of the peasants and the poor in their own education—have resulted in great gains in literacy and laid the foundation for social development.[9] While the leaders of these campaigns are optimistic that curriculum can develop a critical consciousness in students and prepare people to reinvent society, others are more pessimistic.

Wendy Griswold maintains, for instance, that curriculum has not altered much the structural problems of inequality, poverty, or the domination of the many by the few.[10] She finds little evidence that educational reform has had a positive influence on economic development; most curriculum reforms support the status quo. Even leaders of revolutionary regimes use the curriculum to consolidate their power. In fact, the political revolutions in Cuba and Nicaragua preceded literacy; literacy did not contribute to revolt. Curriculum can, however, contribute to the building of a social order by promoting political awareness and strengthening challenges to the existing society.

Neo-Marxists

A new left has evolved that seeks social reforms using the schools to awaken allies in labor, civil rights, and other groups with the need for control and power. These revolutionaries accuse older social reconstructionists of being naive in their belief that they could transform society by using a "new wave of students who have been nurtured [in the schools]." According to the neo-Marxist, the older reconstructionists "fail[ed] to recognize that oppression and exploitation are a fundamental characteristic of class structure in the United States and cannot be altered by tinkering with the school." The neo-Marxists advocate that curriculum specialists recognize that the success of the schools is tied to conditions in the larger society. Just as the conflicts over the curriculum arise outside the school, so the solutions to these problems require efforts by the larger society. Parents, concerned citizens, organized labor, students, and other groups must be involved in studying, for example, the prevailing patterns of financing, ways to create more jobs, and the possibility of redistributing income.

1975 Manifesto. Indeed in 1975 an ASCD Yearbook committee presented a call to action, encouraging educators to protect their own living

---

[9]Special issue "Education: A Transformation, Identity, Change and Development," *Harvard Educational Review* 51 (February 1981).

[10]Wendy Griswold, "Education as Transformation," *Harvard Educational Review* 52, no. 1 (February 1982): 45–53.

standards by uniting with other educators, students, workers and minority organizations. The manifesto in the yearbook urged educators to demand democracy for students and a curriculum designed to serve the interests of the dominated—the broad working class. Public school educators were given guidelines for action:

1. Develop a core of progressive teachers in each school for the purpose of examining instances of class discrimination—materials, tests, methods, policies—that show differential bias.
2. Encourage students to study the presence or absence of democracy in the school and to report whose interests are being served by existing policies and procedures.
3. Present the findings of dominant class interests at meetings with progressive parents, members of other schools, the teachers' union, and other professional organizations.
4. Expose the class content of your school program publicly—for example, at PTA and union meetings.
5. Enlist the help of community and working-class organizations in developing a curriculum based on the interests of the working class. The curriculum at a minimum would include (a) the teaching of modern history focused on the struggles of Western-dominated Third World countries, the working classes, oppressed minorities, and women against exploitation; (b) full equality for the language and culture of oppressed national minorities; (c) instruction in fundamentals of socio-economic analysis of social relations; and (d) development of cultural activities aimed at the acceptance of working-class culture.
6. Establish an areawide committee for a curriculum based on the interests of the dominated groups, enlisting students in the struggle for liberation.
7. Introduce a plan for disseminating revolutionary demands and form a united front among all dominated groups against the increasingly centralized and rigid control by the power structure.[11].

"Reproductive" Theory. More recently Michael Apple and Henry Giroux have argued that the knowledge "reproduced" in schools produces a stratified social order and perpetuates the values of dominant social class interests. Only rarely has the curriculum not reflected what is happening outside of school.[12] Both authors believe that we should broaden the curriculum to include community action. Through community action, they hold, students develop social and political responsibility and skills while learning to question the ethics of their institutions and to criticize

[11]James A. MacDonald and Esther Zaret, eds., *Schools in Search of Meaning,* ASCD Yearbook (Washington, D.C.: National Education Association, 1975): pp. 158–61.
[12]Michael Apple, *Education and Power* (Boston: Routledge, Kegan Paul, 1982).

them when they fail to meet ideals. Giroux wants teachers to change the nature of schooling so that it is more emancipatory and less a feeble echo of the demand for social order.[13] He holds that teachers have the potential to overcome the social form that oppresses them. Giroux feels that schools are sites where personal opinions and beliefs are formed and reformed. Teachers may oppose the official curriculum based upon their own experiences, critical reading, and discussion with others. Although it is naive to think that the school can create the conditions for changing the larger society, teachers and students must try to transform their own practices and consciousness as part of a larger strategy to change society.

Evidence in support of the "reproductive" theory of curriculum—that the knowledge taught in school perpetuates existing political and economic structures—has been provided by Jean Anyon.[14] In her case study, Anyon collected data on school knowledge in five elementary schools in contrasting social class settings. Her data suggest that while topics and materials are similar among working-class, middle-class, affluent, and elite schools, there are dramatic differences in pupils' experience of the curriculum in these schools.

In the working-class schools, students were not taught their own history—the history of the working class—and the curriculum emphasized rote behaviors rather than creative thinking. The dominant theme was student resistance. The teacher had to discipline the class—physically at times—in order to impose a curriculum consisting only of the basics and worksheets. In contrast, the middle-class school students viewed knowledge as facts and generalizations which could be exchanged for college entrance or a better job. Possibility was the dominant theme.

In the affluent school, students perceived knowledge as a personal activity having to do with things or ideas. They were taught ways of using ideas or their own interests. The dominant theme in the affluent school was individualization. Since students thought for themselves and engaged in creative projects and personal discovery, their schooling stressed individual values over collective ones.

In the executive elite school, excellence was the theme. Students viewed knowledge as the result of rational rules, not personal discovery. Children were provided with socially prestigious subject matter and were given analytical insights about the social system.

Though Anyon concluded that the curriculum reproduced the main-

---

[13]Henry Giroux, *Ideology, Culture and the Process of Schooling* (Philadelphia: Temple University Press, 1981).

[14]Jean Anyon, "Social Class and School Knowledge," *Curricular Inquiry* 11, no. 1 (1981): 3–41.

tenance of class roles in society, she felt it also offered possibilities for transformation. The resistance of working-class pupils might lead to a restructuring of capitalistic ideology. The middle-class students, on the other hand, might become disillusioned with false promises about big rewards for working hard and become critics of the system. Students in the affluent school might recognize irrationalities in society as they engage in their individual efforts at making sense of the world. Pupils in the elite school might discover the difference between using knowledge for pleasure and using it to maintain power in the face of competition from others. Further, elitist learners might perceive the need for destroying the system because they might see how under capitalism one must exploit others.

Futurologists

Curriculum futurologists advocate making deliberate choices about the world of the future (Utopia). They would study trends, estimate the social consequences foreshadowed by the trends, and then attempt to promote probable futures seen as "good" and prevent those seen as "bad."

There are many futurologists in society at large. The World Future Society, a nonprofit, nonpolitical organization, alone has 16,000 members ranging from economists and philosophers to Venus watchers. Generally, futurologists do not attempt to predict what is going to happen in 10 or 15 years but attempt to decide on what they want to happen so that they can then make more intelligent choices.

The Use of Future Planning. Harold G. Shane, professor at Indiana University, is representative of those social reconstructionists who would use future planning as a basis for curriculum making.[15] He urges planning the future, not planning for the future. As with other social reconstructionists, he stresses the power of persons to shape their own destiny and to believe that they are not bound to an inescapable future to which they must conform.

Shane would obligate curriculum developers to study trends first. Trends may be technological developments that have been identified with the help of specialists in academic disciplines. Such trends include reduction of hereditary defects, three-dimensional philosophy, increase in life expectancy, chemical methods for improving memory, and home

---

[15]Harold G. Shane, *Educating for a New Millennium* (Bloomington: Phi Delta Kappan, 1981).

education via video and computers. Trends also may be inventoried problems such as those found in the literature of disaster (for example, famine, dwindling resources, pollution). Shane would have educators who have studied trends engage with a wide number of participants in analyzing their consequences. Such consequences might be mandatory foster homes for children whose natural homes are harmful to their physical or mental health; psychological prerequisites for candidates seeking public office; use of biochemical therapy for improving mood, memory, or concentration; reversal of counterecological trends; controlled growth; and concern for equity rather than equalitarianism. Professional specialists—those with expert knowledge—would decide whether the promised consequences would humanize or dehumanize. Final judgment about desirability, however, must rest with the people concerned.

Most social reconstructionists are very clear about the role of the professional expert in the determination of social policy. Although they use experts in analyzing complicated social problems, they do not entirely relegate the solution of these problems to the experts. "In the realm of social policy, the decisions of the whole people, when they have full access to the facts, are in the long run typically wiser than those made by any single class or group. The cult of the expert is but the prelude to some form of authoritarian society."[16] Reconstructionists favor pressing society for decisions and for the development of a clearer social consensus as to what the "good life" is. In achieving this consensus, the ideas of children, parents, administrators, and teachers should be considered. Those ideas that the group sees as having merit must become the basis for "mutual coercion"—control for a socially worthy purpose.

Typical Recommendations. Futurist curriculum focuses on the exploitation of resources; pollution of the air and water; warfare; the effect of the population increase and the unequal use of natural resources; propaganda, especially in press and screen; and self-control in the interests of one's fellows.

For example, in his view of the future Neil Postman sees television as a dangerous curriculum—an information system specially constructed to influence, teach, train, or cultivate the mind and character of the young—competing with the school's curriculum. It is a dangerous curriculum because it is (a) present centered (does not encourage deferred gratification, (b) attention centered (entertainment takes precedence over content), (c) image centered (weakens ability to use abstract, propo-

[16]B. Othanel Smith et al., *Fundamentals of Curriculum Development* (Yonkers, N.Y.: World Books, 1950), p. 638.

sitional reasoning), (d) emotion centered (nonintellectual), and (d) largely incoherent (it creates discontinuity). Postman would create a future in which the curriculum of the school would counter TV, offer a sense of purpose, meaning, and the interrelation of disciplines. The historical development of humanity, for instance, could be used to integrate the teaching of philosophy, science, language, religion, and cultural expression.[17]

Social Adaptation

Both social adaption and social reconstruction derive aims and content from an analysis of the society the school is to serve. Curriculum development in response to social needs—career education, sex education, ecological studies, parenting programs, energy conservation—are often more adaptive than reconstructive. Such curriculum represents a mechanism for adjusting students to what some groups believe to be an appropriate response to critical needs within society. Social adaption differs from social reconstruction in that usually no attempt is made to develop a critical consciousness of social problems and to do something about them. The approach of social adaptionists is to give students information and prescriptions for dealing with situations as defined rather than to seek a fundamental change in the basic structure of society. While social adaptionists look at society to find out what students need to achieve in the real world—to fit into society as it is—social reconstructionists look at society with the intent of building a curriculum by which students can improve the real world.

CRITICISMS OF SOCIAL RECONSTRUCTIONISM

Reconstructionism is appealing because of its faith in the ability of humankind to form a more perfect world. Further, it claims to use the best of science in determining status and possibilities. Among the reconstructionists' difficulties, however, is the fact that scientific findings permit varied interpretations. Established empirical conclusions are scant. Even the futurologists have been grouped into the "bleak sheiks" (pessimists) and the "think-tank utopians" (optimists). Further, there are no direct implications for curriculum. What one sociologist or economist considers true may be refuted by another. Few agree about what conduct is best for a planned society.

[17]Neil Postman, "Engaging Students in the Great Conversation," *Phi Delta Kappan* 64, no. 5 (March 1983): 310–17.

Reconstructionists with a Marxist orientation fault older reconstructionists for failing to recognize that oppression and exploitation are fundamental characteristics of class structure in the United States and cannot be altered by teachers within the schools. While older reconstructionists did not speak of the school as remaking the society in any total sense, they did believe that the school might influence behavior in regard to social problems. They realized that attitudes and beliefs would not be sustained unless supported by changes in the structure of society. However, they thought that the primary task of the school was a moral and intellectual reconstruction. Unlike the neo-Marxists, they did not believe that the school should be an instrument for subversion and political revolution. Instead they wanted to use the school to extend the ideals to which the people were already committed.

Neo-Marxists also have been faulted. Their theory of cultural reproduction has been challenged because no evidence shows that schools have been deliberately oppressive in the interests of the larger society.

Although the work of Freire in developing curriculum through dialog with learners is generally highly regarded, he too has his critics. Jim Walker, for instance, doubts that Freire's educational ideas and methods are truly liberating because they do not give enough attention to effecting a revolution. Freire has little to say, Walker charges, about the nature of political leadership and how to achieve unity among a divided people.[18]

C. A. Bowers, on the other hand, believes that Freire's approach reflects Western culture and, therefore, might undermine the traditional world views of people in non-Western cultures. Brown questions whether Western assumptions such as knowledge is power, change is progressive, and people are the masters of their own fates are appropriate in non-Western traditional societies.[19]

CONCLUDING COMMENTS

Social reconstructionists are concerned with the relation of the curriculum to society as it *should* be as opposed to society as it *is*. Many of the tenets of this group are consistent with our highest ideals, such as the right of those with a minority viewpoint to persuade a majority, and faith in the intelligence of common people and in their ability to shape their own destiny in desired directions. Neo-Marxists within the social

---

[18]Jim Walker, "The End of Dialogue," in *Literacy and Revolution,* ed. Robert Mackie (New York: Continuum, 1981), pp. 120–51.
[19]C. A. Bowers, "Cultural Invasion in Paulo Freire's Pedagogy," *Teachers College Record* 81, no. 4 (Summer 1983): 935–55.

reconstructionist ranks would pit class against class and advocate a biased socioeconomic analysis. The futurists in the movement are far less ideologically oriented and would be quite happy if the curriculum would help learners "want well"—that is, conceive of a desirable future after taking into account crucial social trends.

The reconstructionist commitment to particular social ideas determined by "social consensus" may have difficulty being accepted in an individualistic United States. Americans have so many competing interests and different views regarding moral, religious, aesthetic, and social issues that it would be difficult for them to agree on an ideal. Some also voice concern about the reconstructionists' efforts to change our political structure in the direction of totalitarianism, to create a collective society in which solutions are reached through forced social consensus.

We can expect accelerated curriculum development along reconstructionist lines whenever there is a need to resolve a conflict in values. Such a need often exists in multicultural neighborhoods. Cultural groups frequently have different interpretations of history, different conceptions of nature, different levels of aspiration, and different views of social conduct. The prediction also applies whenever there is a breakdown in the barriers that isolate the school from the community. Accelerated curriculum development should thus occur when parents and community members become involved in teaching and social service roles, when students and adults participate in effecting changes outside the school building, when community members assess local social and economic needs or deficiencies and decide how the institutions in the community can contribute to the improvement of the selected priority needs.

The close tie of some reconstructionists with professional teacher organizations makes it likely that they will clash with reconstructionists favoring local community groups and parents. Rivalry between teacher and parent power movements regarding *what* should be taught and *how* it should be taught has already surfaced. The challenge, therefore, will be to apply the principle that calls for a "community of persuasion," probably by including teachers in the decision-making process but also by giving the community—parents and others—more of a controlling voice.

QUESTIONS

1. What circumstances would be most likely to give rise to a curriculum along social reconstructionist lines?
2. Paulo Freire speaks of the curriculum obstacles preventing a clear perception of reality (for example, control of learning from the outside, content

and method that foster learner dependency, and standardized ways of thinking). Can you provide specific examples of these obstacles in schools you have known?

3. Consider computer literacy, career education, and multicultural courses known to you. Was their approach social adaptionist or social reconstructionist?

4. Are you optimistic or pessimistic about the ability of curriculum to change existing social structure? Why?

5. What predictions about the world future appear "good" to you? Which ones appear "bad?" How should a curriculum be designed in order to prevent the bad future?

6. Whose interests are best served by the curriculum with which you are familiar?

SELECTED REFERENCES

Apple, Michael W. *Education and Power.* Boston: Routledge & Kegan Paul, 1982.

Brameld, Theodore. *Toward a Reconstructed Philosophy of Education.* New York: Dryden, 1956.

Freire, Paulo. *Pedagogy in Process—The Letters to Guinea-Bissau.* New York: Seabury, 1978.

Gireaux, Henry. *Ideology, Culture and the Process of Schooling.* Philadelphia: Temple University Press, 1981.

MacDonald, James B. and Zaret, Esther, eds. *Schools in Search of Meaning.* ASCD 1975 Yearbook. Washington, D.C.: National Education Association, 1975.

Mackie, Robert, ed. *Literacy and Revolution: The Pedagogy of Paul Freire.* New York: Continuum, 1981.

Shane, Harold G. *Educating for a New Millennium.* Bloomington: Phi Delta Kappa, 1981.

3 / TECHNOLOGY AND THE CURRICULUM

Educational consumers are familiar with technology in the form of computer-based instruction, individualized learning systems, and video and audio cassettes. Many have been exposed to Seymour Papert's program for the promotion of technological literacy. In the program primary grade children learn to program robots and learn mathematical concepts by giving "turtle talk" commands to a computer—teaching the turtle to draw a square, for example.

Most persons are less aware, however, that technology is also helpful in the analysis of curriculum problems as well as for the creation, implementation, evaluation, and management of instructional solutions. Technology as a curriculum perspective focuses on the effectiveness of programs, methods, and materials in the achievement specified ends or purposes. A technological perspective has been applied in many contexts—the development of training programs in industry and the military; the design of instructional systems with matching objectives, activities, and tests; and the development of instructional products or materials. Recently, the technological perspective has been a major factor in the competency testing movement and other responses to public demands for school accountability.

Technology influences curriculum in two ways: application and theory. Applied technology is a plan for the systematic use of various devices and media or a contrived sequence of instruction based on principles from behavioral science. Computer assisted instruction, systems approaches using objectives, programmed materials, tutors following scripts aimed at teaching a specific skill, and criterion-referenced tests are all examples of applied technology. A defining element of technology is that its systems and products can be replicated. That is, the same results can be attained on repeated occasions, and the system itself is exportable—useful in many situations.

Technology as theory is useful in the development and evaluation of curriculum materials and instructional systems. In the developmental process technologists formulate rules which, if followed, will result in more predictable products.

General systems philosophy is a technological framework for viewing problems of curriculum. It emphasizes the specification of instructional objectives (usually derived by needs assessment, a study that contrasts the student's level of achievement with the learning goals), precisely controlled learning activities or instructional sequences to achieve these objectives, and criteria for performance and evaluation. Developing a general systems philosophy also requires stressing feedback to modify the learner's behavior and to adapt instruction (i.e., measurement of the achievements of the program), recognizing the interaction between components of the instructional system, and paying attention to the complex interactions between the program and the larger environment in which it is to be implemented.

At first glance, technology appears to be concerned with *how* to teach rather than *what* to teach. Technologists think of themselves as finding efficient and effective means to achieve specific ends. A second glance shows that the instructional sequences produced by the technologist's model are primarily concerned with what is or is not learned. In focusing upon a specified objective, though, the technologist is less likely to develop flexible instructional sequences that contribute to a range of desirable outcomes.

This chapter includes a description and analysis of technology as a learning system as well as procedures for using technology as the basis for curriculum development. The chapter should help in understanding the characteristics of the approach and in discerning the strengths and weaknesses in the technological concepts of curriculum.

EXAMPLES OF TECHNOLOGICAL CURRICULUM

Personalized Systematic Instruction in Higher Education

Over 90 percent of the nation's colleges and universities use highly sophisticated electronic devices to transmit some portion of their curriculum to students. As the use of educational technology becomes more widespread, the teacher tends to relinquish the role of imparter of knowledge for that of manager. The content of instruction and its applications are set in advance. In contrast to traditional higher education, the boundaries of knowledge are not fluid, and the results obtained are more important than the process. When course content is viewed as finite, it can be packaged in advance, duplicated, and transmitted. While the view may narrowly define content, it also allows students to work at their own pace. One popular use of technology as a means to more effective instruction is the personalized system of instruction (PSI). This system is a soft technology involving persons, content, materials, and organizations as opposed to a hard technology, which involves only devices such as television, projectors, and computers. PSI utilizes the principles of behavioral science that call for frequent active responses from students, immediate knowledge of results, and a clear statement of objectives. It also allows for individualization; different students may use different amounts of time and different approaches for attaining mastery of the instructional tasks.

With PSI a course or subject is broken into small units of learning, and at the end of each unit learners take tests to determine whether they are ready for new material or should receive additional instruction. Whenever students believe they are ready, they go to a "proctoring room" staffed by advanced students who administer the test, score it, and give feedback to the students. If less than "unit perfection" performance is shown, the proctor becomes a tutor, explaining the missing points and guiding the student in restudy. There is no penalty for failing a unit, but one must study further and try again. Frequent interaction with proctors often develops affect and contributes to understanding.

PSI permits one instructor to serve as many as 1,000 students, or possibly more. Instructors are responsible for conducting one- or two-hour weekly large group sessions for motivating and clarifying. They also have overall responsibility for planning the course, including the procedures and procurement or development of materials and examinations.

Individually Prescribed Instruction and Mastery Learning

Individually prescribed instruction (IPI) and mastery learning are other examples of curriculum produced by technologists. Instructional objectives, arranged in an assumed hierarchy of tasks, are the keystone of the system, and lesson materials are built around that arrangement. The objectives are the intended outcomes of instruction. Each pupil must master them before going on to the next step in the learning hierarchy. Mastery is indicated by successful responses to criterion-referenced tests matched to the content and behavior specified in the objective. Objectives in the teaching of mathematics, for example, are grouped by topics such as numeration, place value, and subtraction.

Lesson materials are matched with the objectives and allow the pupil to proceed independently with a minimum of teacher direction. The pattern for involving the pupil with the system has three parts.

1. Finding out what the pupil already knows about the subject. Usually a general placement test is administered to reveal the pupil's general level of achievement. The pupil is also given a pretest to reveal specific deficiencies.

2. Giving the pupil self-instructional materials or other carefully designed learning activities. Such activities focus on one of the specific deficiencies previously identified.
3. Giving the pupil evaluative measures to determine his or her progress. Such measures help the teacher decide whether to move the pupil ahead to a new task or to provide additional materials or tutoring.

Materials usually include placement tests, pre- and posttests (criterion-referenced), skill booklets, response booklets, a record system, games and manipulatives, and cassettes and filmstrips. Paid aides and volunteers, such as parents, assist pupils, check response sheets, and help to keep the materials organized.

At the secondary level, technology is a frequent remedy for skill deficiencies found through mandated competency or proficiency testing. Accordingly, students who have been identified as lacking particular mathematical, writing, or reading skills are given self-instructional booklets and student study guides. The booklets offer opportunity to practice both the enroute skills and the terminal performance of separate skills; the study guides describe in simple language each basic skill and include practice test items and their answers as well as a brief exposition of the skill and a set of selected textbook references for student use. The secondary school teacher, too, is given a skill-focused guide including a thorough explanation of what the skill calls for, a test item format, content delineation, and an accounting of the requisite types of intellectual operations. A set of appropriate instructional tactics is also included.

GENERAL CHARACTERISTICS OF CLASSROOM TECHNOLOGICAL SYSTEMS

Objectives

Objectives have a behavioral or empirical emphasis. They specify learning products or processes in forms that can be observed or measured. There is no inherent reason, though, why technological systems cannot employ affective as well as psychomotor and cognitive objectives. Indeed, some technological systems do feature affective objectives. Typically, however, the objectives are detailed, specific, and skill-oriented. Commercially available materials feature objectives that are likely to be appropriate for most children in this country. Those skills that most curriculum developers believe useful in learning to read and in solving mathematical problems, for example, are often focuses of instruction.

The instructional objectives of technological systems thus tend to reinforce the importance of conventional goals and the traditional divisions of academic subject matter. With the exception of locally designed materials, such as Unipacs, learning centers and learning activities packages (LAPs), objectives more appropriate for local social conditions are seldom treated. Neither are there many opportunities for pupils to generate their own objectives.

Methods

Learning is viewed as a process of reacting to stimuli—attending to relevant cues—rather than as a transactional process in which the learner influences the stimuli. The learner is directed to attend to more significant features and is reinforced for appropriate behavior. Goals of instruction are predetermined rather than emergent.

Individualism is restricted to pacing, corrective feedback, and supplementary tasks when deficiencies and misconceptions are noticed. Some children can make their responses more quickly and require fewer exercises in order to learn a generalization. Individual children need not spend time on tasks leading to behaviors already in their repertoire.

Typically, learners work alone, although there may be occasional periods of small group work. There is a set of common objectives, which all pupils are expected to master. The paradigm of instruction follows these principles:

1. *Perceived purpose and advanced organizer.* Learners are told why it is important to learn a certain objective or at least are given a clear explanation of what they are to learn. They are made aware of the standards of successful performance.
2. *Appropriate practice.* Learners have opportunities to practice both the prerequisite skills not already attained and the behavior specified by the objective. The desired response is frequently obtained by prompting. Eventually, however, the prompts are removed and the child responds to the problem using the concept or principles taught.
3. *Knowledge of results.* Pupils are given feedback indicating whether their responses are adequate and are helped to make them more appropriate, if necessary.

Organization

The technologist's curriculum is usually related to subject disciplines such as mathematics, sciences, reading and other language arts, arts, and to applied technical fields. Usually only a few aspects of these fields are selected for treatment at any one time. Decimals in mathematics, for example, are treated in a separate program, not as mathematics in general. The objectives of instruction are arranged in a fixed continuum or hierarchy of skills—an end-of-program objective such as the ability to multiply would follow enroute objectives of addition and subtraction. End-of-program objectives are precisely and operationally stated, and these objectives are the basis for organizing instruction. The objectives are analyzed in terms of prerequisites; each prerequisite in turn is then stated as an enroute objective, and these enroute objectives are arranged in an assumed hierarchical order. A learner may follow a series of activities or tasks such as the following:

1. Define a given concept.
2. Recognize instances of the concept.
3. Combine two given concepts into a principle.
4. Combine given principles into a strategy for solving new problems.

Complex subject matter, in short, is sequenced by the simple components. A particular sequence may vary in length from a single lesson to a course of instruction for a year.

Task analysis—breaking down an objective into its basic elements, steps, or rules—is the chief procedure for designing technological curriculum as well as for determining enroute tasks and the order of their acquisition.

Evaluation

Unique to the technologist is the assumption that if the intended learner (the kind of person for whom the program was designed) does not master the specified objectives, the program maker is at fault. Learners are not responsible for their own success or failure. Programs are developed, tried out on a sample of the intended population of learners, and revised according to the findings until the program attains intended results.

Until recently, technologists usually evaluated their programs only in terms of their own objectives. Unanticipated side effects were seldom sought. Neither was the validity or justification for end-of-program objectives established by considering the full range of criteria that various consumers might apply to both process and product. Technologists examined achievement but sometimes did not consider whether attaining the objective produced desirable or undesirable effects on the community or whether the individualized techniques inadvertently impaired learners' social skills. The technologist, as such, is concerned more with the effectiveness of the process than with the validity of the objectives.

Generally, the technological approach is most effective for conventional, easily measurable tasks. Students achieve more with these techniques than they would otherwise. Edmond Gordon finds that "the tightly structured programmed approach including frequent and immediate feedback to the pupil, combined with a tutorial relationship, individual pacing, and somewhat individualized programming are positively associated with accelerated pupil achievement."[1] According to B. S. Bloom, the typical result of mastery learning studies in the schools is that about 80 percent of students with mastery learning reach the same level of achievement (A or B +) as approximately the top 20 percent of the class under conventional instruction.[2] Again, however, it must be remembered that most of the positive evaluation rests on achievement defined either by scores on standardized tests or by tests designed for the program, which treat aspects of traditional school subjects.

TECHNOLOGY IN THE DEVELOPMENT OF CURRICULUM MATERIALS

The development of textbooks, courses, lessons, and other curriculum materials formerly involved art and politics more than technology. Curriculum development has been a search for some general value—an important idea, problem, or skill—around which content and activities could be organized. Newer criteria for technological curriculum making have only recently been accepted as guides to practice. These criteria are: (1) the developmental procedures used should be reviewed and validated by other developers: they should be able to be replicated; (2) products developed in accordance with models that can be replicated should produce similar results.

The heart of the technological revolution in curriculum is, however, the belief that curriculum materials themselves, when used by those learners for whom the materials are developed, should produce specified learner competencies. This belief is a great advance over the belief that curriculum materials are mere resources that may or may not be useful

---

[1]Edmond W. Gordon, "Utilizing Available Information from Compensatory Education and Surveys," *Final Report* (Washington, D.C.: Office of Education, 1971), p. 24.
[2]B. S. Bloom, *All Our Children Learning* (New York: McGraw-Hill, 1981).

TABLE 3.1   Comparison of Criteria for Selection of Instructional Materials

Old Criteria	New Criteria
Do authors have professional reputations?	Where and how extensively have materials been tried out?
Are materials based on sound pedagogical principles? Are they consistent with established suggestions for instruction and practice? Will the content broaden the children's view of the world?	Is information available about the number of students who started and completed the materials? Does the information say how much time learners of different ability spent on portions of the material and give differential results?
Are selections arranged by level to satisfy the needs and interests of children as they mature? Is the art imaginative and appealing?	Do the materials specify intended-learner characteristics including enumeration of prerequisites? Does the art contribute to affective learning?
Are type faces and sizes, lengths of lines, and space between lines appropriate for the maturity of the children at each level?	Are materials being revised to reflect trial results? How are student responses used in revising the material?
Do materials use high quality paper, clear print, and sturdy binding?	How effectively do students learn specified skills? Do appropriate criterion-referenced tests show student gains?

or influential in a certain situation. The change in concept can be seen in two different ways for judging curriculum materials (see Table 3.1).

Publishers' Response

A major force in the production of curriculum materials, the publishers usually agree that teachers need help in deciding which new and unfamiliar materials are most appropriate for their particular needs. Further, they recognize the vague feeling that education needs to be protected from big government and big business, since either one could foist ideas and products on the educational community before they are properly tested.

Although some limited field testing occurs, textbook publishers admit that their materials are designed and evaluated intuitively rather than systematically. They do their best intuitively to prepare materials that will be productive in the classroom. Then they listen attentively to what the users of these materials have to say about them, and modify succeeding revisions to take this experience into account. Sometimes the revision is better; sometimes it is merely different.

Although they agree with technologists that there is a need for better evaluations and more consistent results, publishers still have many questions. *Who* would do the field testing—developers or outside agencies? *What* constitutes a reasonable sample? *Who* will pay for the higher costs incurred for the more expensive trials and revisions? Will producers publish complete data or only positive findings?

A nonprofit corporation, Educational Products Information Exchange Institute (EPIE), has attempted to make impartial studies of the availability, use, and effectiveness of educational materials, equipment, and systems. EPIE reports tend to be descriptive. They indicate the effects of the materials on teacher time, costs, and staffing, and state the underlying assumptions or philosophy of the materials. They also reveal the extent to which there has been learner verification of the materials.

Federal funds have supported technological curriculum development at a number of places. For example, individually prescribed instruction was developed at the Learning Research and Development Center of the University of Pittsburgh, and Project Plan was developed by the American Institute for Research of Palo Alto, California. Typical of the developmental process used by such institutions is that of the Southwest Regional Laboratory for Educational Research and Development.[3] In the development of a reading program, more extrinsic efforts were made at formulating a product, that is, a communication skills program, than in formulating the goals of the program. The decision to emphasize reading was a policy matter, and once it was made the following kinds of developmental activities were undertaken:

1. Decisions about content were made.
2. There were general decisions about the nature of the materials (for example, it was decided to feature story books in order to provide opportunities to practice the skills of reading).
3. Brief trials of segments, modifications in selection of words, book format, and typography were undertaken.

[3]Eva L. Baker, "The Technology of Instructional Development," in *Second Handbook of Research on Teaching,* ed. Robert M. W. Travers (Chicago: Rand McNally, 1973).

4. Instructional support materials like games, practice sequences, and lesson plans were developed. During this phase, specific objectives were stated. Materials were tried out on small groups of learners and reviewed by experts and teachers.
5. Field trials were initiated with modest teacher training, followed by observations of classroom procedures and use of techniques for obtaining teacher comments.
6. Both teacher comments and results from interim criterion tests provided a basis for revision.

Common Elements

There are five common elements in the technologist's process of curriculum development:

1. *Formulation.* The foundation of an idea for a product rests on the decision that that product is needed. Need may be based on a presumed market. Court and legislative action, for example, may demand a changed emphasis. Bilingual materials were formulated in response to court decisions giving impetus to teaching non-English-speaking pupils in their own language.
2. *Specification.* Specification of outcomes is undertaken both to guide the development of the product and to provide a basis for product evaluation. Delineation of the measures to be used in determining the effectiveness of the program is helpful in planning for evaluation. Specification includes a description of the situation (stimuli) to which the learner will be expected to respond (the domain). Standards for determining the adequacy of a response are also stipulated. Specifications describing component skills requisite for the achievement of the objectives are usually stated and ordered. The characteristics of the intended learners are also specified. Learners' entry skills and other attributes that may bear on the development and use of the product should be listed. The models should also tell whether the product will be self-instructional or require the use of tutor, parent, or teacher; and they should indicate the extent of involvement of instructors.
3. *Prototype.* Variations in learning sequences are produced and tried out with a few learners. Decisions about composite formats, media, and organization are made during this phase.
4. *Initial Trials.* Segments of instruction are tried out with a sample of learners to determine whether the component achieves its objectives and to reveal weaknesses. The use of data to improve the product is essential to the technologist. Data include not only per-

formance on end-of-sequence tests but errors made while responding to the material. Modest revisions of a component usually increase overall performance of the system.

5. *Trial of Product.* The product is put into use with existing school instruction. Data are collected about training, special problems in implementation (such as the need for teacher training or unanticipated side effects), and results achieved.

ISSUES IN A TECHNOLOGICAL APPROACH TO CURRICULUM DEVELOPMENT

On the one hand, many claim that the technological approach leads to products that are consistent with the learner's predispositions because the developer must be attentive to the learner and not rely on armchair planning. The approach is also said to provide procedures for curriculum making that can be replicated and manipulated, helping us learn what works and what does not.

On the other hand, people are concerned about the technological approach's costliness, which has resulted in a greater need for government financing. Such funding is automatically suspect when people fear governmental influence on what their children learn and view federal influences as antagonistic to local development of the curriculum. Also, the technologist's logical approach, which attempts to help the learner achieve mastery of specified objectives, has been faulted for excluding more potential influences on learning outcomes than it includes. In many ways, the older notion of providing rich environments without specific objectives may have had more fruitful results.

Special Problems

Three major problems plague most technological curricula: their invalid hierarchies of prerequisites and arbitrary standards of mastery, their unsuitability for uncertain situations, and their limited concepts of individualization.

Invalid Hierarchies. Technologists have not fully succeeded in defining essential prerequisites and learning hierarchies for complex subject matter. Neither have they been able to determine the degree of mastery required for programs. Attempts to determine mastery or competency through statistical or psychological means have not been satisfactory. In fact, Gene Glass and Mary Lee Smith have argued that the attempt to set standards of performance for promotion is futile except as a political endeavor.[4] Although technologists have contributed greatly to equity among students by introducing criterion-referenced tests, which assess students by their progress toward a defined task rather than by their achievement relative to a peer, the validity (content and construct) of many of these tests is suspect. Many reasons may account for poor performance on a criterion-referenced test, and successful performance on the test may not predict success in situations that demand transfer.

Inappropriateness for Uncertain Situations. Gary Klein asserts that the usefulness of the technological approach is limited to certain kinds of tasks and to lower levels of proficiency.[5] Its limitation rests on the distinction between procedural and nonprocedural tasks. Procedural tasks can be broken down into steps or rules that, when followed, accomplish the tasks. After learning the rules for a task, students have achieved a mediocre level of competence. By contrast, the rules or procedures a person needs to follow in order to perform nonprocedural tasks— producing a work of art, writing a critique, solving a problem, and making a decision—are unclear. It is difficult to break down such tasks into basic steps and rules, and, even if they were, it is not clear that a student who learned the rules could perform at a satisfactory level.

When it is effective, technology is usually aimed at a procedural task. It is a limited tool for nonprocedural tasks and may even hinder proficiency. Forcing proficient people to follow prescribed steps appropriate for novices, for example, would probably impede performance. On nonprocedural tasks, highly proficient persons do not follow abstract rules but use a repertoire of analogies from experience to guide their performance. Experts can perceive a current task as similar to a previous situation and thus use what they know about that situation to predict outcomes, determine what is relevant, and decide what action to take. They do not go through calculations of formal elements. (Imagine someone trying to use Polanyi's rule for riding a bicycle—"At any given angle of unbalance, the rider should turn the front wheel to the degree inversely proportional to the square of the speed."[6] Further, there is the question of whether complex tasks can be analyzed into simple, discrete elements. Elements may exist only in the context of the overall task and the goals of the person performing it.

---

[4]Gene V. Glass and Mary Lee Smith, "The Technology and Politics of Standards," *Educational Technology* 18, no. 5 (May 1978): 12–18.

[5]Gary A. Klein, "Curriculum Development Versus Education," *Teachers College Record* 84, no. 4 (Summer 1983): 821–36.

[6]M. Polanyi. *Personal Knowledge* (Chicago: University of Chicago Press, 1958), p. .

Organizational plans of the technologists' curriculum usually make no real contribution to the problem of helping learners transfer what they learn to new subject matters and to the real world. The technologists' curriculum is usually tied to the achievement of traditional or static goals, to those things that schools have long been attempting to do. Its main contribution is to allow schools to do these things more effectively.

Limited Concept of Individualization. The technological curriculum may be best for helping students who would never be expected to gain proficiency—for whom following rules represents a higher level of performance than they could otherwise achieve—but not for students capable of becoming highly proficient if free from restrictive rules and procedures. Individualization in the technological curriculum seldom allows the learners to generate their own objectives. Also, technologists have not given sufficient attention to learners' predispositions toward specific methods. Students with low aptitude, for example, may respond differently to some technological features than do students with high aptitude. Technologists might take their responses into consideration by developing alternative programs rather than expecting all to learn from the same materials. Tightly structured programs, for example, may be more effective for those with lower aptitude.

CONCLUDING COMMENTS

Technology has greatly improved curriculum. Its emphasis on objectives has led curriculum makers to ask what kinds of objectives are most valuable. Some people question the tendency of the technologists' curriculum to maintain objectives consistent with conventional fragmented or compartmentalized subject matter areas. We are likely to have more warranted objectives as a result of such objections.

The technologists' influence on curriculum developers has been great. Without the technologists' prodding for evidence of results, most developers would have been satisfied to provide what they thought were valid educational environments, never taking responsibility for the consequences. More clearly to be seen is the technologists' contribution to instructional effectiveness, the ordering of instructional sequences, and the monitoring of pupil progress. It is reasonable to suppose that more persons can now produce an effective curriculum by following the technologists' model. Many of these persons may not, however, do any better or as well as the rare creative developer following his or her own intuition.

People who make decisions about how to develop curriculum, such as publishers and school officials, will have to weigh the value of the technologists' model against its heavier development costs (often a threefold time increase over traditional approaches to curriculum development). They may find that the higher costs are balanced by increased learning for more pupils when the model is implemented.

One weakness in the technologists' model for curriculum development is that it does not give sufficient attention to implementation of the products and the dynamics of innovation. Just developing a more effective product is often not enough. Unless attention is given to changing the wider environment (school organization, teachers' attitudes, community views), the good product may not be used or at least not in a way that will fulfill its promise. Efforts to improve the conditions of implementation, however, are likely to draw resources away from efforts to improve the product itself.

Lest this chapter present technology in too grim a light, a reviewer reminds us that there are affective aspects "of keeping the pupil's nose against the content grindstone," citing the computer program "The Dove" that is an aesthetic experience and the computer versions of "Dungeons and Dragons" and the "Star Trek" games as fantasy adventures.

In *Mindstorms: Children, Computers, and Powerful Ideas,* Seymour Papert offers a fresh alternative in the technological curriculum. Papert arranges the computer so that young people learn to control, not be dominated by, their technological environment. To him, the computer is a vehicle for Piagetian learning by which children are encouraged to integrate new concepts into their existing repertoires as they manipulate objects defined as figures on an interactive computer display. Thus children "take new knowledge and make it their own by playing with it and building on it."[7]

Using a Logo language program, a triangular shaped "turtle" can be made to appear and move on a television screen. By giving "turtle talk" commands to the computer, the child can learn geometry. In controlling the position and heading of the turtle, for example, children deal automatically with concepts such as "angle" and "variable." Learning then is a result of controlling and being controlled by the computer, a good example of the environment affecting people but also one of people affecting their environments. Children create their own program for

[7]Robert McWergney, "The Influence of Computers on Children and Vice Versa," *Curriculum Inquiry* 12, no. 3 (1982): 301–3.

geometrical designs, learning new mathematical concepts while developing a sense of power over the machine.

Papert's use of computers may seem a free-form curriculum structure, but the structure is imposed by the need for language. Pupils must talk "turtle" in order to operate the machine. Papert's idea is a far cry from using computers as electronic workbooks and drill exercises. His idea is that children will manipulate the computer to create their own vision of the world and thus prepare themselves for the future by learning about learning.

QUESTIONS

1. How might school environments have to change in order to take maximum advantage of microcomputers, hand calculators, video discs, computer-assisted instruction, televised sequences of instruction, and other materials that commonly use programs created by technologists?
2. What possible side effects or indirect consequences might follow the use of technologists' products that elicit and confirm particular responses from the learner?
3. How does a technologist show that a teaching method, procedure, or product works? How do the technologist's criteria differ from criteria traditionally used in judging material?
4. Most schools use the computer for drill and practice rather than for teaching students how to do programming for their own purposes. What arguments can you make for and against this trend?
5. Technologists speak as if their focus were on *how* learning should take place rather than *what* is to be learned. They conceptualize the curriculum function as finding effective means to predetermined ends. In what ways, however, might this commitment to procedure have consequences for goals and content as well?
6. In order to sense the difficulty in identifying the elements of a non-procedural task, compare your lists of basic elements for learning to manage a classroom with the elements identified by other students.

SELECTED REFERENCES

Association for Educational Communications and Technology. *Professional Development and Educational Technology.* Washington, D.C.: AECT, 1980.

Bloom, B. S. *All Our Children Learning.* New York: McGraw-Hill, 1981.

Briggs, Leslie and Wager, Walter W. *Handbook of Procedures for the Design of Instruction.* Englewood Cliffs, N.J.: Educational Technology Publications, 1981.

Meyrowitz, Joshua. "Instructional Technology and the Multiversity." *Educational Forum* 43, no. 3 (March 1979): 279–89.

Northwest Regional Educational Laboratory. *Stages of Product Development and Installation.* Portland, Or.: Northwest Regional Educational Laboratory, undated.

Papert, Seymour. *Mindstorms: Children, Computers, and Powerful Ideas.* New York: Basic Books, 1980.

4 / THE ACADEMIC SUBJECT CURRICULUM

Depending as it does on public financial support and the political climate of the country, the curriculum vacillates between the goals of equity and social justice at one time and academic excellence at another. In the late 1950s, national anxiety about keeping ahead of the Russians generated a curriculum reform movement that enlisted the talents of the nation's leading scholars in the cause of an academic curriculum. The National Science Foundation, for example, funded 53 separate curriculum projects. These new programs updated the content of subject matter so that it reflected what scholars thought was important. Moreover, the programs featured laboratory practices and discovery methods so that students would be introduced to the modes of academic inquiry practiced by the specialists in major academic fields.

In the 1970s, the crises of domestic, economic, and social strife became more important than scientific rivalry with the Soviets. Monies were shifted to curriculum projects aimed at new social concerns—multicultural education, career education, functional literacy—and to curriculum developers outside academic fields. Humanistic psychologists also weakened the academicians' hold on the curriculum by stressing subjective and personal knowledge as an alternative to objective knowledge that can be tested through reason and empirical evidence.

Just as suddenly in the early 1980s, the emphasis upon social and personal relevance was disparaged. One reason for the change in emphasis was Americans' perception that the Japanese educational system was better equipped to produce workers for the future economy with its requirements for high levels of mathematical, scientific, and technical knowledge. Declining achievement scores, dropping enrollment in academic courses, insufficiently challenging texts, and weakened college entrance and graduation requirements further encouraged the change.

Worried parents, educators and politicians began to call for academic excellence and quality. How to achieve these goals, however, remains a problem. Is it to be just more academic subject matter or a different kind of subject matter? Is it to be academic subject matter for all or just for those students who will be future scholars and scientists? Can the academic curriculum be made relevant to daily living and current social issues without at the same time diluting it? And can such a curriculum encourage clear thought and critical thinking rather than merely demand the memorization of facts? This chapter will show the answers some are finding for these questions and the ways curriculum developers are strengthening the academic curriculum.

KNOWLEDGE AND THE CURRICULUM

Academic Orientation

Just as the heart of schooling is the curriculum, the irreducible element of curriculum is knowledge. The nucleus of knowledge and the chief content or subject matter of instruction are in academic subjects such as language and literature, mathematics, the natural sciences, history, social sciences, and the fine arts.

These disciplines represent a range of approaches to truth and knowledge. Academicians define knowledge as *justified belief*, as opposed to ignorance, mere opinions, or guesses. Paul H. Hirst is an example of a curriculum theorist who represents a current academic orientation.[1] As with other academicians, he believes that the curriculum must develop the mind. His message is that the development of a rational mind is best achieved by mastering the fundamental rational structure of knowledge, meaning, logical relations, and criteria for judging claims to truth. In answer to the classical curriculum question, "What knowledge is of most worth?" Hirst proposes seven or eight forms of cognitive knowledge for understanding the world. Each of these forms is said to meet four criteria: (1) certain concepts are peculiar to the form (for example, gravity, acceleration, and hydrogen are concepts unique to the physical science form); (2) each form has a distinct logical structure by which the concepts can be related; (3) the form, by virtue of its terms and logic, has statements or conclusions that are testable; and (4) the form has methods for exploring experience and testing its statements (for example, in mathematics the "truth" of any proposition is established by its logical consistency with other propositions within a given system, while in physical science, knowledge is validated by data from observation). The forms of knowledge discerned by these criteria are: mathematics, physical sciences, knowledge of persons, literature and the fine arts, morals, religion, and philosophy. This range in forms allows for many different kinds of meaning.

[1]Paul H. Hirst, *Knowledge and the Curriculum* (London: Routledge & Kegan Paul, 1974).

In proposing forms of knowledge rather than stipulating a particular fixed substance of subject matter (particular facts and operations), such as in basic skills programs, Hirst argues for a dynamic curriculum. His forms do not, however, encourage a subjective or relative view of knowledge. To him, knowledge consists of ways to structure experience so that it can be public, shared, and instrumental or useful in daily living.

Criticisms of Hirst's views of knowledge and the curriculum center on whether he has indeed discovered distinct forms and whether he has slighted the idea of subject matter as substance. Jonas Soltis, for instance, worries that a focus on the forms of knowledge will result in an absence of attention to specific knowledge of what has been learned about the world.[2] Soltis believes that learning a form should include learning the substance within it, not just acquiring knowledge of concepts, rules, and criteria for claims to truth. Hirst admits that there is no complete agreement on the descriptions of the forms of knowledge and that mastery of the formal features of a discipline should not be mistaken for mastery of a particular area of knowledge itself.[3] He therefore wants pupils to acquire both substantive knowledge that has significance for them and knowledge of the general principles and ways of thinking that are the inherent features of the forms by which knowledge is gained.

Curriculum developers working within the academic orientation have two choices with respect to theories of knowledge. They may accept recent theories explaining the tentative nature of knowledge—that it is subject to change, modification, and evolution—or they may favor a traditional view that knowledge is not created but that it already exists, independent of persons. The latter view leads to the belief that certain truths or principles that have been discovered through intuitive reason are fixed and eternal. According to the traditional view, the curriculum content consists of principles and ideas that have always been true and in all essential matters will always be true.

Current Views

As is true of Hirst, most curriculum theorists today reject this fixed view of knowledge and instead hold that knowledge can be constructed. The creation of knowledge—valid statements, conclusions, or truths—occurs by following the inquiry systems of particular disciplines or cognitive forms. The acquisition of disciplinary forms for creating knowledge constitutes the most valid aspect of the modern academic

[2]Jonas A. Soltis, "A Review of Knowledge and the Curriculum," *Teachers College Record* 80, no. 4 (May 1979): 785–89.
[3]Paul H. Hirst, "A Reply to Jonas Soltis," *Teachers College Record* 80, no. 4 (May 1979): 785–89.

curriculum; the recitation of conclusions apart from the methods and theories by which they are established is less defensible in a period characterized by both expansion and revision of knowledge—new truths departing from older principles.

Those with humanistic conceptions of curriculum and those with a social reconstructionist orientation reject the traditional view of knowledge and the view that knowledge is best gained through cognitive forms. Instead, humanists claim that all knowledge is personal and subjective. For them, knowledge is the result of an individual's unique perceptions of the world. Social reconstructionists, on the other hand, see knowledge not only as a human product, but as a product of particular social groups. They think socially constructed knowledge is ideology. Hence, they regard attempts to impose a particular content on students in the same way as they regard imposing a particular ideology—a form of social control.

RECENT HISTORY OF THE ACADEMIC CURRICULUM

Academic Curriculum Reform in the 1960s

The so-called curriculum reform movement of the 1960s was identified with the shock that came with the Russians' first satellite launching. In the cold war climate, fear moved government to emphasize the teaching of science and mathematics. Scholars in colleges and universities prepared materials focused on single subjects. These programs began as early as kindergarten and were designed on the assumption that all pupils should understand the methods of science and the basic properties of mathematics. This was in contrast to the prevailing practice of teaching scientific facts and a style of treatment in mathematics best characterized as rote and applied. Algebra, in the "reform" course, was treated as a branch of mathematics dealing with the properties of various number systems rather than as a collection of manipulative tricks.

The Structure of Knowledge Approach. In his celebrated book, *The Process of Education,* Jerome Bruner proposed that curriculum design be based on the structure of the academic disciplines. He proposed that the curriculum of a subject should be determined by the most fundamental understanding that can be achieved of the underlying principles that give structure to a discipline. The basis for his argument was economy. Such learning permits generalizations, makes knowledge usable in contexts other than that in which it is learned, and facilitates memory by allowing the learner to relate what would otherwise be easily forgotten, unconnected facts. "The school boy learning physics is a physicist, and it is easier for him to learn physics behaving like a physicist than doing something else."[4] (Incidentally, ten years later, Bruner, caught up in the social movements of the day, urged a de-emphasis on the structure of history, physics, mathematics, and the like and instead called for an emphasis on subject matter as it related to the social needs and problems of the American people.[5])

A Basis for Curriculum Content. The concept of *structure in the disciplines* was widely heralded as a basis for curriculum content. This concept refers to rules for pursuing inquiry and for establishing truth in particular disciplines. Three kinds of structure are posited: (1) *organizational structure*— definitions of how one discipline differs in a fundamental way from another. A discipline's organizational structure also indicates the borders of inquiry for that discipline; (2) *substantive structure*—the kinds of questions to ask in inquiry, the data needed, and ideas (concepts, principles, theories) to use in interpreting data; and (3) *syntactical structure*—the manner in which those in the respective disciplines gather data, test assertions, and generalize findings. The particular method used in performing such tasks makes up the syntax of a discipline. Sociologists, for example, generally observe in naturalistic settings, identify indicators believed to correspond to the theoretical framework guiding the inquiry, and often rely on correlational data to show relations among factors observed. Experimental psychologists, on the other hand, manipulate their treatment variables in an effort to produce desired consequences. Experimentalists believe they have found knowledge when they are able to produce a predicted result.

The structure of the disciplines concept was widely used in designing curriculum whereby students were to learn how specialists in a number of disciplines discover knowledge. An intellectual emphasis was the basis for most nationwide curriculum development projects of the 1960s. Curriculum builders of this period were primarily subject matter specialists who organized their materials around the primary structural elements of their respective disciplines: problems or concerns, key concepts, principles, and modes of inquiry.

What little debate there was regarding the "new programs" centered on the argument that what was being taught would be needed only by students who were to become professional scientists and mathematicians. The rebuttal offered these arguments:

[4]Jerome S. Bruner, *The Process of Education* (Cambridge: Harvard University Press, 1960), p. 31.

[5]Jerome S. Bruner, "The Process of Education Revisited," *Phi Delta Kappan* 53, no. 1 (September 1971): 18–22.

1. There is need for appreciation from the general culture for well-trained scientists and their fields.
2. It is better to develop a deeper comprehension of the fundamentals than to touch on many facts that are often the outdated conclusions of science. A discipline approach, for example, can help the learner deal with the "knowledge explosion."
3. True understanding of the facts in more fields of learning comes only from an appreciation of various interpretations, and a continuing investigation is far more interesting to the student than a set piece. There is a growing realization that the process of inquiry itself is a form of knowledge to be acquired.
4. A discipline is an internal organization, a subject matter suitable for efficient learning.

In virtually every field—English, social studies, art, health education—there was an updating of content, a reorganization of subject matter, and fresh approaches to method. Typically, the stress was on a separate entity: not science, but biology, chemistry, or physics; not social studies, but history, geography, or economics; not English, but literature, grammar, or composition.

Reaction Against a Structure of Knowledge in the 1970s

Not all went as well as hoped. Teachers who themselves had never produced knowledge—who had not made an original scientific finding or historical interpretation—had difficulty leading students in the ways of discovery. The validity of the concept of structure as a basis for curriculum development was questioned—that the concept was only an after-the-fact description of the way knowledge can be organized by mature scholars and not the way it was really won, and that such structure is not necessarily the best way to organize knowledge for instructional purposes or start and direct significant inquiry and reflection. Enrollments in advanced physics courses declined. Many students, in both high and low ability groups, did not achieve as well as intended. The public was dissatisfied with the decline in mathematical skills. A National Assessment Educational Progress Report in 1975 revealed that only 35 percent of the nation's seventeen-year-olds could solve a simple multiplication problem with decimals, and 40 percent could not do basic work in addition, subtraction, multiplication, and division.[6] Separate assessments of students' academic achievement indicated that United

---

[6]Education Commission of the States, *National Assessment of Educational Progress, Second Report on Knowledge of Science and Math Skills* (Denver, 1975).

States public school students were learning less than they did a decade ago. The College Entrance Examination Board decided that a decade-long decline in scores on the Scholastic Aptitude Test was "real" and caused by a decline in student reasoning ability. The National Assessment of Educational Progress reported that students knew less about science than similar students in 1969 to 1970.[7]

No causal relation was shown, however, between reform projects and lower student interest or achievement. Other factors, such as students' changing social attitudes in an era of social discontent, might have been more influential.

The availability of numerous programs created problems of maintaining balance and organization. By 1971, there were, for example, more than 100 curriculum projects in the social studies alone. Many subjects had to be omitted from a school's offerings. Further, the subject specializations were so narrowly focused that it was difficult to combine their concepts into broader fields.

The 1970s saw a decline in the academic approach to curriculum making. The popularity of a disciplined approach to the science curriculum, for example, waned with a growing distrust of science. It was argued that scientists should be doing more to solve humanity's problems. Also, those with nonacademic curriculum bents attacked the structure of knowledge approach to curriculum development through an attack on a well-publicized exemplar of this approach: MACOS.

MACOS, the acronym for *Man: A Course of Study*,[8] was to have been the primer for curriculum in the 1970s. Bruner himself established the initial guide for this curriculum and directed much of its development, which was supported by the National Science Foundation (NSF) and the United States Office of Education in order to reform the teaching of social sciences and humanities. MACOS is a curriculum designed for students in the elementary school, and consists of books, films, posters, records, games, and other classroom material. More important, it sets forth assumptions about humans. Three central questions define the intellectual concerns and reveal the assumptions of MACOS: What is human about human beings? How did they get that way? How can they be made more human? The developers of the course wanted children to explore the major forces that have shaped and continue to shape humanity: language, tool use, social organization, mythology, and prolonged immaturity. Through contrast with other animals, including the

[7]*Phi Delta Kappan* 61, no. 9 (May 1975): 652.
[8]*Man: A Course of Study* (Washington, D.C.: Curriculum Development Associates, 1970).

baboons, children examine the biological nature of humans. By comparing American society with that of a traditional Eskimo group, they explore the universal aspects of human culture.

The intellectual models used to get ideas across to children are disciplinary. Children are given examples of field notes and encouraged to construct their ideas about animals and humans in the ways ethnologists and anthropologists do. The principal aims of MACOS are intellectual: to give children respect for and confidence in the powers of their own minds and to provide them with a set of workable models that make it simpler to analyze the nature of the social world. Its values include the scientific mode of observation, speculation, hypothesis making and testing; understanding of particular social science disciplines; and the joy of discovery.

Attacks on MACOS came from those with different curricular concerns. Richard Jones, a humanist, in *Fantasy and Feeling in Education,* criticized Bruner for failing to recognize MACOS' potential for fostering emotional growth.[9] Social reconstructionists opposed MACOS on the ground that it was created by a scholarly elite. A ruling class should not foster ideas in teachers and students, they said. The topics that children are asked to study are not related to improving the social life of the community in which they live. Congressman John B. Conlan blasted the course on the House floor as depicting "abhorrent and revolting behavior by a nearly extinct Eskimo tribe." Conlan said the material was full of references to adultery, cannibalism, killing of female babies and old people, trial marriage, wife-swapping, and violent murders. Many congressmen and others began to view the National Science Foundation as indoctrinating children and showing preference for certain scientists and curriculum makers. The controversies surrounding MACOS led to restricted NSF funding for educational research and greater surveillance of NSF by Congress. In 1979, a suit in federal court asked that the state be enjoined from compelling children to participate in MACOS. The plaintiffs charged that this curriculum espoused secular humanism and that the United States Supreme Court had defined this as a religion. They argued that this course violated the First Amendment.

Revival of the Academic Curriculum in the 1980s

A revival of the academic curriculum is now occurring. For example, in 1982, Harvard University implemented a new undergraduate *core curriculum* designed to bring purpose and coherence to courses of study.

[9]Richard M. Jones, *Fantasy and Feeling in Education* (New York: Harper and Row, 1968).

This curriculum requires students to meet academic requirements in five areas: literature and the arts, history, social analysis and moral reasoning, science, and foreign cultures. The new curriculum replaces a list of 80 to 100 highly specific courses, ranging from the historical origins of inequality to lectures on law and social order. It requires also that students show proficiency in writing, mathematics, and the use of computers.

Harvard curriculum reform is partly a response to a laissez faire curriculum policy in the 1970s that encouraged an educational smorgasbord in which a student's tastes alone determined choice. This reform aims at helping the student to see how the various parts of education fit together and at presenting important legacies for a citizen of the world—the knowledge of the past that illuminates the present. Knowledge is not to be conveyed by rattling off facts but by helping students understand the modes of thought employed by a range of disciplines in a spectrum of fields. Other universities are following Harvard's lead.

APPROACHES IN THE ACADEMIC CURRICULUM

Currently at least three approaches are discernible in the academic subject curriculum: the first approach teaches the forms of knowledge; the second focuses on integrated studies; and the third employs basic education.

Forms of Knowledge

Under this approach, pupils learn how to acquire or justify facts rather than merely recall them. It is estimated that 20 percent of the nation's school districts, for example, are using materials for teaching a "new history," in which each student compiles his or her own version of an historical event. The new history uses an inquiry approach that seeks to teach pupils to judge conflicting evidence and draw their own conclusions. Each student's position is valid if researched, reasoned, and articulated well. New history minimizes the importance of chronology and memorization. Advocates stress that they do not want students to reach absolute conclusions but to learn how to judge evidence, to see the other side, and to recognize the biases of other interpreters. Secondary school students are questioning traditional views of Jefferson, Jackson, and Lincoln. They are comparing capitalism with socialism. They are examining the United States' treatment of the Indians and the historical records of the Spanish-American War as well as Vietnam and other recent events. The approach is not without criticism. Some scholars fret about the loss of chronology and absence of traditional historical content. Others believe the approach develops cynics; they say that students need belief in heroism and virtues to build clear ideals and confidence.

Integrated Studies

The second approach marks a renaissance of ideas prominent in curriculum proposals of the 1930s—integrated studies. *Integrated studies* is a generic term applied to any curriculum development effort in which two or more previously separate subjects are combined. It is a response to the changes in society and the need for more comprehensive models of knowledge. Science educators, for example, have identified 170 unified science programs in which boundaries between the specialized sciences are dissolved in favor of pervasive ideas and characteristics. Organizing themes for instruction are major concepts, scientific processes, natural phenomena, and persistent problems. Most of these science programs have been developed locally and are designed to be conducted over a period of more than one year.

Among persons committed to the new patterns of subject matter and reduced redundancy are members of the Federation for Unified Science Education (FUSE), the International Council of Scientific Unions (ICSU), and the Science Teaching Division of UNESCO. These groups use the following approach in developing an integrated curriculum:

1. *Choosing a unifying theme.* The unifying theme is generally either a major idea (concept) that permeates all sciences, or a process of science, a natural phenomenon, or a social problem inviting scientific interpretations.
2. *Incorporating learning activities from several specialized sciences.* Activities that involve content and process from one or more of the behavioral or social sciences and related to the theme are offered.
3. *Incorporating a variety of learning modes.* Concrete experiences that reflect the interests and needs of learners in the particular area and deal with local phenomena are to be used.

One such program is found at the Laboratory School, University of Florida, where high school students over a three-year period acquire interdisciplinary concepts and abilities to investigate scientific questions of social concern. Concepts like order, change, equilibrium, models, and quantification are important in all sciences. These concepts have become the basis for the selection and organization of subject matter. The older system of studying separate subjects has been replaced by one in which chemistry, physics, biology, and technology are combined in trying to understand a complex question.

In order to understand equilibrium, for example, the student should study how the body maintains internal balance. In studying the processes and phenomena occurring in the human body, students will draw on content from different fields. They may use Newton's Laws (balance); center of gravity, rotational and linear equilibrium, forces, and torques; biomechanics (explanation of vertigo); body structure; anatomy; roles of body systems in maintaining homeostatis; and "feedback systems models" as applied to their own body functions. Students are led to consider the role of body chemicals in maintaining a stable body and to explore the meaning of chemical equilibrium and acid-base regulation processes in the body. The knowledge needed to teach such a course normally requires team teaching, and teachers learn from one another. Student response is positive, with dramatic rises in course enrollments, successful advanced work in science, and increased ability to see relationships.

Basic Education

A third approach in the academic curriculum can be found in the "back to basics" movement and in the increasing number of *fundamental* offerings. Accordingly, school subjects are taught *directly*, with an emphasis on learning to read, write, and solve mathematical problems. Grammar is part of the English curriculum. Latin, French, mathematics, and science are presented without attempts at relevance or interesting project designs. Fundamentalists disapprove of both courses that emphasize methods and concepts of inquiry without imparting facts, and courses that encourage pupils' expression of opinions and value preferences. They oppose what they see as a nihilistic tendency, the offering of a curriculum in which good and bad are merely subjective opinions and all ideas are equal.

An interesting proposal urging a single-track academic core curriculum for all elementary and secondary pupils is that offered by the Paideia Group.[10] According to the proposal, there should be the same course of study for all in which students learn their own language, a foreign language, literature, fine arts, mathematics, natural science, history, geography, and social studies. They would take 12 years of physical education as well as industrial arts; they would be involved in drama, music, and the visual arts; and they would learn how to exercise critical

[10]Mortimer J. Adler, *Paideia Problems and Possibilities* (New York: Macmillan, 1983).

and moral judgments. To follow the proposal would require the jettison-
ing of many current offerings, such as vocational education, electives,
specialized courses, and tracking.

This mandatory curriculum emphasizes three modes of teaching
(learning at successive graduations of complexity): didactic instruction
for acquiring organized knowledge; coaching, exercises and supervised
practice for developing intellectual skills; and Socratic dialogue for
understanding of ideas and values.

Chief among reactions to the proposal are those claiming it would
require major societal and economic supports, that it borders on elitism,
and that it mistakes the value of vocational education.[11]

Few schools offer a curriculum based on the proposition that there is a
body of eternal and absolute truth, valid under all conditions, or that
reason can be enhanced by familiarity with the most profound and
grandest of humankind's intellectual works. St. John's College in Mary-
land is an exception. When students take biology at St. John's College,
they are handed a stiff frog and an Aristotelian treatise. In this school an
older view of academic education—including science, mathematics, Greek,
French, music, and the Great Books seminars—is maintained. In precep-
torals, similar to electives, seven or eight students and a tutor work
intensively on one of the Great Books or on a limited subject like Freud.
In the all-required curriculum, third- and fourth-year students study
physics, measurement theory, and chemistry in their science course.
Sophomore biology emphasizes anatomy, embryology, and genetics in
the framework of evolution. When they dissect their frogs, students
read Aristotle's book *On the Parts of Animals* and ponder his notion of
aliveness. They also read Galen, the second-century physician whose
works were definitive for more than a thousand years, while they
dissect rabbits. When they progress to the rabbit's circulatory system,
they discuss William Harvey's treatise, "On the Motion of the Heart and
Blood in Animals," published in 1628. Rather than presenting only the
most current research to students to memorize and repeat in exams,
tutors encourage students to practice scientific inquiry. To do that, they
believe, students must confront the great minds. Almost half of the
biology sessions are spent in laboratory dissections and experiments
that demonstrate genetics and embryological theory. Although students
read from a half-dozen contemporary books, they also read and discuss
the works of such trailblazers as Claude Bernard, Gregor Johann Mendel,
and Karl Ernst Von Baer.

[11]Symposium, "The Paideia Proposal," *Harvard Educational Review* 53, no. 4 (Summer
1983): 377–407.

CHARACTERISTICS OF CURRICULUM AS ACADEMIC SUBJECT MATTER

Whether it is presented as forms of knowledge, compartmentalized disciplines, integrated subjects, or Great Books, academic curriculum has certain attributes. These attributes are related to purpose, method, organization, and evaluation.

Purpose and Function

The purposes of the academic curriculum are to develop rational minds and to train students to do research. Some educators would separate cognitive development from the mastery of academic disciplines. Psychologists tend to have a cognitive conception of curriculum whereby intellectual skills are developed independently of any academic subject matter. In my opinion, the present evidence does not warrant the employment of the cognitive conception. Efforts to measure cognitive processes without regard to content have been unsuccessful. Persons do not think thoughts, they think subject matter. One of the oldest attempts—15 years—at teaching students how to think, or at least to show students how the instructor thinks, is found in the curriculum of Brown University. Brown does not offer typical "survey" courses, courses regularly criticized for trying to cover too much material in too short a time. Instead students take "modes of thought" seminars on a single subject of interest to the instructor whose job is to provide a model for students of the intellectual processes needed for the subject. Those educators who favor the academic curriculum believe that students who become knowledgeable in the forms of knowledge and the methods for continued intellectual growth after graduation should learn to cultivate reason and perhaps even to control their appetites. Schools, they feel, should allow pupils to recognize the finest achievements of their cultural heritage and, when possible, to add to these achievements through their own efforts.

Methods

Exposition and inquiry are two techniques commonly used in the academic curriculum, although inquiry may be less prevalent in the curriculum of the fundamentalist. Indeed, the ideals of the academic curriculum are violated by teachers who rely upon textbooks and factual questions instead of seeking problems that involve the students' understanding and higher level cognitive processes. Ideas should be stated and elaborated so that they may be understood. Main ideas can be ordered, illustrated, and explored. Problems that fall within certain disciplines may be formulated and pursued. Appropriate methods for validating truths in the different disciplines are important to teach. Students should discover that reason and sense perception are used to gain knowledge in the sciences, logic in mathematics, individual form and feeling in art, and coherence in history (a fact must be consistent with other known facts). They should examine statements to ascertain their meaning, their logical grounding, and their factual support. The academician wants students to read the greatest works in order to stretch their minds, to come into contact with great minds from the past as well as those in their own age.

Organization

Alternative organizational patterns for improving the academic curriculum are many. A few are listed here:

1. *Unified or concentrated.* Major themes serve to organize the subject matter from various disciplines. The concept of energy, for example, can be studied from biological, physical, chemical, and geological perspectives.
2. *Integrated.* Skills learned in one subject are used as tools in another field. Mathematics, for instance, is taught for the solving of scientific problems.
3. *Correlated.* Disciplines retain their separate identities, but students learn how concepts in one discipline are related to those in another. For example, history, geography, and English may be taught so as to reinforce one another.
4. *Comprehensive problem solving.* Problems may be drawn from current social interests such as consumer research, recreation, and transportation. Students must draw on skills and knowledge from the sciences, social sciences, mathematics, and art in the attempt to optimize a solution.

Within a course, academic subject matter is typically organized in a linear fashion based on some provision for the progressive development of a concept or a method. Organizational principles that guide this development include: simple to complex (one-celled animals before many-celled animals); whole to part (allowing for topographical study showing the overall scheme of the course before studying detailed topics); chronological narration (events are arranged in a time sequence);

TABLE 4.1   Levels of Schooling and Forms of Subject Matter

School Level	Subject Matter Emphasis
Primary	Varied subject matter through concrete experiences.
Upper elementary	Mastery of fundamental tools of inquiry and communication—reading, writing, arithmetic, observation, investigation.
Secondary	Differentiation of subject matter—systematic instruction in separate fields.
	Views of how each subject is related to another (encyclopedic survey).
Higher education	Subject matter in accordance with individual capacity and interest.

learning hierarchies (learning to place cells in empty matrices comes before learning to infer the characteristics of the object needed to fill an empty cell).

With respect to sequence within total school programs, it is interesting to recall John Dewey's views that the learner should be reintroduced to certain forms of subject matter at different school levels. He stressed the continuity of subject matter and illustrated how subject matter can be adapted in light of the learner's maturation (see Table 4.1).

Evaluation

At the classroom level, the means of evaluation vary according to the objectives of the different subject matters. In humanities, essays are preferred over multiple-choice tests, and answers that reflect logic, coherence, and comprehensiveness rather than a single right or wrong choice. In the arts, the expression is judged by faithfulness to personal subjectivity and to standards for beauty and taste, such as adherence to the principles of unity and balanced contrast. The highest grades in mathematics are given to the students who learn to appreciate the formal axiomatic nature of the field. In science, numerous criteria are used. Value is placed on the learner's use of given processes and modes of thought as well as knowledge of facts and themes. Logical rigor and experimental adequacy are highly prized.

Academic specialists are often ambivalent toward evaluation of their curriculum. They see evaluation as valuable, providing useful information, yet they often worry that it will interfere with the realization of broad teaching objectives. They also believe that evaluation may antagonize the teacher and students, take time that can be spent in other ways, and demand a compulsive attitude toward record keeping, which is not compatible with a spirit of enthusiasm. Further, they share the fear that short-run evaluation may focus on simple skills rather than the complex skills of inductive reasoning. Ideally, the academician would survey not a term, but five or ten years of work. They want the child to change, not for a weekly examination, but for life.

ISSUES IN THE CURRICULUM AS ACADEMIC SUBJECT MATTER

Selecting Among Disciplines

There is a problem in selecting from among the more than 1,000 disciplines those that could become part of the school curriculum. The problem is not new:

> Good Lord! how long is Art,
> And life, how it goes flying!
> . . . .
> It is so hard to gain the means whereby
> Up to the source one may ascend.
> And ere a man gets half-way to the end,
> Poor devil! he's almost sure to die![12]

It is impossible for an individual to delve very deeply into many disciplines. How shall those administering the curriculum decide which disciplines to offer? A number of measuring rods are proposed: (1) comprehensiveness with respect to ways at arriving at or justifying truth or knowledge; (2) social utility—the usefulness of the discipline for all citizens; (3) prerequisite knowledge—the importance of certain disciplines as a basis for others or for subsequent education.

In the interest of comprehensiveness, it would be well to sample disciplines that emphasize different avenues for justifying knowledge. This is the intent of Hirst in offering forms of knowledge. Philip Phenix

[12]Goethe's *Faust*, trans. and ed. J. F. L. Raschen (Ithaca: Thrift Press, 1803) pp. 29–31.

has illustrated how to achieve comprehensiveness in the fundamental disciplines. His *Realms of Meaning* describes and analyzes six basic types of meaning, each of which has a distinctive logical structure.[13] Art, with its concern for subjective validation, can balance a discipline like science, which uses objective observations to confirm an expected occurrence. History can be used to illustrate the criteria of coherence and verifiability—to show that ideas have to fit together and that new conclusions can be weighed against past events. Mathematics can prepare learners to gain knowledge through reason and logic. It may be possible to find a form that will help students recognize that some forms of knowledge can be validated by intuition and divine revelation. Such a curriculum would preclude the exclusivity of contemporary schools, which tend to emphasize the scientific mode of learning.

Few people contend that a discipline is an end in itself. Specialists in each field believe that knowledge in the field will be relevant to some aspect of a better life. The phrase "knowledge for knowledge's sake" is not taken seriously. However, not all disciplines will serve equally well the educational needs of persons in every social context. Some very narrow specialties have little to contribute to problems that directly touch all lives. Newer disciplines claim to be more relevant than older ones. Psychology, for instance, is challenging literature for the honor of interpreting human nature. Anthropology begs admission on the ground that it can better help pupils gain a valid world view than can history, a field known for reflecting parochial interests.

Including certain subjects as prerequisites is sometimes defended on the ground that there is a logical dependency between fields of knowledge, which supersedes learner interest or relevancy to social problems. There are scientists, for example, who would not make biology the first course in the secondary school curriculum in science; they believe that to learn biology one needs to understand the principles of chemistry and that to understand chemistry, one must, in turn, know the basic concepts of physics. Others believe that a prerequisite discipline should help the learner know what posture to assume, what sources to consult, and what to admit as relevant for a point at issue. Because philosophy leads to an understanding of all fields of knowledge, it has been suggested as the initial course in the academic curriculum to prepare learners to see similarities and differences among the disciplines they will meet.

A powerful instance of the prerequisite criterion is found in the requirements for college admission. These requirements have set the

[13]Philip H. Phenix, *Realms of Meaning* (New York: McGraw-Hill, 1964).

standard for the high school curriculum for many years. Many schools gear their curriculum to the subject matters demanded by the College Board's Admission Testing Program which until recently has been broadly conceived as: four years of English, mathematics, science, and foreign language, and three to four years of social studies.

Now the College Board specifically outlines what college entrants are expected to know and to be able to do.[14] This outline of academic preparation is divided into two sections: (a) Basic Academic Competencies and (b) Basic Academic Subjects. The academic competencies are the broad skills of reading, writing, speaking, listening, mathematics, reasoning and studying. Illustrative competencies expected are the following:

Reading—The ability to interpret a writer's meaning inferentially as well as literally.

Writing—The ability to vary one's writing style for different readers and purposes.

Mathematics—The ability to formulate and solve a problem in mathematical terms.

Reasoning—The ability to draw reasonable conclusions from information found in various sources.

Studying—The ability to accept constructive criticism and learn from it.

Basic academic subjects and illustrative expected outcomes are:

English—The ability to read a literary text analytically, seeking relationships between form and content.

The Arts—The ability to express one's self in one or more of the visual art forms—drawing, painting, photography, weaving, ceramics, and sculpture.

Mathematics—The ability to draw geometrical figures and use geometrical modes of thinking in the solving of problems.

Science—The ability to understand the unifying concepts of the life and physical sciences, such as cell theory, geological evolution, organic evolution, atomic structure, chemical bonding, and transformation of energy.

Social Studies—The ability to retain factual knowledge of major political and economic institutions and their historical development.

Foreign Languages—The ability to cope with typical situations in another culture, such as greeting, leave taking, buying food, and asking directions.

[14]College Board, *Academic Preparation for College* (New York: College Board, 1983).

Making Subject Matter More Appealing to Growing Minds

The academic curriculum has been indicted for putting the logic and orderliness that appeals to the academic mind over the psychological logic of the learner. The failure of the subject organization to inspire learners is a common challenge. The fact that teachers often are not willing or able to carry out the curriculum plans of the academic scholars with the intended enthusiasm and insight is related to this criticism. Academicians are also said to be guilty of two curriculum fallacies: the fallacy of content and the fallacy of universalism.

Those who commit the *fallacy of content* are preoccupied with the importance of *what* students study rather than *how* they study. They overemphasize content that they believe to be intellectually rigorous and difficult and that they presume will make the necessary demands on students. As indicated in Chapters 1 and 13, the goal of teaching science as inquiry is rarely observed. Instead textbook information is emphasized—terminology and definitions. Laboratories tend to be used for demonstrations of information already presented rather than for discovery.

There is concern about the lack of emphasis upon application. Academic studies are treated as if they are important chiefly for future studies—a means of advancing up the academic ladder. Certainly students should have access to the very best concepts, principles, and generalizations that civilization has created, but they should seldom be instructed before they are prepared to engage in examining and testing what they are being taught. The process of learning is more important than the content. It is not *declarative* knowledge—knowledge of facts—that students lack. The deficiency is in *operative* knowledge—understanding of how the facts are known and the capacity to apply this knowledge in new situations.

The *fallacy of universalism* rests on the belief that some content areas have universal value regardless of the characteristics of particular learners. One extreme of this view has been given by one of America's best known educators, the late Robert Maynard Hutchins, who said that "Education implies teaching. Teaching implies knowledge as truth. The truth is everywhere the same. Hence education should be everywhere the same."[15] Another instance of universalism is the presumption that academicians can adapt the disciplinary mode of university scholarship

[15]Robert Maynard Hutchins, *Higher Learning in America* (New Haven: Yale University Press, 1936), p. 66.

for wide use in elementary and secondary schools by pupils who are anything but budding knowledge specialists.

Partly in response to these criticisms, efforts are being undertaken to improve the academic subject matter curriculum. Curriculum in newer academic subject matter encourages intuition—clever guessing—as a handmaiden to the recognized analytical thinking of the disciplines. School people are supplementing, adapting, and developing the scholars' curriculum materials, not regarding them as panaceas for given local educational needs. For example, teachers are preparing extra resources for less able pupils, as well as additional ways to stimulate the gifted child. Local facilities are being organized for introducing more creative elements into programs and for alternative studies illustrating the disciplines' techniques in a different environment than that intended by the original planners. Instead of studying biology solely from a textbook, students learn the nature of biology from studies of tidepools and animal husbandry. Home-grown academic programs are flourishing. Indeed, they may survive better than the national transplants.

The new curriculum designed by the Biological Science Curriculum Study for kindergarten through high school is a good example of how subject matter—genetics—can be made valuable in the personal and public lives of students.[16] In this curriculum, kindergarten and first-grade children are provided opportunities that introduce basic scientific concepts and modes of investigation. For example, as the basis for the concept of continuity, children observe the growth and development of seeds, sort organisms of various species into family groups and identify physical resemblances between parents and their offspring in human and non-human families.

In grades two through four, pupils have experiences with the idea of variety by comparing body measurements and individual preferences for foods, color, hobbies. They are helped to be made aware of the concept of change by studying their own patterns of daily living, making predictions about certain days and times of day in their routines. The principle of continuity is reinforced for students in the middle grades by their study of families and other organizations and their constructing of family trees.

Fifth and sixth graders begin population studies considering their own class and other classes as prototypes. They conduct scientific

[16]Biological Sciences Curriculum Study, "You, Me, and Others," "Genes and Surroundings," "Basic Genetics: A Human Approach," and "Living with Cystic Fibrosis," (Boulder, Co.: BSCS, 1982).

experiments with preschoolers to see how little ones think about problems. The principle of continuity is extended as the children examine the transmission of specific traits from generation to generation.

The curriculum for the junior high or middle school learners, "Genes and Surroundings," stresses individuality, continuity, variability (both in time and in relation to others), and adaption. Variability is featured because it is an important developmental concept for the adolescent. The activities in this curriculum require students to apply knowledge about human genetics to their personal growth and to the local physical and social environment.

"Basic Genetics" for the high school and adult learner emphasizes the physical, psychological, and social delineation of health created by new knowledge in genetics. Although students learn as a traditional class would about gene segregation, blood types, pedigrees, and genetic disorders, they also learn the content from a human point of view. In the study of inheritance, for example, human beings are featured in preference to animals. More important, students learn the principles of genetics, not as ends in themselves, but in connection with personal and familial concerns—genetic counseling, prenatal diagnoses, prenatal care—and with social concerns—the ethical issues of such matters as prenatal screening and abortion.

Improvement in the quality of the academic curriculum will require attention to four interdependent parts: learning, application, consequence, and value. Learning—especially what students should learn—receives much attention, and some attention is given to helping students criticize academic assertions and to help design tests for refuting them. More attention is needed in helping students learn strategies for applying knowledge and predicting consequences—"What must I do with what I know?" "How do I take action?" "How do I make desirable outcomes more likely?" "Do I know what would happen?" Lastly, teachers must develop an academic curriculum that students will value. Currently, few academic programs exploit the need for students to answer questions they themselves regard as important—"Where do I fit in?" "Do I care?" "Do I value the outcome?"

In short, some curriculum makers are attempting to provide learning opportunities that are appealing and well within the learners' capacities to serve as the starting point for organizing subject matter intellectually as the specialist does. They are able to differentiate between those activities that lead to growth and those that do not. These developers have taken a long look ahead. They know the academic forms—the facts, principles, and laws—to which the children's present activities belong. They are giving children opportunities for intelligent activity—for seeing how things interact with one another to produce definite effects—instead of aimless activity.

CONCLUDING COMMENTS

Academic specialists have at different times attempted to develop a curriculum that would equip learners to enter the world of knowledge with the basic concepts and methods for observing, noting relationships, analyzing data, and drawing conclusions. They wanted learners to act like physicists, biologists, or historians so that as citizens they would follow developments in disciplines with understanding and support and, if they continued their studies, become specialists themselves. One weakness in the approach was the failure to give sufficient attention to integrative objectives. Learners were unable to relate one discipline to another and to see how the content of a discipline could be brought to bear on the complex problems of modern life not answerable by a single discipline. Two current movements to overcome this weakness are (1) "integrated" studies in which content from several fields is applied to important social problems, and (2) the teaching of the forms of knowledge so that learners acquire a range of perspectives for understanding experience.

A second weakness in the academic conception of curriculum has been a tendency to impose on pupils adult views of the subject matter. Academic specialists have often given insufficient attention to the present interests and backgrounds of particular learners. They might have used those interests as sources for problems and activities by which learners might acquire the intellectual organization that constitutes academic subject matter. There are signs that this weakness is being corrected in curriculum, too.

Because of a growing concern that science education should meet the personal, social, and career needs of students, the National Science Foundation provided support for Project Synthesis, a group of experts developing a new approach to science education.[17] The experts concluded that the present curriculum is organized around the structure of separate disciplines, with only marginal emphasis being given to social problems or personal application of knowledge. In contrast, the experts predicted that the life science curriculum of the future will be organized around the theme of human adaptation in both scientific and social senses and

---

[17]P. D. Hurd et al., "Project Synthesis," in *What Research Says to the Science Teacher*, eds. Norris C. Harms and Robert E. Yaer. (Washington, D.C.: National Science Teachers Association, 1981).

that the use of biological knowledge in making decisions will be an important goal along with values and ethics.

QUESTIONS

1. Science and English successfully challenged the classics—Greek and Latin—as useful academic subjects in teaching students to think. What are the possibilities that knowledge of the computer and ability to use it in problem solving may become a leading contender for a basic academic competency?

2. The capacity to discriminate and judge is a central goal of all education. For centuries, languages, literature, history, philosophy, and the arts have been viewed as the sources of knowledge for best attaining this goal. Is this true today? Why? Why not?

3. The issue of "elitism" versus "populism" shows clearly in curriculum changes from personal and social relevance to academic excellence. Are the goals of relevance and excellence mutually exclusive? Is it possible for the curriculum to reflect the different directions simultaneously? If so, how?

4. The daily lives of most people are going to be complicated and constantly changing. They will be assailed by new laws, new traffic schemes, and new sex-roles; and these will loom larger in their lives than the works of Shakespeare or the Third Law of Thermodynamics. They will not be able to find textbook answers to their daily problems. Neither will they be able to categorize the problems into subjects like history or physics. So more value should be placed on education for ordinary life than on academic education. How would you respond to both the premises of this argument and the conclusion which believes in educating students for life rather than for academic achievement?

5. Judge each of the following definitions of the academic curriculum in terms of feasibility (ease of learning and teaching), utility (extent to which it contributes to learners' basic needs for survival, independence, and respect), and idealism (degree to which it is consistent with the highest ideals about human nature).

   a. Academic subject matter consists of the intellectual tools—the questions, methods, concepts, processes, and attitudes—by which knowledge is currently acquired.

   b. Academic subject matter consists of conclusions—the facts, principles, and laws—carefully chosen from those derived by specialists on the basis of their relevancy to the conduct of daily living.

   c. Academic subject matter consists of the finest achievements of our cultural heritage, the works of those great minds that have had an effect on civilization.

6. Both John Dewey and the new developmentalists have held that it is important both (a) to bring subject matter to bear on the interests, problems, and progress of the child and (b) to attend to activities like drawing, performing music, nature walks, and manual construction so that they lead or lure the learner to the abstract, systematic, and theoretical ideas of which these activities are a part. What competence in subject matter would a teacher need in order to achieve both?

SELECTED REFERENCES

Bernstein, Jeremy. "Science Education for the Non-Scientist." *The American Scholar,* 29, no. 2 (Winter 1982-83): 7–12.

The College Board. *Academic Preparation for College—What Students Need to Know and Be Able to Do.* New York: College Board, 1983.

Commission on the Humanities. *The Humanities in American Life.* Berkeley: University of California Press, 1980.

Diorio, Joseph A. "Knowledge, Truth and Power in the Curriculum" *Educational Theory* 27, no. 2 (Spring 1977): 103–11.

Hirst, Paul H. *Knowledge and the Curriculum.* London: Routledge & Kegan Paul, 1974.

Keller, Phyliss. *Getting at the Core: Curriculum Reform at Harvard.* Cambridge: Harvard University Press, 1982.

Kyle, William C., Jr., Shymansky, James A., and Alport, Jennifer. "Alphabet Soup Science: A Second Look at the NSF-Funded Science Curricula." *The Science Teacher* 49, no. 8 (November 1982): 49–53.

National Science Foundation. *Today's Problems, Tomorrow's Crises: A Report of the National Science Board Commission on Pre-College Education in Mathematics, Science, and Technology.* Washington, D.C.: National Science Foundation, 1982.

Phenix, Philip H. *Realms of Meaning.* New York: McGraw-Hill, 1964.

II / CURRICULUM DEVELOPMENT

This part of the book features what curriculum specialists consider the core of curriculum knowledge. Chapter 5 presents modern answers to the old question of what to teach. More precisely, the chapter indicates directions for finding justifiable answers to the question.

Chapter 6 is a guide to the selection and creation of learning opportunities—activities, instructional sequences, interventions, experiences—which put students in touch with valued content.

Curriculum organization is the topic of Chapter 7. Organization in curriculum refers to the sequence, arrangement, and integration of learning opportunities so that learners profit from them. Persons attend to organization because they believe that relating learning opportunities to one another makes a difference in both what is learned and how easily it is learned. Curriculum organization influences the way students view their studies, their attitudes toward learning, and their ability to learn on their own after leaving school. It makes possible the illumination of essentials, less obvious attributes, and generalizations. Good curriculum planning allows for events to be ordered so that patterns rather than individual entities are seen and so that significant concepts and skills are enlarged over time.

5 / DECIDING WHAT SHOULD BE TAUGHT

The decision about what should be taught in an institution, corporate training program, academic department, classroom, or other instructional situation is a decision about curriculum purposes and goals. Individuals differ in their desire to determine what should be taught. On one hand, there are those who flee from curriculum responsibility. They acquiesce to the decisions of others—teachers sometimes accept without question and justification the static goals of boards, administrators or textbook writers; trustees and administrators sometimes avoid making decisions about curriculum and what should transpire in classrooms, excusing themselves on the grounds of academic freedom. Responsibility is sometimes avoided by denying the need for the decision, claiming that the present curriculum is good enough.

A more subtle way to avoid responsibility is to apply a technological approach. In such an approach the determination of curriculum ends is treated as unproblematic. Content is determined by the ratings that respondent groups give proposed goals; the highest rated goal is designated the priority.

On the other hand, many individuals and groups want to propose what should be taught. They may have special interests—career education, drug abuse, ethnic studies, computer literacy. Similarly, prospective employers and those at the next rung in the academic ladder often are eager to say what should be taught in preparation for future jobs.

Rather than avoiding responsibility and mandating curriculum purposes without justification, those at all levels of schooling should constantly question the purpose of curriculum. Changing circumstances make even the most enduring of subject matters questionable. Of course, some situations offer instructors little freedom to determine ends—the military instructor ordered to train recruits a certain task, for instance. However, having curriculum goals chosen by the largest number of people involved in an educational enterprise is still the best general principle. Thus, in this chapter basic approaches to setting curriculum purpose are stressed. Although not all the approaches give equal opportunity to discover new directions, why one or another of the approaches is more appropriate in a situation should be recognized.

ARENAS FOR DECIDING WHAT TO TEACH

Levels of Decision Making

Curriculum planning, including decisions about what to teach and for what purpose, occurs at different levels of remoteness from intended learners. These levels are *societal, institutional, instructional,* and *personal.* Participants at the societal level include boards of education (national, local, or state), federal agencies, publishers, and national curriculum reform committees. At the institutional level, administrators, and faculty groups are the prominent actors. Parents and students, too, play a role in institutional decision making about curriculum. The instructional level refers to teachers with specific groups of learners. Recently the personal or experiential has been recognized as a fourth decision level in curriculum making. This level is consistent with the view that learners generate their own meanings from their classroom experiences and are not merely passive recipients of curriculum ends and means.[1]

Different techniques and personnel are involved in curriculum making at the different levels. Curriculum making at the national level includes development of goals and objectives as well as textbooks and other instructional materials for wide use: for example, federally financed curriculum projects in universities and educational regional laboratories, the curriculum work of nonprofit organizations, and the objectives that accompany school materials produced by publishing houses in cooperation with professional educators. Often curriculum designers at this level do not focus on a wide range of educational goals such as social adjustment, self-expression, manual dexterity, and general social attributes. Instead they center on domains and objectives that are specific to a single subject area, grade level, or course. In this arena, specialized personnel—subject specialists, curriculum specialists, and editors—make most of the decisions about *what* should be taught and *how.* These specialists do, however, attend to professional and public opinion as reflected in the yearbooks published by national subject matter organizations such as the National Council for Social Studies (NCSS), professional journals, and popular

---

[1]Louise Tyler, "The Personal Domain," in *Curriculum Inquiry: The Study of Curriculum Practice,* John I. Goodlad and associates (New York: McGraw-Hill, 1979), pp. 191–208.

media. They also seek the advice of representative teachers, textbook salespeople, and other consultants. Results from marketing efforts and trials of preliminary versions also bring about changes in both the ends and means of their curriculum.

Curriculum development at the state level involves the production of curriculum guides and frameworks. These materials are prepared by professional staffs in state departments of education assisted by representative teachers, college and university personnel, and curriculum specialists. The purposes and goals set forth in these materials are usually formulated by advisory committees composed of professional educators, representatives from educational agencies, and selected laypersons. State department personnel also engage in curriculum making in response to state laws pertaining to the teaching of such topics as narcotics, health, and physical education.

Beginning in 1977 and continuing into early 1980, legislation in most states mandated minimum competency testing for elementary and secondary students. The mandates concentrated on the skill areas to be tested, the grade levels to be covered, and the elaborate procedures for test selection. State departments of education were given responsibility for the implementation of competency-based education programs. These statewide actions and similar testing programs initiated independently in many local school districts had an implicit but inevitable effect on curriculum. By the mid 1980s, states increasingly prescribe courses of study, graduation requirements, and academic curriculum offerings.

The most common arena for curriculum planning is the school district, although there are signs that curriculum decision making at individual schools is increasing. Districts usually involve specialized personnel in curriculum as well as curriculum generalists, subject matter specialists, consultants, representative teachers, and some laypersons. Ideally, these persons should be concerned with adapting and designing curriculum to local situations and problems. They should consider the implications of regional economy, history, and arts for learners in the local schools. Curriculum making at the individual school level should involve all classroom teachers and administrators, and representative parents and students. Their activities should focus on goals, materials, organization, and instructional strategies. Within the self-contained or nongraded classroom, the individual teacher or teaching team should develop the curriculum objectives and activities that are most appropriate for particular pupils, keeping in mind the general goals of the school. Although many teachers rely on an outside source, such as a textbook or course of study, to determine the concepts to be taught, they frequently expand on this curriculum, reflecting on pupil responses.

The relative importance of the levels of decision making varies from country to country, state to state, and school to school. Centralized educational systems such as those in Japan and France give the ministry of education more authority over curriculum ends. Less centralized educational systems such as are found in the United Kingdom have established local organizations to explore aspects of the curriculum and to develop new schemes or projects intended to improve the quality and relevance of what is offered to pupils. In the United States, local authority for curriculum decisions has been greatest in New England and among the states of the Midwest. State control has always been more evident in such states as Texas, Florida, New York, and California. Now, however, the central role of the teacher in curriculum planning and development is increasing everywhere, partly because of a growing belief that no curriculum derived from outside agencies would be successful without teacher commitment.

Different Curriculum at Different Levels

Casual readers about curriculum get inconsistent messages. On one hand, they read that the curriculum is rapidly changing—a new program in mathematics, health education, more appropriate content for the gifted, and mastery learning for the slow. On the other hand, there are reports indicating that schools are teaching the same thing in the same way as always—reading, writing, arithmetic in the elementary school and vocational and college preparatory programs in the secondary school.

One explanation for the conflicting reports is that the reports do not all refer to the same curriculum. A curriculum formulated at one level is not necessarily adopted and implemented at another. John Goodlad and his associates, for example, have proposed five different curricula, each operating at a different level.[2]

1. *Ideal Curriculum.* From time to time foundations, governments, and special interest groups set up committees to look into aspects of the curriculum and to advise on changes that should be made. Curriculum recommendations proposed by these committees might treat multicultural curriculum, a curriculum for the talented, early childhood curriculum, and career education curriculum. These proposals might represent ideals or describe desired directions in curriculum as seen by those with a particular value system or special interest. The proponents of such ideal curricula are

[2]John I. Goodlad and associates, *Curriculum Inquiry,* pp. 344–50.

competing for power within the society. It should be clear, however, that the impact of an ideal curriculum depends on whether the recommendations are adopted and implemented.

2. *Formal Curriculum.* Formal curriculum includes those proposals that are approved by state and local boards. Such a curriculum may be a collection of ideal curricula, a modification of the ideal, or other curriculum policies, guides, syllabi, texts sanctioned by the board as the legal authority for deciding what shall be taught and to what ends.

3. *Perceived Curriculum.* The perceived curriculum is what the teachers perceive the curriculum to be. Teachers interpret the formal curriculum in many ways. Often there is little relation between the formally adopted curriculum and the teachers' perception of what the curriculum means or should mean in practice.

4. *Operational Curriculum.* This curriculum is what actually goes on in the classroom. Observations by researchers and others who make records of classroom interaction often reveal discrepancies between what teachers say the curriculum is and what teachers actually do.

5. *Experiential Curriculum.* The experiential curriculum consists of what students derive from and think about the operational curriculum. This curriculum is identified through student questionnaires, interviews, and inferences from observations of students.

ELEMENTS IN THE DEVELOPMENT OF CURRICULUM

Range of Activity

Curriculum developers' efforts are directed at producing programs of study, catalogs of goals and objectives, curriculum guides, course outlines, and lesson plans. They also produce more specific instructional materials: textbooks, taped and filmed programs, and instructional sequences. These materials often require the curriculum developer to detail steps for the teacher or child to follow and to prepare tests and record-keeping systems, as well as procedures for training the teacher on how to use the materials.

Before undertaking the production of any materials, the curriculum developer will consider time and the intended learners. Will the material serve an hour's lesson, a year's work, a six-year program? What are the ages, mental and physical characteristics, and experiential backgrounds of the future users of the materials?

In determining what the individual or target population should learn, curriculum developers take either a restricted or unrestricted approach. In the restricted approach, the developer looks for possible objectives from within a domain of knowledge and practice. Mathematics, health, intellectual development, and vocational education are typical domains. In an unrestricted approach, the curriculum developer is willing to regard any problem, idea, or situation as having possible implications for what should be taught. The curriculum maker's task of conceiving possible and desirable outcomes does not mean that all proposed ends will be accepted and acted upon. Boards of education, principals, teachers, and pupils all have ways of rejecting the best conceived purposes. However, persons who propose outcomes should be able to justify them. Later in this chapter, we will describe the ways in which developers justify ends.

Institutional Purposes

Those who plan to develop curriculum within a given institution must attend to the nature of that school, especially to the school's manifest purposes. Why? One reason is that the selection of an appropriate model or set of procedures for the formulation of objectives depends on the central purpose of that school. Vocational and other training schools, for example, are expected to prepare students for specific jobs. Hence, the use of *job analysis,* a technique for deriving objectives that directly contributes to helping students find jobs and keep them, is warranted. This technique seeks to ensure a match between what the student learns and what he or she will do on the job. The method can be amplified, of course, with procedures for collecting data that will help one anticipate likely job requirements. Job analysis would, however, be a less appropriate tool to use in the formulation of objectives within an institution whose mission is to further humanistic goals. Such an institution should use a different technical tool to formulate objectives, one more consistent with actualizing learners as individuals.

Illustrations of how institutional purposes match procedures for curriculum development can be seen in the familiar practices of the community college. There is more freedom in the formulation of curriculum goals in a community college than in a traditional school devoted to the liberal arts. Community colleges frequently have a very broad goal—community service, an invitation to meet the educational needs of the community. Because of such goals and the state legislature's practice of funding community colleges on the basis of student enrollment, the curriculum problem becomes a search for courses that will attract students. Anything that appeals to the aged, young mothers, veterans, and immigrants must be considered. The appropriate technical tool for the formulation of objectives in this case is needs assessment, a procedure for uncovering local deficiencies and trends to decide what might be taught, and a way to sample and stimulate interests in various kinds of learning.

Some curriculum leaders do not want curriculum objectives to be shackled to institutional purposes. Indeed, some people believe that curriculum specialists should be trying to change the purposes of institutions. Some experts believe that curriculum developers have been shaped by the bureaucratic nature of the schools, and thus have formulated objectives that serve an industrial model of education with an emphasis on efficiency. They would prefer curriculum workers to advance both futuristic and humanistic ends, helping institutions focus on getting people to define problems that were not perceived before and to make contact with one another in stronger ways.[3] In contrast, the role of the curriculum worker is not determined by the constraints of educational institutions; instead curriculum workers create new institutional forms and environments. The introduction of forms such as non-directive teaching roles, pupil goal setting, self-instructional systems, and therapeutic modes of working may broaden the function of a traditional school to include humanistic ends.

Functions of the Curriculum

Before preparing any curriculum plan, whether for a textbook, lesson, course of study, document, product, or program, one should be clear about the functions the proposed curriculum will serve. Those persons responsible for total curriculum offerings of a school will also find a functional concept useful in bringing balance to their programs of study. Typically, four functions have been recognized:

1. *Common or General Education.* This function is met through a curriculum that addresses the learner as a responsible human being and citizen, not as a specialist or one with unique gifts or interests. It means, for instance, including as content the ground rules—Bill of Rights—for participating in the civic affairs of the community and developing those minimal competencies essential for the health, welfare, and protection of all. Successful general education enables everyone to support and share in the culture; hence, a curriculum worker must decide what the individual needs in order to com-

---

[3]Bruce R. Joyce, "The Curricular Worker of the School," in *The Curriculum: Retrospect and Prospect,* NSSE Yearbook (Chicago: University of Chicago, 1971), pp. 307–55.

municate with others. The planner must consider what outcomes
and experiences all should have in common.

2. *Supplementation.* Individuality is the key to understanding supplementation. Objectives consistent with it deal with both personal
   lacks and unique potentials. To serve this function, a curriculum
   might be designed for those whose talents and interests enable
   them to go much further than the majority or those whose
   defects and deficiencies are severe enough to require special attention. Such a curriculum is personal and individual, not common or
   general.

3. *Exploration.* Opportunities for learners to discover and develop personal interests capture the meaning of exploration. When well
   executed, it enables learners to find out that they do or do not
   have either the talent or zeal for certain kinds of activities. Exploring experiences should *not* be organized and taught as if their purpose were to train specialists. Neither should they be conceived as
   shoddy and superficial. Exploration demands a wide range of con-
   tacts within a field, realization of the possibilities for further pursuit, and revelation of one's own aptitudes and interests.

4. *Specialization.* A specializing function is rendered by a curriculum in
   which the current standards of a trade, profession, or academic
   discipline prevail. Students are expected to emulate those who are
   successfully performing as skilled workers or scholars. Entry into
   such a curriculum requires that students already have considerable expertise and drive.

The balance among the different functions and the curriculum conceptions associated with them varies every few years. With secondary
schools, for example, academic specialization was in the ascendancy in
the 1960s. In the early 1970s, there was a weakening of general education
in favor of exploration; minicourses, optional modules, alternative curriculum, and other electives were used. In the early 1980s, the demand
for basic skills by parents and some educators pushed the curriculum
back in the direction of general education. Vocational specialization, too,
received more attention, particularly training on the job site itself.

In higher education too newer curriculum policy favors general
education—often said to be an unwelcome chore. Opposition to general
education comes from humanists and academic specialists who (albeit
for different reasons) believe it best for teachers and students to select
their own areas of interest for study. As a counter to the charge of
narrowness, the academic specialist says that by understanding one field
in depth, the student will learn to appreciate a wider array of intellectual

tools and artistic achievement. This notion has not gone unchallenged. Elliot Eisner, for instance, views it with skepticism.

> I am not convinced by the thesis that specialization breeds general under-standing, or that it cultivates an appreciation of the variety of ways in which meaning can be secured. . . . If attention to a wide range of problems and fields of study is necessary for the type of personal and intellectual range one wished to develop in students, how then can one cultivate, in depth, those idiosyncratic interests and aptitudes which almost all students have?[4]

The return to general education was spearheaded by a professor at Harvard University, Henry Rosovsky, who bemoaned the absence of a core of general studies—a missing common denominator—and the lack of a broad perspective for sense of purpose. His recognition of the problem was a clear signal to the schools of higher learning in the nation that it was time for a reexamination of their function.

The curriculum also performs less recognized functions. They include the *consummation* function (whetting the student demand for material things such as a car or the latest microcomputer, the *custodial* function (keeping students from job markets and entertaining them), and the *socializing* function (allowing students to meet members of the opposite sex).

MODELS FOR DETERMINING WHAT TO TEACH

The power to frame educational purposes is central in the curriculum field. Those who are not sensitive to the need for this power—who merely accept ends that others have proposed—are in one sense instruments. The following paragraphs describe the ways individuals and groups generate and select curriculum ends—aims, goals, and objectives. These ends indicate the purposes for which our programs and lessons are undertaken. They give direction to what would otherwise be blind activities and enable us to prepare plans of action. A curriculum goal is more than a whim or desire. Its formulation is a complex intellectual operation involving observation, study of conditions, collection of relevant information and, most of all, judgment. There can be no true curriculum ends without an intellectual anticipation and evaluation of consequences.

---

[4]Elliot W. Eisner, "Persistent Dilemmas in Curriculum Decision Making," *Confronting Curriculum Reform* (Boston: Little, Brown, 1971), pp. 168–69.

Needs Assessment Model

Needs assessment is the process by which educational needs are defined and priorities set. In the context of curriculum, a need is defined as a condition in which a discrepancy exists between an *acceptable* state of learner behavior or attitude and an *observed* learner state.

Needs assessment is one of the most frequently used ways for justifying curriculum goals and objectives. Several reasons underlie the popularity of needs assessment as a tool for formulating desired outcomes. Some people are motivated by efficiency. They want to identify and resolve the most critical needs so that resources can be employed in the most efficient manner. They want to avoid the practice of trying to do a little bit in many problem areas and solving none of them. Other people are concerned about social disorganization, the lack of consensus among the school community. They see needs assessment as a way to effect shared values and mutual support. The discussion of alternative ends by parents, students, teachers, and other citizens is an educational activity in itself. Other people want new value orientations to be reflected in the curriculum and see needs assessment as a vehicle for influence. Cultural pluralists, for example, use needs assessment to ascertain the values of subcultures such as those of Mexican-Americans, blacks, or the Chinese. They also try to persuade the dominant society to accept these values as worthy goals to be advanced through the curriculum.

Steps in Needs Assessment. A needs assessment requires four steps: formulating a set of tentative goals statements, assigning priority to different goals, determining the acceptability of learner performance in each of the preferred goals, and translating high priority goals into plans.

1. *Formulating a Set of Tentative Goals Statements.* Comprehensive sets of goals that reflect the dominant culture are readily available.[5] Such goals statements are collected from curriculum guides, textbooks, evaluation studies, and basic research studies by psychologists and educators. These goals refer to the conventionally sought outcomes in most schools: fundamental competencies for reading, writing, mathematics, health, citizenship, aesthetics. Goals may be found in four areas: academic, social and civic, vocational, and personal. Goals statements may also include attributes of character such as friendliness, respect, and independence.

Should one want to apply needs assessment to a cultural minor-

[5]Roger A. Kaufman, "Needs Assessment" in *Fundamental Curriculum Decisions*, ASCD 1983 Yearbook, ed. Fenwick W. English (Alexandria, Va.: ASCD, 1983), pp. 53–67.

ity, additional goal statements that reflect subculture values are necessary. Cross-cultural investigations reveal fundamental differences among the values of different cultural groups. Many Mexican-American parents, for example, believe that learners should make their choices in terms of family interests rather than personal desires. Some Mexican-Americans do not want their children to express personal feelings in the presence of an adult. These goals often contrast sharply with those of many in the dominant culture and with goals of other subcultures. Sometimes, goals statements from minority group members reflect a desire to gain better treatment for their children in majority-dominated schools. Such a goal might be that learners should see school as a friendly and helpful place.

Goals statements about community values must also be obtained. Those conducting needs assessments must consider more than the conventional goals available from lists of commercially prepared statements. They must focus on their own perception of what they want their learners to think, feel, or be able to do as a result of school instruction.

Typical techniques for eliciting data for needs assessment are *concerns conferences* and *sponsor speakups*. Concerns conferences, organized by school administrators and curriculum specialists, are attempts to identify local problems as most people in the community perceive them. At a large convocation, community members are prepared for the task of identifying community problems, and later, in small discussion groups, problems are articulated and suggestions made for their solution. Frequently, new educational goals are proposed in order to attempt a solution of the identified problem. In sponsor speakups students are organized into groups so that they work cooperatively to identify the most pressing needs of their school situation. Efforts are made to encourage uninhibited student expression. Although many of these needs may be met by actions that are not curricular in nature, it is important to consider the curriculum goals that might contribute to resolving the perceived difficulties. A perceived problem in health, for example, may involve a different goal for medical or health agencies than for a school. The school's curriculum goal might be limited to helping students understand the reason for the health problem and explaining some ways the learner can cope with it; a medical agency might take more direct action—inoculate the students to prevent disease.

2. *Assigning Priority to Goal Areas.* The second phase consists of gathering preference data, typically from parents, staff, students, and
   community members. Members of these groups are given goal
   statements and asked to rank them in terms of importance.
   Opportunities are provided for the respondents to add to the set
   of goals presented. Usually they rate the goals on a five-point scale
   (a rating rather than a ranking allows more goals to be considered). Samples of goals can be given to different individuals to
   effect average group estimates. Later, the combined ratings of all
   the people sampled will reveal those goals considered very important, important, average, unimportant, and very unimportant.
3. *Determining the Acceptability of Learner Performance in Each of the Preferred
   Goal Areas.* In the third phase either a subjective or an objective
   approach can be taken. A subjective approach calls for a group of
   judges to rate the acceptability of present learner status on each
   goal. No direct measure of the learners with respect to the goals is
   undertaken; judges estimate the present status of learners with
   respect to each goal. Their impression might be gained by whatever they have observed or been led to believe by the media and
   reports from the children and other neighbors. Judges' ratings
   become indices of need. The objective approach requires actually
   measuring the status of students relative to each goal. Measures
   must be congruent with the goals, of course. To this end, instructional objectives within each goal area are selected. Matching
   assessment devices are chosen and administered to representative
   samples of pupils. If the students' level of performance on a measure is less than the acceptable level, a need is indicated. Levels
   obtained on each measure are compared. Those showing the wid-
   est gap indicate a greater priority. However, one must also consider the relative importance of the goal as indicated by preference
   data.
4. *Translating High Priority Goals into Plans.* In the fourth phase, goals
   that are preferred and for which a need has been identified
   become the bases for new curriculum instructional plans. The
   selection of new target outcomes, goals, and objectives has implications for course offerings and for instructional materials and
   arrangements because the realization of new goals requires new
   facilitating means. Learning activities, teaching strategies, and evaluation techniques must be changed. For example, having once
   identified a need for pupils to learn to read and write in Spanish
   and acquire minority cultural values as well as positive attitudes

toward school, the school may need to develop a bilingual program. Consequently, the staff must acquire new materials in the Spanish language and offer activities consistent with minority values—group cooperation and family involvement. Further, teachers must be helped to use teaching strategies which are effective with the culture, such as learning how to indicate non-verbal acceptance through touching.

Problems in the Needs Assessment Technique. Technical and philosophical problems need to be resolved before needs assessment can fulfill its promise. One technical problem involves making the meaning of the goals clear so that respondents are choosing the same goals. A vague goal, such as citizenship, creative fluency, or application of scientific methods, indicates only a general direction. On the other hand, making a vague goal specific often results in numerous objectives, so many in fact that no one person could rank them according to their value. More than fifty years ago, Boyd H. Bode commented on Franklin Bobbitt's claim that some 1200 high school teachers in Los Angeles had given an almost unanimous judgment on a long list of objectives. Bode said, "If the list really represents common judgment, we are bound to conclude that men and women are more amenable to reason in Los Angeles than anywhere else on the globe.... One almost wonders whether the teachers of Los Angeles did not mistake Bobbitt's list of abilities for a petition to be signed."[6] One answer to the problem of how to discriminate among objectives is to rely on precise and observable objectives that represent significant competencies rather than to stipulate the many objectives that contribute to the general competency. Another answer is to have different individuals rate different goals and objectives, no one person having to evaluate carefully more than seven, a digestible number.

It is helpful to ask all who are to rate goals to engage first in common discussion and to ascertain that particular goals or objectives satisfy these three criteria: (1) that the goal is needed for future learning and contributes to fundamental needs, such as making a living and gaining the respect of others; (2) that the goal is teachable; and (3) that it is not likely to be acquired outside the school.

Needs assessment is frequently used by those with adaptive conceptions of curriculum who see it as a way to ensure that the curriculum is responsive to changing social conditions. It can also be used by social reconstructionists who want not so much to prepare students for

[6]Boyd H. Bode, "On Curriculum Construction," *Curriculum Theory* 5, no. 1 (1975): 39–59, reprinted from *Modern Educational Theories* (New York: Macmillan, 1927), 47.

changing conditions as to alter the social institutions that are creating undesirable social conditions. Group deliberation and judgment thus become factors in needs assessment. There must be opportunity for sharing facts and logical persuasion—facts and ideas brought by the participants themselves, not by outsiders—and there must be deliberation involving normative philosophical considerations. That something exists does not mean it is desirable. The reflective curriculum worker inquires about not only what is desired but also whether it is worthwhile, right, and good. Those who regard needs assessment as nothing more than a scientific information gathering procedure see it as a way to avoid ethical issues by justifying the curriculum merely on the basis of the popularity of certain goals and the magnitude of the discrepancy between where learners *are* and where learners *should be* with respect to these popular goals. Needs assessment has been opposed when it is regarded solely as an information gathering procedure on the grounds that "No scientifically derived information can yield a judgment about 'what should be' because science deals not with normative considerations but with facts."[7]

It remains to be seen whether the dominant groups in schools will attend to the goal priorities of minority groups. Can the curriculum reflect the priorities of all groups within the community or must a consensus be reached? If there is group conflict, how will the conflict be resolved?

The Futuristic Model

There is a growing realization that the world of the future is going to be very different from the present, that it will demand new kinds of people, and that the time is short to prepare the citizens of the future. Hence, efforts have been made to develop educational objectives consistent with this realization and specific enough to imply action.

Common Ingredients. Although there are slight differences among authors' conceptions of the model, the following techniques and phases are regarded as important:

1. *The multidisciplinary seminar.* Professional educators and specialists from outside education—political scientists, economists, medical psychologists—meet for several days to discuss possible future developments that would affect curriculum planning. Members of this seminar prepare papers examining the research frontiers in

[7]Maurice L. Monette, "Need Assessment: A Critique of Philosophical Assumptions," *Adult Education* 29, no. 2 (1979): 83–95.

their field. The results of literature searches on educational innovations and goals are also presented.

2. *Judgment of projected trends.* Major anticipated changes are ordered
according to their importance to society and probability of occurrence. The difficulty of bringing about these changes in terms of
time, money, and energy is considered. A period of occurrence is
estimated. The potential social effects of these changes are classified as good or bad on the basis of carefully examined opinions on
which there is a consensus. Participants rate each change from
"very desirable" to "very undesirable."

3. *Educational acceptance for creating the future.* After the social consequences of trends have been established and rated, school persons and
others suggest how they think the schools should respond. In
deciding the educational responsibility to be taken, consideration is
given to the certainty of a future occurrence, the social consequences of that occurrence, and the possibility that educators can
effect it or can prepare students for it. Educational objectives, thus
formed, should support "good" futures and resist "bad" ones. The
educators also decide what items in the present curriculum are
unlikely to prepare students for the future world and suggest that
these items no longer be supported.

4. *Scenario writing.* A group of writers prepares at least two descriptions. One is a description of what learners will be like if action is
taken on the decision in phase 3 and implemented by the school.
The second is a description of the necessary related changes in
subject matter, learning activities, curriculum organization, and
methods. Attention is also paid to institutional arrangements that
will bear on the new curriculum.

A Strategy Planning network, consisting of 23 schools and sponsored
by the Association for Supervision and Curriculum Development attempts
to analyze changes for which the schools should be planning if they are
to have a program suitable for all students in the next century. An
example of strategy planning within the network is "Project 2001"
undertaken by Lake Washington School District, Washington. In this
project futurists were commissioned to write reports on what skills
schools should teach in 2001, so they asked other members of the
community for their views on what schools should be doing.

The Delphi method is used by curriculum workers to obtain a consensus on goals and objectives for the future. By this method one tries to
obtain the intuitive insights of experts and then uses these judgments
systematically. In vocational education, content is often selected through
Delphi as a way to find what is likely to be useful to future graduates of

the school. Members of an employers' advisory council to the school are sent a series of questionnaires. The first questionnaire indicates present content offerings and asks participants to indicate their recommended course subject areas in light of anticipated futures and to state the amount of time to be spent on each. In an attempt to gain consensus, more questionnaires are sent, providing information about how all participants responded to the previous ones. Participants are asked to reconsider their first recommendations and to give their reasons. Usually survey participants begin to form a consensus.

Problems With the Futuristic Model. The difficulty any group of people faces in trying to predict or invent the future is problem enough. However, there are also difficulties associated with getting a broad enough base of participation within and outside school systems and with understanding the complex factors that affect school curriculum. Different community contexts and different views of the school's role delay consensus. There is no consensus about what different educational institutions should be trying to achieve. A related aspect of the problem is that many people do not like to make choices, and many find it difficult to make even hypothetical choices. Even when groups arrive at a consensus on some preferred alternatives, many dissensions remain unresolved. Educational objectives frequently are not consistent with other objectives or have more than one meaning even for one person. One objective may call for the learner to show initiative; a second objective may call for the learner to follow directions. Respondents experience a tension in deciding between creativity on the one hand and order and tradition on the other.

The Rational Model

Ralph Tyler's rationale is the best-known rational model for answering questions about formulating educational purposes, selecting and organizing educational experiences, and determining the extent to which purposes are being attained.[8] It is called an ends-means approach because the setting of purposes or objectives as ends influences the kinds of activity and organization most likely to assist in reaching the goal. Evaluation, too, according to this model, is undertaken to see how the learning experience as developed and organized produces the desired results.

[8]Ralph W. Tyler, *Basic Principles of Curriculum and Instruction* (Chicago: University of Chicago Press, 1950).

Deriving Objectives. Tyler's assumption is that objectives will be more defensible—will have greater significance and greater validity—if certain kinds of facts are taken into account. One source of facts consists of studies of the intended learners. A second source is found in studies of contemporary life outside the school, and a third source is made up of suggestions about objectives from subject matter specialists regarding what knowledge is of most worth for citizens. The following will elaborate how objectives are derived from data provided by the different sources.

1. *Learners.* In order to derive objectives from this source, one would study learners in terms of their deficiencies with respect to knowledge and application of a broad range of values in daily living; their psychological needs for affection, belonging, recognition, and a sense of purpose; and their interests. Essentially, the process of deriving an objective from studies of the learner demands that an inference be drawn about what to teach after looking at the data. Making inferences also involves value judgments. If the data show that learners are chiefly interested in reading comic books, one still must decide whether this is a desirable interest to be extended or a deficiency to be overcome.

   Let us assume that the curriculum worker has discovered this fact: "During adolescence, learners are likely to have the cognitive skills of intuition, generalization, and insight; and their sensibilities toward justice are awakened." The curriculum planner can use this information to infer what to teach, perhaps deciding that learners should acquire knowledge of Utopian thought and the methods for effecting a more perfect social order. The curriculum planner might also infer that students should suppress the tendency to believe that wars, tyrannies, and the like are caused by human nature and believe instead that changes in social structure may preclude injustices.

2. *Social Conditions.* Facts about the community—local, national, or world—must be known and taken into account if what is to be taught is to be made relevant to contemporary life. Again, one needs to make a value judgment in deciding what kinds of facts to collect. Comprehensiveness is sometimes sought: one might collect data on health, economics, politics, religion, family, and conservation. The educational responses to these facts often provoke controversy. After discovering from health data that venereal disease is at an epidemic level, the curriculum worker might make inferences that range from: (1) learners should be taught the causes and means for preventing communicable diseases; to

(2) learners should be taught those moral principles governing sexual conduct which uphold the sanctity of marriage. One can easily see that a curriculum worker's responses in such a case could be controversial.

3. *Subject Matter Specialists.* In rational curriculum making, scientists and scholars, the discoverers of knowledge, are consulted in order to find out what the specialist's subject can contribute to the education of the intended learners. Suppose a curriculum planner asked this question: "What in your field might best contribute to the aim that learners generate new questions and that they conceptualize alternatives and their consequences?" He or she would receive different answers from specialists in different fields. A historian might reply: "You should teach the principles for interpreting historical events. Help students to comprehend such schemes as the great–man theory, cultural movements, and economic determinism as explaining factors." A linguist's response might be: "You should teach concepts that show the unitary and meaning–bearing sequences of language structures, such as intonation patterns." An anthropologist might want to stress the processes of inquiry that illuminate culture or might say, "Be sure learners understand the difference between the symbolic devices, institutions, and things constructed by people and by nature."

Selecting from Among Educational Objectives. After formulating tentative objectives, the rationalist applies the following criteria to the objectives before accepting them as suitable for the selection of learning activities:

1. *Congruency with values and functions.* Objectives must relate to the values and functions adopted by the controlling agency. If authorities for the institution value general education, objectives must further common understanding; if they value specialization, then objectives must be related to the development of specialists in a field.
2. *Comprehensiveness.* Objectives that are more encompassing, that do not deal with a minuscule sort of learner behavior, are more highly valued. Often many such objectives can be coalesced into a single powerful objective.
3. *Consistency.* Objectives should be consistent with one another. One should not have objectives stressing both openness or inquiry and dogmatism or unconditional acceptance.
4. *Attainability.* Objectives should be achievable by the intended learners.
5. *Feasibility.* Objectives should be capable of being reached without

great strain. The curriculum maker should consider teacher and community concurrence, costs, and availability of materials.

As guides to instructional planning, educational objectives are then stated in a form that makes clear the content that the learner must use, the *domain* or situation in which the knowledge is to apply, and the kind of *behavior* to be exhibited by the learner. The following objective is an illustration: "In different writing samples (domain), the learner will be able to recognize (behavior) unstated assumptions (content)."

Learning activities must allow the learner to work with the defined substantive element at a level of behavior consistent with that called for in the objective. Activities designed to teach prerequisites to that terminal task can also be provided, of course.

Problems with the Tyler Model. The Tyler model represents conciliatory electicism. In recommending the three sources to use in formulating objectives, Tyler confronts the decision maker with three warring conceptions of the curriculum. The learner as a source is consistent with the humanistic conception—especially when data regarding the learners' own psyche needs and interests are considered. Society as a source is in keeping with social adaptive and some reconstruction orientations, while the subject matter specialist as a source tends to recognize the academic conception of curriculum.

Little help is given in the way of assigning weight to each source when one must take precedence over another. On the other hand, the model offers the possibility of treating learners, society, and subject matter as part of a comprehensive process rather than as isolated entities.

The criteria by which one excludes some objectives is not stipulated by the model. Users of the model must identify their own set of philosophical axioms for screening objectives. The fact that objectives must be consistent with one another does not in itself indicate the value of the objectives formulated.

The role of values and bias is not highlighted in the model. Values and bias operate at all points in the rationale—in the selection of particular data within the sources, in drawing inferences from the data, in formulating the objectives, and in selecting from among the objectives.

Three other criticisms remain. The model tends to lock curriculum making into the "top-down" tradition, with those at the top setting the purposes and functions that narrow the school's objectives; the objectives, in turn, control classroom instruction. Those who favor teacher or learner autonomy in the selection of ends and learning opportunities oppose the model. They charge that the predetermined objectives which guide all other aspects, such as learning experiences, are like a production model with its input (students), processes (learning experiences), and output (prespecified objectives). The second criticism, that the model takes time to implement, is related to the third: the resolving of disagreement over values. The practical difficulties of getting the right data sources and being able to infer appropriate implications for schools require imaginative thinkers. The model does not resolve the political conflict in curriculum policymaking even if common values are accepted. Even those characterized as devout members of the same value persuasion may have their disagreement over methods:

> Those who agree that the truths honored in our tradition should be the primary curriculum elements may still disagree over whether certain classics should be taught in English translation, Latin translation, or the original Greek. They may argue whether to include Virgil together with Tacitus and Julius Caesar in a fixed time of study. They may differ over the amounts of time to be allotted to the Bible and other more strictly oriented texts. The resolution of such problems requires a decision procedure in addition to a value base.[9]

Curriculum specialists have tried to improve upon the Tyler model. Usually the improvement consists of reversing the order of procedures by placing the statements of educational values or aims as the first step and then refining these aims in light of information about learners, social conditions, and new knowledge in the subject fields. In working with students of curriculum, I often randomly divide the students into two groups—(a) those who will follow the procedures as outlined by Tyler beginning with sources and ending with the application of philosophical and psychological screens and (b) those who follow the revised procedures, making value orientations explicit before looking at data from the sources. I give both groups the same facts or generalizations from each of the three sources and then observe how variations in ordering of the procedures influences the number and kinds of objectives generated. Table 5.1 illustrates the contrast in procedure.

The difference in number and kind of objectives generated by the two procedures is considerable. The Tyler model results in many more objectives and objectives that are more responsive to the range of data available about learners and the community. The difficulty experienced by the revisionist group in getting agreement on educational aims is much greater than the difficulty of establishing a philosophical framework after forming tentative objectives.

[9]Michael W. Kirst and Decker F. Walker, "An Analysis of Curriculum Policy Making," *Review of Educational Research* 41, no. 5 (December 1971): 485. Copyright 1971, American Educational Research Association, Washington, D.C. Reprinted by permission.

TABLE 5.1 Comparison of Tyler and Revisionist Procedures for Generating Objectives

Tyler	Revisionist
1. *Data* Facts about learners indicating that they do not feel responsible for their successes or failures in school. Facts about the community indicating perhaps ideological confusion about traditional ways of doing things and newer technology.	1. *Philosophy* State educative aims of importance to you (cognitive development, development of respect for the rights of others, desire for continuing education, ability to enter world of work) and the aims most relevant for the school you have in mind (general, remedial, or vocational).
2. *Tentative Objectives* Suggested objectives in response to the facts and generalizations.	2. *Data* Facts about learners indicating that learners do not feel responsible for their successes or failures in school. Facts about the community indicating perhaps ideological confusion about traditional ways of doing things and newer technology.
3. *Philosophy* State your educative aims (cognitive development, development of respect for others, desire for continued learning, ability to enter the world of work) or the aims most relevant for the school you have in mind (general, remedial, or vocational).	3. *Objectives* Objectives are derived by keeping in mind detailed educational aims and functions and responding to facts in light of these aims.
4. *Final Objectives* Acceptance or rejection of the tentative objectives or the basis for your educational values, educational aims and functions of schooling.	

The Vocational or Training Model

Training usually implies narrower purposes than educating. Educating allows for objectives that include the wholeness of a student's life as a responsible human being and a citizen. Training tends to look at the student's competence in some occupation. Although these two sides of life are not altogether separable, different procedures are used in deriving training objectives than in formulating educational objectives. The training model for formulating proposed outcomes has essentially two functions: one is to reveal particular manpower needs or occupations which the institutions or programs should serve. A second purpose is to determine the specific competencies that must be taught in order for learners (trainees) to take their place within the target occupations.

Determining Occupational Targets. Procedures for determining needed occupations rely initially on existing studies and plans. Most states release detailed area manpower requirements for more than four hundred key occupational categories, reflecting for each category current employment, anticipated industry growth, and personnel replacement. The annual *Manpower Report of the President* issued by the United States Department of Labor gives an overall picture of the employment problems facing the nation. Specific organizations such as the military, large industries, and business have projected their own manpower needs, which indicate the types of training that will be necessary. State and regional planners attempt to estimate future employment opportunities and to foresee fluctuations in mobility within the area and in mobility likely to result as firms enter or leave an area. These planners try to coordinate the programs that determine vocational services with those aimed at developing jobs. They take into account job market analysis, program reviews, curriculum resources, and state, local, and national priorities.

It is customary to use advisory councils in connection with planning vocational programs. These councils are composed of parents, students, representatives from labor, and potential trainees. Members of these councils help supply more information on both what will happen in a community and what kind of employee employers are seeking. Further, they help inform the community of the forces that are affecting the job market.

Determining the Objectives for Training Programs or Courses. Job descriptions and task analysis procedures are used to enhance the relevancy of the training program to the job to be performed. A job description is a paragraph or two listing the tasks involved and any unusual conditions under which those tasks are carried out. All classes of tasks are listed. The task analysis begins with a study of the particular job or jobs. The curriculum developer tries to answer these questions: What tasks are required on this job? How frequently are they required? What skills and information is the graduate of the training program expected to bring to each task?

A task is a logically related set of actions required by a job objective. The first step in the task analysis is listing all tasks that might be included in the job. Second, for each of these tasks an estimate is made of the frequency of performance, relative importance, and relative ease of learning. Third, the task is detailed by listing what the person does when performing each of the tasks. Note that what is done is not necessarily the same as what is known.

Task identification occurs through interviews, questionnaires, reports of critical incidents, and hardware analysis. Observation shows what the employees *do* while being observed; questionnaires and interviews reveal what they *say* they do. Critical incident techniques also indicate what people say they do. A critical incident report may describe a specific work assignment which an employee carried out very effectively or very ineffectively. Such reports are especially valuable in identifying unforeseen contingencies, difficult tasks, and interpersonal aspects of a job. Reports are sorted into topics such as equipment, problems, or groups of incidents that go together. The features common to these incidents are categorized. Each incident is judged effective or ineffective and characterized by the presence or absence of some skill or knowledge. The records may be further classified by such dimensions as "work habit," "management effectiveness or ineffectiveness," and "method problem." From these data one derives new training objectives for courses. Critical incident reports are completed by representative samples of job holders and of persons who interact with job holders.

The job analysis and a knowledge of the characteristics of the intended learners are all that one needs for the blueprint of expected student performance. By subtracting what the student is already able to do from what he or she must be able to do one can obtain the course objectives. Course objectives are not the same as task analyses. Objectives specify the abilities that a beginning learner must have after training; task analyses describe the job as performed by a highly skilled person. Subtracting what students are already able to do from what they must be able to do helps one to decide the course objectives. However, one cannot go directly from a task analysis to the formulation of objectives for a course. It is necessary to decide which of the skills demanded by the occupation may be better taught on the job and which are best taught in the course.

Problems with the Vocational Model. There are several criticisms of the training model. First, the objectives derived from it usually prepare a learner for work as it *is* rather than as it *should* be. Related to this criticism is the charge that the model is associated with *presentism,* a focus on the current situation rather than on a likely future condition. Most critics admit, however, that the model is ahead of the practice of deriving objectives only from tradition, convention, and the curriculum maker's personal experiences.

A second criticism is that the task analysis procedure is only valid for aspects of jobs that are certain. If we know what an employee must do in a situation, the training model is effective. However, there are many aspects of jobs that are uncertain—what to do in light of unanticipated circumstances, what to do when the situation is altered. Further, not many developers know how to make task analyses for situations demanding political, economic, or moral judgments. Preparing students for instances when the grounds for decision are unclear or unique requires a different model for curriculum development—one that is unrealized but probably will take the form of critical inquiry as suggested by Habermas.[10] Briefly, the model will call for opportunities by which learners (a) relate proposed decisions to common norms, (b) question the validity of the common norms in light of satisfying human needs, and (c) employ the weight of evidence and reason in arriving at the best solution.

Disjointed Incrementalism

Disjointed incrementalism is not really a model; it is a nonmodel. It occurs when curriculum decisions are made without following a systematic procedure. In the nonmodel, decisions about what will be taught occur through a political process. Advocates of a particular curriculum try to justify the ends they already have in mind. Advocates of great works and fundamental skills appeal to tradition; advocates of cognitive skills appeal to psychological and educational research; advocates of relevant vocational skills appeal to community; advocates of self-improvement appeal to personal judgment. Those who must resolve the conflicting pressures—school boards, advisory councils, textbook publishers, professional educators—tend to use informal methods of decision making. Disjointed incrementalism is a strategy, and it has these rules:

1. Contemplate making only marginal changes in the existing situation.

[10]Thomas McCarthy, ed. *The Critical Theory of Jurgen Habermas.* (Cambridge: MIT Press, 1981).

2. Avoid making radical changes and consider only a few policy alternatives.
3. Consider only a few of the possible consequences for any proposed change.
4. Feel free to introduce objectives consistent with policy as well as to change policy in accord with objectives.
5. Be willing to look for problems *after* data are available from implementation.
6. Work with piecemeal changes rather than making a single comprehensive attack.

Decisions made under disjointed incrementalism are not based on much objective data. Hence, political processes are used to resolve conflicts. In Chapter 11, we shall describe this process in detail.

Problems with Disjointed Incrementalism in Curriculum Making. Disjointed incrementalism in making curriculum decisions about what to teach is not too different from what occurs in other areas of government and industry. It tends to result in a fragmented curriculum that lacks continuity. Many, however, prefer such an irrational model over a more logical and effective model that might be more appropriate in a totalitarian society. The main defect in the procedure is one associated with the democratic process: the lack of well-informed citizens who will exercise wide participation, assume responsibility for starting social improvements, and show competency in the skills of political action.

Disjointed incrementalism is the approach used most frequently in times of affluence; programs and courses are added rather than hard choices being made about their elimination. It represents a realization that conflict over what to teach is not just a conflict of ideas but of persons, groups, and factions. Under disjointed incrementalism, conflicts over goals and objectives are not resolved on the basis of principles, logic, and evidence but by political power. Future fiscal and demographic trends will make disjointed incrementalism more difficult to practice, so scrutiny of curriculum offerings should increase.

A COMMENT ON MODELS FOR CURRICULUM BUILDING

Thus far we have focused upon models for determining the purposes that curriculum should fulfill. Other decisions must be made—decisions about what is necessary to achieve stated purposes and how best to evaluate progress toward intended goals. The choice of emphasizing purpose as a first step in curriculum development is somewhat arbitrary.

Alan Purves has been building curriculum for over twenty years. When asked to think about the processes by which he developed and arranged materials to effect people's learning, he realized that existing models are a fine way to look at curriculum but that they don't tell one how to proceed any more than a blueprint tells where to begin building a house. Purves realizes that curriculum reflects the maker's view of the society, the people who are to be affected, and the nature of what is to be learned. However, he thinks the metaphor of a game is the best way to describe the process by which one builds curriculum.

Rules for playing the curriculum game center on these pieces: legal constraints and administrative structure. Who is the decision maker in the school—the principal, the teachers, or some more remote body? How does the proposed curriculum fit with other curricula? Other pieces include teacher attitude and capacity, student interests, principles for sequencing activities, activities themselves, and the constraints of time and resources. Obviously, formulating objectives and anticipating possible outcomes are important pieces. Purves believes that the formulating of objectives and outcomes might take place at the same time as the selection and arrangement of materials, just as evaluation can take place during the course of devising the curriculum.

Curriculum is, however, like a game board. Just having the pieces does not mean one knows how to play the game. Some start with a sense of what the classroom should look like, structured or open. Others begin with a view of how society should be. Purves says, "A number have started with evaluation and built a dog to fit the tail."[11] Some begin with behavioral objectives and others with a set of materials. Others start with a theory about subject matter.

Purves's rules indicate that a player may start with any piece, just as long as all the pieces are picked up. His next rule is that all pieces must be perceived in some relationship to one another. Activities should relate to objectives and theories of learning. A final rule is that there are several ways to win the game. One way is to have the pieces all placed in some relation to one another. Another way is to have the finished board approximate a model of rationality with objectives determining learning activities, organization, and evaluation. One can also win by showing that the intended outcomes were achieved by the learner. If the learner achieves the stated purposes, no matter what else is learned, it is a winning curriculum. It is even possible to have a winning curriculum by virtue of the attractiveness of the materials or their intellectual modernity.

[11]Alan C. Purves, "The Thought Fox and Curriculum Building," in *Strategies for Curriculum Development*, eds. Jon Schaffarzick and David Hampson (Berkeley: McCutchan, 1975), p. 120.

Conflicting views of winning make curriculum one of the most controversial games in town.

CONCLUDING COMMENTS

The needs assessment model for determining curriculum has been a popular means of curriculum making. It is seen as one way of restoring community confidence in the school and of advancing the interests of previously ignored groups when it allows clients to determine what they want to learn and not just select from among a list of meaningless choices. It is closely associated with the adaptive and social reconstructionists' conception of curriculum, but may also be used by those with other philosophical orientations.

As the name implies, the futuristic model emphasizes future conditions more than present status. It is a form of needs assessment in that future needs are anticipated. For this model, one decides what students should be like in light of some desirable future.

Few models are as idealistic and comprehensive as the rational model. It is appealing because it gives attention to the interests of learner, society, and the fields of knowledge. In practice, however, curriculum makers often fail to respond equally to these interests. Once specialization is accepted as the overriding function of a school program or course, the outlooks of subject matter specialists carry the most weight. Similarly, when those in an institution prize the general education function—wanting to develop shared values and to make schooling relevant to social needs—they tend to respond to generalizations about society to the exclusion of other considerations. Almost no curricula have appealed to the learner in order to decide what to teach.

The vocational training model is most appropriate in institutions claiming to prepare students for jobs. Those using this model must be aware, however, that its use may tend to perpetuate the status quo.

Curriculum ends should not be narrowly conceived. Objectives that are relevant to present and likely future conditions, to the concerns of the learners, and to a wide span of cultural resources are better than those that rely solely on tradition. The final acceptance of educational ends is a value judgment. The decision to accept, however, should be influenced by evidence that shows that the end—the goal or objective—will be of value to the learner, that it is attainable, and that it probably will not be achieved without deliberate instruction.

To keep curriculum workers in touch with reality, let us admit that disagreement on the proper base for assessing the worth of the curriculum is likely. Hence, political processes are used for dealing with the value conflicts.

QUESTIONS

1. Consider the mission of an institution known to you—a training center, junior college, or elementary school. Which model for formulating goals and objectives is most appropriate for that institution? Why?
2. In using the needs assessment model, would you want the preferences of special groups—parents, teachers, students—to be given equal or weighted importance? Why or why not?
3. State an aim of importance to you, such as health, conservation of resources, self–worth, vocational skill. How would you refine this aim into an educational objective? What might be taught in order to help learners make progress toward this aim?
4. Read the following generalizations and then infer what should be taught in light of each generalization.
   a. Secondary school students construe moral issues in terms of power relationships and physical consequences. They see morality as something outside their control.
   b. Adults are strangers who grant neither substance nor interest to one another and do not see a society larger than their private world.
   c. The cry for law and order is a fundamental demand for cognitive order, for normative clarity, and for predictability in human affairs.
   d. Within humans are powerful forces leading toward diversity and variety rather than uniformity.
5. What do you believe is the function of the school? Is there something the school can do better than any other agency? Indicate how your answer might be used in deciding what and what not to teach.

SELECTED REFERENCES

Brandt, Ronald and Tyler, Ralph W. "Goals and Objectives." In *Fundamental Curriculum Decisions,* ASCD Yearbook, ed. Fenwick W. English, pp. 40–52. Alexandria, Va.: 1983.

California State Department of Education. *Curriculum Review Handbook.* Sacramento: Education Department, Instructional Services Unit, 1981.

Glatthorn, Allan A. *A Guide for Developing an English Curriculum for the Eighties.* Urbana: National Council of Teachers of English, 1980.

Goodlad, John I. and associates. *Curriculum Inquiry.* New York: McGraw-Hill Book Company, 1979.

Kaufman, Roger and English, Fenwick. *Needs Assessment: Concept and Application.* Englewood Cliffs, N.J.: Educational Technology Publication, 1979.

Larson, David H. "Designing School Curriculum for the Twenty-First Century." *NASSA Bulletin* 67, no. 464 (1983): 10–15.

McNeil, John D. "Deriving Objectives" and "Selecting Among Educational Objectives—Defensible Choices." *Designing Curriculum: Self-Instructional Modules.* Boston: Little, Brown, 1976.

Schaffarzick, Jon and Hampson, David, eds. *Strategies for Curriculum Development.* Berkeley, Cal.: McCutchan, 1975.

Shevach, Eden. "The Translation of General Educational Aims Into Functional Objectives: A Needs Assessment Study" *Studies in Educational Evaluation* 1, no. 1 (Spring 1975): 5–11.

6 / SELECTING AND DEVELOPING LEARNING OPPORTUNITIES

This chapter has two general purposes. One is to show the different considerations involved in deciding on learning opportunities—books, materials, experiences, activities, programs. To illustrate the considerations, the nature of instructional decisions at societal and institutional levels is contrasted with decisions at classroom levels. The conflict between those who see learning opportunities as having inherent worth and those who see them as means to be appraised is also treated. Consequently, a sense of the strengths and weaknesses of some arguments used in justifying learning opportunities should be gained.

A second purpose is to analyze and compare the procedures used by technologists, humanists, social reconstructionists, academicians, and teachers in developing instructional materials and programs. The description of the procedures should stimulate criticism and discussion.

A CURRICULUM CONFLICT: LEARNING ACTIVITIES AS MEANS OR ENDS?

In the curriculum field, as in travel, some people value the journey (the learning process) and others prize the destination (knowledge). The latter value the learning opportunities involved in the journey only to the extent that the opportunities contribute to the attainment of goals.

Theorists in the first group, such as Maxine Greene, tend to prize those learning opportunities—sometimes called learning experiences, activities, interventions—as valuable in their potential for having personal significance for learners.[1] These theorists are concerned that learners

[1]Maxine Green, "Public Education and the Public Space," *Educational Researcher* 11, no. 6 (June-July 1982): 4–9.

care enough about the opportunity to do something with it and to create meanings from it. The use of classical exemplars—great books, paintings, drama, sculpture—is common among these theorists. So, too, is the practice of placing students in challenging situations and helping them better understand themselves as they grapple with the challenges. These theorists value a rich environment. They define worthwhile opportunities as those that are relevant to the students' purposes, that give students opportunities to make informed choices, that provide a moral quality, that offer aesthetic satisfaction, and that display other indicators of quality of life.

Theorists in the second group, such as Mauritz Johnson, define curriculum as the destination—the intended outcomes of instructional activity.[2] They regard the planning and implementation of strategies for achieving goals as instruction. Further, they see the instructional component as consisting of both planning and interactive phases. Planning involves formulating intended objectives and instructional activities and stipulating the characteristics of instructional materials to be used. Interaction refers to actually carrying out the plans, such as a teacher presenting a lesson.

Implications of Conflict

Those who view learning activities as valuable in themselves are *expressives* or humanists; they see learning activities as expressions of individuality, significant as such. They tend to be interested in the learning process and believe that the curriculum person can accept responsibility only for offering the best of conditions, not for controlling the behavior of others or effecting outcomes that are likely to be unpredictable. The expressives do not try to control what students are to become but take responsibility for what students undergo. They view learning opportunities as aesthetic experiences that break the bonds of dead custom.

In contrast, those who view learning opportunities as instrumental select and design activities that are most likely to have specified consequences. *Instrumentalists* are oriented to product or outcome rather than to activity as an intrinsic value; they appraise activities by results, not by inherent attributes alone. Their distinction between planning and teaching allows them to assess the effects of the plan separately from the way the plan is carried out. A plan might be quite effective with one teacher who follows it carefully but ineffective as executed by another.

[2]Mauritz Johnson, Jr., *Intentionality in Education* (Albany: Center for Curriculum Research and Services, 1977).

An expressive prizes particular experiences or opportunities which reflect the values of the designers, tending to assume that desirable experiences have desirable but unspecified consequences rather than to appraise systematically the learning that follows. Measurement of results in terms of predetermined objectives is incompatible with the view of the expressives. Once it is decided that certain things are to be learned, an instrumentalist selects or designs activities on the basis of their likely contribution to specific purposes. An activity is justified on the basis of results produced.

PLANNING FOR INSTRUCTION

The range of learning activities is infinite, which is why curriculum making and teaching are creative fields. We can, however, distinguish types of learning opportunities that are common at different levels of instructional planning.

Macro Level

Those responsible for curriculum development at the macro level—for an entire school system or an institution—select general categories of opportunity that are called domains or areas of study. Domains indicate what kinds of programs will be offered students and suggest what is likely to be learned. They can be considered planned activities although they are general. Breadth and variety of classroom activities are somewhat limited once the domains are established. Examples of sets of domains are: (1) symbolic studies, basic sciences, developmental studies, and aesthetic studies; (2) academic disciplines—English, mathematics, science, social science, the arts; and applied fields—agriculture, business education, industrial arts, vocational education; (3) the personal, the social, and the academic; and as was mentioned in Chapter 5, domains that correspond to functions of the school, general education, exploratory and enrichment studies, specialization studies, and remedial studies.

Other categories of instructional opportunities selected at the macro level are: (1) programs of study, such as a foreign language program or a program in physical education, and (2) course offerings, such as introductory Spanish or advanced German. Note that a program indicates continuities over a longer period of time (two or three years or more) while a course may be of shorter duration (a quarter, semester, or year). The teacher's selection of classroom activities is sometimes further constrained by the problems, projects, themes, centers of interest, and topics selected at macro levels as important for a course. In a curriculum developed by a rational model, categories of activity are consistent with the school's goals or functions. In a curriculum developed in accordance with humanistic tenets, the offerings must elicit the enthusiasm of students as well as serve the major goal of individual self-realization.

Chapter 8 indicates how curriculum planning can best be implemented at the macro level.

Micro Level

At the classroom or micro level, planned learning opportunities become more specific, and in the case of a rational curriculum allow learners to practice what is called for in predetermined instructional objectives. An instrumentalist defines a learning activity as a specification or product delineating content or method intended to influence or shape the learner. To the expressive or humanist, it is a situation that gives learners the opportunity to have valued experiences. Particular books, films, games, and manipulative and other instructional products are selected as the means for instruction. Field trips, debates, projects, demonstrations, and the like are common activities at this level. Interestingly, although learning opportunities at macro and micro levels differ considerably in form, the criteria used in justifying their selections are the same. Values such as inquiry and personal or social relevancy can serve in the justification of domains, programs, and course offerings at the macro level as well as in the justification of texts, lessons, and excursions at the micro level. Individuals making decisions at any level, however, often do not employ the same criteria. One person may, for example, put more value on practicality whereas another may give greater weight to tradition.

CRITERIA FOR SELECTING LEARNING ACTIVITIES

Five kinds of criteria are used in guiding and justifying the selection of learning activities; philosophical, psychological, technological, political, and practical. Each curriculum orientation tends to place priority on different criteria. Humanists, for example, are more interested in the inherent qualities of a learning activity than in data indicating that the activity has had an effect in some specific but limited way. Learning activities are judged as good or bad when they meet our value expectations or philosophical assumptions. If one holds human variability, for instance, to be of great worth, then one will favor activities that advance learner variability rather than activities that stress common outlooks and capacities. Learning activities are also judged in accordance with psychological criteria. Those who differ on whether learning should be painful or pleasant will differ on their assessments of learning opportunities. The technologists' studies of learning and instruction have resulted in a number of new criteria to use in designing and evaluating learning activities. Technologists claim that their criteria are empirically based principles for effective learning rather than canons established by philosophical beliefs.

Philosophical Criteria

Values are the chief basis for judging proposed learning activities at both macro and micro levels. Typically, these value positions appear as options as indicated in the curriculum maker's dilemma seen in Table 6.1.

TABLE 6.1   Curriculum Maker's Dilemma

Learning Activities Should:	But They Also Should:
Be immediately enjoyable.	Lead to desirable future experiences.
Show the ideal: the just, beautiful, and honorable.	Show life as it is, including corruption, violence, and the profane.
Treat the thought and behavior of the group to which the learner belongs.	Treat the thought and behavior of the groups other than those to which the learner belongs.
Minimize human variability by stressing common outlooks and capacities.	Increase variability by stressing individuality.
Stress cooperation so that individuals share in achieving a common goal.	Stress competition so that the able person excels as an individual.
Allow students to clarify their own positions on moral and controversial issues.	Instruct students in the values of moral and intellectual integrity rather than allowing students to engage in sophistry and personal indulgence.

TABLE 6.2   Conflicting Views of How to Enhance Learning

Closed View Learning Activities Should:	*Open View* Learning Activities Should:
Be under the direct influence of the teacher who demonstrates the learning activities so that the learner will imitate and acquire.	Be removed from direct teacher influence, allowing self-actualization by finding meaning in a situation where the teacher is a resource person.
Be pleasant and comfortable for the student.	Allow for hardship and perplexity so that significant growth can take place.
Teach one thing at a time but teach it to mastery, simplifying the environment and giving enough instances to help the learner abstract desired generalizations.	Bring about several outcomes at once, helping students develop interests and attitudes as well as cognitive growth.
Allow the learner to acquire simple basic patterns before being exposed to higher orders of learning.	Allow the learner to grasp the meaning and organization of the whole before proceeding to study the parts.
Allow the learner to see and imitate the best models of talking, feeling, and acting.	Allow the learner to create and practice new and different ways of talking, feeling, and acting.
Feature repetitive practice on a skill not mastered. Don't let the learner practice error.	Feature novel and varied approaches to an unlearned skill. Recognize that learners can learn from error.

Psychological Criteria

Psychological beliefs about how learning best takes place often determine whether a learning activity is acceptable or not. Not all people agree, however, on the particular learning principles to employ. Some examples of conflicts are shown in Table 6.2.

Technological Criteria

Recently, technologists studying instructional variables and procedures have gained great influence over the kinds of factors used in both judging and developing learning opportunities.[3] Persons like Benjamin Bloom have adapted constructs of programmed learning and behavioral and contiguity psychology to instructional development.[4] Hence psychological and technological criteria often overlap—practice and knowledge of results can be both psychological and technological criteria. These persons accept the revolutionary idea that all students can master a learning task if the right means for helping the student are found. Chief among the means they turn to are careful analysis and sequencing of tasks so that prerequisites are provided. They make sure learners understand the task and the procedures they are to follow, and adapt instruction to the characteristics of individuals. One way to adapt to these characteristics is to give more examples, frequent testing with immediate knowledge of results, reteaching if necessary, alternative procedures, and variation in time allowed for learning.

The technologists' criteria are found increasingly in instruments for assessing instructional materials, as indicated in the following list of criteria selected from widely used instruments:[5]

1. The objectives for the activity or material are stated in behavioral terms including the type of behavior, conditions, and level of expected performance.

2. A task analysis—identification of components of a complex behavior—has been made and a relationship between the tasks and the final objectives has been specified.

---

[3]Robert Greer, "Contingencies of the Sciences and Technology of Teaching and Pre-Behavioral Research Practices in Education," *Educational Researcher* 12, no. 1 (January 1983): 3–9; Geneva D. Haertel et al., "Psychological Models of Educational Performance: A Theoretical Synthesis of Constructs," *Review of Educational Research* 53, no. 1 (Spring 1983): 75–91.

[4]Benjamin S. Bloom, *All Our Children Learning* (New York: McGraw-Hill, 1982).

[5]Meridith D. Gall, *Handbook for Evaluating and Selecting Curriculum Materials* (Boston: Allyn and Bacon, 1981).

3. Learning activities are directly related to the behavior and content of the specified objectives.
4. Evaluation procedures are comparable to these objectives:
   a. There is immediate feedback regarding the adequacy of the learner's responses.
   b. There are criterion-referenced tests that measure stated objectives.
   c. Attention is given to evaluating both process, by which the learner learns, and the product, or what the learner learns.
5. The product or activity has been carefully field-tested. A technical manual might cite sources of available evidence to document claims about effectiveness and efficiency, including reports of unintended outcomes.

Political Criteria

Some pressure groups have been very successful in promoting new criteria for guiding the adoption of instructional materials. Although many of these new criteria reflect the philosophical belief that every human being is important, legal and political actions were necessary before the portrayal of racial, ethnic, and cultural groups, the handicapped, and the sexes began to change nationally. Typical of criteria that reflect the political efforts of minorities are the following legal requirements:

1. Teaching materials must portray both men and women in their full range of leadership, occupation, and domestic roles, without demeaning, stereotyping, or patronizing references to either sex.
2. Material must portray, without significant omissions, the historical role of members of racial, ethnic, and cultural groups, including their contributions and achievements in all areas of life.
3. Materials must portray members of cultural groups without demeaning, stereotyping, or patronizing references concerning their heritage, characteristics, or life style.

As a consequence of these standards, publishers and teachers count the pictures of boys and girls to be sure that both sexes are depicted in a range of roles, rather than traditional masculine and feminine ones. In addition, they are careful not to attach a color to an animal serving as the antagonist in a tale. They also modify the language by making changes in affixes and other structures. The singular *he* is replaced with *they* and *person* substituted for *man*.

At macro levels, curriculum planners attempt to meet the political criteria by designating curriculum domains or areas such as women's studies, American Indian studies and Chicano studies. Curriculum planners at a macro level also confront the special interests of conservationists, religious and veterans' organizations, auto-related industries, and other groups. Numerous admonitions to curriculum developers are the direct result of such pressures. They are told to teach the responsibilities of individuals and groups in preserving or creating a healthful environment, including appropriate and scientifically valid solutions to environmental problems; to present the hazards of tobacco, alcohol, narcotics, and drugs without glamorizing or encouraging their use; and to be sure the curriculum reflects and respects the religious diversity of people.

Practicality as a Criterion

At the macro level, practicality generally takes the form of economy. Planners weigh the cost of providing a certain learning opportunity. In times of a financial pinch, for instance, curriculum planners at macro levels might consider the cost of initiating an expensive laboratory course prohibitive. Instead, they might suggest a science course that features a less expensive instructional process such as a lecture and video demonstration format. Curriculum programs can be expensive in many ways. There are the outright costs of purchase of materials, the costs of maintaining the materials, the costs of purchasing necessary supplementary materials, and then the further costs of acquiring or training personnel.

It is important to weigh costs of purchase and installation against the expected level of goals or objectives to be achieved. If powerful forces outside the school are working against the attainment of a goal, the purchase of new means for attaining that goal is impractical. In times of economic austerity, curriculum planners must also consider diminishing returns in learning opportunities. There is a level of educational attainment beneath which dollars invested show a return in student progress. Beyond that level, however, gain occurs only at rapidly increasing cost.

At both macro and micro levels, there are other practical concerns. Safety, durability, and adaptability of the activity must be considered. There also is the factor of *conditions of use*: Does it demand that a teacher interact with pupils or does it free the teacher from direct instruction? Is it appropriate for learners with given abilities and motivational levels?

Criticisms of Criteria for Selecting Learning Opportunities

Criticisms may be directed both at the criteria themselves and at their use. Simply having criteria does not take care of the problem of who will use them in making decisions; it may make a difference whether they are used by state curriculum committees, individual teachers, or boards of education. Further, little thought has been given to decision rules. Seldom are answers given to these questions: How many criteria must be satisfied before adoption? What should the planners do if two alternative opportunities meet the same number of criteria? Will the decision require agreement among evaluators?

It is often difficult to obtain agreement on the evidence that a particular criterion has been met. Criteria demanding few inferences, such as the specification that objectives be stated in behavioral terms, present little difficulty. Criteria requiring high levels of inference, however, such as the requirement that materials be appropriate for the learners' motivation levels allow for more subjective and varied judgments.

Many people also disagree on the relative merits of the respective criteria. Kenneth Komoski, president of the Educational Products Information Exchange Institute, would put primary emphasis on learner verification—data showing the learning effectiveness of the opportunities.[6] No clear basis exists for claiming the superiority of materials that have provisions for feedback, behavior objectives, task analysis, or criterion-referenced tests; there is little conclusive evidence that these variables are directly related to the attainment of particular goals and objectives.

Disagreement on the worth of learning opportunities occurs because the value of activities and content depends upon the time, place, and the individuals concerned. What was deemed worthwhile in the past is not necessarily worthwhile today. For example, the supremacy of calculus in the freshman mathematics curriculum is being challenged by those who would substitute discrete mathematics on the grounds that calculus deals with continuous problems whereas discrete mathematics allows one to treat individual values—something more appropriate for use with computers that manipulate individual symbols and quantities. However, trying to justify an activity or content on the grounds that it is instrumental to the pursuit of other ends leaves much to be desired. The instrumental argument is of little consequence if the ultimate justification cannot be sustained. Generally an activity is justified if it satisfies a range

[6]Personal correspondence.

of impulses, rises above mere partisan considerations, meets a social norm, and is highly prized by experts who have reflected on the activity and its value.

DEVELOPING LEARNING OPPORTUNITIES

Selecting learning opportunities is not the same as developing them. Some people can apply criteria in deciding among various textbooks and other materials but are not able or willing to produce them. Similarly, the ability to carry out opportunities in the interactive phase with learners calls for additional skills. It is true that developers should keep in mind the criteria given for selection. Commercial developers do so because they want their products adopted. Development, however, is a creative art and allows for personal expression of the developer's values and style. As indicated in Part I of this book, techniques of development can be categorized by the four major categories of curriculum.

Major Orientations

Social Reconstructionist Guidelines. The social reconstructionist wants the learners to use knowledge and intelligence to help improve the quality of public decision that determines the conditions under which they live. In the late 1950s, the Carnegie Corporation funded a project to develop a guide by which teachers and others could choose activities that would combine knowledge and action in effecting change in the community. Although no longer in print, the guide was widely used and found to be practical. The following are ten key steps in the processes suggested by the fund.

1. *Select an idea for a learning opportunity.* The developer might reflect on a topic or problem such as public opinion, elections, media, or conservation, which makes sense to the students and is related to school and course goals. Issues and problems in the community are among the best sources of ideas for learning opportunities. Persistent struggles and value premises also suggest areas for learning. One might want to consider apathy toward general welfare or the importance of keeping informed on public issues and informing others.

2. *Explore the idea.* Here one must ask, "What can students do about the issue or problem besides studying about it?" A learning opportunity for the reconstructionist requires the students to take

responsible action, whether working with community groups, informing people, or taking a stand on issues. Students may provide information to people about a public issue, try to influence people to a point of view, serve the community, or work with and as adult citizens.

3. *Plan for action.* Surveys, field trips, and interviews are not what the reconstructionist means by action. Although these activities may contribute to the action phase, they don't constitute *taking action* in a political sense. Since the essence of the civic act is carrying knowledge into action, a student activity that omits persuasion, decision making, and so forth, is not viewed as satisfactory. Planning means thinking of the action or project desired; for example, organizing a public forum and indicating how students will carry it out.

4. *Test the idea or project for realness.* Work in the community—helping to get out a vote, campaigning for a candidate, talking on issues—is real. Mock trials, mayor for a day, reading, and taking straw votes are not real to the reconstructionist; they are only role playing. To the reconstructionist, action must promise to contribute to the solution of the situation and be seen by students as important.

5. *Specify the instructional objectives that will also be served by the project.* The objectives might stress competencies such as persuasion, getting information, arriving at valid conclusions, predispositions toward recognition of others, acceptance of responsibility, or knowledge of function and structure in institutions.

6. *Limit the scope of the learning opportunity.* The project must be subject to reasonable limits of time and effort. Enough time must be allowed for students to complete the action phase. For most effective results, the project should be focused. One idea is to plan the project around the action of the city council on a particular issue rather than around some broad interest such as government. Include only those activities that are necessary to achieve the goals of the plan. Decide on the termination date at the outset and keep it in mind daily. The sixth consideration is met when teaching has limited student actions to a specific job, enumerated what students are to do, and justified the time needed for completing the project.

7. *Involve others in the project.* Get the school administrator and other persons in the community whose help is desirable to participate.

8. *List the sources of firsthand information needed.* Consider interviews, polls, surveys, filming, and making visits.

9. *Select study materials.* Collect textbooks, pamphlets, films, and other materials on the subject matter of the project and pertinent to the instructional objectives.

10. *Plan for evaluation.* Select the evaluation devices that will be used to determine what gains and losses will have accrued as a result of the project.

Technological Guidelines. In Chapter 3, the technologists' product development procedures were delineated. Technologists identify four stages in developing learning activities:

1. Specify terminal objectives. The instructional objective guides all development. This objective must be specific enough to remove ambiguity about what the learner will be expected to know and do in particular situations or classes of situations. A posttest or other procedure for indicating achievement of the desired terminal behavior is often created in order to further designate all dimensions of the learning task.
2. Make a task analysis. An effort is made to list all prerequisite skills and knowledge believed necessary before one can perform in accordance with the objective. After this list is prepared, the developer must indicate which of these prerequisites will be taught in the learning opportunity and which will be considered "entry behaviors" (requirements that the learner is expected to demonstrate on entrance to the learning opportunity).
3. Specify the intended population. At this point, an idea of the anticipated learners can be gained. In addition to entry skills, characteristics such as cultural differences, learning styles, personality, and interests are used to guide the developers.
4. Formulate rules for development of the product. These questions give direction to the developer and determine the characteristics of the product.
   a. Concept presentation. Will the concept be taught through examples leading to a generalization (inductive) or will a generalization be given followed by examples (deductive)?
   b. Response mode. Will the learner be actively involved by speaking, writing, touching? In addition to overt responding, are there anticipated covert responses? How often will learners be expected to respond overtly?
   c. Elicitation of correct responses. How will the learners be helped to make a correct response and learn? Will all answers be confirmed as right or wrong? Will they be confirmed with reiteration of the reasons for correctness? How? Will the learner be prompted to make the right answer by hints, as through visual cues, questions, metaphors, and other verbal means?

d. Learning sequences. How will enroute objectives be ordered and reviewed? Will all learners be required to follow the same order? Will there be provision for "branching" (a point of choice at which students are sent to alternative material depending on their prior responses)?

Early use of the computer featured computer-assisted instruction (CAI), a technological approach to curriculum in which the designer focused on specific objectives, made a task analysis of enroute objectives and then decided upon a presentation strategy. The designer might consider whether the program will give the learner examples and ask for a generalization (examples to rule), or present a generalization and ask the learner to recognize examples that match the generalization (rule to examples)? Other decisions included *pacing* and *branching* (Will the learner be advanced to more difficult material when responses indicate mystery?); *response format* (multiple choice or constructed?); and *feedback* (Will the learner simply be told whether an answer is right or given additional explanation if there are errors?).

As described in Chapter 3, newer uses of the computer give the student more control over the machine by applying LOGO and the word processor to one's purposes. The development of educational games by teachers and students is another way to gain control of one's learning. Procedures for designing instructional games for the computer are as follows:

1. Define a subject theme area.
2. Create a list of games that lend themselves to the subject: Hangman, puzzles, Tic–Tac–Toe.
3. Stipulate the capabilities of the computer: graphics and animation, counters and timers, number of words or letters that can be displayed at one time, keyboard layout, voice activation, memory available for use.
4. List rules for program construction:
   (a) justification for educational content
   (b) population of problems
   (c) problem generation—problems shall be randomly generated and consist of new instances of the family of problems rather than particular problems whose answers have been confirmed previously.
   (d) Feedback—How will correct responses be determined and information regarding performance be presented to the user? How will progress be charted? Will a summary of user's strengths and weaknesses be available?
5. Specify player rules. Will it be a cooperative or competitive game? If competitive, will it be against the machine, peers, or self? Can player select a particular game or level of difficulty?

6. Specify computer decision rules: Does the computer respond to player's input? How does play change after correct responses? How does play terminate?
7. Prepare preliminary story board for each activity generated. Indicate display format and specify sounds.
8. Select the best set of activities within constraints of the computer.
9. Outline the flow of the activity using a flow chart showing message, prompts, and paths for user's replies. A partial example of such an outline is as follows:

$$\boxed{\text{SAME SUM}}$$

Players try to find one number that will fit in the corners of the puzzle so that each side will add up to a given total.

$$\boxed{\text{1 or 2 players?}}$$

1 player - player vs. machine/computer problems
2 players - player vs. player/player's problems

$$\boxed{\text{2 players}}$$

Player 1's SUM			
	5	4	
8			2
1			7
	9	0	

Prompt for player 2 to enter player 1's sum.

$$\boxed{\text{Player 1's SUM is 21}}$$

Player 2 has entered the sum "21" for player 1. Player 1 must find the one number that will fit in the corners of the puzzle so that each side adds up to a total of 21. Use the same number in all four corners.

	5	4	
8			2
1			7
	9	0	

5	5	4	5
8			2
1			7
5	9	0	5

Player 1 misses sum. Computer emits a razz sound and the puzzle reappears.

6	5	4	6
8			2
1			7
6	9	0	6

If player 1 is correct, a fanfare is sounded.

(1)				0	9	0
(2)				1	4	0

Scoreboard shows cumulative score for rounds.

Humanistic Guidelines. The humanistic curriculum has its roots in both the individual humanism of the Renaissance with its stress on personal culture, individual freedom, and development as the best way toward a full and rich life, and the naturalism of the eighteenth century which was a revolt against the cold aristocracy of intellect. The naturalists worshiped feelings and regarded education not as a preparation for life but as life itself. They believed that the activities which spring naturally from the interests of the pupils, from the needs of life, should make up the curriculum.

In contrast to other curriculum orientations, learning opportunities in the humanistic curriculum are not planned in the framework of a means–ends continuum. Indeed, many humanistic educators believe that only *after* an opportunity has been experienced can an objective be formed. How then does one create a more humanistic experience? The answers from the neo–humanists fall into three categories:

1. Emphasize teaching procedures. Instructional plans, textbooks, courses of study, and other artifacts designed to shape learners in specified ways are all seen as less important than the actual teaching. The teacher is seen as the primary source of learning; the interpersonal associations experienced with a teacher influence the pupils' growth. The humanists give more attention to method and the interactive phases of instruction than on advanced planning. Indeed, the planning of opportunities, activities, and experiences should be a cooperative process by students and teacher in which the pupil's own purposes are respected.

   This emphasis takes many directions. It may mean that the teacher will prepare by developing procedures of reflective teaching, group dynamics, and sensitivity training—methods that may be of value in releasing the creative capacity of learners. It may mean that teachers will anticipate what they will bring to students by "knowing" themselves. They will try to recognize their prejudices, biases, fears, loves, strengths, and other attributes that bear on the ability to care, feel, and relate to students.

2. Create an environment that will not impede natural growth. The most general guide to developing learning opportunities is focused on the conditions of learning. On the positive side, creating good conditions for learning includes attending to conditions such as: the characteristics, interests, and growth patterns of each student; the richness of the environment; the opportunities that stress wholeness, putting all our senses to work; the opportunities to wonder and be puzzled; and the opportunities for the learner to feel independent by facing problems alone.

   On the negative side, some warn that such an environment implies that learners do not have to meet standards beyond their abilities, endure great tension, face destructive criticism, think in terms of previous solutions to problems, conform to tradition, regard achievement as the production of a similar rather than a unique product, and be denied choices.

3. Arrange situations in which learners determine what they will learn. The teacher as arranger considers physical conditions

including safe facilities as well as natural objects of beauty, and uses those from which the learner can benefit. The cultural environment, too, is a responsibility of the humanistic teacher. Cultural excellence in music, painting, and literature, and scientific equipment, musical instruments, and art supplies may constitute an invitation to learning. Arrangement of the social environment may also be planned. Association with others in a variety of shared enterprises may permit self-activated students to respond and by their own urge toward self-realization, bring the learning process to fulfillment.

Academicians' Guidelines. To the academician learning opportunities are chiefly textbooks, films, teachers' guides, as well as laboratory apparatus. The textbook is most important. Development of these tools is seen as an effort to convey the authenticity of content and method of given subject fields. Organizing centers, rather than instructional objectives, are central to academic developers. These centers are topics, questions, or problems that will guide the class activities. Until about the 1930s, for example, textbooks by scholars were descriptive and usually consisted of a mass of disconnected facts and primitive generalizations. Between the 1930s and the 1960s, textbooks were more often written by professional educators rather than by specialists in the disciplines. Their books were criticized as being too busy with many topics to treat any in depth. The student was given many conclusions but had little opportunity to understand how these findings were achieved and how they were interrelated. About 1960, distinguished scholars began to select and guide the development of textbooks as well as courses and materials. They used five steps.

1. Choose organizing centers. Organizing centers relate text, lab, films, and the context for study of a field over a year-long span. The following criteria should guide the selection of centers: Do they stress major achievements, that is, powerful ideas? Do they show ways in which the powerful ideas were conceived and sometimes improved on? Do they show how the ideas are interrelated?
2. Lay out the ordering of the centers. Usually this step rests on an assumed principle of dependency in which the basic concepts are given so that the student can have the understanding necessary for further study. The presentation is through general concepts rather than specific definitions so that the students make some contact with the subject matter they will deal with later in greater depth.

3. Develop suggested units of instruction. Each unit deals with a particular topic and has its own purposes. Each unit also includes an outline of suggested information to be presented and a bibliography suggesting other sources of information.

4. Recommend specific instructional content. This content consists of a wealth of information for each unit. Some examples of recommendations are: methods that will help students interpret data; suggested examples that will lead to important generalizations; background information that will encourage generalizations; opportunities that will lead students to apply generalizations; suggested demonstrations that will show the limits of the generalizations; and listing of useful materials, such as maps, apparatus, and collections that might be used.

5. Recommend teaching strategies. Unlike the technologists, academicians do not specify in detail the methods teachers are to follow; each teacher must adapt the material to his or her methods. Academicians do, however, prize the method of choice, learning how to inquire by doing it. Hence, they not only suggest different ways for students to discover important principles, they provide training materials, workshops, and films to help the teacher move from didactic methods to those of discovery. Further, they preface with a variety of step-by-step solutions the experimental and theoretical problems presented to students. However, the communication of method has turned out to be one of the weakest aspects of the academic curriculum. Teachers who have never themselves developed skill in scientific reasoning and problem solving have difficulty in teaching methods of inquiry to others. Also, each teacher may have a favorite method and is likely to stress different ideas and concepts than other teachers. The instructor interested in laboratory methods, for example, will emphasize laboratory procedure. Teachers filter the materials through their own perceptions.

One can infer from the classic monograph on text material by Lee Cronbach that academicians and others do not know how to achieve a perfect learning opportunity in text materials. Cronbach thought, however, that creative developers might make real progress if they kept these questions in mind:

> Does the text create readiness for the concepts and accomplishments to be taught in subsequent grades? Does the text assist the pupil to understand why certain responses are superior to others for given aims, rather than present them as prescriptions? Does the text make provisions for

realistic experience, through narration, proposal of supplementary experiences, and laboratory prescriptions, so that students will be able to connect generalizations to reality? Does the text formulate explicit and transferable generalizations? Are the text explanations readable and comprehensible? Does the text provide for practice in application either by suggesting activities or by posing sensible problems in symbolic form? Do these problems call for the use of generalizations under realistic conditions and require the student to determine which principles to use as well as how to use them? Does the text provide an opportunity to use concepts from many fields of study in examining the same problems? Does the text help the learners recognize the intended outcomes from the study?[7]

The classroom activity into which the text fits should make it possible for the student to acquire emotional attitudes and skills of group membership. The text should fit as closely as possible the readiness of the students for whom it is intended and help develop their readiness.

The Role of the Teacher

Adapting Learning Opportunities to Individual Differences. There is no simple method to achieve optimal learning in a diverse population of learners; neither is there a consensus about the best strategies to use in responding to individual differences. Curriculum goals can be matched to individuals (general science to some, physics for others), but this usually results in unequal opportunity to learn. Adaption by remediation (same goals for all, but extra time and compensating activity) is difficult to implement. Pupils who are pulled out for remediation seldom get equivalent opportunity and because of finite time and lack of social stimulation tend to lag farther behind in the attainment of common goals. Adaption by matching instructional strategies to learning styles (teaching different pupils with different methods) is often touted as a panacea, but in practice it is a disappointment.

From their review of the literature on individual differences in the classroom, Thomas Good and Deborah Stipek concluded that status variables, including sex, race, and socioeconomic factors, do not provide a systematic basis for planning instruction.[8] The idea, for example, that

[7]Lee J. Cronbach, *Text Materials in Modern Education* (Urbana: University of Illinois Press, 1955), pp. 90–91.

[8]Thomas L. Good and Deborah J. Stipek, "Individual Differences in the Classroom: A Psychological Perspective," in *Individual Differences and the Common Curriculum*, NSSE Yearbook, eds. Gary D. Festermaker and John I. Goodlad (Chicago: University of Chicago Press, 1983): 9–37.

all girls or boys need a particular level of learning opportunity is likely to be incorrect at least 60 percent of the time. Similarly, the problem of matching activity to high and low ability students is considerable. In classrooms composed of students of unequal ability, the outcomes are determined only in part by ability; the teacher and pupil expectations for success, effort, and other factors are as important in the selection of content and its organization.

The idea of teachers offering opportunities suited to their own personalities and educational goals may be more powerful than adapting instruction to the personal needs of students. At least it should be tried. Although there is some evidence that students perform better when taught by a method consistent with their preferred learning style, it is not clear that curriculum should always be matched with learning style. Under some conditions, mismatches may be beneficial; in some instances it is desirable to increase a learner's ability to learn a variety of content under different circumstances. Also there is danger that in offering a curriculum for students who have particular learning styles, other important variables will be ignored: learner variables like ability, cultural background and motivation; and classroom variables like teacher knowledge, subject matter, and peer influences.

Adaption of instruction is best undertaken by the teacher's sensitivity to learner responses, the ability to learn from students and to vary instruction according to hypotheses about how learning takes place.

Developing Learning Opportunities. In hundreds of ways, teachers modify curriculum for the needs of a class—mimeographing materials, making arrangements for visiting speakers, creating learning games, designing learning packets, planning field trips, arranging original displays, suggesting individual studies, and posing novel questions. Teachers recognize the inadequacies of available instructional materials in matching the requirements for each child. It is as if textbooks, curriculum guides, and other instructional material developed by those outside the particular classroom are highways, satisfactory for general planning, yet highways from which the teacher must at times turn off, taking a different route in order to provide something more appropriate for a learner or a group of learners. Usually the development and modification of curriculum by teachers is undertaken for the following reasons:

1. The particular learners require learning opportunities that are closer to their present background and level of attainment. Pupils may need explanations drawn from familiar instances or more simple or more advanced tasks than have been provided. The

development of a skill lesson in the language of a non-English-speaking child is one example.

2. The particular learners or their community have pressing questions or problems that require the experiences, facts, or the introduction of new activities and material.

3. Teachers desire to provide opportunities that are motivating. Hence, they create learning opportunities in accordance with motivational principles such as:

    choice—Learners choose from among activities. A range of opportunities is offered in order to accommodate the learners' style or mode of learning.

    utility—Opportunities encourage learners to use what is learned in satisfying unmet physical and psychological needs and to satisfy motives such as curiosity, exploration, and manipulation.

    link to other values—Opportunities place learners in contact with highly valued persons or activities.

    interests—Opportunities are related to special interests of learners at hand.

    models—Older peers, parents, and other significant persons are selected as exemplary models.

    success—Adaptations in conventional materials are made in order to ensure success, including prompting, flexible standards, and provision for learners to recognize their own success.

4. Teachers' interests, capabilities, and style make departures from standard materials desirable or necessary.

Developing Learning Centers. As a further illustration of procedures used by teachers in developing learning opportunities, consider the development of a learning center. (A learning center may consist of interesting activities that offer opportunity for children to practice and apply skills already acquired and to learn concept relationships.) In general, the teacher begins with a view of learning from a child's perspective, including a predisposition or desire to be active, to manipulate—touch, grab, fondle—things, to socialize, to contemplate, to speculate, and to discover. Next, the teacher asks how concepts of mathematics, art, science, and other subject fields can be presented so that they are consistent with children's predispositions. One answer might be to create a center that encourages manipulation in mathematics, where a young child is asked to guess how many sets of four are in a plastic pill bottle containing twenty-four beads. The child can write down a guess, count the beads out into cups of an egg carton and check the answer against an answer card. After the beads are put back in the bottle, other written directions can ask the child to guess how many sets of three, eight, and six there will be. Or the task can be made harder by not disclosing how many beads are in the bottle.

Other answers might feature using a word processor, engaging in social interaction, making a product, speculating through "just suppose" activities, discovering through activities involving simple experiments, and learning about one's self through responsive activities in which children indicate their feelings or reactions to stories, music, and the like, through their drawings as well as through oral and written comments.

In developing the learning center, the teacher answers such questions as:

1. What purpose will the center serve? What will children learn from it?
2. What subject area will be enhanced? What skills should be strengthened? Where is motivation the weakest? What attitudes are lacking? What concepts should be applied? What extra interests should be encouraged?
3. What kinds of tasks are appropriate—listening, recording, experimenting, writing, discussing, constructing, or what?
4. What materials are available?
5. To what extent should the activities of the center be designed so that children may proceed without the immediate presence of the teacher? Should the center allow pupils to decide on a strategy or direct them to use a particular process?
6. How long will each child or group have at the center? What will be the life span of the center?

As indicated previously, the teacher's curriculum orientation will reflect the planning procedures used. Those teachers who begin with objectives follow a technological approach, those who commence with the quality of experiences use a humanistic procedure.

John A. Zahorik studied how teachers actually go about planning lessons and courses.[9] His findings indicated that teachers of adults were more likely to focus first on objectives or purposes than were other teachers. Secondary school teachers were more likely first to make decisions about materials or resources to be used, while elementary teachers first make decisions about pupils' readiness—ability and interest—for the particular lesson(s). Decisions about the subject matter to be taught—fact, idea, content—are among the first decisions made by

[9]John A. Zahorik, "Teachers Planning Models," *Educational Leadership* 33, no. 2 (November 1975): 134–39.

most teachers in their planning. The first and most frequently asked question generally seems to be, "What are the ranges and particulars of the subject matter of the lessons that I must teach?"

In their review of research on teachers' thoughts and decisions, Richard Shavelson and Paula Stern summarize the elements teachers consider in planning curriculum—content, goals, students, materials, activities, and social community.[10] The teachers' fear of management problems in schools where the administration expects them to enforce rules of discipline, for example, has been found to influence planning in the direction of simplistic, teacher-controlled activities requiring little student discussion and other stimulating activities. The sequence of elements and the compromises that must be made are as yet unknown, but probably depend on the task at hand as well as the personality of the particular teacher. Some teachers appear to be incremental planners who proceed in a series of short steps based on day-to-day information. Others are comprehensive planners who develop an abstract general scheme for the long run.

Teachers are instructional designers when they engage in such tasks as designating lessons for a particular grade or content area, writing a rationale for a specific instructional unit, or developing criteria for evaluating a commercial instructional program. However, teacher participation in curriculum decisions about goals and planning the scope and arrangement of a projected educational program for a school or district is not always attractive to classroom teachers. The major function of teachers is often viewed as carrying out district central office curriculum decisions in their particular classrooms and selecting or creating instructional materials (means), rather than participating in establishing district- or schoolwide goals (ends). Only as teachers are relieved of full-time classroom responsibilities does their interest in curriculum decision making expand. The teachers' classroom orientation prevents the development of a long–range perspective and sense of community that are essential to planning overall school or systemwide courses of study. In his celebrated study of schooling, John Goodlad found that circumstances of teaching make it difficult for teachers to plan collaboratively.[11]

An alternative context for curriculum decision making that promises to enlarge teacher participation in curriculum making is to change the

[10]Richard J. Shavelson and Paula Stern, "Research on Teachers' Pedagogical Thoughts, Judgments, Decisions, and Behavior," *Review of Educational Research* 51, no. 4 (Winter 1981): 455–98.

[11]John I. Goodlad, *A Place Called School* (New York: McGraw-Hill, 1983).

context for curriculum decision making from the school district to the individual school. Each individual school would have responsibility for development of the school's educational programs, money for the development and implementation of the programs, and accountability for the results that follow. The proposal would require teachers to expand their role beyond their own classroom and to engage in curriculum making on a continual basis. All members of the staff would be expected to work toward common goals that they set with parents and others in the school community. There still would be districtwide goals and required subjects in the curriculum of every school because the school district is responsible for the educational programs of the district. Teachers would, however, organize these subjects, and possibly others, into a curriculum suitable for the particular community. The school staff would plan the ways in which it would achieve the common goals and how each subject would contribute to the total curriculum.

UNFINISHED BUSINESS: RELATING CURRICULUM PLANS TO TEACHING MODELS

The previous discussions should have illuminated the kinds of choices that can be made among the instructional means available. What has not been made clear is that there should be some consistency between these different guides to instructional planning and both the curriculum domains and teaching modes to be employed. Just as failure to match a domain with the right learning opportunities makes an ineffective curriculum, so too does a mismatch between goals and teaching modes. Currently, for example, a teaching mode appropriate for teaching basic skills is being widely promoted as an exemplary teaching model. The inappropriateness of this mode for use with social reconstructionist, humanistic, and inquiry goals within an academic curriculum is not considered by those promoting it. In evaluating this model, M. Frances Klein indicates the limited focus of a skills model for teaching and at the same time suggests that the use of activities representing a number of different curriculum orientations within a single classroom might be confusing to learners.[12]

A serious deficiency in curriculum planning is the gap between concepts

[12]M. Frances Klein, "A Perspective in Curriculum and the Beginning Teacher Evaluation Study," *Newsletter 4 Beginning Teacher Evaluation Study* (Sacramento: Commission for Teacher Preparation and Licensing, June 1979), pp. 1–7.

for designing learning activities and concepts for guiding teacher preparation. Paradigms for teaching are not often related to particular curriculum domains or to the wide range of criteria for selecting learning opportunities. Hence we see teacher training programs preparing teachers in methodologies that do not correspond to the curriculum designs those teachers are likely to encounter or use in their particular school settings. Teachers are given methods for conducting inquiry lessons only to find themselves later responsible for designing and implementing didactic lessons or managing instructional systems.

Some indication that the problem is being addressed is found in the writings of Bruce Joyce and Marsha Weil, and Fenwick English.[13] Joyce and Weil have described models of teaching within four major families that correspond closely to prevailing views of curriculum, thereby relating teaching strategies, curriculum structures, and educational goals. For example, they match the learning opportunity approach of Carl Rogers with the domain of personal development, the academic modes of Bruner with information processing and the goal of intellectual development. By clarifying alternative purposes and domains and by using the appropriate sets of criteria for developing the activities and instructional strategies, curriculum workers will be engineering a consistent curriculum. In the process, they will be encouraging broad conceptions of purposes and extending options in order to attain those purposes. In contrast to Joyce and Weil, English would align the curriculum by *mapping*—a technique for recording instructional and learning time given to tasks and then analyzing the data recorded to determine its suitability to the officially adopted curriculum and testing program.

CONCLUDING COMMENTS

The chapter is divided into two parts. The first part dealt with how best to select the learning activities to attain the ends of educational programs. It also considered whether activities should be considered as means to ends or whether they should be judged valuable in their own right. Differences were shown between the learning opportunities— categories or domains—commonly chosen at macro or societal levels and the opportunities selected at micro or classroom levels. Several criteria for selecting learning activities were presented as was an analysis

---

[13]Bruce R. Joyce and Marsha Weil, *Models of Teaching*, 2nd ed. (Englewood Cliffs, N.J.: Prentice Hall, 1980); Fenwick English, "Curriculum Mapping," *Educational Leadership* 37, no. 7 (April 1980).

of the strengths and weaknesses of different arguments used to justify learning activities.

The second part focused on development of learning opportunities—products and materials. The ways in which social reconstructionists, technologists, humanists, and academicians develop learning opportunities were described, and attention was drawn to the special problems of relating curriculum plans to teaching modes.

Development of learning opportunities will continue at both macro and micro levels. It is not known, however, which set of procedures will dominate. There is, for example, a question as to whether the technologists' more expensive procedures that have guided the developmental projects of regional laboratories will be adopted by publishers or whether less rigorous operational standards will prevail. We need to study what happens when different procedures are followed. Are different ends promoted by different approaches? Do some procedures pay off in demonstrably superior programs? What is the relative economic and procedural efficiency of the different approaches?

QUESTIONS

1. How do technologists, humanists, academicians, and social reconstructionists differ in their models for developing learning opportunities?
2. To what three criteria would you give greatest weight in selecting among textbooks?
3. How would you expect the issue of accountability to be treated by expressives and instrumentalists in their attitude toward learning opportunities? Accountability is defined here as the selection of goals, the assessment of learner status with respect to these goals, the efforts directed at improvement of weaknesses revealed in the assessment, and the assessment of responsibility for results.
4. Contrast the nature of learning opportunities at macro levels of planning with that at micro levels.
5. Consider a learning opportunity that you might like to introduce as an innovation within a school system. What factors would you use in defending the proposed innovation? How would you justify the proposal? Would you use costs as a criterion?
6. Consider a classroom objective that you think is important for a given learner. Describe a learning opportunity for this learner consistent with the objective, illustrating the following principles: (a) appropriate practice (opportunity to practice what is called for in the objective), (b) learning satisfaction (provision for the learner to find the opportunity rewarding), and (c) learner readiness (assurance that the learner has the necessary prerequisites for participating in the opportunity).

SELECTED REFERENCES

Briggs, Leslie J., ed. *Instructional Design: Principles and Application.* Englewood
Cliffs, N.J.: Educational Technology Publications, 1977.

Chiarelott, Leigh. "The Role of Experience in the Curriculum: An Analysis
of Dewey's Theory of Experience" *Journal of Curriculum Theorizing* 5, no. 3
(Summer 1983): 29–41.

EPIC Report. *Improving the Selection and Use of Instructional Materials: A How-To
Handbook.* New York: EPIC Institute, 1979.

Gow, Dovis and Casey, Tommye W. "Selecting Learning Activities" In *Fundamental Curriculum Decisions,* ASCD Yearbook, pp. 112–126. Alexandria,
Va.: ASCD, 1983.

Komoski, P. Kenneth. "The Realities of Choosing and Using Instructional
Materials" *Educational Leadership* 36, no. 1 (October 1978): 46–51.

Read, Donald A. and Simon, Sidney, eds. *Humanistic Education Sourcebook.*
Englewood Cliffs, N.J.: Prentice-Hall, 1975.

Schutz, Richard E. "Learning About the Costs of Instruction and the Benefits of Research and Development in Education" *Educational Researcher* 8, no.
4 (April 1979): 3–8.

7 / DESIGNING CURRICULUM

The prior chapter focused on learning opportunities that are satisfying, and that teach students concepts for which they are developmentally ready. This chapter considers the organization of learning opportunities so that the goals of the instructional activity are clear and so that the different lessons reinforce each other. Curriculum designers relate purposes, contents, learning opportunities and organizing structures to one another. Learning opportunities can be grouped by two kinds of devices: (1) organizing centers and (2) organizing elements.

Organizing centers indicate the scope of the curriculum. Centers may consist of topics, problems, questions, and projects that are important in their own right but also valuable in motivating students and developing their skills, concepts, and attitudes in pursuing the selected focus. Organizing elements are threads or strands of knowledge, generalizations, and skills that are to be extended in breadth and depth throughout a course or program. These elements clarify and illuminate less glorious meanings.

Curriculum designers are concerned about the disarray and fragmentation that have overtaken instructional programs. Too often curriculum takes on the kaleidoscopic quality of television in presenting isolated pieces of information and sensations without cultivating the meaning behind them.

Finally, this chapter describes two major criteria for the organization of learning opportunities—*sequence* and *integration*. Sequence requires that each successive learning opportunity builds upon the preceding one and goes more deeply and broadly into the subject matter. Integration aims at having students see the links not only between ideas and processes within a single field but also between ideas and processes, in separate fields, and to the world outside of school.

ORGANIZING STRUCTURES

An organizing structure divides time spent in the school into a series of periods for activities. The kind of structure used depends on (1) the level (institutional or classroom) at which curriculum decisions occur; (2) the conception of curriculum (academic, humanistic, technological, social reconstructionist), and (3) the chosen domain or purpose of the curriculum (exploration, general education, specialization).

Structure at the Institutional Level

Institutions use a number of options in structuring curriculum. A *broad fields* structure focuses on fields of study—social studies, language arts, vocational education—while *specific subjects* structure concentrates on individual subjects—science, mathematics, business, English. A *core curriculum* structure draws content from a range of subjects or fields by addressing general problems or unifying themes. Amherst College, for example, once organized a program around "Problems in American Democracy" involving the entire faculty and student body. The arts, humanities and sciences were all related in addressing the problems selected. Lastly, a *free-form* structure, common in affluent times and when individuality and choice are priorities, offers a potpourri of courses to reflect different students' needs.

At intermediary levels, such as within departments, structures feature discrete courses—Health Care and the Law, Women's Movements, Modern Dance—as well as courses that make up a unified program—first-year science, second-year science, and third-year science.

Whatever structure is chosen, it should be part of an over-all design relating purposes (functions, domains, goals, objectives) to organizing elements (concepts, values, skills) and to specific learning opportunities or activities. Such a design is shown in Figure 7.1. The designers in the school depicted in Figure 7.1 show that they have a wide range of purposes, domains, and objectives. They provide several organizing structures: broad fields for general education, undifferentiated or open structure for self-realization, and subjects or disciplines for specialization. The organizing elements derived from purposes indicate the kinds of learning opportunities that must be created within the structures.

Structure at the Classroom Level

Open Structure. A popular structure in humanistic classrooms within the elementary school is an *open structure*. Time, space, materials, and

FIGURE 7.1   Outline of a Curriculum Design

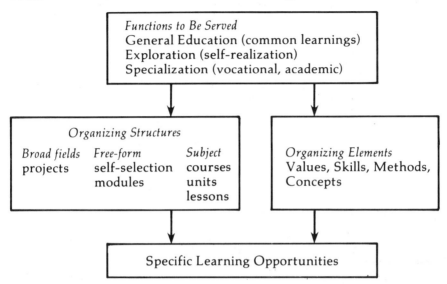

human resources are arranged to integrate skills learned in isolation and develop social skills. At Beavers Lane Infant School, for example, the curriculum is divided into three major areas: language, numbers, and drama. The thrust of most activities is to involve the children in their own learning. Observers of the school sense a tremendous enthusiasm on the part of both teacher and pupils as they work together in small groups or as a whole class. The following account records one man's observations of such a class during a typical school day.

The Integrated Day—A Number Class

In the number class three children were measuring flour, water, and orange juice in order to make cookies. After measuring the ingredients, they became involved with additional number activities by cutting out squares for each member of the class. After these children finished their project, other children became involved with the same procedure.

At the same time, another child was coloring numbers, another was counting, two other children were painting and finishing their projects, four children were individually taking a number count regarding an upcoming sports event, four others were working with the teacher with counters. There was an abundance of activity, interest, and sustained effort on the part of each of the 31 children in the classroom. Those children who were not involved were questioned by the teacher as to their activity or lack of it. The room was alive with number concepts and activities, but also there was ample evidence of language and creative activities present, such as science interest centers, art projects, writing, and verbalization. Other activities included:

Measuring each other to find the tallest, and the shortest, boy or girl
Measuring hand spans—number of hand spans—needed to fill the inside of a truck
Motor skill development
Questions on who wants to be a nurse, a hairdresser, a fireman, or a policeman
Art
Drawing pictures of their concept of football players on the field
The flower shop—using tissue to make flowers, and selling them, which entails using money
Using the water table to measure water—how many cups in a gallon jug, etc.
A visual diagram shows a usual day in a number class.

Flow of Activities in a Number Class

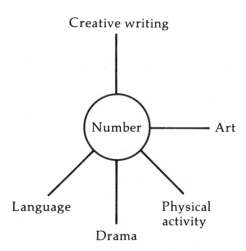

The same type of diagram could be drawn for the language and drama areas. A typical day at Beavers Lane Infant School is arranged according to a schedule which allows each child intensive involvement with all three areas—language, number, and drama. At the same time the schedule allows the teacher opportunity to explore any other area that teacher and pupils decide upon.

                        9:00–10:30 language
                                   number
                                   drama
                       10:30–11:00 free play
                       11:00–12:00 language
                                   number (change)
                                   drama
                       12:00– 1:30 lunch
                        1:30– 2:35 number (change)
                        2:35– 3:15 play and activity

Structured Openness
   The use of this integrated approach, coupled with vertical grouping
(that method of organization in which individuals of different ages are
placed together in the same class), ensures heterogeneity and expands
opportunities for freedom of choice, flexibility, facilitation of PIES (physical,
intellectual, emotional, and social) development, and individualization of
instruction. Furthermore, progressiveness and personalization of learning
experiences are enhanced through this type of school organization. Of
course, the integrated day approach or unstructured day, can be achieved
only by careful planning to ensure that materials are ready and pupils are
prepared for participation.[1]

   Lesson Plan. Although the lesson plan can reflect humanistic, academic,
or other orientations, teacher education programs have tended to foster
the technological view with a prescriptive model of planning. The
format is also found in contingency management and competency-based
organizational structures. Typically, the plan has these features:

1. Diagnosis—A major objective is identified and there is some
   provision—a quick quiz or question perhaps—for determining the
   status of the learners in relation to the objective.
2. Specific objective—On the basis of the diagnosis, a specific objective for a day's lesson is selected.
3. Anticipatory set—There is a plan for focusing the learner's attention, giving brief practice or relating learning previously achieved,
   and developing readiness for the instruction to follow.
4. Perceived purpose—Learners are informed of the objective and
   told why it is important and relevant to their present and future
   situations.

[1]Alan Wheeler, "Structuring for Open Education," *Educational Leadership* 31, no. 3
(December 1973): 251–53. Reprinted by permission of Alan Wheeler and ASCD.
Copyright by ASCD, 1973. All rights reserved.

5. Learning Opportunities—Activities are selected that promise to help achieve the objective.
6. Modeling—This is a demonstration or visual example of what is to be attained—product or process—and a verbal description of the critical features involved.
7. Check for Understanding—This provision checks whether or not learners have acquired the essential information or skill.
8. Guided practice—Activities to test whether or not students can perform the task successfully are given so that the teacher can decide if students are ready to study on their own.
9. Independent practice—Once learners can perform the task without major errors, they are given opportunity to practice the new concept, skill, or process with little or no teacher direction either at school or outside the school.

According to Shavelson and Stern,[2] this prescriptive model of planning is consistently *not* used in teacher's planning in schools. There is a mismatch between the demands of classroom instruction and the prescriptive planning model. Teachers must maintain the flow of activity during a lesson or classes might become unruly. Teachers must give first priority to planning activities that will capture the attention of students during the lesson. The focus of teacher planning is on the learner's interest while attending to the content.

The Unit. There are two kinds of units: the *resource unit* and the *teaching unit*. The difference between the two lies in how closely the recommended practices are tailored for particular learners. The resource unit is a guide for teaching a potential and general population of learners. The teaching unit is developed for known individuals. Both units have the same components: rationale (justification for the unit presented as an overview), goals, objectives, topics, activities, and materials.

The unit's length is usually from two to six weeks and the body of the document includes activities to introduce the major topics and to prepare for the activities that will follow. Problems, demonstrations, and guest speakers are common initiating activities. Developmental activities comprise the major portion of the unit. In these activities, students interact with the content, raising and formulating questions, collecting data, and trying to resolve the initially proposed problem.

In preparing such activities, the designer considers what resources—field site, materials, resource persons—will be necessary as students carry out their investigations, and what skills they will need to gather

[2]Shavelson and Stern, "Research on Teachers' Pedagogical Thoughts," pp. 6–28.

information and complete their projects. Culminating activities in the unit give opportunity for students to evaluate and synthesize what has been learned, to summarize and to formulate new questions for further study.

Topics for units should reflect one's curriculum orientation—subject matter, personal concerns, social problems, and basic skills. These topics are cast as organizing centers and arranged in a sequential order thereby constituting a course of study.

The following example illustrates the different components in a resource unit for teachers in the middle grades entitled "Providing Education."

Organizing Elements—relation of physical environment to quality of life (generalizations)

Language skills—reading, writing, speaking

Organizing Centers—the focus of the problem. "What is the function of education?" "How do the differences in living conditions between modern and earlier cultures account for differences in the educational system?"

Activities—Compare a contemporary school with a colonial one, showing the contrast in enrollment, lessons, discipline, and materials. Read and write stories about the school days of pioneer children. Exhibit old textbooks and show how these books differ from current books.

Dramatize a day in a colonial school.

Teacher's materials—

Cubberly, E. P. *History of Education.* Boston: Houghton, Mifflin, 1920.

Mayhew, K. and Edwards, A. *The Dewey School.* New York: D. Appleton-Century, 1936.

Children's Materials—

Dunton-Lucy. *School Children the World Over.* New York: Stokes, 1909.

Gordy, W. P. *Colonial Days.* New York: Scribner, 1908.

Wilson, Howard. *Where Our Way of Living Comes From.* New York: American Book, 1937.

Community Resources—

Schools (public and private), libraries, museums

The Module. A module is a short course of between 20 and 60 hours, designed in terms of objectives, content, skills required on entry and anticipated at the end of the course, assessment techniques, and suggestions for methodology and resources. Modules are not mere chunks of content, but develop knowledge and skills in a balanced way. The key quality of the module is its relative brevity. The brevity allows students more choices about the composition of their whole course of studies than would be the case if they were committed from the start to a one-year or two-year block of work. Often students can negotiate the specific curriculum they need and want.

Centers and Course Development

An organizing center for a unit gives focus to the learning opportunities in that unit. A series of organizing centers and the accompanying learning opportunities comprise a course. Although each center has educational significance of its own, the instrumental value is paramount. Centers are vehicles for introducing the key content of the course. As in the case of learning opportunities, the center should appeal to prospective learners, give opportunity to practice desired outcomes, and be appropriate in terms of the learners' backgrounds. The center differs from the learning opportunity in that it contributes to multiple objectives or outcomes. A field trip to a local archeological dig, for example, could be a learning center. Preparation for the trip would teach different skills— studying the historical context, learning how to recover artifacts, learning how to interpret findings and to recognize special problems. Conducting the trip would require additional activities—applying the new skills and knowledge—while posttrip evaluation would contribute to reflection and the generation of new questions and plans.

The organizing structure of the institution influences the choice of centers. For example, a subject structure would have a concept or topic of importance to an academic subject. For physics, *light* or *motion* might be used as a center. A broad field structure would probably focus on a social problem; a free-form structure would center on personal concerns and interests of learners, such as self-image, isolation from others, or control over one's life.

The arrangement of centers within a course follows some principles of sequence. Humanistic designers often put as an early center one that will foster awareness, next they put centers that lead to an abstract thought about the matter, and finally they put centers that result in the learner taking action. Consider how teachers might arrange centers in a course of literature: fiction (novel, short stories); poetry (popular songs, folk songs, religious songs); drama (comedy, tragedy); journalism (articles, advertisements, editorials). They might start with the center they think is less complex or with a center which best represents the interests of the learners.

ORGANIZING ELEMENTS

In order for opportunities to be related, there must be some common element between them. Elements are the threads, the warp and woof of the fabric of curriculum organization. They need to be woven together, or organized. If they are not, we will have this situation, described by Edna St. Vincent Millay:

> Upon this gifted age, in its dark hour,
> Rains from the sky a meteoric shower
> Of facts ... they lie unquestioned, uncombined.
> Wisdom enough to leech us of our ill
> Is daily spun; but there exists no loom
> To weave it into fabric ...[3]

Common Elements

Some of the more common elements used as the basis for organization are:

Concepts. Many academic curriculum plans are built around such key concepts as culture, growth, number, space, entropy, metaphor—the ruling ideas in respective fields.

Generalizations. Generalizations are conclusions drawn from careful observations by scientists. Two generalizations are: "In stable societies all educative influences operate consistently upon the individual; in heterogeneous societies, there are inconsistencies and contradictions." "A person is both participant (subjective) and observer (objective) in all human behavior."

Skills. Skills are generally regarded as proficiency plans for curriculum organization. They are commonly used as the basis for building continuity in programs. Elementary schools, for example, sometimes organize learning experiences around word recognition or comprehension skills, fundamental skills or operations in mathematics, and the skills for interpreting data. Metacognitive strategies in problem solving are the latest organizing elements in skill programs.[4]

Values. Philosophical values are cherished beliefs that are not ques-

[3]Edna St. Vincent Millay and Norma Millay Ellis, *Collected Poems,* 1967; reprinted ed., Harper and Row, 1939), p. 51. Reprinted by permission.
[4]J. D. McNeil, *Reading Comprehension: New Strategies for the Classroom* (Chicago: Scott Foresman, 1984).

tioned but taken as absolutes for governing behavior. Two examples are: "respect for the dignity and worth of every human being regardless of race, nationality, occupation, income, or class" and "respect for self." When organizing a curriculum plan around values, most of the activities must be designed so that they reinforce the particular value selected.

Understanding organizing elements is a distinguishing attribute of the curriculum expert. A child may be immediately aware of learning activities or centers only in their concrete form, but the insightful teacher or curriculum writer is always conscious of their deeper significance. When one asks children what they are learning, they are likely to respond, "We're learning about the Indians" or "We're learning to speak a foreign language." The curriculum person, however, sees, in addition to such direct study, the key abstractions to which the present activity points. The activity dealing with Indians may be pointing toward a generalization about basic needs that all people have always had. Learning to speak a foreign language may be most important for what it illuminates about one's own language, language in general, language acquisition, or even some more fundamental element, such as communication among people.

Organizing elements are, of course, selected in light of the goals and objectives of the curriculum. When the curriculum goals are technical and vocational, skills are an appropriate element to use. When the curriculum goals emphasize moral and ethical domains with an integrative function, values are the preferred element for organization.

Table 7.1 gives an example of the use of organizing elements in relating an objective to experiences or opportunities.

Objective: Given new situations from life, the learner can predict the likely effect of technology on these situations. Characteristics, limitations, and capabilities of modern technology will be used by the learner in determining the effect.

Within the first center or unit of instruction—defining technology—students are introduced to a systems approach for reducing complex problems. Students acquire one definition of technology and in the next unit they glimpse the ways that technology helps people, the limits to its use, and its side effects. The concept of technology is further extended and the student begins to judge the way in which technology decreases or enhances the value of people. Subsequent units involve students in problems about the application of technology to human uses, to societal needs, to natural and manmade environments. Prior elements are extended and a new element—the relation of resources to the quality of life—is introduced. Opportunity for students to assess the future effect

TABLE 7.1 Relating Organizing Elements or Organizing Centers

Organizing elements	Organizing Centers or Units of Instruction					
	Defining technology	People	Jobs	Society	Environment	Quality of life
Technology (concept)	X	X	X	X	X	X
Value of persons (value)		X	X	X	X	X
Relation of natural resources to quality of life (generalization)			X	X	X	X

and value to persons is given in all subsequent units. The quality of life unit allows for an unusually large number of activities related both to individuals and to societal values. As indicated in the matrix, no provision is made for treating value in the first unit; and the relation of natural resources to quality of life is not dealt with until the third unit.

To illustrate how the element is used in connecting different fields, consider how learners taking a course in technology might be helped if teachers in other courses exchanged elements with the teacher of the course in technology. In their mathematics course, they could acquire other basic concepts for understanding technology and systems, such as algorithms, probability, and binary systems. In their English course, they might be able to examine the interaction between technology and society in the mass media. They could appraise American societal values as reflected in newspapers, advertisements, and modern fiction. They could be helped to see how language is related to thought in both persons and machines.

There are two ways to extend the meaning of an organizing element through learning opportunities. The designer can provide for more complex situations to which the element applies, or the complexity of the situation can remain constant but the level of competency expected from the learner becomes more demanding. For example, in early learning opportunities, the learners might be asked only to define and give examples of a concept; in later centers the learners will be given opportunity to apply the concept; and in a final unit they might be asked to evaluate the concept or show its limitations.

PRINCIPLES FOR SEQUENCING CONTENT

Traditional Principles of Sequence

Principles for sequencing learning opportunities go back hundreds of years. Comenius in 1636, for example, admonished teachers to order activities from the simple to the complex. The principle *simple to complex* means introducing learning activities involving a few factors before activities involving many factors. It also means going from a part to a whole or from general to more detail. There are other traditional principles of sequence. Generally, it is best to go from *familiar to unfamiliar*. Activities that involve what the learners know should precede completely novel activities. Children should study their neighborhood before learning about their state and nation, and about foreign lands, for example. One should also progress from *concrete to abstract*, by presenting opportunities for children to see, touch, taste, hear, or smell a phenomenon before asking them to verbalize and categorize. It is also best to teach *dependent factors* first. Addition and subtraction, for example, should precede multiplication. There are also several ways of sequencing a series of facts or subjects. Ordering by *chronology* means presenting events as they occurred in time. Ordering by *usefulness* means teaching particular school subjects at the time they are needed in everyday life.

In Chapter 14 there is a discussion of the *theory of culture epochs*, which was used as the basis for sequencing studies at the turn of the century. This theory states that the learning processes of children follow the same pattern as the learning process of the human race. The notion is still very much alive. Some modern curriculum writers in the field of music are interested in the ideas of Carl Orff, a German composer who developed new plans and materials for teaching music to children based on the cultural epoch hypothesis. Orff reasoned that primitive people used free bodily movement in dance and also simple rhythmic drum patterns, so children should begin with drums suited to their size and skill. Bodily movements should be combined with the beat of the drum and rhythmic chants should synchronize the spoken rhythm with other movements.

Since primitive peoples first employ only one or two pitches before finally progressing to the use of the five-tone scale, the musical experiences planned for children should include songs with only two or three notes and, at most, five notes from the pentatonic scale. Melodic vocabulary includes other steps only after many opportunities with the simple melodies.[5]

Newer Principles of Sequence

Some recent principles for sequencing learning come from psychological models like those of Robert Gagné,[6] and from developmental schemes like those by Robert Havighurst, the late Jean Piaget, Erik Erikson, and Lawrence Kohlberg.

Gagné's View. Gagné orders activities according to types of learning. He believes that children learn an additive series of capabilities; that is, the simpler, more specific capability must come before the more complex and general one. Gagné would order learning activities in this fashion:

[5]Carl Orff and Gunhill Keetman, *Orff-Schulwerk: Musik fur Kinder,* 5 vols. (New York: Associated Music, 1950–53).
    [6]Robert Gagné and Leslie J. Briggs, *Principles of Instructional Design,* 2nd ed. (New York: Holt, Rinehart and Winston, 1979).

1. *Multiple discrimination.* The student learns to make different responses to stimuli that are similar in appearance. Children in kindergarten, for example, learn to tell the difference between the letters *d* and *b*.
2. *Concept learning.* The student makes a common response to a class of stimuli. A student may learn, for example, to classify or identify different types of literature or to recognize consonant–vowel–consonant spelling patterns.
3. *Principle learning.* The student acquires a principle, rule, or chain of concepts. The student learns, for example, to predict what word will follow in a given sentence structure according to rules for sequencing English.
4. *Problem solving.* The student learns to combine two or more principles to produce a solution and in the process acquires the capability to deal with future similar problems with greater facility.

Gagné believes the child comes to school with many capabilities for making multiple discriminations and building further concepts and higher order capabilities. He also realizes that the order of attaining complex behavior is not universal, that it is possible to subordinate capabilities.

Curriculum ordered in accordance with Gagné's theory, like *AAAS Science—a Process Approach,* a number of commercial programs using a cumulative approach to the teaching of reading and mathematics, and mastery learning strategies, sequence learning opportunities according to assumed hierarchies. Children at different levels of a hierarchy are given opportunities to learn prerequisite subordinate and superordinate capabilities as appropriate.

Gagné's model is deficient, though, in one respect. It does not take into account the unique ways children look at a task. Children differ from adults not only in the amount of previously learned subskills, but in the number of subskills they are capable of coordinating at one time and in their ability to avoid applying incorrect subskills or concepts. In making a task analysis or hierarchy, the structure of the task *from the learner's point of view* is important. When such an analysis shows a mismatch between the capacities of the learner and the demands of the task, the sequence should be redesigned either to reduce the hierarchy to differentiate concepts that are confusing to children.

The Developmentalists' View. Developmental tasks form an important basis for sequencing curriculum events. Robert J. Havighurst created the concept of a developmental task from (1) the idea that the maturation of the biological organism sets the conditions for learning social tasks, (2) the fact that social and cultural patterns demand that certain things be learned at a given time, and (3) the fact that there is often a sequential pattern of preferences and dislikes dictated by the individual personality. He defined a developmental task as "a task which arises at or about a certain period in the life of an individual, the successful achievement of which leads to his happiness and to success with later tasks, while failure leads to unhappiness in the individual, disapproval by society, and difficulty with later tasks."[7]

Hence, the activities selected for the late childhood curriculum might be those which help one form friendships with peers, learn rules and abstractions for fairness, identify with peers of same sex, and accept a changing body. Developmental tasks of the adolescent might be forming new relations with age mates of both sexes, gaining emotional independence from parents and other adults, selecting an occupation, and preparing for marriage.

In a simple way most schemes outlining developmental stages and tasks support the commonsense notion that health, safety, and physical survival must be attended to first; then can come opportunities that will enable learners to gain the capacity for economic self-maintenance in maturity, which, in turn, is likely to bring the ability to maximize cultural values like morality, prestige, wealth, and self–realization.

Erik Erikson has been credited with originating the idea of charting both the desires of the learners and the demands placed on them by cultural expectations.[8] Erikson's chart of life cycle states, from infancy through senescence, has been proposed as a way to organize the curriculum. Children would be given opportunities to deal with the emotional issues that are salient at particular stages of the life cycle. Children in the latency period (about 8 to 12 years), for example, whose central growth crisis is "mastery versus defeat," would be given opportunities to use newly acquired skills in logical thought to interpret a long-standing conflict with one of their parents.[9] Erikson has defined crucial tasks for each of the major seven life states. The selection and arrangement of learning activities addressed to these crises might better serve the needs of learners. While the specific tasks of each age are the same for boys and girls, the content and length of each stage differs in each society and from generation to generation in the same society.

Lawrence Kohlberg, too, has created a developmental scheme for ordering learning opportunities in the area of moral judgment. According

[7]Robert Havighurst, *Developmental Tasks and Education*, 3rd ed. (New York: McKay, 1973).

[8]"A Conversation with Erik Erikson," *Psychology Today* 17, no. 6 (June 1983): 22–32.

[9]Richard Jones, *Fantasy and Feeling in Education* (New York: New York University, 1968).

to him, learning opportunities must take into account both the learner's existing stage of development and a next higher stage.[10] Kohlberg believes that changes in moral thinking progress step by step through six stages and three levels.

Preconventional Level

Stage 1. Goodness or badness is determined by whether or not one will be punished for an act (punishment and obedience orientation).

Stage 2. Right action is that which satisfies one's needs (instrumental relativist orientation).

Conventional Level

Stage 3. Good behavior is that which pleases others and is approved by them ("good boy-nice girl" orientation).

Stage 4. Right behavior consists of doing what family, group, and nation expect ("law and order" orientation).

Postconventional Level

Stage 5. Right action means obeying legal standards agreed on by the whole society and, in areas where there is no agreement, following personal values and opinion. Right action also includes taking action to change the law (social contract, legalistic orientation).

Stage 6. Right action is exercising one's conscience in accordance with universal principles of justice and rights (universal ethical principle orientation).

Developmentalists have the central idea that development—physical, social, intellectual, and emotional—is fairly orderly and internally regulated. This idea has generally had a salutary effect on curriculum. It has kept before us the fact that some things can be more easily learned after minimum levels of maturity. It may be dangerous, however, to give too much credence to the view that capacities are genetically predetermined and unfold automatically. By manipulating environmental factors, we may alter the concept of readiness—the assumption that there is an optimal age for every kind of learning.

The idea of a developmental sequence sometimes leads to a curriculum organization in which children's interests are taken as an adequate index of their developmental needs. However, such a selection process is unreliable since the students' interests would reflect their prior learning opportunities more than their stage of development, and would in turn

---

[10]Lawrence Kohlberg, *Recent Research in Moral Development* (New York: Rinehart & Winston, 1984).

create an inadequate curriculum. The tyranny of fixed age level norms can both lower our sense of what is possible under different learning conditions and keep us from remembering large individual variations.

The late Jean Piaget's ideas on the stages of mental growth are probably the best known among developmentalists. He has postulated the following stages: a *sensory motor stage* (birth to about 2 years), in which the child begins to "symbolize and to represent things by words or gestures"; *representational stages* (approximately 2 to 4 years), in which the child learns to represent objects by symbolic means and (4 to 7 years) in which the child begins the initial stage of logical thought and can group objects into classes by noting similarities and differences; a *concrete operations stage* (approximately 7 to 11 years), in which the child learns to solve physical problems by anticipating consequences concretely; and a *formal operations stage* (usually 10 to 15 years), in which the youngster learns to use hypothetical reasoning and to perform controlled experimentation.[11]

One implication of Piaget's stage theory of mental development is that learning opportunities should match or nearly match the child's thought structure. This means analyzing each opportunity in terms of the level of reasoning required and then testing to see whether the intended learner has this level of ability. It is often assumed that learning can be induced when the learning activity requires reasoning that is slightly above the predominant level at which the child is operating. However, about the only way one could develop a curriculum that would allow for matching (in most classrooms, children will be at different operational levels) is to provide opportunities that have solutions at each level and let each child choose the level at which he or she will experience the activity.

Developmental schemes for sequencing learning opportunities are subject to two criticisms. First, there is a question about the validity of the principle underlying the scheme. Not everyone believes that Piaget has established valid stages of growth. Contrary to Piaget's findings, there is evidence that young children can think reflectively, recognize fallacies in logic, and make and apply generalizations.[12] Second, it is difficult to relate developmental sequences to the sequences of learning opportunities. The variation in individual needs, interests, and levels of thought makes it necessary to test all intended learners across a wide range of interests and concepts to assess individual developmental

[11]Jean Piaget, *The Psychology of Intelligence* (New York: Harcourt, Brace, Jovanovich, 1950).

[12]Robert H. Ennis, "Children's Ability to Handle Piaget's Propositional Logic: A Conceptual Critique," *Review of Educational Research* 45, no. 1 (Winter 1975): 1–43.

profiles. Further, it is difficult to select principles that are both effective in teaching a particular subject matter and important in promoting cognitive development. Definitions of cognitive competencies are not precise enough for constructing curriculum, and we lack a means of measurement that characterizes a developmental stage across a range of subject matter.

Categorizing Sequencing Principles

George Posner and Kenneth Strike have devised a scheme for showing how different principles of sequence relate to views of knowledge, views of learning, and views of how content is to be used.[13] By way of example, the category for *relating content to phenomena*—people, events, things— includes:

1. *Space.* Principles of closest to farthest, bottom to top, east to west (for example, used in relating such diverse content as parts of a plant, geography, and positions on a football team).
2. *Time.* Principles of cause and effect, chronological—early to most recent events (for example, used in relating content of history).
3. *Physical attributes.* Principles of softness to hardness, smaller to larger, greatest to least brightness, less to more complex structure (for example, used in teaching the properties of things in the natural world; science).

The category of sequence principles useful in the *teaching of concepts* includes:

1. *Class relations.* Principles that call for teaching about a general class before teaching about its members (for example, teach about mammals before teaching about specific animals in that group).
2. *Sophistication.* Principles by which the less abstract matter is presented first (for example, real numbers before imaginary numbers) and basic ideas before refinements (for example, Newton's laws before Einstein's refinement of these laws).
3. *Logical prerequisites.* The principle that the arrangement of concepts depends on the relations among concepts rather than the relations among their referents (for example, teach the concept of set before the concept of number).

The category of *inquiry-related* sequences includes principles for se-

---

[13]George J. Posner and Kenneth A. Strike, "A Categorization Scheme for Principles of Sequencing Content," *Review of Educational Research* 46, no. 4 (Fall 1976): 665–90.

quencing learning activities for generating, discovering, or verifying knowledge.

1. *Logic of inquiry.* Principles of sequencing based on induction (instances before generalizations) and principles based on deduction (hypotheses before evidence is collected).
2. *Empirics.* Principles calling for a general survey of an area before consideration of special problems.

Learning-related content sequences are similar to those mentioned previously as coming from the works of psychologists like Gagńe, Piaget, and Erikson. Learning sequences stress ordering of experiences according to familiarity (most familiar to most remote), difficulty (less difficult before more difficult), interest (most interesting first), development (according to developmental stages), and internalization (opportunity to recognize certain features in others before recognizing it in themselves).

The category of *utilization-related* sequence principles includes:

1. *Procedure.* Principle of sequencing steps in the order in which they will be used when carrying out a procedure (for example, teach golf grip before teaching address of the ball).
2. *Frequency.* Principle of basing sequence on predictions of likely future encounters (for example, teach the use of chi square and correlation coefficients before factor analysis; teach a television repairer how to change a tube before teaching how to change a resistor).

You will note how the above categorization system corresponds to different conceptions of the curriculum. Those with an academic conception use the categories of sequence for (1) relating content to phenomenon, (2) development of concepts, and (3) generating and discovering knowledge. Those with a technologist orientation select sequencing principles from the category of learning-related sequences, such as those of Gagné or Bloom, and from the category of utilization, when their interest is in developing curriculum for vocational training. Humanists tend to draw their sequencing principles from the developmental category, such as the sequences for moral development, values acquisition, and stages of growth. Some humanists are trying to apply John Dewey's principles for sequencing of curriculum content by attending to the individual learner's prior experiences—the cumulative result of the learner's use of knowledge gained from one experience to understand more fully the meaning of the next experience.[14] Although social recon-

---

[14]Chiarelott Leigh et al., "Basic Principles for Designing Experience Based Curriculum" (paper presented at AERA annual meeting, San Francisco, April 1979).

structionists might find the sequencing principle of internalization useful, they give less attention to sequence than to integration of the curriculum. One principle of sequencing sometimes used by reconstructionists, however, is the *principle of graduated responsibility* in ordering learning opportunities for children. This principle is illustrated as follows: *observe→ play act→perform useful service→work as equal partners with adults→carry responsibility for a project on a limited budget of power→exercise full adult responsibility.*

PRINCIPLES FOR INTEGRATING CONTENT

Integration

Curriculum integration is a response to the desire to make curriculum socially relevant and personally meaningful. Proponents of curriculum integration argue that if knowledge is to be important and relevant to students growing up in contemporary society, there must be a departure from traditional forms and organization. Exploration of topics of crucial social and personal concerns, such as relations between the sexes, life in cities, and war requires introducing content and organizational patterns not found in conventional subject areas. An interdisciplinary approach is required.

Integration of subject matter becomes controversial because it usually means giving up fixed subject matter boundaries and conventional content, emphasizing breadth rather than depth and showing more concern for application of knowledge than for the form of knowledge.

There are several schemes for effecting curriculum integration. In some schemes, academic content is fixed and in others the individual student has much freedom of choice. The teacher is a generalist in some schemes; in others each teacher contributes as a specialist while team teaching. There are also integrated schemes within a discipline, such as integrated science, as opposed to schemes whereby all kinds of subjects— science, art, technology, and so forth—are combined.

Integration is a logical problem when we allow a rigid view of knowledge to dominate curriculum planning. As indicated in Chapter 4, there are those with a narrow academic conception of curriculum who view knowledge as fixed. Such persons will oppose curriculum reorganization along integrated lines for epistemological reasons. On the other hand, social reconstructionists and humanists who view knowledge as tentative favor integration as a way of ensuring that knowledge and curriculum fit changing social and human needs.

We have fewer principles for integrating activities than for sequencing them. When content is integrated, subjects are related with one another, with out-of-school experiences, and with personal needs and interests.

Integration usually means applying organizational elements to an ever widening variety of situations. Organizing principles commonly in use call for increasing breadth of application and range of activities, and for fitting parts into larger and larger wholes. Sometimes the learner's problems and interests serve as the framework or organizing center within which knowledge from many fields can be brought together. Similarly, opportunities to attack social problems and to conduct projects require concepts and methods from different fields of knowledge. The subject matter is featured then, not as a system of ideas or concepts, but as ideas that have relevance to a practical problem. *The Chicken Book,* a popular nonfiction book, is an excellent example of how an organizing center, the chicken, can be used to bring together a wonderful compendium of history, literature, science, medicine, religion, technology, economics, fact, and lore.[15] One of its authors teaches a course on the fowl dedicated to the idea that what is divided may once more be made whole.

The use of such content elements as key ideas in subject fields, broad concepts, major questions, and methods of inquiry may effectively interrelate courses and out-of-school experiences. In the *Carnegie colloquium on general education,* for instance, the members report new academic alliances as inquiry blends what traditionally have been isolated fields of study.[16] Sociologists, psychologists, biologists, and chemists found themselves seeking answers to the same or closely related questions such as the role of chance in the arrangement of life on the planet.

Typical arrangements for facilitating integration are:

1. *Concentration.* Students are not expected to take more than four courses at any one time so that they may gain the depth of preparation necessary for seeing the ramifications of each subject on the whole curriculum.
2. *Correlation.* Subjects keep their separate identifies, but the concepts of one subject are related to the concepts of another (for example, concepts from history and literature are taught at the same time to reinforce each other).
3. *Integration of a tool subject.* Skills learned in one subject are used as tools in another field (for example, mathematical concepts are used in social science).
4. *Fields of study.* Fields or areas of study differ from forms of knowledge and disciplines in that they do not have a distinctive rational structure of knowledge (for example, the fields of geography and

---

[15]Page Smith and Charles Daniel, *The Chicken Book* (Boston: Little, Brown, 1975).
[16]Carnegie Foundation for the Advancement of Teaching, *Common Learning,* ed. Ernest Boyer (Washington, D.C.: Carnegie Foundation, 1981).

health draw on mathematics, the physical sciences, and the human sciences).

5. *Comprehensive problem solving.* Problems such as those of energy and conservation are predicted which require a combination of skills and knowledge from such forms of knowledge as science, mathematics, and philosophy to best solve them.

ISSUES IN CURRICULUM ORGANIZATION

Curriculum organization is difficult because the fields of knowledge have not been organized in a way that makes them useful in daily life. Also, those in different disciplines express their findings in different terms so that the consumer does not know how to relate the findings. Curriculum efforts to integrate concepts from various disciplines have not been very successful.

Practical problems of curriculum integration center on (1) the teachers' loss of identity and security as isolated teachers of English, science, history, or other subject fields; (2) the need for flexible scheduling during the school day along with freedom for student choice of work and movement within the school building and community; (3) the need for material resources that go beyond the normal stock of books and equipment found in separate departments; (4) the difficulty of learning the teaching roles, skills, and attitudes required by curriculum; and (5) the need to answer the objection that an integrated curriculum will not prepare students for external examinations based on separate subject matter.

Curriculum integration is now an overriding concern. The curriculum reform movement of the 1960s extended the scope of content to include new areas of knowledge, but neglected to evolve a unifying purpose. Pluralistic and humanistic interests as well as governmental programs aimed at social and political causes of the 1970s extended even further the range of electives and the scope of content. Curriculum fragmentation resulted. We are in a wave of curriculum organizational reform in response to the fragmentation. Some of the difficulty involved in responding to this situation and to the lack of shared skills and values can be seen in efforts to build an integrated curriculum. Designers at the Education Development Center in Newton, Massachusetts, tried to organize learning opportunities around interests that appear to be important to the prospective students—child-rearing practices, love and affection, expressions of fear and anger, parent–offspring conflict. Using these interests, the staff sought content from different disciplines (biology, anthropology, psychology, sociology, linguistics) that would help students to meet these interests and at the same time gain an understanding of their own uniqueness, of their kinship with others of the culture, and of the characteristics that unite the human race.

The curriculum developers found that no academic discipline was adequate to cope with the questions they wanted to raise. They also found that academics from different fields use different words to discuss similar phenomena and that these words are invested with different meanings. A biologist speaks of "bonding" when examining relationships between male and female or between parent and offspring; a psychologist may use words like "love" and "attachment" to describe the same relationships. A third problem was that the disciplines not only represented separate languages and analytic tools, but also drew from bodies of data that did not overlap. A final and deeper problem was the difficulty of trying to combine different points of view regarding human nature. There is, for example, much conflict over whether cultural evolution proceeds independently of biological factors or whether biological forces determine the direction of evolution.

Several solutions have been offered as broader approaches to the problem. Philosophers of science have argued that integration can be achieved by using concepts of knowledge about knowledge. One can draw from disciplines the content that represents the field as a whole. The curriculum person can select ideas and instances that exemplify the method of inquiry in these disciplines and offer instruction in *synoptics*—the integrative fields, like history, religion, and philosophy. These disciplines have as their function the making of coherent wholes.

A second proposal is that we live with the fact that the scholars in any one discipline are incapable of resolving any complex human problem. In other words, students should try to examine personal and social problems from multiple perspectives, realizing that no one of these views is entirely satisfactory. Perhaps the conclusion that students reach after attending to the different perspectives will be more valuable than any one discipline's answer to the problems.

A third proposal is that we forget about curriculum organization as a way to effect meaning for students. Even when there is a careful attempt to simplify and relate content so that students can follow it, the organization will fit any one student imperfectly. Students individualize their experiences anyway. This position puts the burden on the learners to make sense out of learning opportunities in any order. More positively stated, it challenges individuals to pose their own questions, seek their own answers, make their own synthesis, and find satisfaction in so doing.

Peter Freyberg and Roger Osborne think that curriculum developers have erred in structuring curriculum from the perspective of the teacher.[17] They propose that no matter what curriculum framework is employed, learners are going to structure the subject matter in their own way. What is learned can be very different from what is taught. Progress in curriculum development rests upon finding out the concepts and cognitive structures that learners bring with them to the learning opportunities. Usually, there are only three or four distinctly different viewpoints regarding a matter. However, ascertaining the learners' conceptions takes time and the procedures for dealing with conflicting preconceptions so students can be helped to accommodate more adequate conceptions are not well known.

Curriculum design has been accused of preventing learners from comprehending content in any other order and from learning content that is incompatible with adaptive teaching. Underlying most organizational issues, however, are disputes about purpose. Curriculum workers who favor academic specializations value organization as it relates to sequencing for depth, but they are not impressed by integrative arrangements. Those who seek integrated approaches, usually humanists and social reconstructionists, distrust prearranged sequences within a single field.

A final point of view about the problems of integration warns of the political danger of unified and integrated curricula. The integration of separate subjects and the destruction of subject departments in schools often marks a shift of power from the staff in separate fields to the administrator who directs the new master plan. One can argue that modern societies are better served with power on the periphery and a diversified curriculum—many separate subjects—but with specialists coming together to decide on common objectives.

CONCLUDING COMMENTS

In this chapter emphasis was placed upon two ways to organize learning opportunities: by a center of interests and by organizing elements. Curriculum design was viewed as a plan showing the relationships among purpose, organizing structures, organizing elements, and specific learning opportunities. Illustrations of curriculum design were presented

---

[17]Peter Freyberg and Roger Osborne, "Who Structures the Curriculum: Teacher or Learner?" *Science Information for Teachers* 12, no. 2 (1981).

with special attention to the designing of classroom curriculum structures. Principles for sequencing and integrating content were critiqued. Issues in curriculum organization—particularly concern about the integration of subject matter—were discussed. The problem of linking curriculum planning undertaken at two levels of decision making—institutional and classroom—was also introduced.

Since the planning of a curriculum is a management and political matter as much as a technical one, the connection between the curriculum and these matters is treated more fully in Part III.

QUESTIONS

1. Think of a familiar learning task such as tying shoes, operating an auto-mobile, playing a game, composing a musical or literary piece. Into what units would you divide the task you have in mind? In what order would you teach these steps? What principle of sequence determines your ordering?

2. State an organizing element—a concept, value, or skill—that you would like to build on throughout a number of activities in a course or program of interest to you.

3. Curriculum constructed in accordance with hierarchical theories (that is, curriculum where there is an attempt to specify prerequisites and to place them in a simple-to-complex order) is sometimes criticized for being boring and ineffective. Critics charge that there are too many unneces-sary steps for some learners and that many learners who successfully complete the enroute steps fail at transfer tasks at the end of the pro-grams. What is your response to this criticism?

4. What consequences (good or bad) would be likely from a curriculum in which learning opportunities are ordered on the assumption that there is an optimal age for acquiring particular capacities?

5. Arno Bellack once suggested a program that would include basic instruc-tion in the humanities, natural sciences, and social sciences together with a coordinating seminar in which students dealt with problems "in the round" and in which a special effort is made to show the relationships between the systematized fields of study as materials from these fields are brought to bear on a topic. What are the likely advantages and disad-vantages of Bellack's suggestion? What conditions would have to exist in order for the proposed plan to work?

6. Assume that you are a member of a planning committee charged with a new curriculum organization for a school. You have been asked whether or not the new organization plan should attempt to provide for integra-tion of subject matter and, if so, how it can best be achieved. What is your reply?

SELECTED REFERENCES

Gibbons, J. A. "Curriculum Integration" *Curriculum Inquiry* 9, vol. no. 4 (Winter 1979): 321–37.

Posner, George J. and Strike, Kenneth A. "A Categorization Scheme for Principles of Sequencing Content" *Review of Educational Research* 46, no. 4 (Fall 1976): 665–90.

III / MANAGING CURRICULUM

In recent years the question of who shall control the curriculum has gained more attention than any other aspect in the field. The issue of control is often behind curriculum mandates, achievement tests and studies of school effectiveness.

The chapters in this part examine the issue of control. Chapter 8 treats the relation between the institutional character of curriculum to external powers and to the individual classroom teacher.

Chapter 9 focuses on ways to implement and generate curriculum innovations in the school setting. It also considers curriculum change in some detail.

In Chapter 10, curriculum evaluation is reviewed from both the perspectives of traditional evaluations which measure effectiveness with tests and pluralistic evaluations which favor a broader means of evaluation and wider participation in the evaluation process.

Chapter 11 explains the formulation of curriculum policy and points out potential sources of conflict among policymakers. A study of the politics of curriculum making may help foster concern about the decision-making processes at local, state, and federal levels. It may also focus attention on the interest groups making curriculum decisions and the consequences of political solutions to curriculum questions.

8 / ADMINISTERING CURRICULUM

For decades school administrators—superintendents, deans, principals, curriculum directors—have been asked to act in accordance with models of curriculum which assume a close tie between decisions and implementation. Now, however, schools are viewed as systems being run with indeterminate goals, limited supervision, and little knowledge of their success or failure. Administrators are asked to bind the system to a common purpose and to embrace new modes of operation in an environment characterized both by change and a lack of consensus about policies and procedures.

This chapter focuses upon aspects of curriculum management, giving special attention to the policies and factors associated with effective programs. The chapter also notes two responses to the lack of coordination in curriculum management. On one hand, some administrators would integrate the system by increasing accountability with standardized tests. On the other hand, others would leave the system as it is. They welcome the freedom it offers as an opportunity to solve curriculum problems through local initiative.

POLICY FRAMEWORKS

In the previous chapter we said that schools do not have an integrated, coherent curriculum but a collection of classes and teachers. In part the confusion is a result of federal and state policies for curriculum. Federal and state agencies have failed to consider overall curriculum policy. Instead the policymakers have reacted to lobbyists, such as advocates of bilingual education, handicapped children, women's rights, and industry. As a result, programs and courses have been added rather than balanced and organized into a coherent pattern of instruction. To complicate matters, teachers often make their own curriculum policies; they decide what topics should be taught and which students will study what content.

Concern about the direction and deterioration of overall curriculum policy has increased with the decline in federal aid, rejection of categorical funding of special programs, and fiscal limitations. Necessity demands that administrators decide on the content students most need to learn rather than evade the issue and simply add more courses. At the same time, the curriculum must accommodate all students.

Questions for Administrators

Michael Kirst has proposed two sets of questions that administrators might ask as they try to establish a coherent program.[1] The first set attempts to ensure that all students have access to the courses. The second set helps the administrator appraise the quality and coherence of the courses:

Student Access. Questions to determine access can include:

1. What courses and subjects are offered? How and why have course offerings changed in the past five to ten years?
2. What are the trends in enrollments for courses by student subgroups? Why have enrollments in some subjects increased or decreased?
3. What courses are required for graduation? What courses are recommended? Are there minimum graduation standards?
4. What are the criteria for student access to courses? Do students and others know these criteria? What do students see as barriers to taking particular courses? Do some students miss out on elements of the common curriculum because certain courses cannot fit into their schedules?
5. When and how do students select or become assigned to courses, sequences, and tracks? Why do they take the courses they do? Especially why do they *not* take advanced courses?
6. How much is course access affected by scheduling, number of periods per day, electives, and work experience programs?
7. What information is provided to students about the relationships between courses, sequences, requirements, and college and job

[1]Michael W. Kirst, "Policy Implications of Individual Differences and the Common Curriculum," in *Individual Differences and the Common Curriculum*, NSSE Yearbook (Chicago: University of Chicago Press, 1983): pp. 282–300.

entrance? When is this information provided? Is it provided prior to high school? What characterizes the student's process in planning courses?

8. What are the sources of information and influence on students' course planning? How are parents involved in the planning process? Are they aware of curricular choices and consequences?

9. Do students and parents feel well informed and confident about getting information? Are they satisfied with courses and their qualifications to choose them? How do they assess the planning process?

10. Are students tracked, laned, or otherwise grouped? How many tracks are there and what characterizes both the students and the courses? What effect does tracking have on instruction, content, student self-image, aspirations, and so forth?

11. Do courses in all tracks prepare students for advanced course work or is the track a barrier to advancement?

Nature of Courses and Content. Questions in this area would be:

1. How consistent is course content across teachers and schools in terms of (a) materials covered (texts, topics), (b) number of assignments (writing, reading), and (c) entrance and exit criteria?

2. How do policies or views regarding the common curriculum and individual needs influence the findings in answer to the above question?

3. Why do teachers focus on the particular questions they do?

4. How do teachers and others assess adequacy of course content, difficulty, and achievement? Is there a periodic analysis of these matters?

5. How much do teachers modify their courses to accommodate student characteristics? What are the student characteristics that most affect teacher planning?

6. Are courses sequential or otherwise articulated or coordinated? Do students, teachers, and others see connections and continuity in sequences?

7. Do students experience continuity in skills and subject matter? Do they get instruction in areas of deficiency when needed? What barriers do they see to learning the content, receiving assistance, and achieving good grades?

8. What criteria are used to determine students' mastery of content and access to appropriate instruction? Who decides which courses fit into various tracks?

9. Are remediation, special assistance, and lower track courses designed to provide students with skills for more advanced work? Or are they dead ends?

Curriculum Policy at College and University Level

Policy is urgently needed for reforming curriculum at many colleges and universities. For more than a decade, institutions of higher education have merely responded to external and internal pressures on the curriculum, and have failed to develop coherent curriculum policies. However, signs of more sustained thought about the curriculum of the future are found in *Common Learning*, a Carnegie colloquium on general education.[2] The colloquium members feel the need for reform and propose a means for the development of a general curriculum for all students. Many faculty members support a general curriculum and recognize the need to drop courses as a result of declining revenues and enrollments. In order to establish a program of general education, though, everyone must agree on what it means: Is it general in the sense of having learning opportunities (a Shakespearean play, a particular law of thermodynamics) shared by all students? Does general education mean meeting the common needs of all in a particular time and place (political and civic knowledge)? Or does it mean emphasizing the methods of inquiry and key ideas from representative fields (as Hirst indicated in Chapter 4)?

Some even feel a general education should apply to people in all cultures. All courses might stress how different societies address the need for food, shelter, aesthetic experience, and respect. On the other hand, all courses might stress certain values like creativity, critical thinking, and clear, written expression. Notably, the latter alternative needs no additional courses; existing courses emphasize these values already perhaps.

ADMINISTRATIVE ARRANGEMENTS

In organizing the curriculum, administrators must decide how students are grouped, how much time is devoted to each subject, and how it will be taught. Since the needs and functions of schooling change, each of these factors require frequent alteration. The need for constant adjustment can be illustrated in a comparison of the organization of curriculum during the 1960s, 1970s, and the present.

[2]Carnegie Foundation for the Advancement of Teaching, *Common Learning* (Washington, D.C.: Carnegie Foundation, 1981).

Traditional Administrative Arrangement

A typical small high school in the early 1960s was divided into three or four nine-month grade levels. Each level offered semester or year-long courses. Each course met five days a week for forty-five minutes, and each student took five or six courses in a number of subjects or departments, usually mathematics, social studies, English, physical education, foreign language, science, homemaking, or fine, industrial, or commercial arts. All students were expected to take some required courses, like tenth-grade English, world history, and physical education.

However, different sections of the required academic courses were established. Hence, students of lower and higher academic, social, and economic background were separated by being assigned to different sections of the required courses where the content and method differed considerably; this was called *tracking*. Tracking also occurred when students were counseled into either a vocational or college preparatory program. Further separations of students occurred when they elected a major, a subject area in which one completed continuing work of three- or four-year duration.

There were opportunities within the typical school of the early 1960s for students to explore their interests in electives and through student activities. Often there were courses within departments, which were designed to introduce students to a certain aspect of a field (for example, drama or ceramics in the arts). Student activities—clubs, sports, games, hobbies—were usually considered extracurricular. They seldom carried credit and usually took place before or after school. Some of these activities, however, such as student council or the annual staff, had curriculum status.

Innovations During the 1960s and 1970s

Several different scheduling and staffing approaches were advocated by the Ford Foundation and by persons like J. Lloyd Trump.[3] Let us examine the most important of these changes.

Grouping. Instead of grouping thirty-five students with one teacher on the basis of ability or achievement, one can use different sized groupings for three different purposes. There is *independent study*, allowing

---

[3]J. Lloyd Trump and Delmas F. Miller, *Secondary School Curriculum Improvement* rev. ed. (Boston: Allyn and Bacon, 1973); J. Lloyd Trump, *A School for Everyone* (Reston, Va.: National Association of Secondary School Principals, 1977).

for an individual activity or, on occasion, for two or more pupils to work together. It may take the form of remedial or advanced work in the library, at resource centers, in conference areas, and in outside work experiences or study projects. There is *large–group instruction* by which presentations are given to motivate, inform, and direct students. Large-group instruction is often followed by independent study and small discussion groups. The size of the class does not matter and is often 100 or more. In *small–group discussion* students apply the knowledge gained in large groups and from independent study. Twelve to fifteen student members usually constitute a small group. Membership, however, may change weekly, monthly, or at other intervals depending on the nature of their study. The groups are supervised by a teacher, although students may assume leadership. Such groups usually meet once a week for about forty minutes.

Scheduling. It is possible for some classes to have more time than others or to meet less often, but for longer periods of time, on certain days. In the *modular concept* of flexible scheduling, for instance, there is a fifteen–, twenty–, or thirty–minute time module within a twelve–, sixteen–, or twenty–four period day. Various subjects are scheduled for a different number of modules. Schedules can be rotated by days and periods, and students can take more than six subjects by scheduling subjects to meet fewer than four times a week. True flexible scheduling depends on a sequence of content not divided by grade level and large blocks of time for independent study. One school, for example, introduced ten-week minicourses and scheduled them in the middle of the day. These courses were regarded as extensions of the main curriculum stream and as exploratory areas. Students could choose from among courses in genetics, sports in literature, local political issues, vocabulary building, preparation for college examinations, home maintenance, and others. In addition, courses were offered during one period a day for a full year or in a double period block for half a year. Half-year courses were joined and taught in tandem blocks during the year as well as in their conventional time segment. Hence, students had more opportunity to alter their schedules to meet their career needs. Further, the summer school program was broadened to continue the school year, allowing for a modified trimester plan. A broadening of course offerings was also made possible by offering independent study via an educational contract system. The system allowed a teacher and student or group of students to set an objective in agreed-on areas. The plan, in turn, was approved by the department chairman and principal. Both vocationally and colle-ge–bound students could move at a pace other than that of the conventional program. Self–scheduling allowed parents and students to assume more responsibility and allowed departments to make their courses more appealing. Indeed, 75 new courses were introduced during a two-year period.[4]

About 15 percent of secondary schools in the United States used flexible modular scheduling (FMS) at its zenith in the mid 1970s; by the 1980s not more than 3 percent used FMS.[5] Changes in the social milieu and problems with facilities, materials, staff development, and student responsibility contributed to its wane in popularity. Nevertheless, some form of flexible scheduling is necessary to tailor instruction to students.[6]

Team Teaching. Team teaching occurs when, for example, six teachers accept responsibility for 180 students for a two-hour block of time each day. This allows the staff to assume different roles, such as planning, lecturing, leading discussion, and counseling. A teacher in a team may be involved with a large class, with a seminar–sized group of fifteen, or with pupils engaged in individual study. Teaching teams determine in advance what pupils they need to teach, in what size groups, for what lengths of time, and with what materials. Team leaders provide information for preparation of a master schedule for student guidance. Often, in a daily twenty–minute period, pupils determine their own daily program from the choices available on the master schedule.

One brand of interdisciplinary teaming is found in some middle schools where four-person teams are composed of one specialist from among the areas of language arts, mathematics, social science, art, or science. Each specialist serves as the resource person for an area, doing much of the planning and teaching of that subject. Each teacher on the team, however, teaches all four of the academic subjects. The advantage of this arrangement is that correlation of subject matter areas is easier and teachers are better able to attend to individual students.

Team teaching is not supposed to be a labor-saving device, like cooperative or rotating turn teaching. It is intended to bring about clear joint acceptance of objectives and better conditions for achieving them. Teams of teachers and groups of students can be together, for example, for approximately three hours each day in what is called a *fluid* block. Two of the hours are devoted to interdisciplinary activities, and the

---

[4]Richard A. Berger et al., "A Redesign Experience for Sachem High School," *The Clearing House* 49, no. 2 (October 1975): 84–87.

[5]Mary B. Tubbs and James A. Beane, "Curriculum Trends and Practices in the High School," *High School Journal* 64, no. 2 (February 1981): 206.

[6]Jeri J. Goldman, "Flexible Modular Scheduling: Results of Evaluations in Second Decade," *Urban Education* 18, no. 2 (July 1983): 191–228.

TABLE 8.1   A Team Teaching Outline

	Fluid Block	Individualized Labs
Hour 1	Fluid block: 100-120	Music
2	students in course	Math
3	(minicourses or	Driver Ed.
	planning)	Art
		Drama
		Typing
		etc.
4	Elective	
5	Elective	or three-hour
6	Elective	vocational block

additional hour is given to one or more open labs in a variety of
subcourse content. With twelve teachers operating across three teams
for at least two of the three different hours, as many as twenty-four
different minicourses can be offered during a nine-week period. Students
from each of the three fluid blocks are able to schedule the minicourse of
their choice. The fluid block team also schedules large–group, small–
group, and individual student activities, always with an option for
student placement in the open labs, which operate concurrently on an
individual basis. The balance of the school day is given to elective courses
such as physics and typing, or to a vocational block in any of a number of
different areas (see Table 8.1).

Each student is assigned to a specific team or faculty member for the
entire day, hence meeting accountability concerns. The organization of
the team, advisement, and individualized labs offer several ways to meet
student needs.

Supplementary Personnel. Pupil tutors, adult volunteers, and inexpensive
paraprofessionals allow teachers to serve more pupils effectively and
efficiently. Cross-age tutoring, whereby older students tutor younger
ones to the benefit of both, has become very popular across the country.
No other innovation has been so consistently perceived as successful.
Ideally, tutoring is a regular class assignment rather than a voluntary
activity. Instructional modules are selected that will induce academic
growth of the tutor as well as tutees. Ninth-graders, for example, may
teach fractions to fourth-graders if the ninth-grade teacher believes the

tutors need to learn and practice fractions and the fourth-grade teacher would like his or her students to learn fractions.

Scheduling of one-to-one tutoring can occur when two classes get together regularly on two or three occasions per week. A room set up with pairs of desks (carrels) is most desirable, but regular classrooms, cafeterias, or libraries will suffice. The sending teacher prepares the tutors in special training sessions. In these sessions, tutors learn exactly what they are to teach. They may also practice their methods and prepare materials such as flash cards and tests for their tutees.

The tutoring sessions themselves should be supervised by the teachers concerned. Tutors should be free to ask for assistance, and the teacher can check that the work is being taught correctly.

Nongrading. Nongrading occurs when content and experience are offered on the basis of learner interest and ability and are not restricted to a given grade level. The lack of grade levels permits students to progress at different rates and lets them take advanced or additional courses. A student may wish to take correspondence courses, for example, or participate in advanced placement programs, taking college level courses for credit while in the secondary school. Also, instead of offering world history, United States history, and problems of democracy to tenth-, eleventh-, and twelfth-graders respectively, schools may offer one of these courses each year to all students.

Facilities. Building, grounds, supplies, and equipment should correspond to both the educational objectives and the means by which teachers and pupils achieve these objectives. Facilities for independent study means pupils must have a place to work and a place to use the special materials of the subject matter they are learning. There may be a need for places in which to view films, read, practice music, and work with metals and clay.

Classroom walls should not define the limits of the learning environment. Facilities should encourage communication, and there should be variations in lighting—less in small group discussion space than in independent study rooms. The budget for supplies and equipment should be increased as the cost of school building increases. Unlike industry, which wisely puts only 25 percent of total capital outlay into structure, schools have put 75 percent of capital outlay into the building shell and only 25 percent into instructional tools. Although modernization procedures are less costly than building new structures, the politics of education usually means that school persons are vulnerable to the pressures of real estate and building contractors for expensive sites and buildings that are not necessary.

The Middle School. A major institutional change with implications for curriculum organization is found in the rise of the American middle school. This type of school has grown from a smattering of schools in the 1950s to more than 5,000 in 1979. This school is characterized by service to the eleven- to fourteen-year-old age group. Typically, such schools are centered on the child rather than on subject matter. The schools usually offer the design components of a subschool within a larger middle school and an interdisciplinary teaching team. The team operates as a small four- or five-teacher school. The same group of students in the subschool may stay together for a period of three or four years. Another team of teachers offers a related unified arts program to students from all subschools. The unified arts program gives all students experiences in such subjects as art, shop, homemaking, music, physical education, as well as focusing on career opportunities. Exploratory experiences on a nongraded basis are also provided to enrich the students and supplement their needs.

Alternative, Magnet, and Specialized Schools. Modular scheduling, team teaching, flexible group instruction, and similar plans did not prove to be ideal solutions or lead to more effective curriculum. Some call these innovations superficial tinkering and are demanding a much more basic reform.

Active groups began to take daring steps toward the reorganization of schooling in the late 1960s. Convinced that public schools were instruments of a racist and oppressive society, some community activists opened storefront schools that emphasized both basic skills and black culture. They also tried to enroll school dropouts from the street and prepare them for college. These "freedom schools" were financially supported by foundations and dedicated individuals. Such schools encouraged a close, nonauthoritarian teacher-pupil relationship and an open concept of learning. Not surprisingly, content focused on the ills of the capitalistic society.

By 1971, there were over 200 free schools, but with the calmer atmosphere of the early 1970s and the loss of available monies during the economic slump, the free school movement lost much of its original impetus. Although alternative schools had no uniform philosophies, they continued to increase in number. By 1977, the National Education Association reported 10,000 alternative schools in 5,000 districts across the country.

It is impossible to generalize accurately about alternative schools. By definition, each one is different. Much of the movement is directed toward making schools effective for students who have been school dropouts. Some alternative programs are organized to allow students to work in a congenial atmosphere consistent with their work style. Most people in alternative schools today are not working as social revolutionists but as humanists who want pupils to have a choice, not only in what is to be studied, but in styles of learning.

Alternative schools have made us conscious of whether or not we should allow students to select freely a formal or an informal school; a structured or an individualized curriculum. An alternative school—whether a separate institution or a unit within a comprehensive school—is an organizational answer to the old problem of fitting the curriculum to the enormous range of talents and traits students bring to school and the diverse expectations they and their parents have for schooling.

Today's alternative school movement has broadened the definition of an elective from a choice of a subject to a choice in ways of working. Generally, people in the movement recognize the need for structure, sequence, and discipline but assert that, for many students, a choice about the degree of structure in a learner's school life is as crucial as a choice between studying Spanish or stenography.

In some of the alternative schools, students seldom enter a classroom. They pursue their individual interests outside the school. They may study the stars at an observatory, work with computers at a local firm, learn to make bread at the corner bakery, and discuss medicine with a physician—all for academic credit. Sometimes students travel from place to place in the city, learning from a variety of paid and unpaid teachers. A student may take physics at a university, Elementary Functions and World Cultures from the school staff, Contemporary American Literature and French II from students at another university, Museum Methods from the school staff, and Understanding the Stock Market from a broker.

Recently an *options* system has been introduced. In an options system, the choice of school curriculum—methods, activities, or environment—is left to individual students and their families. Instead of a single alternative to an existing program, there are many options. In Minneapolis, for instance, students may attend the school selected by themselves and their parents. In most large cities, there are "magnet" schools which are consistent with the concept of options. These schools offer an especially strong curriculum in some areas such as science or business education, as a way to further court-ordered integration by attracting students from different ethnic and socioeconomic populations.

Other changes are occurring in response to the international competition in mathematics and science. Some "exemplary" schools specialize in mathematics and science—1000 at the elementary level and 1000 at the secondary level—in the most ambitious of organizational plans on the national level. State networkings, such as the Louisiana School for Math, Science, and the Arts at Natchitoches where the most talented juniors from the state's 66 school districts are brought together for an elite education, are becoming more common.

Unlike the early 1960s, public schools currently available to students, parents, and teachers offer incredible variety. Some schools emphasize different instructional approaches (open schools, Montessori schools, continuous progress schools, behavior modification schools); some feature distinctive curriculum (centers for world studies, environmental study centers, vocational centers); and others focus on special students (maternity schools, bilingual schools, schools for the gifted and the dropouts). Yet, throughout the country, schools are putting more emphasis on basic skills and college preparation. Concern is expressed that optional and elective courses have gone too far and some schools are returning to a standard curriculum. Alternative classes are being established, however, for students who fail competency examinations in reading, mathematics, and writing.

Across the country national studies lamenting lax school standards and mediocrity have spurred organizational reform. Typical of these changes are those in the Florida school system:

1. *Upgraded curriculum* - High school juniors must have 22 credits (24 by 1987) to graduate, including three years of mathematics and science. Some students must drop electives such as art and typing to take more mathematics and science. Students who want to play sports must earn 2.0 grade point average on a scale of 4.0.
2. *Longer days* - More high school students have a seven-period schedule instead of six.
3. *Academic competition* - The state is carved into 5 school regions, which are pitted against each other to inspire better results.

DIRECTIONS IN THE REFORM OF SCHOOL ORGANIZATIONS

Options in the Schools

Two directions of organizational reform have emerged out of the ferment over social policy dilemmas and the innovations both from those who would make the school more humane and from those who would make it more productive. Various commissions and study groups bent on studying secondary schools in order to restore them to full strength and vitality agree on two directions.

First, reduce barriers between adolescents and opportunities in the community. Work or volunteer experience outside the school building is seen as desirable in increasing students' independence and helping them to encounter a broader range of people and experiences. Students' time should, however, be well planned, and off-campus programs should be organized to allow for reflection. The study groups also realized that tracking can occur outside as well as inside the school. A combination of action and reflection is believed necessary in order for adolescents to mature in an integrative manner.

Second, create smaller schools or subschools with more specialized courses of study. Students who are unlikely to get training beyond high school should leave school with enough skill to procure a job. Rather than each offering training in fifteen or twenty skills, different schools might each offer three or five trades in depth. To facilitate such specialization, the school, satellite, or cluster within schools should be smaller, with each unit focusing on fewer but more specific areas and skills. Basic academic subjects would still be offered in all schools, but students would select a magnet school on the basis of the training it offers.

John Goodlad has recommended the reorganization of junior and senior high schools into houses.[7] Each house has its own curriculum. The students in each house are at all grade levels; that is, each student spends his or her entire junior and senior high school career affiliated with one house through several grade levels. Teachers have the chance to adjust to the student's present attainment, and all students have opportunity to reach mastery in the general curriculum; slower students would not be tracked into different courses. Further, the longer association of the students and their teachers is likely to reduce both student alienation and teacher frustration.

Teachers within smaller schools, with some of their students on alternating work and study programs outside the school, would have more time to spend with fewer students. They also would perform more varied roles, like that of advisor, work supervisor, and role model. The reports from the various commissions and panels trying to reform secondary education emphasize options in high school organization and the need for instruction in informal settings. These reports are not truly plans for curriculum development because they fail to attend to the questions of what should be taught and how. If we return to our metaphor of curriculum as a game, as found in Chapter 5, we might say that the authors of these reports fail to pick up all the curriculum pieces. Like so many administrators and policymakers, they make the mistake

[7]John Goodlad, *A Place Called School.* (New York: McGraw-Hill, 1983).

of assuming that if the structure and organization are changed, or if the setting and scene of schooling are moved, then appropriate and effective education will result. This is not so. The learning in the various settings must be coordinated with that of the school, and one should not assume that all work settings are appropriate for learning. The task of improving the learning of students in specific tasks has yet to be done. Unfinished, too, is the development of a conceptual framework for the creation of learning activities and the training and deployment of personnel.

Accountability Movement

Concurrent with the movement toward alternatives or options in the school are the accountability movements and academic reforms. Whereas the accountability movement demands minimum competencies for all students, the academic reform movement stresses more mathematics, science, and writing for all. Accountability demands arise out of fears that students are graduating without necessary skills; fear that encouragement of individual values over social ones will result in a fragmented society. Reformers at federal and state levels often fuel these fears so that they can control the curriculum at the institutional and classroom level. The academic reform movement, as indicated in Chapter 4, arose out of concern about the decline of test scores, the rise of competition with Japan, and the lack of equal access to cultural resources. These conflicting concerns require different organizational plans. Some demand a fixed structure focused on specific ends; others an open structure trained on a wide variety of ends. Accommodating these conflicting requirements has not yet been accomplished.

ADMINISTRATION FOR INSTRUCTIONAL EFFECTIVENESS

The last decade has seen substantial growth in our understanding of what accounts for achievement in individual schools. Studies such as those conducted by the late Ron Edmonds tend to define achievement as pupil performance on standardized tests of reading and mathematical skills, not creativity nor critical thinking.[8] These studies suggest that coordination and management of the instructional program and a sense of shared values among students and staff are important to instructional effectiveness.

[8]Ronald Edmonds, "Programs of School Improvement," *Educational Leadership* 40, no. 1 (1982): 4–5; Wilbur Brookover and Lawrence Lezoth, *Changes in School Characteristics Coincident with Changes in School Achievement* (East Lansing: Institute for Research on Teaching, 1979).

Coordinating the Curriculum

The different aspects of the curriculum in effective schools (effective as defined by achievement tests) is carefully coordinated or "tightly coupled." School goals, classroom objectives and activities and measures of pupil performance are all aligned. Curriculum alignment has become the most popular way to improve test scores. Alignment consists of three steps: First, the essential skills to be taught are defined and the lists of skills are distributed to teachers. Second, test items for the essential skills are developed. In these tests the item format is the same as those found in the textbooks so that the skill is being measured, not the ability to handle a new format. A system for easily scoring the tests is developed and presented to teachers, principal, and district administrators. Teachers and the principal receive reports on student achievement for each grade level in the school. Teachers also receive a separate report for individual students.

Third, teachers must be certain to focus their teaching on the desired skills. To this end, teachers work in grade–level groups, discussing each skill and making sure they agree on what each objective means in terms of classroom instruction. Although all the skills are included in the curriculum, a small number of skills might receive special attention when prior results show the need for emphasis. Once priorities are set, groups of teachers plan instruction for the year, ensuring that adequate time and appropriate materials and methods are available. During the year, teachers monitor the program and meet to discuss how well plans are being carried out. Near the end of the year, teachers assess their accomplishments in teaching the skills, discuss problems and develop plans for improvement.

Tight-coupling requires instructional goals which are clear, public, and acceptable. Such a program must minimize differences in the treatment of students' allocated time to certain content, and expose all students to the same curriculum. It also means that the work of outside specialists—resource teachers, reading teachers, counselors—must support the efforts of the classroom teacher.

Although the integration of objectives, tests, and instruction may seem an obvious way to improve test scores, few schools have done it. Porter, for instance, found that the percentage of textbook topics covered by tests ranged from 14 to 29 percent, while the percent of tested topics covered by 20 or more exercises ranged from 21 to 50 percent.[9]

[9]Andrew Porter, "The Role of Testing in Effective Schools," *American Education* 19, no. 1 (1983): 9–12.

Shared Values

Effective schools have a strong sense of community with shared goals and high expectations for student and staff performance.[10] In a successful school more members of the teaching staff discuss their teaching. The teachers are organized as a team, making collective decisions about instructional matters for a common population of students. Shared values also follow from the teachers' acceptance of the need for continuous improvement through analysis, evaluation, and experimentation. A school with shared values is often characterized by (a) talk among teachers about *manipulative variables*—methods of teaching, materials—and *external variables*—pupil background, community attitudes; (b) frequent observations by teachers of each other's teaching; and (c) teachers working together planning, designing, and preparing teaching materials.

Effective Principals

Principals can contribute to the development of collegiality and continuous improvement in several ways: They can express clearly the expectation that all staff members are to be knowledgeable about teaching and to participate in activities for instructional improvement. Principals should themselves participate in instructional improvement activities and support such efforts by providing encouragement, time, and materials. For example, effective principals protect teachers who are trying curriculum innovations from competing demands and possible criticism.

Principals in successful schools tend to emphasize achievement, set instructional goals and performance standards for students. They are optimistic about the ability of students to meet goals. They are able to work well with others, manage conflict, and cope with ambiguity. Compared with less effective principals, they take more responsibility for instruction—observing teachers, discussing teaching problems, and protecting teachers from distractions.

Effective Classroom Practices

A number of research findings about effective classroom practices are consistent with conventional wisdom.[11] Highly successful teachers believe

[10]Patricia Ashton et al., *A Study of Teachers' Sense of Efficacy,* NIE Report 400-79-0075 (Gainesville, Fla.: University of Florida, 1982).

[11]David A. Squires et al., *Effective Schools and Classrooms: A Research Based Perspective* (Alexandria, Va.: ASCD, 1983).

in the importance of teaching particular curriculum content and accept responsibility for reteaching, if necessary, until all students acquire the material. They create an environment with clear goals and instructions, close supervision, and appropriate materials and activities. Effective teachers are less likely than ineffective teachers to transmit low expectations to low achievers.

Effective teachers are distinguished by their planning and organization. They move through activities at a good pace because their materials are prepared in advance; they do not have to backtrack or stop to consult a teacher's manual. They ignore minor distractions and deal with potentially serious problems without interrupting the flow of the lesson. Successful teachers give direct instruction—structuring the learning activities, giving detailed explanations, providing examples, and allowing for much student practice.

Effectiveness Research and Curriculum Policy

Caution must be exercised before translating research on effectiveness to curriculum policy. In the first place, most of the findings are only correlational, not causal. The fact that principals who concern themselves with instruction and students who try to accomplish clear learning goals are associated with high test scores may mask the underlying reasons for success. What is it in the school environment or training of the principal that makes it likely that the principal will be concerned with instruction in one school and not do so in a different school? How can teachers engage uninterested students in learning? The answers to such questions are more important than the mere association of an instructional variable with learning.

Further, many of the associations are misleading. The use of time in school, for example, has been often discussed in connection with teaching. However, there is evidence that the amount of time spent on a task by itself is meaningless.[12] We need to know how much time is needed and to consider time spent in relation to decisions on content, mode of instruction, and the students' willingness and ability to pay attention. In a well–organized school, trying to improve a time–on–task rate of 65 percent is probably constructive. But in a school where the average attendance is less than 70 percent and the school day characterized by disorder, more pressing issues than time on task should receive attention.

A serious limitation to the effectiveness studies is that they ignore

[12]Center for Social Organization of Schools, *Time on Task: A Research Review* (Baltimore: Center for the Social Organization of Schools, 1983).

achievement in important areas—creativity, desire for further learning, ability to deal with uncertainty. Standardized achievement tests (most of which are skills for reading and math) focus on known tasks for which there are known procedures for teaching. Those interested in good education must also attend to the problem of teaching complex concepts and a range of subject matters for which the teaching strategies are not known. Indeed, there are indicators that the focus upon mastery of isolated skills such as decoding in reading is detrimental to the attainment of higher level cognitive processes—comprehension and critical reading.[13] The heavy emphasis upon answering correctly may reduce curiosity and critical thinking in students. Investigators have found strong resistance from students as teachers make an effort to shift from routine or procedural tasks (teacher directed) to understanding tasks (student directed).[14]

Several implications follow from the findings of the effectiveness studies. The use of achievement test scores, profiles of school practices, needs assessment and other tight–coupling mechanisms may help the staff to identify a curriculum problem. Sources for proposed solutions should include the effectiveness literature as well as the best thinking of the staff itself. If a school is not successful in a certain area, the first place to look for reasons might be the amount of time each teacher is allocating to that content area. Once a solution is proposed, a plan outlining staff responsibilities and procedures for evaluating progress should be developed and put into effect.

Central administrators have several mechanisms for coordinating the curriculum. Districtwide testing programs can focus the curriculum on important goals. The practice of focusing on a limited set of goals and aligning these goals with objectives, content, materials, and tests is a powerful tool. However, efforts to coordinate the system from above are insufficient. Enlistment of the faculty in each school will be necessary because different circumstances exist at each site and because staffs need to develop shared values within each school. Principal and teachers must work together to plan, design, and prepare curriculum materials in order for a school to be effective. Rather than imposing school improvement plans from above, administrators should allow individual school faculties sufficient latitude to adapt new policies and practices to their situations, their unique problems. Along with autonomy, the

[13]W. C. Becker and R. A. Gersten, "A Follow-up of Follow-Through: The Later Effects of the Direct Instruction Model on Children in Fifth and Sixth Grades," *American Educational Research Journal* 19 (Spring 1982): 75–92.

[14]R. S. Brause and J. S. Mayher, "Teachers, Students, and Classroom Organizations," *Research in the Teaching of English* 16, no. 2 (1982): 131–148.

development of group norms requires time for the staff to talk with each other, observe each other, and engage in planning and preparation. There is need both for trust and the type of communication framework specified in Chapter 9.

As school superintendent, Larry Cuban successfully coordinated the curriculum at his school. However, he also recognized that the concentration on academic achievement and the coordination of the organization with this goal resulted in undesirable consequences.[15] There was a press toward standardization, a uniform curriculum, and adoption of the same materials for each class in a grade level. (Fewer materials were appropriate for the range of individual differences in each of these grade levels.) Teachers tended to assume that there was a single best way of teaching (usually involving lecturing, recitation, and whole-group instruction). Teaching seemed to be focused on tests rather than on teaching students to think. There was teaching to the test and forgetting about responsibility for dealing with such serious matters as being sensitive to the welfare of others.

In brief, tightly-coupled procedures narrowly focused on standardized tests are a limited answer to the achievement of the broader and more complex goals of education. Major improvement in academic work will depend on learning (a) to teach higher order tasks that may not lend themselves to direct instruction; (b) to present difficult material so that slower students will learn it; (c) to ensure that subject matter is meaningful to teachers and students, not just material to be memorized for tests.

CONCLUDING COMMENTS

There is a need for more coherent school programs. Reform by addition—costly innovations and courses for special interest groups—is not as effective as improving the curriculum by setting priorities, focusing on certain subject matter, and abolishing the tracking system in favor of a common core of knowledge. Guidelines have been presented in this chapter for establishing common purposes and making hard choices about what *not* to teach.

As the purposes of schooling change, so must organizational arrangements. When personal interests and social concerns are foremost, the curriculum features flexible scheduling, electives, and minicourses. As the mode turns to challenging students in basic subjects, fewer electives

---

[15]Larry Cuban, "Effective Schools: A Friendly but Cautionary Note," Phi Delta Kappan 64, no. 10 (June 1983): 695–7.

are offered and the requirements for mathematics, science, and English are strengthened. Remedialism and pluralism, however, have not disappeared. Administrators often arrange through networks, magnet schools, and schools within schools to help students with special needs even amidst widespread standardization.

Finally, effective schools are characterized by shared values among staff and students. Curriculum development activities within local schools should be conducted and supported in the interest of developing shared values. Further, magnet schools, schools in which parents, teachers, and students choose the curriculum that best represents their values, are likely to be effective schools. Institutions that offer different curriculums are welcome safeguards against narrowly conceived educational ends.

QUESTIONS

1. There is much interest in ensuring that all students have equal access to knowledge of mathematics, science, literature and language, social studies, the arts, and the vocations. How does the practice of tracking students on the basis of achievement and ability deny some students access to these domains? Should a tracking system that divides students into academic and vocational programs be abolished in favor of a core program that allows flexibility for all students in both work and further education?

2. The National Commission on Educational Excellence gives highest priority to mathematics and science. The report by the Carnegie Foundation for the Advancement of Teaching recommends strengthening the curriculum by emphasizing English language proficiency—especially writing. Try applying the following three criteria to the two sets of recommendations:
   a. Frequency of use—teach that subject matter which everyone must use regularly and which requires formal instruction.
   b. Flexibility—select subject matter that can function in the greatest variety of situations.
   c. Liberal education—select subject matter which best promotes the ideals of humanity.

3. Consider an educational situation familiar to you and describe whether the following mechanisms were used in order to focus the curriculum: a testing program aimed at specific goals; a school-wide plan for educational goals, materials, methods as well as for policies of student promotion and student achievement.

4. Shared educational values among administrators, parents, teachers, and students are important to the success of the school. What are some ways to foster shared values in a local school?

5. How will tests, textbooks, school and classroom organization have to

change if understanding, innovation, and creativity are to become the educational target rather than rote tasks?

SELECTED REFERENCES

Cohen, Michael. "Instructional, Management, and Social Conditions in Effective Schools." American Educational Finance Association Yearbook. In *School Finance and School Improvement: Linkages in the 1980s,* eds. Allan Odden and L. Dean Webb (New York: Ballinger, 1983).

Doyle, Walter. "Academic Work," *Review of Educational Research* 53, no. 2 (Summer 1983): 159–199.

Goodlad, John. *A Place Called School.* New York: McGraw-Hill, 1983.

Squires, David A., et al. *Effective Schools and Classrooms: A Research-Based Perspective.* Alexandria, Va.: ASCD, 1983.

9 / IMPLEMENTING CURRICULUM CHANGE

The purpose of this chapter is to introduce several approaches for bringing about curriculum change. The strengths and weaknesses of the approaches are also presented. This chapter provides a perspective on such serious issues as whether curriculum change should start with the teacher, with the administrator, with education committees, or professional reformers at local, state, and federal levels. It emphasizes the importance of considering a wide range of conditions in implementing curriculum change, of matching innovation with the realities of the school, teachers' perspectives and abilities, and the prevailing social climate.

One might think that teachers would welcome the chance to formulate a curriculum for their classrooms. However, teachers are often reluctant to develop a curriculum and put it into practice for several reasons. They are constrained by lack of time and heavy teaching loads, and they might perceive a resistance to change from parents, peers, or a principal. Even if others are not actually opposed to teachers implementing a new curriculum, the anticipation of resistance might be enough to preclude innovation. Most curriculum innovations, further, do not affect a single classroom, but an entire school or school district. Without the means for developing shared norms and goals, teachers are more interested in planning for their own classroom rather than for the entire school or school district. Hence, it is difficult to effect a school system's curriculum revision through teacher initiation.

Administrators, on the other hand, often feel helpless in initiating a new curriculum, finding it difficult to persuade staff and others to respond enthusiastically and to carry out the proposed changes. It is not easy to control the classroom when one is outside it. Even when administrators have money to stimulate curriculum improvement, the results are frequently insignificant.

Those who develop curriculum at the state or national level also run into problems. Their first challenge is getting the curriculum adopted. They must clear the political hurdles of textbook committees, curriculum commissions, boards of education, and other groups so that the curriculum can be made available to teachers. Their next, and even larger, challenge is ensuring that their curricula are properly put into effect in the schools. Teachers do not always have clear-cut ideas about the requirements for enacting the curriculum innovations of others. At best, the innovations are only partially implemented. The novel features often are blunted in the effort to twist the innovation into familiar ways of doing things. Top-down planning generally fails because it does not generate the staff commitment necessary for success and the planning does not take into account the special knowledge and suggestions of those who will be responsible for implementing the curriculum.

What understanding and practical suggestions are available to help those who would implement curriculum changes? Some believe that theories of educational change give fresh interpretations of how to achieve it while others distrust solutions, models, and designs for change because they believe these strategies do not correspond with the reality in the schools. Rather than taking a single position on the argument over the need for theories of change or prescriptions for it, we will present both.

CONCEPTUALIZATIONS OF THE CHANGE PROCESS

Kinds of Changes and Difficulties in Implementing Each

Scientists who interpret the change process have found it useful to look at five kinds of change.

1. *Substitution.* One element may be substituted for another already present. Substituting a new textbook for an old one is an example. This kind of change is readily made.
2. *Alteration.* Alteration occurs when a change is introduced into existing material in the hope that it will appear minor and thus be readily adopted. The curriculum person who modifies the activities accompanying a popular textbook in the interest of student initiative and independence as opposed to student dependency is engaging in alteration. Such changes are easily made but may lead to unanticipated consequences. For example, altered activities may be accepted but the initiative and independence may hamper other classroom objectives.
3. *Perturbations.* These irritating changes are disruptive, but teachers can adjust to them within a fairly short time. Most teachers, for instance, can quite easily make allowances for a change in scheduling of classes and the length of time allowed for teaching.
4. *Restructuring changes.* These changes lead to modification of the sys-

tem itself. Decentralization and new concepts of the teaching role
are examples of restructuring. When students and parents begin
to participate in selecting objectives and designing learning opportunities, there is a change in the system.
5. *Value orientation changes.* These are shifts in the fundamental value
   orientations of participants. When a school begins to be staffed
   with new teachers who value student personal growth or social
   reconstruction more than academic achievement, value orientations are changed.

Curriculum workers will find these conceptualizations useful
in making decisions regarding the requirements for implementing
particular innovations. Before introducing a change, they should classify
it and recognize the probable difficulty and consequences. Such
anticipation will facilitate planning of the resources necessary to
effect the change. Indeed, in some cases, one may decide that the change
should not be undertaken.

SOCIOLOGICAL FINDINGS ABOUT CHANGE

Sociologists study stability and changes in organizations. They have
found that both formal and informal channels of communication are
features of curriculum change. They tell us that most curriculum innovations in a school are borrowed rather than invented. The borrowing
may take the form of direct imitation or the importation of new personnel.
The former is exemplified by those who visit another school or district
to see an innovation, such as a new writing program and subsequently
start a similar one, perhaps avoiding many of the errors and costs
associated with the initial development. Observation of results in classroom situations and the exchange of opinions with fellow teachers are
also important in getting teachers to change, particularly when the
validity of information is in doubt. Importing occurs when a group of
persons from a subculture—for example, minority group members not
previously represented—become members of the staff.

For teachers, there is little financial incentive for accepting an innovation. Indeed, disadvantages are often associated with such acceptance.
The teacher might have to work longer hours in order to make the
change and might attract criticism from those who are opposed to it. It is
much more comfortable and a lot safer to be conventional most of the
time. It is remarkable that many teachers are as open to innovation as

they are, considering the basic reward system which discourages risk taking, experimentation, and responsiveness to some pupils.

School administrators are viewed by sociologists as persons in the middle, with little possibility of being primary advocates for major curriculum change. In the formal organization, school administrators must maintain equilibrium among different forces. They cannot alienate significant segments of the public and remain in charge. Thus, institutional change cannot rest mainly with the administrator. To say that administrators may not be major advocates is not to say that they may not be key figures in innovation, however. On the contrary, when they are both aware of and sympathetic to a change, the innovation tends to prosper. When administrators are uninformed, apathetic, or hostile, an innovation tends to remain outside the school. Implementation of new curriculum is directly related to immediate administrator support. Teachers alone cannot innovate and implement curriculum. Department and grade level faculty, possibly under the direction of a chairperson or team leader and operating with the backing of the principal, often are influential.

One problem in effecting change is the conflict between the school organization and its external environment. Often, for example, tension arises between those who seek to maintain the values of the school staff and those who would respond to the conflicting values of a changing community. A somewhat different situation arises when some want the curriculum to be more responsive to local concerns than to larger relevant social issues. Though there is vigorous interest in local autonomy over curriculum matters, wider sociocultural problems also receive attention and can further be a source of conflict.

Major curriculum decisions are being made at the national level relating, for example, to bilingual education, early childhood education, and special education. Few persons would deny that we should be sensitive to national interests and to the larger society. Professional reformers supported by federal and foundation funding have raised the consciousness of local communities and influenced curriculum change in the interests of the non-English-speaking, handicapped, and other students. Yet the concept of the school as a community operation is not dead. Most of us sympathize with those who want to see local lay participation in curriculum planning. The school has been one of the few institutions in which a scattered public could recognize itself and express its interests. Because citizens feel remote from many civic, national, and international affairs, it is desirable to preserve those neighborly vehicles by which the individual can influence a crucial public matter. Further, such participation makes possible the innovations and creations that are essential in implementing more general plans. The task, therefore, is to find a way to interest the community in curriculum change without jeopardizing the right of pupils to acquire the knowledge, skills, and attitudes necessary for participation in a larger world.

Groups and individuals in the community can also aid in devising supplementary learning situations. They can plan opportunities out of school in which pupils can apply the intellectual skills being taught and can attack those conditions shown to be detrimental to the instructional program. There is, however, a danger that in collaborating with the community, administrators will make incidental functions dominant and respond to pressures that attenuate the systematic organization of learning.

Conditions Conducive to Change

Curriculum change is most likely to occur when one or more of the following conditions exist:

1. A prevailing social change is in the same direction as the proposed change. When the nation is in technological competition, for instance, it is easier to introduce programs in computer literacy than programs for personal enrichment.
2. There is imbalance in the traditional power structure. The use of "student power" in the late '60s was connected with the offering of new high school and college courses appealing to student interests.
3. A crisis develops in a time of change. When California community colleges met severe economic cuts in 1983, vocational programs were eliminated but not academic courses leading to more advanced education.
4. Faculty and administrators see the change as beneficial to their own interests. Reading specialists, for example, quickly adopt procedures and terms that sound scientific so that their innovations are more likely to be introduced. Their terms—diagnosis, remediation, intervention—often associate teaching with medical practice.
5. A change in the physical arrangements of the institution—a new facility, for example—offers the opportunity to rethink curriculum offerings.

Although any one of the five conditions may be sufficient for introducing a curriculum change, the simultaneous existence of several of the conditions signals a propitious time for introducing change.

Introducing New Materials into the Classroom

Ronald Lippitt long ago gave us a model that has proven effective in introducing new materials and activities.[1] Lippitt is one of the few to show the importance of involving pupils in the change and to specify the aspects that lead to greater teacher acceptance and use of innovations. If the following guidelines for curriculum committees were followed, our schools would be using more effective curriculum materials.

Student Use of New Material. The decisions students make about their involvement with a new curriculum are the most crucial in the process of curriculum change. Such decisions are determined by *internal supports.* If students perceive the learning opportunity as relevant to their values, interests, and curiosities and they receive feedback from their responses, they are more likely to learn from the material and experience the excitement of active search and discovery. Other determinants of student involvement are *external supports.* The innovator must take into account peer norms about student participation and cooperation in working with the teacher. Teachers also need to be aware of peer norms and to be willing to share leadership with peer leaders if pupils are to become involved. Also, the extent of collaboration of parents and other adults in the community will influence student involvement with the changed curriculum.

Teacher Use of New Material. In order to get teachers to use the new curriculum, it is recommended that the curriculum leader first involve the teacher in the review, evaluation, and exploration of the new materials. This means asking teachers to apply criteria for the evaluation of learning opportunities and objectives. Second, the teacher should have freedom to explore the new skills needed for utilizing the curriculum material, to learn new concepts and new techniques, and to collaborate with colleagues in sharing practices and learning together. Third, the curriculum changes must equip teachers with the tools for observing their classes' responses and for student involvement in adapting the curriculum.

Adoption of New Material. A curriculum committee's adoption decision should include involvement of appropriate decision makers in a review of the alternatives. There should be a review of the criteria to be used in making the decision and a plan to test alternatives, to judge feasibility,

[1]Ronald Lippitt, "Processes of Curriculum Change," Curriculum Change: Direction and Process *(Washington, D.C.: ASCD, 1966): pp. 43–59.*

and to learn about the learners' responses to the material and method. Learners should be involved in evaluating the new materials. It is important that adoption committees analyze the needs for staff development that would follow if the materials were adopted.

The Search for Curriculum Innovations. In searching for new ideas, curriculum planners should start with the *home school,* recognizing the creative curricula hidden within the school community. Next, planners should consider *neighboring school systems.* They should break down the barriers that keep neighbors from sharing. Finally, curriculum workers should get information regarding promising innovations. Clearing house procedures for identifying creative innovations should be used to obtain information. The National Bank of Validated Programs available through the U.S. Department of Education, The National Diffusion Network, and the report of the Council for Educational Research and Development are examples of such sources. Also, one should ask innovators about their latest experiments, discoveries, failures, problems, and the skills needed to carry out changes in curriculum.

Distribution of New Curriculum. Diffusion of curriculum rests heavily on the staff development available for the teachers. Teachers must have the opportunity to learn the skills for using the new curriculum. They should also have the chance to get excited about new materials and to adapt them.

Development of New Materials. New material may be developed through the work of a team in a school system, the creative efforts of a single teacher, or the project staff of a research and development center. Curriculum development requires identifying priority objectives and core units of knowledge, and relating content to experience, interests, and competence of learners. Teachers should be helped to understand and use the resources skillfully and to evaluate the materials so that the curriculum may continue to improve.

STRATEGIES FOR CHANGE

The level at which a proposed change originates—federal, state, district, school, classroom—determines the strategy for change. Top-down strategies are associated with mandates from the federal and state governments—desegregation, programs for the handicapped and non-English speakers, competency testing, and required course offerings. The implementation of districtwide curriculum policies about goals, content, materials, and testing also employ these strategies. Top-down strategies range from merely issuing the decree and requiring accountability reports or visits, to concern about what the school will require for staff development, materials and other support to implement the mandate.

Bottom-up strategies are found when the local school is the origin of change, the faculty itself examines the school's problems, considers alternatives, and takes action to better the situation.

Top-Down Strategies

Top-down strategies are technological. Improvement is sought by training teachers new techniques and holding them accountable for following these techniques. A change in some part of the technology of the school—a testing program, computers, mastery learning—is the most likely element open to immediate influence from outside the school. However, unless other elements of the school—the teachers' own views of what education should be or the norms of the school—are compatible with the innovation, a technological change is likely to be circumvented or temporary. A researcher was once puzzled in trying to understand a school's curriculum plan. Although there seemed to be careful monitoring of pupil progress, well-stated goals, and reams of paper showing compliance with the mandated program, his own observation of the daily life in the school revealed qualities very different from those in the accountability plan. Only when teachers privately commented, "Oh, you're talking about our official plan—the one we prepared for funding and accreditation—not our real one," did he understand. Often the return to a previous equilibrium follows an attempt to change some part of the technology of the school.

Adoption Strategy

The adoption or research and development (R and D) model has been popular among those concerned with implementing curriculum throughout a region or nation. The strategy takes programs, research, and projects from universities, regional laboratories, and other institutions and disseminates it as an innovative package of material or product. Effective diffusion requires that the consumers be aware of potential benefits and usefulness of the innovation. Influential persons in the schools must be convinced that the innovation will strengthen the school.

The strategy makes use of an aide who first performs the role of salesperson and later that of trainer teaching key school personnel about the program so that they can train others—the "multiplier effect." The innovator, together with school leaders, monitors and assists with problems that arise during initial installation.

Criticism of the adoption model centers on its lack of attention to political factors that might interfere with acceptance. A teachers' union, for example, might oppose the change because of increased paperwork. Mammoth curriculum innovations often leave their advocates frustrated. The planned treatments become distorted, lacking in standardization when used by teachers and pupils with different backgrounds. Variation between schools often wipe out any noticeable effect of the innovation, making it difficult to say with certainty that the change is valuable.

Mutual Adaptation and Multiple Element Strategies

Efforts to improve the adoptive model have been made. Richard Schutz, for example, at the Southwest Regional Laboratory revised the R and D strategy by giving more attention to political, social, and economic factors. He introduced a new era in which the researcher and developer conduct participatory activity *with* the school community rather than provide answers *for* the school community.[2]

The newer top-down strategies try to overcome the limitation of "single element change by acting upon three organizational elements— social norms, teacher perceptions, and the technology to be introduced." Susan Loucks and Ann Lieberman, for example, who have long been engaged in curriculum implementation, employ three key concepts in addressing teacher perception and the technology:[3]

Developmentalism. Developmentalism refers to the way teachers change as they confront new ideas. It means giving different kinds of help to teachers at different stages in the change process. As teachers implement new curriculum, they change in their feelings about the new ideas. At first, they are self-oriented—"Can I do it?" "What will I have to do differently?" Later they are more task-oriented—"It takes so long to prepare." And still later, after mastering the new procedure, they focus on the impact of the curriculum—"Is this new curriculum working well with all my students?" "Are there ways I can make it better?"

One implication of developmentalism in effecting change is to follow

[2]Richard E. Schutz, "Where We've Been, Where We Are, and Where We're Going in Educational R and D," *Educational Researcher* 8, no. 8 (September 1979): 6–24.

[3]Susan F. Loucks and Ann Lieberman, "Curriculum Implementation," in *Fundamental Curriculum Decisions,* ASCD Yearbook, ed. F. W. English. (Alexandria, Va.: ASCD, 1983): pp. 126–141.

a sequence in ordering training activities. First, focus on personal concerns, clarifying expectations and planning for individual input and consultation. Second, attend to management concerns, modeling and giving hands-on training, answering questions, and third, reflect on the impact of the innovation and how to improve upon it.

Participation. Participation is related to the need for understanding how teachers see their work. When teachers participate in decision making during the process of implementation, there is a greater chance of success. Trust between those encouraging the innovation—superintendent, principal—is a necessary starting point. Peer demonstrations, observation of others, and team planning are all forms of participation that contribute to a mutual adaptation to a change.

Support. Different kinds of support are needed at various times of the implementation process. Material support is of primary importance initially. Human support—ensuring that parents, administrators, peers, students view the change favorably—is very important at all stages. Time for teachers to plan, confer, demonstrate, critique, and revise is also critical. Three to five years must be allowed for the implementation of a complex innovation. One year may be needed to learn what innovation is appropriate and to assess what changes it would bring in a particular school. Teachers need to learn whose help is required and what skills are to be acquired. Curriculum change will require organizational changes, particularly in the staff and students. The shift in roles is often difficult for both. For example, I once visited a classroom where a teacher was trying to implement a curriculum that required interaction among pupils. The furniture had been arranged to accommodate the small group work demanded by the new materials. The teacher, however, had not recognized the need for changing from a didactic role to a resource role. Consequently, the teacher was frustrated in ability to control the attention of pupils working in groups with the new materials.

Bottom-Up Strategies

Bottom-up strategies of change start locally. They may either attempt to get a school staff to look at its problems and to consider options as a means of bringing about innovation in the curriculum or they may start with individual teacher-innovators who contact other teachers, forming teacher-to-teacher networks of change. Examples of bottom-up strategies follow:

The Integrative Development Strategy

The strategy in the integrative development model is to handle the immediate concerns of teachers and then move out of the classroom, perhaps even to reorganize the school system. An assumption underlying this approach is that a climate for eliminating clouded vision and fears must accompany change. The model encourages involvement by starting with the concerns teachers face. The first step in the strategy is to help teachers identify their problems. The problems selected, however, should be within the competence of the teacher. The second step is to study the cause of the difficulties. Using the analysis of the teachers' data, the curriculum leader introduces the teachers to new insights and abilities. The integration of theory with the analysis of problems stimulates bolder departures and the transition of general ideas into practice.

A sequential process begins as faculties cope with change. First, people talk about the possibility of bringing about change. Expectations rise and there is uneasiness as teachers feel the pressure to act. Second, some teachers begin to take action. Third, justification for the new departure brings: "Why was I doing this?" "Is the new system better than what I did before?" Fourth, problems with the innovation arise and teachers question the basic assumptions of the program: "What is the relevancy of the program for my students?" "Is the program consistent with educational goals?"

Difficulties with the approach include a lack of time and expertise on the innovator's part both to handle human relations and to relate the theory to the specific problems each situation develops in adapting the innovations. Changes in teacher attitudes and skills take time. An experimental attitude is especially slow to develop at first. Also, there are teachers who feel insecure about engaging in group problem solving. To lessen such problems, productive groups should be composed of persons with good social skills and expertise in several areas: the curriculum, the principles of learning, the realities of the classroom, pertinent subject matter, inquiry skills, and interpersonal relations.

Teacher as an Agent of Change

The teacher as an agent of change was proposed long ago by Hilda Taba.[4] She wanted curriculum making to start by planning specific units of instruction. The results of experimentation with these units would provide a basis for a general design to be created later.

[4]Hilda Taba, *Curriculum Development—Theory and Practice* (New York: Harcourt, Brace and World, 1962).

A recent demonstration of the value of teacher as an agent of change is found in IMPACT II, an experimental teacher-to-teacher network.[5] The Exxon Education Foundation created a program by which teachers who wanted to refine classroom innovations could receive "developer" grants of $300. Other teachers who would try out the developer's innovations could apply for "replicator" grants of $200. About 500 grants were made. Each developer chose a particular innovation to refine; the only restriction was that the project must focus on classroom instruction. Informal interchanges were made among teachers through the network. Teachers met other teachers, had opportunity to be trained and to train others, and the chance to visit other schools and be visited. Publishing their ideas, receiving college credit, and gaining recognition were important factors in the success of the program. The evaluation of this program was positive. There were significant changes in the instructional procedures after participation in the program; the work of the teachers was disseminated and attitudes toward teaching improved.

Suggestions for Successful Implementation

Newer views on staff development, along with modified organizational and role expectations, are among the best answers to curriculum implementation. Curriculum innovations that rely heavily on technology tend to be short lived. Unlike business or industry, which seek to eliminate the need for human services, education is a labor intensive field that requires teachers more than machines. Hence, a key to educational change must include staff development.

Staff development is now a central focus in successful curriculum implementation. As a result of recent studies, staff development is taking the following directions.[6]

Intensive *staff development* rather than single one-day workshops is an important strategy. Staff development is seen as part of curriculum planning tied to a school site. The principal serves as the instructional leader, strengthening the school curriculum by clearly encouraging teachers to take responsibility for their professional growth. *Staff training*

[5]Dale Mann, "The Impact of IMPACT II," *Phi Delta Kappan* 67, no. 9 (May 1982): 612–615.

[6]Milbrey W. McLaughlin and David D. Marsh, "Staff Development and School Changes," in *Staff Development,* eds. Ann Lieberman and Lynne Miller (New York: Teachers College, Columbia University, 1979), pp. 69–94; and Michael Fullan and Alan Pomfret, "Research on Curriculum and Instruction Implementation," *Review of Educational Research* 47, no. 2 (Winter 1977): 335–97.

activities are skill specific, such as instruction in carrying out a new reading program or introducing new mathematical material. This contrasts with many old in-service programs where training activities were isolated from the teachers' day-to-day responsibilities, thus having little impact. There are also *support activities*. In order that staff training results in more than transient effects, the contributions of staff training must be reinforced and extended through: (1) classroom assistance by resource personnel and outside consultants (provided these resource persons are perceived by teachers as being helpful), and (2) project meetings whereby teachers learn to adapt the new curriculum to the realities of the particular school and classroom. In addition to feedback between users and consultants, peer discussions seem to be vital for working through the problems of innovation.

Curriculum innovation may require a change in the principal's role. Teachers follow a new curriculum more closely when the principal plays an active role in the implementation; a new curriculum does not flourish when the principal remains in an office, verbalizes support, and lets the teachers struggle with the problems.

Active involvement of the teachers in the development process—in developing guides and materials—is more important in persuading teachers to implement plans than their participation on the curriculum committees that decide on the plans. The roles of students and parents as decision makers in relation to the degree of implementation have been largely unstudied.

Central policymakers should emphasize programs with wide support and provide a base for the local development of the specific forms of implementation. Social experimentation should be encouraged during implementation to develop variants that are more appropriate in particular circumstances.

We should recognize that while professional reformers are rewarded for proposing controversial, innovative curriculum changes, school practitioners are usually rewarded for innovations that promote social stability. Therefore, professional reformers are likely to be frustrated in their efforts to persuade schools to implement controversial curriculum.

In order to illuminate the problems that come with curriculum implementation, one need only reflect on these considerations: What is the desirable number of new curriculum installations for any one year? What should be the timing of installations and requisite experience of the staff? Must there be agreement on humanistic, technological, and subject matter orientations? What relations between administrators and teachers are necessary? In what way does a school district's history of innovation efforts influence the decision to innovate?

CONCLUDING COMMENTS

This chapter raises a number of issues. One issue arises in the approach to innovative curriculum: should it be from the teacher-student viewpoint, the developer's orientation toward the product, or the professional reformers? Recommendations that call for the involvement of students, parents, and community members in school curriculum development, staff problem–solving approaches, and the teacher as an agent of change favor one side of the issue. The manipulation of organization, social structure, competency-based approaches, and R and D adoption models favor the other side. Reformers and R and D developers want teachers to implement a focused curriculum in predetermined ways, although teachers may advise and indicate the factors that must be attended to in order to achieve objectives of a specific plan. Those with a teacher-student perspective assume that users should at least have a hand in deciding what innovations to implement and how to implement them.

Tension develops between those external to the school who would impose innovations that foster greater rationality in the curriculum and those who see merit in individual teachers acting responsibly, making their curriculum decisions in the best interests of their students. One answer is to employ strategies of change that attempt to match curriculum innovations to the school and have the faculties adapt the innovation to their local conditions. Another answer might be to help teachers create a new social climate that will support the change.

A second issue relates to the value of theories in guiding the implementation process. Disenchantment with a single model of change probably rests on the fact that most settings for curriculum implementation are for specific situations. In one case, the social environment or policy may be crucial in effecting the change. In another, group dynamics or individual personalities may be more important. If such differences exist, then broadly conceived models of change and histories of innovations should be in the curriculum specialist's repertoire.

Finally, the frequent triviality and faddish nature of curriculum changes effected from both outside and inside the school indicate the continuous need to consider the value of proposed innovations. Decision makers should be sure that a proposed curriculum will best serve a specified group of learners or aid general education; contribute to interpretive or applied purposes; be relevant to the world the students will live in when they finish school; and relate to the other domains of knowledge that are supposed to be provided by the school experience.

QUESTIONS

1. Preparing effective curriculum materials costs much money. Without broad dissemination, the impact of the materials is minimal. What are the implications of these facts for curriculum development?
2. Give examples for each of the following kinds of curriculum changes: substitution, alteration, restructuring of the system, value orientation.
3. Consider the relative strengths and weaknesses of the R and D adoption model and the integrative development model of curriculum change. Can you indicate how both models can be used together or when one or the other model might be more useful?
4. What kinds of curriculum changes do you think can best occur at national, state, district, school, and classroom levels?
5. Consider the curriculum in a situation familiar to you. How would you like to see this curriculum changed? How would you try to bring about the desired change?
6. Describe a situation where one or more of the following conditions exist: a social climate conducive to change, an imbalance in the power structure, a crisis, an element of self-interest, or a facilities modification. Be specific about the condition. What kind of curriculum change could be successfully implemented in view of the condition(s) described?

SELECTED REFERENCES

Fullan, Michael and Pomfret, Alan. "Research in Curriculum and Instruction Implementation." *Review of Educational Research* 47, no. 1 (Winter 1977): 335–97.

Fullan, Michael. *Implementing Educational Change: Progress at Last.* ERIC ED 221540. Washington, D.C.: National Institute of Education, 1982.

Lieberman, Ann. "Curriculum Change: Promise and Practice." *Theory Into Practice* 22, no. 3 (Summer 1983).

10 / EVALUATING THE CURRICULUM

Curriculum evaluation generates a host of responses. Some fear the power and control it might give central authorities. Local communities have been dismayed by those in government who seem to offer autonomy, yet still demand that the school system be evaluated by standardized tests. Others are reassured by the evaluations. People often expect that evaluation will solve many pressing problems—the public who demand accountability, the decision maker who chooses curriculum alternatives, the developer who needs to know where and how to improve the curriculum product, and the teacher who is concerned about the effect of learning opportunities on individual students all look to evaluation for their answers.

The field of evaluation is full of different views about the purposes of evaluation and how it is to be carried out. Humanists, for example, argue that measurable outcomes form an insufficient basis for determining the quality of learning opportunities. They believe it simplistic to measure higher mental functioning, knowledge of self, and other life-long pursuits at the end of the school year. Curiously, however, they perceive no difficulty in evaluating the classroom environment. For them, the learning experience is important in itself, not just a rehearsal whose value will be known only on future performance. Technologists, on the other hand, perceive evaluation as a set of verified guidelines for practice. They believe that if curriculum workers use these procedures, essential decisions regarding what and how to teach will be more warranted.

David Hamilton has summarized the ideas and events in curriculum evaluation during the past 150 years, illuminating its relatively unchanging features.[1] According to him, curriculum evaluation falls within the sphere of practical morality. As such, it responds to both the ethical question, "What

[1]David Hamilton, "Making Sense of Curriculum Evaluation: Continuities and Discontinuities in an Educational Idea," in *Review of Research in Education*, ed. Lee S. Schulman (Itasca, Ill.: F. E. Peacock Publishers, 1979), pp. 318–49.

should we do?" and the empirical question, "What can we do?" He recognizes, too, that the importance of evaluation is heightened by social change and politics. Governments make evaluation compulsory, and curriculum evaluation can be seen as part of the struggle by different interest groups—educationalists, teachers, administrators, industrialists—to gain control over the forces that shape the practice of schooling. When more than one person is involved in the selection of criteria for use in an evaluation, agreement cannot be assumed.

Recently, debate has begun over the conduct of curriculum evaluation and over the particular evaluation model to be used. Technologists use *consensus* models and regard evaluation as a technical accomplishment—the demonstration of a connection between what is and what all agree ought to be. They require a consensus on educational goals and on the rules of evidence. If all agree on the ends, the selection and evaluation of appropriate means are only technical problems for them. In reality, technologists have been most active in determining achievement in basic skills and academic knowledge.

Social reconstructionists and humanists, however, have a *pluralistic* view of evaluation. This view holds that evaluators should be sensitive to the different values of program participants and should shift the judgment away from the evaluator to the participants. As evaluators, pluralists tend to base their evaluations more on program activity than on program intent and to accept anecdotal accounts and other naturalistic data rather than numerical data and experimental designs. For them, evaluation is an unfinished blueprint that can point out problems, not solutions. They are more concerned that the evaluation will be fair to all parties than in its effectiveness as measured by, say, changes in test scores. Hence, those with a pluralistic bent advocate handing over control of an evaluation to those who have to live with the consequences and having it conducted *by* the participants rather than *for* the participants.

This chapter shows how to match specific evaluation procedures with specific curriculum decisions, such as how to improve a course, how to decide which program should continue, and how to assess the long-term effects of the curriculum. A major issue raised is whether curriculum evaluation is best served by classical research models and experts in measurement or by adaptable procedures in which students and teachers judge their own curriculum.

In addition to offering information about a number of evaluation techniques, the chapter covers common errors that prejudice evaluative studies and make it difficult to judge the relative effects of different programs. After studying the material, students should be able to take a personal stand regarding controversial technical issues on the role and form of objectives used in evaluation, the value of criterion-referenced and norm-referenced tests, and evaluation and invasion of privacy.

MODELS FOR EVALUATION

Consensus Models

In a general sense, curriculum evaluation to a technologist is an attempt to throw light on two questions: (1) Do planned learning opportunities, programs, courses, and activities as developed and organized actually produce desired results? and (2) How can the curriculum offerings best be improved? These general questions and the procedures for answering them translate a little differently at macro levels (for example, evaluating the citywide results from several alternative reading programs) than at micro levels (evaluating the effect of a teacher's instructional plans for achieving course objectives). Classroom teachers often have an additional set of evaluation questions to guide them in making decisions about individuals:

1. *Placement.* At which level of learning should the learner be placed in order to challenge but not frustrate?
2. *Mastery.* Has the learner acquired enough competency to succeed in the next level?
3. *Diagnosis.* What particular difficulty is this learner experiencing?

Decisions and Evaluative Techniques. If evaluation is to provide information useful to decision makers, evaluative models should be chosen in light of the kind of decisions to be made. In this connection, a useful distinction can be made between formative and summative evaluation. Formative evaluation is undertaken to improve an existing program. Hence, the evaluation must provide frequent detailed and specific information to guide the program developers. Summative evaluation is done to assess the effect of a completed program. It provides information to use in deciding whether to continue, discontinue, or disseminate the program. Summative evaluation is frequently undertaken in order to decide which one of several competing programs or materials is best.

Guidelines for conducting formative evaluation have been given by Lee J. Cronbach in a classic article treating *course improvement* through evaluation. The following prescriptions are among the most important:

1. Seek data regarding changes produced in pupils by the course.
2. Look for multidimensional outcomes and map out the effects of the course along these dimensions separately.
3. Identify aspects of the course in which revisions are desirable.
4. Collect evidence midway in curriculum development, while the course is still fluid.

5. Try to find out how the course produces its effect and what factors influence its effectiveness. You may find that the teacher's attitude toward the learning opportunity is more important than the opportunity itself.
6. During trial stages, use the teacher's informal reports of observed pupil behavior in aspects of the course.
7. Make more systematic observations only after the more obvious flaws in the early stages have been dealt with.
8. Make a process study of events taking place in the classroom and use proficiency and attitude measures to reveal changes in pupils.
9. Observe several results of the new program ranging far beyond the content of the curriculum itself—attitudes, general understanding, aptitude for further learning, and so forth.[2]

Formative evaluation does not require that all pupils answer the same questions. Rather, as many questions as possible should be given, each to a different sample of pupils. Follow-up studies to elicit opinions regarding the ultimate educational contributions of the course are of minor value in improving the course because they are too far removed in time.

Summative evaluation has several purposes. One purpose is to select from several competing curriculum programs or projects those which should continue and those which are ineffective. To this end, an experimental design is highly desirable. James Popham has illustrated such designs.[3] There is, for example, the *pretest/posttest control group design*. As the design's name suggests, students are pretested on whatever dimensions are sought from the programs. Then, after receiving instruction, students in each of the competing programs are tested for their status on a common set of objectives for which each program claims superiority. The posttest used must not be biased in favor of one program's objectives. Objectives important to others, but not those of the designers of a particular program, can also be assessed.

The students are assigned to the programs randomly so that each student has an equal chance to be assigned to any one of them. Differences in the performance of students may be attributed to differences in the programs. However, evaluators may not always know whether the respective programs were carried out as planned. It is desirable to try each of the programs in many settings, since the experimental unit for analysis is likely to be schools or classrooms, not pupils. Only in experi-

---

[2]Lee J. Cronbach, "Course Improvement Through Evaluation," *Teachers College Record* 64, no. 3 (May 1963): 672–83.

[3]W. James Popham, *Educational Evaluation* (Englewood Cliffs, N.J.: Prentice-Hall, 1975).

ments in which the pupils in the same classrooms receive different programs can the pupil be the unit of analysis.

Evaluators should not allow ideas about what must happen in a perfect evaluation to discourage them; they should remember that there have been no perfect evaluations. When faced with frustrations such as student absenteeism or the failure to give tests they should remember that the curriculum evaluator is only responsible for providing the best information possible under existing circumstances.

Purposes of Evaluation. One purpose of evaluation is to decide on the value of a curricular intervention within a course. An *interrupted time series design* is useful for this purpose. In this design, a series of measurements are taken both before and after the introduction of the intervention. Unobtrusive records—absences, disciplinary referrals, requests for transfer—are frequently used with this design, although test scores and other data can also serve. A significant difference in pupil performance during and after the intervention may be taken as evidence that the intervention had a positive effect.

Another important purpose of evaluation is to decide on the long-term value of curriculum offerings. Longitudinal or follow-up studies are undertaken to indicate whether desired objectives are being realized and to reveal shortcomings. One of the better known longitudinal studies was conducted on a national level in Project Talent. This project was initiated in 1960 with the testing of 400,000 secondary school students. Such data as student interests, ability scores, and characteristics of a student's school, including courses offered, were collected. Fifteen years later, a representative sample of these persons were interviewed, and they reported on their satisfaction with their current status on different life activities. One overall generalization from the findings was that educational programs should be improved and modified to enable persons to achieve greater satisfaction in intellectual development and personal understanding.[4] Another example of the findings from Project Talent studies is that, whereas in 1960, 47 percent of the graduating boys and 38 percent of the girls said their courses were not helpful in preparing them for occupations, eleven years later 46 percent of the men and 40 percent of the women still felt high school had been adequate at best.

National Assessment of Educational Progress (NAEP) is an information system designed to furnish information regarding the educational

[4]John C. Flanagan, *Perspectives on Improving Education* (Los Alamitos, California: Southwest Regional Laboratory for Educational Research and Development, 1979).

achievements of children, youth, and young adults, and to indicate both the progress we are making and the problems we face.[5] Unlike Project Talent, NAEP does not follow individual progress but does sample different age groups. The project assesses a variety of curriculum areas. Information on factors that affect student performance is also provided. Reports on test results are reported by age and grade level. Parents, school board members, legislators, and school officials all find the information useful.

A new procedure has been introduced for national assessment—Balanced Incomplete Block (BIB) spiraling. With BIB spiraling, each test exercise is administered the same number of times, as in matrix sampling, but each exercise is located in several different booklets, and many different booklets are administered in an assessment session. Thus, by administering different exercises in a given school and giving particular exercises in many different schools, it is possible to compare schools across the nation.

An illustration of how the NAEP illuminates problems is the 1982 finding that most improvements in mathematics achievement over previous years are limited mostly to lower order skills—simple computation. One curriculum implication from the finding is that our mathematics curriculum is obsolete and should be restructured with the goal of developing more thoughtful students—problem solvers who can apply their knowledge in unexpected as well as routine ways.

Evaluating a Curriculum Project. Technologists evaluate a curriculum project by assessing (a) the merits of its goals, (b) the quality of its plans, (c) the extent to which the plans can be carried out, and (d) the value of the outcomes. Illustrative of such models is the CIPP (Context, Input, Process, Product) model developed by Dan Stufflebeam and others.[6] In the *context* phase of evaluation, the evaluator focuses upon defining the environment, describing the desired and actual conditions and identifying the problems (needs assessment). *Input* refers to the selection of strategies to achieve the educational objectives. Once a strategy has been selected, a *process* evaluation provides feedback to the implementer about faults in the design and the implementation. Finally, a *product* evaluation is undertaken to reveal the effects of the selected strategy on the curriculum.

In his analytical review of evaluation, David Nevo summarized in

[5]Gregory Anrig and Archie La Pointe, "NAEP: The Nation's Report Card," *Phi Delta Kappan* 65, no. 1 (September 1983): 52–4.

[6]William J. Webster, "CIPP in Local Evaluation," in *Applied Strategies for Curriculum Evaluation,* ed. Ronald Brandt. (Alexandria, Va.: ASCD, 1981): pp. 48–57.

question and answer form the nature of consensual models and approaches:

1. What is evaluation? Educational evaluation is a systematic description of educational objects (projects, programs, materials, curriculum, and institutions) and an assessment of their worth.
2. What is the function of evaluation? Evaluation can serve four different functions: (a) formative (for improvement), (b) summative (for selecting and accountability), (c) sociopolitical (to motivate and gain public support), and (d) administrative (to exercise authority).
3. What kinds of information should be collected? Evaluators should collect information about the goals of the object, its strategies and plans, the process of implementation, and the outcome and impacts.
4. What criteria should be used to judge the merits of an object? In judging the worth of an educational object, consider whether or not the object (a) responds to identified needs of clients; (b) achieves national goals, ideals, or social values; (c) meets agreed upon standards; (d) does better than alternative objects; and (e) achieves important stated goals.
5. What is the *process* of doing an evaluation? The process should include three activities: (a) focusing on the problems, (b) collecting and analyzing empirical data, and (c) communicating findings to evaluate audience.
6. Who should do evaluations? Individuals or teams who have (a) competency in research methods and other data analysis techniques, (b) an understanding of the social context and the unique substance of the evaluation object, (c) an ability to maintain correct human relations and rapport with those involved, and (d) a conceptual framework to integrate the above mentioned capabilities.
7. By what standards should an evaluation be judged? Evaluation should strike for a balance in meeting standards of (a) utility (useful and practical), (b) accuracy (technically adequate), (c) possibility (realistic and prudent), (d) propriety (conducted legally and ethically).[7]

Pluralistic Models

Evaluation models with the pluralistic concern of humanists and social reconstructionists have had as yet a relatively limited impact. Pluralistic procedures are less frequently used than the research and technological procedures applied by teachers in course improvement, by school managers in rational decision making, by government evaluators in auditing new social programs in the schools, and by statewide evaluators in monitoring the curriculum for accountability purposes.

[7]David Nevo, "The Conceptualization of Educational Evaluation," *Review of Educational Research* 53, no. 11 (Spring 1983): 117–128.

Pluralistic evaluation models tend to be used only when research and technological models are less attractive for reasons of politics, costs, or practicality. These newer models are chiefly used with curriculum that is out of the mainstream—curriculum associated with aesthetic education, multicultural projects, and alternative schools. Pluralistic models are also increasing in supplementary experimental designs.

The Countenance Model. Robert E. Stake was one of the first evaluators to propose the pluralist argument that the evaluator should make known the criteria or standards that are being employed and who holds them. His model differs from the older technological models by being more extensive in the types of data collected, and more sensitive to the different values of program participants and allowing them more participation in judging the programs. The countenance model calls for attention to three phases of an educational program: *antecedent, transaction,* and *outcome* phases. Antecedents are conditions existing prior to instruction that may relate to outcomes; transactions constitute the process of instruction; and outcomes are the effects of the program. Stake emphasizes two operations, descriptions and judgments. Descriptions are divided according to whether they refer to what was intended or what actually was observed. Judgments are separated according to whether they refer to standards used in arriving at the judgments or to the actual judgments. The model is depicted in Table 10.1.

As a pluralist, Stake believes that sensitivity to the perceived needs of those concerned with the evaluation is essential. Accordingly, he urges initial evaluations to discover what clients and participants actually want from the program evaluation. These concerns should be discovered prior to designing the evaluation project. Stake places less emphasis on precisely specified objectives than do technologists, for he wishes to describe all intentions, even those which are not expressed in terms of student learning. The key emphasis in his model is on description and judgment. For him, an evaluator should report the ways different people see the curriculum. Hence the evaluator's principal activities include discovering what those concerned want to know, making observations, and gathering multiple judgments about the observed antecedents, transactions, and outcomes. A wide variety of persons—outside experts, journalists, psychologists—as well as teachers and students may participate in the conduct of the evaluation.

The Connoisseurship Model. Elliot W. Eisner has argued for an evaluation process that will capture a richer slice of educational life than do test

TABLE 10.1 Stake's Description of Data Needed for Educational Evaluation

	Descriptive Matrix		Judgment Matrix	
	Intents	Observations	Standards	Judgments
Antecedents (student and teacher characteristics, curriculum content, instructional materials, community context)				
Transactions (communication flow, time allocation, sequence of events, social climate)				
Outcomes (student achievement, attitudes, motor skills, effect on teachers and institution)				

Source: R.E. Stake, "The Countenance of Educational Evaluation," *Teachers College Record* 68 (1967). Reprinted by permission of Teachers College, Columbia University.

scores.[8] One of his procedures is educational criticism in which an evaluator asks such questions as: "What has happened during the school year in a given school? What were the key events? How did they come into being? How did students and teachers participate? What were the consequences? How could the events be strengthened? What do such events enable children to learn?"

Other vehicles for disclosing the richness of programs, according to Eisner, are films, videotapes, photography, and taped student and teacher interviews. These useful tools in portraying aspects of school life are, when supplemented by critical narrative, valuable channels for communication.

Connoisseurship is involved in noting what is and is not said, how it is said, its tone, and other such factors that indicate meaning.

Another procedure recommended by Eisner is the analysis of work produced by children, including a critique to help evaluators understand what has been accomplished and to reveal some of the realities of classroom performance.

The fundamental thesis of the connoisseur approach is that the problem of communicating to some public—parent, board, state agencies—about what has happened in school—the good and the bad—can be usefully conceived as an artistic problem. In such an approach an evaluator fashions an expressive picture of educational practice and its consequences.

Connoisseurship and criticism—ways of seeing rather than ways of measuring—have been criticized as abstruse technology requiring special training in acquiring "interpretive maps" and ways to understand the meaning of what has been said. Judgments are established externally by the nature of artistic virtues and tradition. This approach, though informative and highly adaptive to unique local conditions, is subjective and thus potentially controversial.

CONTROVERSIAL TECHNICAL ISSUES IN CURRICULUM EVALUATION

Curriculum specialists, teachers, and administrators often disagree on which techniques to use in evaluation. Many disputes about procedures occur because each party has different purposes and needs in mind. They argue over the merits of procedures and instruments such

[8]Elliot W. Eisner, *The Educational Imagination on the Design and Evaluation of School Programs* (New York: Macmillan Company, 1979).

as formats for stating objectives or specifying goals, norm- and criterion-referenced tests, sampling, and technical hazards. Their controversies will not be resolved by taking an uncompromising attitude but by showing the circumstances in which one approach is better than another.

The Form of Objectives

During the last fifteen years, no issue in curriculum has received more attention than the value of and proper manner for stating objectives. Part of the problem is philosophical. One extreme position is that an objective must specify the exact overt behavior that a learner is to display at the end of an instructional sequence. This overt response is seen as important in itself. A more moderate position is that the objective must specify behavior that will indicate whether the objective has been attained. This position allows for covert responses on the part of the learner, but demands that some overt behavior be specified to indicate whether the desired (perhaps hidden) behavior has occurred. Another extreme position is that there should be no stated objectives at all. It is said that objectives represent external goals and manipulation and that they insignificantly indicate what a learner actually experiences from a situation.

Part of the problem is that these groups try to judge the form and value of objectives without understanding their purposes. There are many uses for objectives. They can communicate general direction at a policy level, provide a concrete guide for selecting and planning learning opportunities, and set the criteria for evaluation of the learners' performance. To illustrate, there are at least four degrees of specificity for an objective. There are very general statements that are useful when trying to get a consensus on direction at a policy level. For this purpose, it is often sufficient to use *general goal statements*: "to learn to respect and get along with people by developing appreciation and respect for the worth of individuals"; "to respect and understand minority opinions"; "to accept majority decisions."

More specific objectives are useful when planning the learning opportunities for courses or when analyzing instructional materials. These objectives are called *educational objectives* and are illustrated in several taxonomies of educational objectives.[9] These taxonomies treat affective,

---

[9]Benjamin S. Bloom, ed., *Taxonomy of Educational Objectives: Handbook I: Cognitive Domain* (New York: David McKay Company, 1956); David R. Krathwohl et al., *Taxonomy of Educational Objectives: Handbook II: Affective Domain* (New York: David McKay Company, 1956); Anita Harrow, *A Taxonomy of the Psychomotor Domain: A Guide for Developing Behavioral Objectives* (New York: David McKay Company, 1972).

cognitive, and psychomotor domains. The *Taxonomy of Educational Objectives: Handbook I*, for example, treats cognitive objectives and classifies them using six major categories and several subcategories. Categories range from simple recall of information to critical evaluative behaviors. One such category is *application*. Application is defined as using abstractions in particular and concrete situations. The abstractions may be general ideas, rules of procedures, or generalized methods. They may also be technical principles, ideas, and theories that must be remembered and applied. The taxonomy also gives sample objectives. The level of specificity of an educational objective can be seen in this example: "The ability to predict the probable effect of a change in a factor on a biological situation previously at equilibrium." The objective can be further amplified by an illustration of the kind of test or test item that would be appropriate.

The taxonomies have greatly influenced curriculum making. More attention is now given to affective, cognitive, and psychomotor domains. Also, curriculum workers are now more sensitive to the level of behavior expected from instruction. They are, for instance, more concerned now that objectives and test items treat higher cognitive processes like comprehension, application, and analysis rather than dealing only with recall of information.

There is an even more specific form for an objective; it is called an *instructional objective*. This form is useful when teaching pupils a specific concept. It is often called a Mager-like instructional objective after the person who advocated its use.[10] These objectives specify the behavior to be exhibited by the student, a standard or criterion of acceptable performance, and the kind of situation in which the behavior is to be elicited. One instructional objective might be, "Given a linear algebraic equation with one unknown [the situation or condition], the learner must be able to solve the equation [behavior and criterion] without the aid of references, tables, or calculating devices [additional conditions]."

An additional degree of specificity can be found in the *amplified objective*, which is used when one desires to communicate to writers and consumers of criterion-referenced tests. Amplified objectives represent a set of rules to generate test items.[11] These rules describe (1) the stimuli or testing situations that can constitute or be used in constructing test items, including the potential content from which items can be generated and the directions to be given the learners; (2) the response options, including the nature of the wrong answers to appear on a multiple-choice test; and (3) the criteria of correctness (the bases for judging responses right or wrong).

---

[10]Robert F. Mager, *Preparing Instructional Objectives* (Palo Alto: Fearon Publishers, 1962).
[11]Popham, *Educational Evaluation,* p. 147.

Special objectives seem valuable in providing guidance for the evaluation of instructional materials and student performance. Other functions of objectives, however, such as giving direction in teaching and aiding learning, arouse much difference of opinion. It is charged that a teacher who uses specific objectives may not give enough attention to the immediate concerns of learners. The research on this issue, however, is inconclusive. Some studies on the effects of specific objectives on learning, for example, have shown positive effects, but an equal number have not shown any significant differences. Objectives sometimes help and are almost never harmful. They seem to assist students in determining what is expected of them and in discriminating between relevant and irrelevant content. However, a question remains about the number of objectives that should be provided to the student. If the list of objectives is extensive and detailed, both student and teacher are overwhelmed. On the importance of stating objectives, a reviewer cites the philosopher George Santayana, "The fanatic is one who re-doubles his efforts when he has forgotten his aim."

Measurement of Intended Outcomes Versus Goal-free Evaluation

In the past Ralph Tyler told evaluators that it was impossible to decide whether a particular test would be appropriate for appraising a certain program until the objectives of the program had been defined and until the kinds of situations that would give an opportunity for this behavior to be expressed were identified. Tyler recommended checking each proposed evaluation device against the objectives and constructing or devising methods for collecting evidence about the student's attainment of these objectives.

More recently, Michael Scriven moved beyond Tyler's concern for data about intended outcomes to a concern for all relevant effects.[12] His approach is called *goal-free evaluation*. Such evaluation does not assess a situation only in terms of goal preferences. It is evaluation of *actual* effects against a profile of demonstrated needs. It is offered as a protection against the narrow vision of those close to the program—against harmful side effects, missed new priorities, and overlooked achievement. To the extent that Scriven's approach is used, more evaluative measures will have to be employed. Selection of these measures will be difficult, for there are thousands of such devices. Practicality will probably dictate the use of measures that assess most intended outcomes and a limited number of possible side effects.

[12]Michael Scriven, "Pros and Cons about Goal-free Evaluation," *Evaluation Comment* 3, no. 4 (December 1972): 1–4.

David Fetterman is also opposed to use of evaluations of programs based on their goals.[13] He believes that such evaluations are misleading. Goals are often part of the political rhetoric; they are often vague, and so misrepresent the program. Focus upon procedures, formulative evaluation, and ethnographic techniques may contribute to more accurate understanding of a program—revealing both the manifest and latent purposes of the program.

Norm-Referenced Tests and Criterion-Referenced Tests

Standardized achievement tests are norm-referenced. They are designed to compare the performances of individuals to the performance of a normative group. The purposes of these tests initially were to find the most able persons and to sort out those who were most likely to succeed or fail some future learning situation. Only those test items which discriminate between the best and worst are kept. The assumption that everyone can learn equally well is rejected in norm-referenced testing. These tests, therefore, tend to correlate very highly with intelligence tests. In order to obtain items with high response variance, writers of norm-referenced tests are likely to exclude the items that measure widely known concepts and skills of schooling.

Although norm-referenced tests do identify persons of different ability, they are of questionable value in curriculum evaluation. They may not accurately measure what educational programs are designed to teach or reveal particular problems that are keeping pupils from achieving. Teachers can sometimes improve scores on such tests, but such improvement usually results from tricks such as (1) telling children to respond to all items so that the possibility of getting more right answers is increased (a child needs to get only three to seven more items right to show one-year improvement on typical achievement tests); (2) testing at a different time of the year than previously to show apparent but not real gains; (3) capitalizing on regression effects that make the poorest scores look better on the second testing; and (4) teaching pupils how to respond to the test items themselves and to the test format.

Criterion-referenced tests are meant to ascertain a learner's status with respect to a learning task, rather than to a norm. These tests tell what learners can and cannot do in specified situations. The tasks selected can be those which the curriculum emphasizes. The items used in the test match the set of learner behaviors called for in the objective and should not be eliminated, as in the norm-referenced tests, merely

[13]David M. Fetterman, "Ibsen's Baths: Reactivity and Insensitivity," *Educational Evaluation and Policy Analysis* 4, no. 3 (Fall 1982): 261–279.

because most students answer them correctly. Hence, these tests can be sensitive measures of what has been taught.

Criterion-referenced tests are also useful in showing whether a student has mastered specific material. Consequently, they are popular in instructional settings using continuous progress plans or other individualized teaching approaches. The tests indicate what instructional treatments are needed by individual learners and also indicate when learners are ready to proceed to other tasks.

Criterion-referenced tests are sometimes faulted because they have been based on objectives that are too narrow. The multiplicity of tests necessary to accompany many objectives has been a management problem for teachers. Trends indicate that particular courses in the future will use perhaps eight to ten very important final tests based on objectives which are applicable to many situations, rather than the large numbers of such tests as is now common. Tests that have items dependent on particular materials or programs will also diminish. Other ways of improving these tests are to include a complete description of the set of learner behaviors that the test is to assess and to increase the number of items for each competency measured in order to have an acceptable standard of reliability.

Tests and Invasion of Privacy

The American Civil Liberties Union has taken up the cause of students who charge that tests are an invasion of privacy. Students have complained about the use of instruments, usually self-report devices, that probe their attitudes in such areas as self-esteem, interest in school, and human relations. Evaluators want such data in order to assess the effects of schooling. Protests against the use of tests to guide the learning process in academic areas are less frequent. ACLU lawyers argue that authorities have not made it clear that pupils may refuse to take tests that they believe to be invading their privacy. Pupils should also be told that the questions asked in a test might require self-incriminating responses which could later be used against them.

This issue is related to a larger problem, that of the effect of tests on students. Do they affect motivation and self-esteem by producing anxiety and encouraging cheating? Do they create labels and determine adult social status? Marjorie C. Kirkland completed an extensive review of the research treating such questions. Her review throws light on test effects. She shows, for example, that how individuals think of themselves and what they believe about a test influences their test behavior. Other examples from Kirkland's review show that students' attitudes about tests in general are negative. The more interested persons are in their test results, the more they perceive positive consequences of tests. Systematic reporting of test results helps students to understand their interests, aptitudes, and achievements.[14] Anyone reading Kirkland's review will conclude that tests are powerful and that their consequences are far-ranging.

TECHNIQUES FOR COLLECTING DATA

Newton S. Metfessel and William B. Michael's list of multiple criterion measures for evaluating school programs is an old but useful survey of ways to collect evidence.[15] One class of indicators of change in learners includes informal devices, short answer techniques, interviews, peer nominations, sociograms, questionnaires, self-evaluation measures, projective devices, and semantic differential scales. The authors also describe the many ways for assessing the effect of programs without influencing the outcomes. These methods are called *unobtrusive measures*; they include attending to absences, anecdotal records, appointments, assignments, stories written, awards, use of books, case histories, disciplinary actions, dropouts, and voluntary activities.

Creative indicators can be devised if persons will think beyond the use of formal tests. Other useful indicators are (1) the learners' products— such as compositions, paintings, constructions; (2) the learners' self-reports on preferences and interests; and (3) the learners' solutions to problems, their conduct in discussions, and their participation in physical games and dances. With these methods, the teacher or evaluator should use an accompanying checklist stipulating the behavior to be exhibited by the pupil and the qualities to be found in the pupil's product.

Michael Patton has written on ways the evaluator can get closer to the people and situations being evaluated in order to understand the curriculum as the students experiencing it do.[16] His suggestions for observation and interviewing are extensive and consistent with pluralistic

[14]Marjorie C. Kirkland, "The Effects of Tests on Students and School," *Review of Educational Research* 41, no. 4 (October 1971): 303–51.

[15]Newton S. Metfessel and William B. Michael, "A Paradigm Involving Multiple Criterion Measures for the Evaluation of the Effectiveness of School Programs," *Educational and Psychological Measurement* 27, no. 4 (1967): 931–34.

[16]Michael Q. Patton, *Qualitative Evaluation Models* (Beverly Hills: Sage Publications, 1980).

notions. Patton stresses the importance of understanding the point of view and experiences of others. For example, he believes that evaluators, with their own personalities and interests, will be naturally attuned to some people more than others. To resist these attractions may hinder the observer from acting naturally and being integrated into the program. The evaluator as observer, then, must decide about personal relationships and group interest, without losing perspective on the experience of other students with whom the evaluator is less directly involved. Similarly, in interviewing, Patton is opposed to having participants fit their knowledge, experiences, and feelings into the evaluator's categories. Instead, the evaluator must provide a framework for the respondents' understanding of the program. Not asking "How satisfied are you with this program?" but asking "What do you think of this program?"

Measuring Affect

Although it is a controversial activity, the assessment of affect is gaining interest. Special techniques are used for this task, because it is believed that individuals are more likely to "fake" their attitudinal responses. Hence, mild deception is often used so that learners will not know the purpose of the inquiry or that they are being observed. A student may be asked, for example, to respond to several hypothetical situations, only one of which is of interest to the examiner. The examiner may ask, "Where would you take a visitor friend from out of town—to the market, the movie, the school, the library, the bank?" If "school" is the answer, it is presumed that the respondent tends to value that institution. Another, less direct approach, is to use high inference and theoretical instruments. The examiner might ask, "Would you play the part of a degenerate in a play?" or "Which of the following names (one of which is the respondent's own) do you like?" (The inference is that students with high self-concepts will play any role and will like their names.) Situations are sometimes contrived, and students' reactions are interpreted to indicate particular attitudes. Student observers may collect unobtrusive data and report their observations later, for example. Audio recordings are sometimes made of student small group discussions and analyzed later.

An illustration of a low inference self-report device follows. This device is an example of how affect can be assessed with criterion-referenced measures. Note how the objective stated in the general description is amplified by sections treating stimulus and response attributes.

PREFERENCES IN MUSIC[17]

General Description

When given the names of a wide variety of types of music, students will select a response for each type that indicates whether they are familiar with it and, if so, the degree to which they like it.

Sample Item

Directions: This is a survey of students' opinions about different kinds of music, such as bluegrass, gospel, and hard rock. If you are not familiar with a type of music, mark choice *a* on the answer sheet. For those types of music with which you have any familiarity, no matter how slight, select an answer from *b, c, d, e,* and *f* that states how much you like each one. Mark the letter of your choice on the answer sheet. In the item below if you have heard some *operetta* music and you *like* it, you would mark *e* on the answer sheet. Since this is an opinion poll, there are no right or wrong answers. Do not put your name on the answer sheet and do not worry if many of the types of music are not familiar to you.

1. Operetta

     a. unfamiliar
     b. strongly dislike
     c. dislike
     d. neutral
     e. like
     f. strongly like

Before answering any of the items below, please look over the names of all of the types of music.

Stimulus Attributes

1. Students will be given the names of categories or types of music.
2. The types will be ones to which Americans are commonly exposed in the U.S. media or where they are living abroad. The categories will represent a wide range of music and will include those types that are currently popular with the student population. The categories may have some overlap since borrowing among types is common and boundaries of types are not distinct.
3. At least 20 different categories of music will be included, of which at least 20 percent will be more formal types, such as classical and chamber. Test constructors will rely on their knowledge of local culture in generating types of music that are found in the home area. No more than 10 percent of the items will be specifically local ones. The following list may be useful in generating test items:

[17]Drawn with permission from *JOX Illustrative Criterion-Referenced Test Specifications: Aesthetics K–12* (Los Angeles: Instructional Objectives Exchange, 1980).

Big band (dance and swing)	Folk rock
Bluegrass	Gospel
Blues	Hymns
Cantata and oratorio	Indian (from India)
Caribbean (calypso, reggae)	Jazz
Chamber music	Latin American
Christmas music	Marches and military music
Classical: full orchestra	Musical show tunes
Concert band	Opera
Country and western	Operetta and light opera
Electronic	Pop (except rock)
Folk dances	Rhythm and blues
Folk songs: international	Rock
Folk songs: American	Soul

Response Attributes

1. Students will respond by selecting one of six multiple-choice alternatives from the following set:
   a. unfamiliar
   b. strongly dislike
   c. dislike
   d. neutral
   e. like
   f. strongly like
2. Point values will be assigned to the response categories as follows: $a = 0$, $b = 1$, $c = 2$, $d = 3$, $e = 4$, $f = 5$, with informed dislike (choices b and c) scoring higher than complete unfamiliarity (choice a). Students may then be assigned three different scores on the survey, as follows:
   a. Average appreciation of familiar types of music: The average of all nonzero value (non-a) responses reveals the degree to which students like the categories of music that are familiar to them.
   b. Breadth of familiarity: The number of different types of music receiving responses other than a, divided by the total number of types on the test, gives the proportion of types that the student is familiar with.
   c. Average appreciation overall: The average rating for all categories, both familiar and unfamiliar, reflects in one score both the breadth and degree of students' likes.

Sometimes, too, individuals are offered ways to respond anonymously. In evaluating the affective consequences of a curriculum, individuals need not be identified. One only has to know what effect the curriculum is having on students as a group. Further, the measures or scores obtained with most high inference instruments are not reliable enough for making predictions about individuals.

In an effort to improve the credibility of their findings, evaluators may use *triangulation* (the use of three different measures in concert). If a similar attitude is found by all three measures, they have more confidence in the findings. Locally developed instruments also are thought to be more valid when two or more persons score students' responses the same and when several samples of student behavior are consistent.

Appraisals of Existing Instruments

There are several sources that both list and evaluate instruments. The Center for the Study of Evaluation, at UCLA, has four publications that describe and evaluate thousands of tests for elementary and secondary schools.[18] The Social Science Education Consortium has analyzed and catalogued 1,000 instruments for use in evaluating programs in the social studies.[19] Many measures of social and psychological attitudes are also described in a publication by John Robinson and Phillip Stover of the Survey Research Center Institute for Social Research at the University of Michigan. Data concerning criterion-referenced tests and instructional objectives can be obtained from the Instructional Objectives Exchange. *Tests in Print III* by J. V. Mitchell, Jr., is available from the Buros Institute, University of Nebraska, Lincoln. This reference includes a bibliography of most known tests published for use with English-speaking persons, a classified index to the contents of mental measurement yearbooks, a description of the population for which each test is intended, and other features. The *Eighth Mental Measurement Yearbook,* edited by the late Oscar K. Buros, is also a good source, containing, among other things, 798 reviews of 546 tests. Finally, the Educational Testing Service is a clearing house for tests, measures, and evaluation, offering information on a wide range of instruments.[20]

Sampling

Sampling is the practice of inferring an educational status on the basis of responses from representative persons or representative tasks. James

[18]The Center for the Study of Evaluation, 405 Hilgard Avenue, Los Angeles, Calif. 90024.

[19]The Social Science Education Consortium, 855 Broadway, Boulder, Colo. 30302; Instructional Objectives Exchange, Box 24095, Los Angeles, Calif. 90024.

[20]J. V. Mitchell, Jr., *Tests in Print III* (Lincoln: University of Nebraska Press, 1983); Oscar K. Buros, ed., *The Eighth Mental Measurements Yearbook* (Highland Park, N.J.: Gryphon Press, 1978); ERIC Clearing House, *Tests, Measures, and Evaluation* (Princeton, N.J.: Educational Testing Service, 1980).

Popham has said, "Sampling should make a Scotsman's values vibrate. It is *so* terribly thrifty."[21] It is controversial mainly because it is sometimes imposed in inappropriate situations. When students are to be graded on their relative attainment of common objectives, for example, it is not proper to assess only certain students nor is it valid to test some individuals on one set of objectives and other individuals on another set.

Administrators rightfully use sampling when they estimate the typical reactions of students from a few instances of their behavior. It is not necessary to collect all the compositions students have written in order to judge their writing ability. Samples will suffice—perhaps one at the beginning of the year and one at the end—to show change, if any, as a result of instruction. Similarly, to determine a student's knowledge in one subject, it is not necessary to ask the student to respond to all the items that are involved in this knowledge. A sample of what is involved is enough to draw an inference about the student's status. To find out whether the student can name all the letters of the alphabet, one can present only five letters at random from the alphabet and ask the student to name them. The responses will indicate ability to respond to the total population of letters. If all five are named correctly, there is a high probability that the child could name all of the letters. If the child cannot name one or more of the letters, obviously the objective has not been reached. Controversy arises over sampling because teachers have concerns that do not lend themselves to sampling. If sampling indicates that a child cannot name all of the letters of the alphabet, then the teacher wants to know specifically which ones must be taught. Sampling is unlikely to reveal this information.

Controversy may also arise between legislators and others who want achievement records of individuals and evaluators who prefer to use a technique like *matrix sampling* to determine the effects of a program. In this sampling technique randomly selected students respond to randomly selected test items measuring different objectives. Thus, different students take different tests. The advantages of the technique are many: reduced testing time required of the student, attainment of information concerning learners' knowledge with respect to many objectives, and reduced apprehension on students' part since examinees are not compared. The disadvantage is that sampling does not tell us the status of an individual on all the objectives. But again, this is not necessary to get an indication of abilities within groups of students.

[21]Popham, *Educational Evaluation,* p. 218.

Technical Hazards

Donald Horst and colleagues of the RMC Research Corporation have identified twelve hazards in conducting evaluations. Each hazard makes it difficult to know whether or not students do better in a particular program than they would have done without it.

1. *The use of grade-equivalent scores.* One should not use grade-equivalent scores in evaluating programs. The concept is misleading; a grade-equivalent score of 7 by fifth-graders on a math test does not mean that they know sixth- and seventh-grade math. Such scores do not comprise an equal interval scale and, therefore, it is difficult to obtain an average score. The procedures for obtaining these scores make them too low in the fall and too high in the spring.

2. *The use of gain scores.* Gain scores have been used to adjust for differences found in the pretest scores of treatment and comparison groups. Using them in this way is a mistake, because raw gain scores (posttest scores minus pretest scores) excessively inflate the posttest performance measure of an initially inferior group. Students who initially have the lowest scores will have the greatest opportunity to show gain.

3. *The use of norm-group comparisons with inappropriate test dates.* A distorted picture of a program's effect occurs when pupils in the new program are not tested within a few weeks of the norm group's tests. Standardized test developers might collect performance scores in May in order to obtain a norm for the test. If the school's staff, however, administers the test during a different month, the discrepancy might be due to the date of testing rather than to the program.

4. *The use of inappropriate test levels.* Standardized norm-referenced tests are divided into levels that cover different grades. The test level may be too easy or too difficult, and thereby fail to provide a valid measure of achievement. The test might differentiate sufficiently among groups at either end of the scale. Such effects may also occur with the use of criterion-referenced tests. Hence, one should choose tests on the basis of the pupils' achievement level, not their grade in school.

5. *The lack of pre- and posttest scores for each treatment participant.* The group of students ultimately posttested is not usually composed of exactly the same students as the pretest group. Eliminating the

scores of dropouts from the post-test may raise the post-test
scores considerably. Conclusion of a program's report should be
based on the performance of students who have both pre- and
post-test scores. The reason for dropping out should also be
reported.

6. *The use of noncomparable treatment and comparison groups.* Students
   should be randomly assigned to groups. If they are not, students
   in a special program may do better or worse than those in other
   programs, because they were different to start with.

7. *Using pretest scores to select program participants.* Groups with low pretest scores appear to learn more from a special program than
   they actually do because of a phenomenon called *regression toward
   the mean.* Gains of high-scoring students may be obscured.

8. *Assembling a mismatched comparison group.* The correct procedure for
   matching groups is to match pairs of pupils and then randomly
   assign one member of each pair to a treatment or comparison
   group. If, for example, one wants to control for age, one should
   choose pairs of pupils of the same age. Each member of the pair
   must have an equal opportunity to be assigned to a given treatment. Do not consciously try to place one member in a certain
   group.

9. *Careless administration of tests.* Pupils from both treatment and comparison groups should complete pre- and posttests together.
   Problems arise when there is inconsistent administration of tests
   to the two groups. If, for example, there is a disorderly situation
   in one setting and a different teacher present, the results may
   differ.

10. *The assumption that an achievement gain is due to the treatment alone.* The
    Hawthorne effects—unrecognized "treatments," such as
    novelty—may be responsible for gain. Plausible rival hypotheses
    should be examined as a likely explanation.

11. *The use of noncomparable pretests and posttests.* Although conversation
    tables allow one to correct scores on one test to their equivalent
    on other tests, it is best to use the same level of the same test for
    both pre- and posttesting. Often it is possible to use the identical
    test as both pre- and posttest. Obviously, this will not suffice if
    teachers teach to the test and if there are practice effects from
    taking the test.

12. *The use of inappropriate formulas to estimate posttest scores.* Formulas that
    calculate expected posttest scores from IQ or an average of grade-
    equivalent scores are inaccurate. The actual posttest scores of

treatment and comparison groups provide a better basis for evaluating treatment effects.[22]

CONCLUDING COMMENTS

Evaluation is useless if conclusions are not drawn from the data and
acted on in modifying the curriculum. Looking at test scores and filing
them away mocks the evaluative process, although admittedly, evaluation
sometimes serves other purposes. Results are sometimes used to gain
support of parents and others.

Evaluation may be also undertaken because it is a necessary basis for
requesting monies or reassuring a public that the school is doing its job.
The principal purpose for using the data, however, should be improvement of the curriculum. Hence, some schools now have curriculum
groups that study the findings and then make plans both for the whole
school and for individual teachers.

Scores or descriptive terms that summarize learner performance give
study groups the opportunity to see the strengths and weaknesses of
their programs. Analyses of different populations of pupils reveal how
well the curriculum is serving major cultural subgroups, such as the
physically handicapped, or to see how different groups compare with
each other. Teachers attempt to ascertain from the data what individual
students need. Diagnosing needs becomes a basis for giving personal
help. Study groups also discuss the reasons for a curriculum's strengths
and weaknesses. Members try to explain the results of particular learning
opportunities, the time spent on an objective, the arrangement of
activities and topics, the kinds and frequency of responses from learners,
the grouping patterns, and the use of space and interactions with adults.
Explanations are verified by determining whether all the data lead to the
same conclusion. Plans are made to modify the curriculum in light of
deficiencies noted and the cause of the deficiencies.

The results from evaluation should be used in at least two ways. First,
they can be used to strengthen ends. Results can be the basis for
deciding on new instructional objectives aimed at meeting revealed
needs. If evaluation of a program or particular learning opportunity
results in the selection of more important objectives than were originally

---

[22]Donald P. Horst et al., *A Practical Guide to Measuring Project Impact on Student Achievement,*
Monograph Series on Education, no. 1 (Washington, D.C.: U.S. Office of Education,
1975).

held, the evaluation was valuable. Dewey put it well: "There is no such thing as a final set of objectives, even for the time being or temporarily. Each day of teaching ought to enable a teacher to revise and better in some respect the objectives arrived at in a previous work."[23]

Results can also be used to revise means. They can serve as a guide to the need for new learning opportunities and arrangements that might remedy deficiencies in the curriculum. That is, evaluation pinpoints needs and guides one in the selection of new material, procedures, and organizational patterns. These innovations in turn must be tried out and their results appraised. In short, evaluation is only one part of a continuing cycle.

QUESTIONS

1. How would you respond if faced with the choice of obtaining important data about the learner through deception or getting less important data in a straightforward manner?
2. What kind of student progress is best revealed by (a) products of learners, (b) self-reports, and (c) observations of pupil behavior?
3. Compare the purpose and construction of norm-referenced and criterion-referenced tests.
4. Think of a learning opportunity that you might select for learners (for example, a particular educational game, lesson, field trip, experiment, textbook article, or story). Then indicate what you would do in order to find out whether or not this opportunity produced both intended outcomes and unanticipated consequences.
5. How might a teacher or principal gain information regarding the progress of students with a large number of objectives without subjecting students to much testing?
6. Whose criteria should be used in an evaluation situation known to you— experts, participants, or those affected by its consequences?
7. Discuss the strengths and weaknesses of each of the following evaluative purposes and accompanying approaches:

Purpose	*Approach*
To measure student progress.	Determine gain by testing.
To resolve crises and increase perception of school as legitimate.	Blue ribbon committee.

[23]John Dewey, *The Sources of a Science of Education* (New York: Horace Liveright, 1929).

Purpose	*Approach*
To understand teachers' and students' perceptions of the curriculum.	Observation and interview.
To make rational curriculum decisions.	A history of options and the costs of each.

SELECTED REFERENCES

Brandt, Ronald S., ed. *Applied Strategies for Curriculum Evaluation.* Alexandria, Va.: ASCD, 1981.

Brinkerhoff, Robert O., et al. *Program Evaluation.* Hingman, Ma.: Klower Boston, 1983.

Cronbach, L. J., et al. *Toward Reform of Program Evaluation: Aims, Methods, and Institutional Arrangements.* San Francisco: Jossey-Bass, 1980.

Eisner, Elliot W. "The Forms and Functions of Evaluation." In *The Educational Imagination,* pp. 168–89. New York: Macmillan, 1979.

Hamilton, David. "Making Sense of Curriculum Evaluation." In *Review of Research in Education 5,* ed. Lee S. Schulman, pp. 318–49. Itasca, IL.: F. E. Peacock, 1979.

Popham, W. James. *Educational Evaluation.* Englewood Cliffs, N.J.: Prentice-Hall, 1975.

Rodgers, Frederick. "Curriculum Research and Evaluation." In *Fundamental Curriculum Decisions.* Alexandria, Va.: ASCD, 1983.

Willis, George. "Studied Naiveté: A Review Handbook of Curriculum Evaluation." *Curriculum Inquiry* 1, no. 9 (Spring 1979): 27–36.

11 / THE POLITICS OF CURRICULUM MAKING

When members of the National Institute of Education (NIE) quizzed officials from more than sixty education and citizen groups, they found the officials more worried about who makes the decisions on school curriculum than about what is being taught. Although NIE's respondents unanimously agreed that it is better to leave the ultimate decisions on curriculum to the local community, opinions differed sharply about who is making curriculum decisions, what the federal and state roles are in curriculum development, and how curriculum materials get into the schools. This chapter addresses such questions. It treats the influence of textbook publishers, testing organizations, and other special groups. The roles of teachers, students, board members, principals, and superintendents are also included in this analysis of curriculum policymaking. The chapter also delineates the underlying struggle between complex political and professional reform apparatus at the national level and "loosely coupled" educational systems at other levels attempting preserving local values and interests.

CURRICULUM POLICY

Curriculum policy is not always rational or based on research. Decisions are not often based on careful analysis of content in the discipline and of societal needs, or on studies of the learning process and concerns of learners.

The Politics Involved

Curriculum decision making is a political process. Different pressure groups are proposing competing values about what to teach. A state board must decide, for example, whether to give in to efforts to have the biblical version of human origin—the creation theory—become part of the content in the school or to follow the pressure of those who want only the Darwinian evolutionary theory to be taught. Members of state and local public agencies legally responsible for these decisions regularly are accepting and rejecting different values in some way. They may bargain and permit new values to enter the program on a piecemeal basis. They may give lip service to the new values, indicating their importance in general terms but not providing concrete ways for their fulfillment. They may reject a proposed curriculum because it does not meet their view of a school's functions. The decision to accept or reject a proposal often depends on the decision maker's own view as to whether the school should emphasize individual growth and enrichment, transmission of subject matter, or preparation for life in the community.

Some idea of the complexity of curriculum policymaking can be gained from this paragraph by Kirst and Walker:

> A mapping of the leverage points for curriculum policymaking in local schools would be exceedingly complex. It would involve three levels of government, and numerous private organization foundations, accrediting associations, national testing agencies, textbook-software companies, and interest groups (such as the NAACP or the John Birch Society). Moreover, there would be a configuration of leverage points within a particular local school system including teachers, department heads, the assistant superintendent for instruction, the superintendent, and the school board. Cutting across all levels of government would be the pervasive influence of various celebrities, commentators, interest groups, and the journalists who use the mass media to disseminate their views on curriculum. It would be very useful if we were able to quantify the amount of influence of each of these groups of individuals and show input-output interactions for just one school system. Unfortunately, this is considerably beyond the state of the art.[1]

Decisions About What Will be Taught

There are several definitions of curriculum that would alter most analysis of curriculum making. To say, for example, that the curriculum is what the learner actually experiences from schools—the outlooks, predispositions, skills, and attitudes—implies that the learner personally has a major role in determining the curriculum. Individual learners can decide to some extent at least what they will learn. To say that curriculum

---

[1]Michael W. Kirst and Decker F. Walker, "An Analysis of Curriculum Policy Making," *Review of Educational Research* 41, no. 5 (1971): 488. Copyright 1971, American Educational Research Association, Washington, D.C. Reprinted by permission.

encompasses everything that influences learning in the schools increases the range of curriculum makers by including peers, custodians, visitors, and cafeteria workers. Further, the definition means that anyone whose actions affect the school experience—either fortuitously or by plan—is engaging in curriculum making.

For this analysis, we will treat curriculum decisions as conscious policy choices that affect what is learned. These decisions pertain to the nature of programs, preinstructional plans, materials, or activities that delineate organized educational programs of the school or classroom. They are made with the intent of controlling the purposes, subject matter, method, and order of instruction. Curriculum policymaking is indeed anticipatory. However, plans and materials are not always used as intended. And learner differences make it difficult to ensure that all will derive the same meaning from a common experience or opportunity.

Not all who influence the curriculum do so in the same way. A school superintendent who persuades his or her board to install a program of career education is influencing the curriculum. Testing agencies that determine what will be called for on standardized tests, thereby guiding the instructional program, are also making curriculum decisions. When deciding to substitute value clarification activities for those involving ecological studies, the teacher is engaging in curriculum policymaking, because each of these learning opportunities probably will lead to different outcomes. The authoritative decision to advance one goal over another is policymaking.

CONCEPTS FOR INTERPRETING THE PROCESS OF POLITICAL DECISION MAKING

Certain ideas and issues provide a framework for understanding the politics of curriculum decision making. Some of these come from studies by sociologists, and some from insightful educators observing how curriculum decisions are being made.

The Professionalization of Reform

Daniel P. Moynihan is credited with the idea of "the professionalization of reform"—the notion that efforts to change the American social system (including schools) have in recent years been undertaken by persons whose profession is to reform.[2] National curriculum reform has

[2]Daniel Moynihan, *Maximum Feasible Misunderstanding* (New York: The Free Press, 1969).

been spearheaded by persons like Jerrold Zacharias, Mario Fantini, Edward F. Zigler, and Ernest L. Boyer. Professional reformers tend to measure their success by the number of changes they begin.

Examples of professional reformers in action are found in: (1) J. Hottois and N. A. Milner's study citing evidence that the initiative for introducing sex education came from educators, although the educators themselves claimed that sex education was added in response to public demands for it; (2) D. Nelkin's complaint that, in connection with the nationwide introduction of the curriculum *Man: A Course of Study*, "an elite corps of unrelated professional academics and their government friends run things in the school;"[3] (3) Norman Drachler's account of how a United States commissioner of education established the Right to Read Program with overtones of a political manifesto, including demands for accountability, minority teachers, cultural pluralism in the curriculum, bilingual education, voucher plans, and competency-based teacher certification; and (4) description of the Reverend Jesse Jackson's Push for Excellence Program with funding from such sources as the Ford Foundation and the federal government.[4]

In his analysis of professional reformers, William Boyd sees them as a controversial new force in educational policymaking. He describes them as pursuing their visions of equal opportunity and a more just society convinced of their expertise and its prerogatives, armed with "solutions looking for problems," assisted by an educational research establishment with its built-in incentive to discover failure, which justifies even more research, supplied by federal and foundation funding, and stimulated by the civil rights discovery of new classes of disadvantaged students and forms of discrimination, such as the non-English-speaking, handicapped, and victims of sex discrimination.[5]

Forces of Stability

In contrast to professional reformers, many communities, school boards, school administrators, and teachers are more interested in maintaining the social values of the current curriculum and the structure

---

[3]J. Hottois and N. A. Milner, *The Sex Education Controversy* (Lexington, Mass.: Heath, 1975); D. Nelkin, "The Science-Textbook Controversies," *Scientific American* 234, no. 4 (April 1976): 36.

[4]Norman Drachler, "Education and Politics in Large Cities, 1950-70," in *The Politics of Education*, NSSE Yearbook (Chicago: University of Chicago Press, 1977): pp. 188–219; Barbara Sizemore, "Push Politics and the Education of America's Youth," *Phi Delta Kappan* 60, no. 1 (1979): 364–70.

[5]William L. Boyd, "The Politics of Curriculum Change and Stability," *Educational Researcher* 8, no. 2 (February 1979): 15.

of the schools. To them, carrying out the curriculum changes proposed by professional reformers is too costly to coordinate, too difficult to guide, and too controversial to avoid conflict. The power of the forces for stability may be eroding, yet Lawrence Iannaccone and Peter Cistone testified to the strengths of constraint in innovation by saying, "Two decades of effort in the area of race, equality, and curricular revision with more federal input than impact speak loudly enough for those who will listen. Schools today are more like the schools of twenty years ago than they are like anything else."[6]

Constraints on Policy

Constraints on policy for curriculum innovation occur through *non-decision making, conflict avoidance,* the *threat of controversy,* and *loose coupling.*

Non-decision Making. This term refers to the ability of powerful interests to control the decision-making agenda, preventing the discussion of "undesirable issues." Wilson Riles, when California State Superintendent of Public Instruction, along with leaders from the California educational establishment, avoided, for example, public exposure of a campaign to place a school voucher initiative on the 1980 ballot. A low profile strategy was laid out at a meeting of educational groups where they also agreed to step up propaganda efforts to improve the public image of public education. Riles turned down numerous invitations to debate the voucher question, saying, "If we were to get into a knock-down drag out fight, it would get attention. If they (voucher advocates) are going to get publicity, they are going to have to do it on their own." Non-decision making is a formidable barrier to change by keeping potential issues from being discussed or recognized.

Conflict Avoidance. This term refers to educators' unwillingness to introduce curriculum changes that conflict with community values and are likely to arouse controversy and opposition. William Boyd found that the degree of latitude for local educators in effecting curriculum change depends on the community.[7] In general, rural school districts and those in the "sunbelt" of the United States are more restrictive about the content of courses such as social studies, literature, and biology. Prevailing controversies center on evolution, obscenity, sex education, and religious views. Methods of teaching reading or mathe-

[6]Lawrence Iannaccone and Peter J. Cistone, *The Politics of Education* (Eugene, Oreg.: ERIC Clearing House on Educational Management, University of Oregon, 1974) p. 64.
[7]Boyd, "The Politics of Curriculum Change," p. 15.

matics are also sometimes a matter of public controversy, especially in conservative communities.

The Politics of Controversy. This is a technique used by those with a minority viewpoint to control the majority. Using a squeaking wheel tactic, those opposed to a curriculum innovation create a controversy in the hope that school authorities will back off from it. Textbook publishers, for example, are known to be sensitive about introducing into their materials content that is likely to be controversial. Thus the threat of controversy results in nonpublication and weak pablum in the curriculum.

Loose Coupling. The goals set by reformers—the ideal curriculum—may not be faithfully followed by local school boards—the formal curriculum—and certainly are not likely to be attained by the procedures of teachers in the classroom—the actual curriculum. Awareness of loose coupling, or the inability of policymakers to implement their curriculum plans, has resulted in what Arthur Wise calls "hyper-rationalization."[8] Since teachers have failed to attain the goals, they must be made accountable for the goals. Classroom methods and procedures for treating handicapped and bilingual children, for example, are now specified in detail by federal and state agencies and by the courts. Compliance is sought through program evaluation, site visits, reviews of classroom records, and learner verification—pupils both displaying desired competencies and reporting to authorities about teachers' practices. Policymakers in federal or state governments now mandate measurable goals (narrow, selective, and minimal) and demand frequent testing of pupil achievement with respect to these goals. Additional control over the curriculum occurs through special staff development of experienced teachers and competency-based education for novices—both types of training programs consistent with the curriculum goals of the centralized planners.

PARTICIPANTS IN DETERMINING CURRICULUM POLICY

School-Based Participants

Teachers. Michael Kirst has shown that the teacher is a crucial maker of curriculum policy.[9] Even in such a seemingly clear-cut subject as elementary arithmetic, the teacher is not simply an implementor of

[8]Arthur E. Wise, "The Hyper-rationalization of American Education," *Educational Leadership* 35, no. 5 (February 1978): 354–62.
[9]Michael W. Kirst, "Policy Implications of Individual Differences and the Common Curriculum," in *Individual Differences and the Common Curriculum*, NSSE Yearbook (Chicago: University of Chicago Press, 1983), pp. 282–299.

policy. Teachers decide, for example, whether to spend time on drill or problem solving. Similarly, John Schwille and others have pointed out that teachers have considerable freedom to employ their own notions of what schooling ought to be even when subjected to the external pressures of state textbooks and district curriculum guides.[10] In deciding which students will get what kind of curriculum content, the teacher takes on a political role.

At the classroom or instructional level, most teachers have the opportunity to define instructional objectives within an overall framework that indicates what is to be taught. Often they can also design and order learning activities to achieve these ends. They make important curriculum decisions when they decide to group activities around particular organizing centers such as a problem, a project, an area of inquiry, a subject topic, or a unit. However, a teacher's freedom in curriculum development varies. Many years ago, Virgil Herrick proposed three different degrees of teacher responsibility for making curriculum decisions.

As seen in Table 11.1, teachers differ in their acceptance of responsibility for decision making. At Degree I teachers do little more than to follow the textbook and school policies. At Degree II teachers take responsibility for decisions regarding learning activities, the time to be spent on particular subjects and in evaluating students. Teachers at Degree III go beyond textbooks, selecting concepts to be taught, designing learning activities, and creating smooth transitions between steps.

In earlier periods, teachers were more involved in courses of study preparation. Teacher participation in curriculum revision was not new even in 1922. Gary Peltier, for example, writes of a program of curriculum construction at that time using teacher participation. The account brings forth most of the arguments in favor of teacher participation in curriculum decision making. As a result of this participation, teachers became better informed about the aims of education and better able to interpret programs for the people, and they accepted suggestions for new methods more readily. Their courses of study then reflected newer views of subject matter, social needs, and attention to the learner.[11]

A radical proposal for curriculum decision making was made by Hilda Taba in 1962. She called for a deliberate inversion of the common procedure. Instead of starting with a general design in which curriculum began at the societal level and rippled down through institutions to the classroom, Taba proposed that curriculum making start at the teaching

[10]John Schwille et al., "Teachers as Policy Brokers," in *Teaching Policy*, ed. Lee Shulman. (New York: Longman, 1982).

[11]Gary L. Peltier, "Teacher Participation in Curriculum Revision: An Historical Case Study," *History of Education Quarterly* 7, no. 2 (Summer 1967): 1209–1215.

TABLE 11.1   Degrees of Teacher Responsibility in Making Curriculum Decisions

Areas of Decision	Degree I	Degree II	Degree III
Concepts to be taught	Text or workbook	Text and course of study	Subject specialist
Experience, facts, activities, materials	Text, workbook, and teacher	Text, teacher, groups of pupils	Teacher, pupils, community
Timing and schedules	Text, workbook, teacher, and school program	Teacher and school program	Teacher, pupils, school program
Evaluation	Text, workbook, teacher, school evaluation program	Teacher, concepts to be learned, evaluation program	Teacher, pupils, school evaluation
Continuities and next steps	Text, workbook, and activities of school program	Text, courses of study, teacher	Teacher, pupils

level with the planning of specific units of instruction. The results of experimenting with these units then would provide a basis for a general design to be created later. Taba's strategy was calculated to infuse theory into the operation of the practitioner from the outset.[12] The concept of teacher participation as given in Chapter 9 is a similar notion. However, school or districtwide coordination of curriculum by teachers is unlikely because of their focused interest in their own classrooms.

Teachers are likely to influence curriculum policy in the larger political arena through their unions. Teacher organizations are beginning to look at curriculum issues. Accountability procedures, differentiated staffing, voucher plans, and other innovations affecting teachers force them to take positions on what shall be taught. Until recently, however, demands from such organizations focused primarily on staff benefits such as pay, class size, or extra assignments. But today, there is an expectation that teachers will use this organized power in the interests of curriculum to exercise authority over such matters as textbook selection. In 22 percent of school districts in the United States, teacher participation in the selection of textbooks is part of the negotiated contract.[13] Teachers want to establish the minimum knowledge that students enrolled in particular courses should derive from the courses and to determine what concepts and values are to be taught in a particular course. Teachers also want the authority to choose the appropriate method for teaching the course. In general, teachers desire to have a modest amount of influence over school policies and practices, particularly those affecting their classrooms. They like to be consulted and to have the opportunity to initiate change as it affects their individual classroom, but not to have large responsibility for the entire school.[14]

Teachers are beginning to influence some curriculum decisions through collective bargaining. For example, innovative programs are being traded for smaller classes and guaranteed jobs for experienced teachers. Van Geel, for instance, wonders whether boards of education should be forced to pay off, in effect, a private group (the teachers' unions) in order to keep control of what they were established to do.[15] Collective bargaining has raised the issue of whether public interests in curriculum—the interests of students, parents, and others—might be

[12]Hilda Taba, *Curriculum Development: Theory and Practice* (New York: Harcourt Brace and World, 1962): p. 529.

[13]Sherry Keith, *Politics of Textbook Selection* (Palo Alto: Stanford University Press, 1981).

[14]Gerald Grant et al., "The Teacher's Predicament," *Teachers College Record* 84, no. 3 (Spring 1983): 593–609; Susan Mones Johnson, "Teacher Unions in Schools: Authority and Accommodation," *Harvard Educational Review* 53, no. 3 (August 1983): 309–26.

[15]T. Van Geel, *Authority to Control the School Program* (Lexington, Mass.: Heath, 1976): pp. 178–79.

trampled on if disproportionate powers are given at the bargaining table to board and teacher groups.

Teachers' organizations also have much influence at the state and federal levels. Teacher political action committees are active in nearly all states raising funds for politicians friendly to teachers' causes. Teacher center legislation, for example, which states that teacher centers must come under the operation of a policy board whose members are represented by a majority of practicing elementary and secondary teachers, was lobbied for and supported by the teachers unions.[16]

Principals. Despite the formal job description as curriculum leader, the principal tends to be little more than a middleman between the central office, parents, and the staff in implementing curriculum. Principals are burdened with such a multitude of managerial activities that it is extremely difficult for them to devote the time and effort required for innovation on a substantial scale. Principals can be actively engaged in curriculum making only in schools where their planning responsibilities can be carried out without heavy managerial responsibilities.

The role of the principal in curriculum making is not settled. Some people think that the principal should initiate curriculum change. Others believe that principals can be more effective and influential by implementing curriculum decisions already made. One would expect principals working in centralized school systems to be more likely to accept the latter role. To date, however, they have not. Although the principal now has the power to make some decisions that were formerly made at the central office, accountability is still directed upward, not toward the community. Decentralization has probably made some principals more responsible to their communities and more attentive to system–wide goals and to ways of tailoring local school objectives to meet these goals. Esra Staples, for instance, found that, under decentralization, the principal's influence was the greatest in selecting materials, altering programs in content areas, and in determining the school goals.[17]

Mainly, curriculum development has not improved in decentralized school systems because teachers and principals lack the technical skills for curriculum making. Decision making has been placed at the local level with very little guidance for the principal. Meanwhile, we continue to hear the platitude that the "greatest amount of power to change and improve the curriculum lies in the hands of local administrators." Older

[16]Douglas E. Mitchell, "The Impact of Collective Bargaining on Public and Client Interests in Education," *Teachers College Record* 80, no. 4 (May 1979): 695–717.

[17]Esra I. Staples, *Impact of Decentralization on Curriculum: Selected Viewpoints* (Washington, D.C.: ASCD, 1975).

studies in support of this belief are found in the work of Henry Brickell and of Paul Mort and F. G. Cornell, who reported that administrators were the vital force in the initiation of change and that neutrality on the part of principals prevented changes.[18] The reason for this conflicting assessment of the principal is that the older studies were referring to the legal authority of the principalship as a power in effecting change. The newer view attends to the principals' lack of expertise, which impedes their ability to make wise decisions about curriculum. Also, as curriculum has become increasingly legalized because of the growing body of legislation, regulation, and judicial doctrine, the principals have had their authority to initiate curriculum diminished.

Superintendents. The superintendent influences curriculum policy by responding to matters before the board of education, initiating programs for the in-service education of teachers, making district personnel aware of changes occurring in other schools, and moderating outside demands for change. The superintendent must take the curriculum demands from state and federal governments and make them acceptable to the local population. Existing studies of the superintendent are outdated. The data we have, however, indicate that school board members tend to feel that superintendents are poor in curriculum planning. Superintendents also rate themselves weakest in curriculum and instruction, as opposed to performance in finance or plant management. Nevertheless, the superintendent is the key figure in curriculum innovation and educational decision making.[19] In large cities, assistant superintendents for curriculum and instruction attempt to influence the curriculum through their work with committees of teachers and their preparation of guidelines, bulletins, and staff development sessions.

The superintendent, like the principal, is losing control over the curriculum to the centralizing forces of state and federal legislators and to the courts. On the basis of his review of research over the past two decades, on the other hand, William Boyd concluded that one of the most effective means for local control of the curriculum was held by communities having superintendents whose values were consonant with those predominant in the district.[20] Superintendents were fired

[18]Henry Brickett, *Organizing New York for Education Change* (Albany: New York State Department of Education, 1961); Paul Mort and F. G. Cornell, *American Schools in Transition* (New York: Teachers College, Columbia University, 1941).

[19]Gordon M. MacKenzie, Harmon Zeigler et al., "Communication and Decision-Making in American Public Education," in *The Politics of Education,* NSSE Yearbook, ed. Jay Scribner (Chicago: University of Chicago Press, 1977).

[20]William L. Boyd, "The Changing Politics of Curriculum Policy Making for American Schools," *Review of Educational Research* 48, no. 4 (Fall 1978): 622.

when they strayed from community values. Recent developments in taking control out of the hands of local superintendents, however, may be eroding the last power of local control.

Students. Students seldom have formal influence over what they learn. There are, of course, schools in which provisions are made for some genuine self-government by students. Student officers can be elected and appointed to policy boards. They may even approve faculty appointments and determine course offerings and academic requirements. The extent of control given students is usually a function of maturity they have attained and the nature of the particular community. Student policymaking is generally derivative rather than absolute, a privilege granted by higher powers and subject to revocation by them. Often student government is an administrator's or teacher's means of securing student cooperation.

Informally, however, students have much influence over what is taught. Often they can vote with their feet by refusing to enroll in courses that feature the curriculum of academic specialists. The failure of students to respond to the Physical Science Study Committee's "Physics" was an argument for curriculum change. Alternative schools and underground newspapers are other instances of student power. The late 1960s saw both college and high school students dissenting against their role as a captive audience and asking for both a social curriculum that would confront the facts of war, racism, oppression, and a personal curriculum to help them discover themselves.

Community Participants.

Local School Board. Political analysis shows local boards of education playing a diminishing role in actual decision making.[21] Members of these boards often rubber stamp the professionals' recommendations. Board members usually lack the technical competence they need to decide on specific programs. Hence, they vote on intuition or the advice of others. Also, growing state and federal pressure has weakened local jurisdiction, and in large districts at least, the less specific policies are not carried out according to the board's mandates. Usually the smaller the community, the more likely the public is to believe that school board members are primarily concerned with the welfare of children. Residents of large urban centers tend to see board members as individuals seeking prestige and power.

[21]David K. Wiles and Houston Conley, "School Boards: Their Policy-making Relevance," *Teachers College Board* 75, no. 3 (February 1974): 309–18.

Lee K. Davies described how the actions of legislators, judges, and lay groups took away the control from local school boards.[22] She finds the courts the focus of the current struggle for control. Special interest groups prefer to go to court if board policies are not to their satisfaction rather than to discuss board policy at public meetings of the board. Law suits are especially popular with those who cannot prevail in ordinary political decision making.[23] Similarly, legislation is viewed as a last resort for the citizen who is in opposition to the local board. The instances of Massachusetts legislation on the local policy for the assignment of pupils to special classes and of Florida legislation in opposition to Orange County's policy regarding sex education are examples of legislation which parents seeking a change in the school system began.

Briefly, federal, state, and local professionals seem to be determining the curriculum and the board is serving as an advisor. The realities of implementing federal and state directives and court orders tend to make board members more dependent on experts, especially those with legal expertise.

The Public. The role of the local lay community in formulating curriculum is minimal. The public knows little about course content and is not involved with general curriculum issues. Vandalism, drugs, and discipline tend to be seen as problems, not as curriculum issues. Until very recently, local communities left curriculum planning to professionals. Only occasionally did the public get involved in curriculum. These occasions are viewed as episodic issues which emerge under special conditions and shortly subside. Thus it is not textbooks that cause concern, but a particular textbook under a special set of circumstances.

Community participation in local curriculum making was thought to increase because of the establishment of such innovations as local school advisory bodies charged with representing community needs and interests and local school site management. To date, however, studies of such councils have shown that most participation has come from parents of successful learners and that not much has been improved by virtue of the school councils. This may have been due to school boards' lack of specificity in stating what they mean by participation or to the reluctance of educators to share in decision making.

Jon Schaffarzick found that citizen participation in curriculum poli-

[22]Lee K. Davies, "The School Board's Struggle to Survive," *Educational Leadership* 34, no. 2 (November 1976): 95–99.
[23]Michael A. Robell and Arthur R. Block, *Educational Policy Making and the Courts* (Chicago: University of Chicago Press, 1982).

cymaking tends to be minimal, perfunctory, reactive, and superficial.[24] Citizens take part very early when general goals are being established or very late when most of the preparation for change has been completed. Citizens can, however, be influential when they become activated. When significant conflicts arise between citizens and school board, lay groups usually win. Most active parent groups represent special interests in the curriculum, working for such programs as those in behalf of the handicapped or those that will strengthen the fields of athletics, art, and music. Together with the professional educator associated with those particular programs, they engage in campaigns to protect and enhance their interests.

Most citizen groups active in school affairs are not parents, however, but members of noneducational organizations, such as business associations and property owners' groups. They are more interested in school policies bearing on taxes and the prestige of the school in connection with property values than in decisions about course content.

State Agencies

During the 1970s, the states increased their role in educational policy at the expense of local school districts. This growth was a result of an increase in the states' fiscal capacity to regulate education and the activities of interstate policy issue networks, which influence federal funding and educational directives.[25]

States exercise leverage on the curriculum in many ways. State legislatures frequently prescribe what shall be taught. Driver training and courses on the dangers of alcohol and narcotics have long been mandated. Insurance, oil, and automobile interests, too, have influence in such matters as driver education legislation. Professional organizations, like those of vocational, special, and physical educators, even of home economics teachers, use their state chapters to maintain their interests by influencing state requirements. Representatives of these special interest groups long ago cemented links within state departments of education.

The most noteworthy evidence of state control of curriculum is in the national minimum competency movement and academic reform by

---

[24]Jon Schaffarzick, "Teacher and Lay Participation in Local Curriculum Change Considerations," (Paper presented at the American Educational Research Association Annual Meeting. San Francisco, Ca., 1976).

[25]Michael W. Kirst, *The State's Role in Educational Policy: Innovation* (Palo Alto: Stanford University Press, 1981).

state legislation. This competency movement is concerned with assessing the basic academic skills of students at the high school and grammar school levels, and, ultimately, with establishing competency standards which all students must meet. By 1980, most states had either adopted legislation on the testing of such skills or had enacted regulations through their state boards of education. Academic reform legislation chiefly in setting tougher standards—more mathematics, science, English and foreign language—was common in 1984.

Unlike the federal government and its chief reliance on fiscal control, states use many controls in shaping the process and quality of the curriculum. Required texts, mandated testing, and requirements for teacher certification and competency are some of their means of control. The monitoring mechanisms are also more informal than those of the federal government—informal conciliation, district self-review, and management by media.

The roles of state departments of education and state boards of education vary from state to state. In New England, the local schools have had much freedom from state control, whereas in most southern states, textbooks and courses of instruction are mandated by the state. The manner of control has also differed. Some states, like New York, have long exercised control through required tests and examinations. Others, like Texas and California, exercise their leverage through state adoption of textbooks and instructional systems. In Texas, for example, the state commissioner nominates the members of the State Textbook Committee, and the State Board of Education has final authority in the selection of texts. State education department personnel specify the criteria for selecting the books, including the topics to be covered. Books that have been selected are distributed to schools at state expense. Districts that want to use other texts must do so with local money.

In 1974, California adopted, for the first time, a multiple list of textbooks in a field instead of a single or very limited list. Further, the criteria used in California reflected new influences on the curriculum, such as from women's rights and ethnic or racial groups. Evaluators were mainly concerned with the structure of the materials, and with portrayal of race and minority relationships. These concerns, in turn, had an effect on the publishing houses, many of which modified their material. Later, California returned to a limited list of textbooks. Reasons for this return to limited choice paralleled the trend to a more centralized curriculum and less attention to individual differences.

Some states use accreditation procedures to maintain a particular curriculum. Accreditation may be done by the state department of education itself, by an association of professional educators (such as the National Association of School Principals), or by a private regional accrediting organization (such as the North Central Association of Colleges and Secondary Schools). Usually these agencies require site visits and evidence of a school's adherence to each of their detailed standards. One of their standards might read, "English courses are organized by themes or experiences with a minimum of emphasis on type or chronology." A standard for social studies might read, "Social studies offerings assist pupils in understanding ideologies that differ from democracy."

Testing Agencies

Testing agencies have helped make a "national" curriculum. Standardized tests for college admission have almost defined what students going to college must know in the way of understanding and reasoning. (See the *College Board Specification of Outcomes*, page 123.) Further, national standardized reading and math tests given in the elementary schools determine much of the specific content of the curriculum. The Educational Testing Service, with an annual budget of more than $52 million, dominates the testing industry and administers a broad range of vocational and college placement tests. Its Scholastic Aptitude Test is considered the most important test the company has. About 1 1/2 million students take the test each year. The test publishers say they try to hold a middle ground; they try not to freeze the secondary school curriculum and not to adopt innovations too quickly. Their practice of involving professionals from secondary schools and colleges in the preparation and review of the tests is intended to keep the achievement tests abreast of important trends.

Publishers

Book publishers are the gatekeepers of ideas and knowledge. Most teaching in our schools is from textbooks or other curriculum material, such as guides, workbooks, and laboratory apparatus. Nearly 75 percent of students' classroom time and 90 percent of their homework is spent with instructional materials.[26] Student achievement—what students acquire from instruction—mirrors to a substantial extent the content in the textbook. Students are more likely to learn what they find in their

[26]Sherry Keith, *Politics of Textbook Selection*.

textbooks than in something else. Once an item of content has been included in a text as important for children to use, Walker and Schaffarzick say,

> the multiple resources of the curriculum in use and the variety of active student learning processes combine to produce a level of achievement that is usually greater than any additional increment that might be produced by any further refinement of the curriculum or any improvement in teaching style or method or medium of instruction or organizational change in the school or classroom.[27]

Often the textbook publisher is only a disseminator, and the actual product is developed by professionals in regional laboratories, universities, and nonprofit organizations paid by agencies of the federal government, private foundations, and professional and scientific associations. At other times, the publisher contracts directly with teachers to develop the company's products. Reference has already been made to the pressure on publishers from state curriculum commissions and groups demanding emphasis on certain content. Publishers also use their sales organizations for information and guidance in the revision and production of texts. "Strangely enough this network of salespeople is the only reasonably dependable comprehensive mechanism for compiling the preferences and prejudices of schools on curriculum matters."[28] Even so, textbook content is generally one decade behind the scholarly fields with respect to knowledge and interpretation.

The Courts

The involvement of the courts in curriculum matters has become a critical issue. Some curriculum specialists are disturbed by what they see as a trend in the courts to exceed their authority in curriculum matters.[29] Recent court decisions have mandated specific tests, methods and materials that schools must use. Some courts have even mandated achievement goals in desegregation cases which, in effect, have made them the evaluators of school curriculum and programs. For example, in San Diego a judge ordered a controversial approach to teaching reading involving mastery learning. In Tucson, a specific teaching method was mandated for use with minority pupils, and in Detroit, a judge ordered

[27]Decker Walker and Jon Schaffarzick, "Comparing Curriculum," *Review of Educational Research* 44, no. 1 (1974): 101.
[28]Kirst and Walker, "An Analysis of Curriculum Policy Making," p. 497.
[29]Nicholas G. Crisculo, "Seven Critical Issues Facing Today's Schools," *Catalyst for Change* 12, no. 2 (Winter 1983): 28–30.

school officials to submit an instructional plan for use by all teachers in the system.

Authority to control public school curriculum resides as a matter of state law primarily with state education officials. However, Gail Sorenson has suggested two practical and legal ways to deal with challenges to curriculum content such as occurs in censorship matters:

1. Consider the fundamental First Amendment Principle of non-suppression of ideas. "Our Constitution does not permit the official suppression of ideas."
2. Recognize that materials used in public schools must be educationally suitable. That is, the decision to accept or reject material must not be on the basis of ideas expressed but on whether the material fosters or hinders the intellectual, emotional, and social development of students.[30]

The Federal Government

In the 1960s and 1970s, the federal government became a very powerful influence on the kinds of materials used in schools. Mainly through the National Science Foundation (NSF) and the United States Office of Education (USOE), it dwarfed all previous curriculum development efforts by states, districts, and private enterprise. Federally supported regional laboratories, academic scholars, and nonprofit organizations produced curriculum materials that have been used in most of our schools. Generally, this material modified the content of existing subject matter—mathematics, science, English, and reading. Also, by specifying the use of standardized tests for evaluating the projects they finance, federal agencies fostered national objectives.

Initially the government seemed to be interested in increasing the number of curriculum options available to schools. Later, however, there were deliberate efforts to ensure that schools used the new curriculum through evaluation requirements and special monies given to disseminate materials developed with federal funds. The government became more interested in producing change than in merely making change possible.

The partnership between government and certain subject matter specialists had effects on the curriculum, some of them dire. Jerome

[30]Gail Paulus Sorenson, "Constitutional Considerations in Content-Based Curriculum Decision-Making" (Paper presented at the Annual Meeting of the AERA, April 11-15, 1983).

Bruner and Jerrold Zacharias were two professional reformers sponsored by National Science Foundation funds. Zacharias gave much of the impetus to the curriculum reform movement of the 1960s, in which subject specialists took it upon themselves to define the structure of subject matter worth teaching to pupils. He argued then that a curriculum based on disciplines was necessary because "our real problem as a nation was creeping anti–intellectualism from which came many of our educational deficiencies."[31] Dissatisfaction with the scholars' curriculum came under attack for reasons ranging from economics to ideology. Evaluation in terms of pupil achievement failed to demonstrate its worth. Test scores declined considerably as did student interest in further study of the subjects taught. Zacharias, the physicist who was partly responsible for the academic emphasis, reversed his judgment and admitted that the impact of the new math, for example, was "on the whole negative." Along with other critics, he said that the proponents of the reform curriculum were too concerned with pure subject matter and paid too little attention to the practical uses of mathematics in the children's present and future lives. Subsequently, Zacharias conceived a new project and received $4 million from the USOE to develop a television series, which stressed the power of mathematics as a tool to cope with such common tasks as baking a cake, leaving a tip, and estimating the amount of paint needed to paint a room.

In 1977 the National Institute of Education (NIE) shifted its budget from curriculum development to support for basic and applied research and efforts to stimulate and coordinate the research and development (R and D) work of other educational agencies. This change in federal reform strategy occurred because of the high costs of curriculum development as carried out by regional laboratories and other R and D agencies, and because of public concern over the nature and effects of federal support for curriculum development. Jon Schaffarzick and Gary Sykes have discussed this shift in government priorities.[32] They recall the issues of federally backed revision efforts—the argument that federal involvement in curriculum contributed to the nationalization of the curriculum versus the argument that such efforts increased the educational alternatives.

The 1977 NIE policy established equalization of educational opportunity for minorities, women, non-English-speakers, the poor, and the geographically isolated as the focus of federal curriculum development

---

[31]J. Koerner, *Who Controls American Education?* (Boston: Beacon Press, 1968): p. 62.
[32]Jon Schaffarzick and Gary Sykes, "A Changing NIE: New Leadership, A New Climate," *Educational Leadership* 35, no. 5 (February 1978): 367–72.

(instructional improvement) efforts. NIE recognizes that there is little consensus about the proper role of government in curriculum development, particularly in the areas where values are so prominent—social studies, moral education, and sex education. The educational community fears that federal sponsorship of development, demonstration, dissemination, and teacher training activities is an illegitimate attempt to weaken state and local control over the school curriculum.

In his analysis of the failure of federal education policy, James Guthrie does not see an expanded role for the federal government in education.[33] Instead he thinks that the responsibility for improving public schools will fall on local districts and state governments. Without the cooperation of special interest groups which are now fragmented and changed public opinion, Guthrie sees federal influence sticking with its long-standing interest in vocational education and equal educational opportunity.

Foundations

The foundations are a major source of funds and influence on the curriculum. The Ford, Rockefeller, Carnegie, and Kettering foundations have been very active in curriculum development. Some indication of the direction and effect of their influence is found in *A Foundation Goes to School*.[34] This report tells of deliberate efforts to change the habits of school systems and to modify the curriculum, both by putting into practice the curriculum reform movement of Zacharias and Bruner and by underwriting the production of locally made curriculum materials. The foundations' effort was only partially successful, mostly in suburban school districts. The effort to package curriculum stalled because teachers wanted to create their own materials. Yet, in many instances, overproduction of inadequate curriculum units at the local level occurred because of failure to estimate the difficulties of curriculum construction.

In terms of both cost and learning, the adoption of professionally developed curricula produced far more substantive change than in-house curriculum development. Without systematic teacher preparation, the use of new curricula tended to be superficial, sporadic, and ephemeral. The most lasting application seemed to occur in middle-sized suburbs, which were small enough to avoid the divisive debate between powerful interest groups but large enough to require that innovative movements be identified with more than individual or simple localized concerns.

[33]James W. Guthrie, "The Future of Federal Education Today," *Teachers College Record* 84, no. 3 (Spring 1983): 672–690.
[34]Ford Foundation, *A Foundation Goes to School* (New York: Ford Foundation, 1972).

Pressure Groups

Kirst and Walker have differentiated between two separate policy-making processes: normal policymaking and crisis policymaking. Groups such as the John Birch Society, Chamber of Commerce, National Association of Manufacturers, and AFL-CIO are regarded as relatively weak in normal policymaking but very powerful in crisis policymaking.[35]

International academic competitiveness, drug abuse, war, depression, violence, energy, and natural disaster are examples of crises which draw the response of different groups. Then there are organizations like the Council for Basic Education, which lobbies consistently for the teaching of fundamental, intellectual subjects, and the American Education Association which is against sex education and atheistic ideas. The political workings of the National Association for the Education of Young Children illustrate a single cause approach.[36] Also, some causes invite the combined pressures of many different groups. Virtually every organization working for the advancement of Afro-Americans, whether militant or moderate, has demanded a more adequate treatment of blacks in books and courses dealing with the history of the United States. Similarly, in protecting against the secular offerings of public schools, members of conservative religious groups challenge the notion that schools teach the truth and that there is such a thing as objective knowledge.

Special interest groups follow a common strategy in influencing curriculum content: (a) they offer their own evaluation criteria for judging instructional materials, in contrast to the criteria given by the state; (b) they politically address the school board rather than go through the bureaucratic structure of the school, and (c) they rely on moral arguments and their own moral positions.

CONFLICTS IN CURRICULUM CONTROL

The control of curriculum in the United States is a shared responsibility. Authority is dispensed throughout three levels of government—local, state, and federal—and curriculum mandates are issued from all three branches of government—legislative, executive, and judicial. These mandates include: (a) federal court actions such as those pertaining to meeting the language needs of non-English speakers and of children

---

[35]Kirst and Walker, "An Analysis of Curriculum Policy Making," p. 498.
[36]Barbara Miller, "Expanding Our Child Advocacy Efforts: NAEYC Forms a Public Network on Children," *Young Children* 38, no. 6 (September 1983): 71-74.

with specific handicaps; (b) federal legislation giving funds to school districts if they agree to meet certain conditions for their use. Examples of such funding are those for disadvantaged children, science, mathematical, and environmental education, ethnic studies, vocational education, career education, gifted education, and consumer education; (c) state courts in their decisions relating to school financing, planning, and implementation of educational programs have triggered mandates that increase state control of programs formerly delegated to local school authorities; (d) court decisions giving participation privileges to parents and students as well as increased use of legal contracts (collective bargaining) which result in mandates directly or indirectly affecting curriculum, preempting the control by local boards and educators.

Shared control has produced conflict. Federal mandates often combine both educational and social or political goals, as in grant programs for special groups. While these mandates draw attention to the poor, minorities, and the handicapped, they also conflict with traditional views of how best to develop understanding, skills, and attitudes among learners. For example, children sometimes are required to travel to distant schools, losing instructional time in order to satisfy arbitrary racial composition percentages.

Contradictory mandates from different levels of authority sometimes occur. For example, the federal requirement demands quotas in vocational education, quotas which often conflict with state guidelines on who is to be eligible for such programs. Mandates for the federal and state governments on behalf of certain special interests have resulted in competition with other special interests and with regular programs, resulting in program fragmentation in the local school. Conflict is triggered by the failure of federal and state authorities to consider the ability of local authorities to carry out the mandates. Although financial incentives are given for starting some curriculum programs, these are mandates which assume that other agencies will provide the necessary funds, or that the local school can implement the mandate without additional resources.

Conflicts over noncompliance are associated with shared control. Intentional and unintentional deviation from the goals and guidelines of a mandate create tensions. Even when there is surface compliance, the intents of the mandate may not be fulfilled. As Richard Elmore and Milbray McLaughlin point out, "We have some perfectly legal but perfectly horrible Title I programs in our state."[37]

As the discussion in Chapter 8 of top-down strategies indicated,

[37]Richard F. Elmore and Milbray W. McLaughlin, "The Federal Role in Education," *Education and Urban Society* 15, no. 3 (May 1983): 316.

mandates cannot create commitment. The motivation of local participants to comply with mandated objectives and their willingness to achieve the project's goals are essential if the project is to succeed. More regulations governing implementation is not the answer. The difficulties arising from increased bureaucratic red tape actually hinder attaining the intent of the mandates. It is true, however, that fiscal audits and compliance reviews are influential in shaping administrative behavior.[38]

Recent studies of shared control, though, are not all pessimistic. Michael Knapp and others, for example, have found that over time, local problem solving and accommodation reduce the conflicts of an external mandate.[39] Most of the burden of particular laws, for instance, diminishes after the first year or two. While intergovernmental conflicts exist, they are neither massive nor common across all programs.

Suggestions for improving shared curriculum control include an idealistic proposal to limit the authority of each agency so that there is no conflict in power.[40] Other more feasible suggestions call for employing implementation strategies emphasizing local technical assistance and capacity building rather than depending upon regulatory or compliance oriented strategies. At least, implementation rather than compliance strategies should be used after a mandatory program has been established. Flexibility for local decision making in designing, managing, and delivering· services is a key factor in the quality of education provided under mandates. Similarly, federal mandates should encourage flexibility in responding to the wide variance among states and local communities.

One final example illustrates the conflict over the control of the curriculum and shows whose interests proposals for overhauling American schools serve.[41] In Table 11.2 the author of each report is shown to allocate greater or lesser curriculum control to the federal or state governments and serves different interests—business or industry, labor or academic, state or national. Noteworthy is the small allotment of control or influence to the local community and the absence of attention to the concerns of learners themselves.

---

[38]Mary T. Moore et al. "Interaction of Federal and State Programs," *Education and Urban Society* 11, no. 4 (August 1983): 452–478.

[39]Michael S. Knapp et al., "Cumulative Effects at the Local Level," *Education and Urban Society* 15, no. 4 (August 1983): 479–499.

[40]Edmund C. Short, "Authority and Governance in Curriculum Development: A Policy Analysis in the United States Context," *Educational Evaluation and Policy Analysis* 5, no. 2 (Summer 1983): 195–205.

[41]J. Lynn Griesmer and Cornelius Bustler, *Education Under Study: An Analysis of Recent Major reports on Education*, 2nd ed. (Chelms Ford, Maine: Northeast Regional Exchange, 1983) and *Educating Americans for the 21st Century* (Washington, D.C.: National Science Board, 1983).

TABLE 11.2 Differences in Emphasis among National Reports on Deducation

Sponsor and Report	Emphasis in Content	Organizational Concern	Special Interests	Other Features
Carnegie Foundation for Advancement in Teaching, *High School*	Language Core curriculum Elective clusters	Flexible schedules One track Residential schools	Citizenship National unity	Requires civic service. Asks for links with community, business, and academia.
Business-Higher Education Forum, *America's Competitive Challenge*	Math Science	Flexible	National interest (Federal government influence) Business-Industry	Encourages private sector initiative.
Twentieth Century Fund, *Making The Grade*	Basic skills Technical capability Science, foreign language, civic	School manager's focus on teaching performance	National (federal government influence in interest of business and industry)	Supports federal aid for special programs for poor and handicapped in literacy or English language, not bilingualism

TABLE 11.2 (continued)

Sponsor and Report	Emphasis in Content	Organizational Concern	Special Interests	Other Features
John Goodlad, *A Place Called School*	Academic studies Prestigious subjects Computer science No electives	Eliminate tracking Rigorous preparation of principals Divide big schools into small units	State control in interest of colleges and universities State determines goals but long-range planning determined in each school	Recommends schooling begin at age 4 and that the graduation age be 16, not 18. General education should replace vocational education
U.S. Department of Education National Commission on Excellence in Education, *A Nation At Risk*	Academic studies related to college admission Reasoning strategies	Extended school day and year	State influence in interest of colleges and universities	Recommends that university scientists and scholars write textbooks for secondary and elementary schools

Commission of the States Task Force on Education and Economic Growth, *Action for Excellence*	Academic basic skills	Stresses management techniques	State control in interest of business, industry, and labor	Puts emphasis upon discipline, homework, grades
National Association of Secondary School Principals *A Study of High Schools*	Shelve traditional subject matter Concentration on Higher order thinking skills	Eradicate age grouping Eliminate teacher specializations Incentives to students	No reference to federal role Emphasis is upon improving the organizational structure of the high school	Recommends out of school opportunities for learning, federal support for special students
National Science Board's Commission on Pre-College Education in Math, Science, and Technology, *Report and Action Plan*	Math, Science, and Technology	12 year plan for math and science education Exemplary schools	Federal influence in the interest of world competition	Recommends national teacher institutes, NSF curriculum development, teacher retraining

CONCLUDING COMMENTS

The debate over the proper division of responsibility among federal, state, and local government shows no sign of being settled. Issues such as a federal mathematics and science program, tax credits, and school prayer keep the focus on the federal role. The tendency of states to require more of everything—legislated excellence—is strong. The need for local commitment on every undertaking gives support for adaptive policies of implementation and local initiative. Intergovernmental relations will remain numerous and complex.

Many groups and individuals are interested in having a say about what should be taught. No single source believes that it has enough influence or power. Each tends to feel that another element is in charge. In reality, it is a standoff. The curriculum decision of a board of education, a federal agency, a state department of education, or a legislature can be changed in spirit and in fact by principals and teachers. Although students are often thought to be without much power in deciding what will be taught in schools, they have a great deal to say about what is learned.

The political link of special interest groups within professional education to those in government is not too different from the more exposed business and government ties. Most curriculum decisions, however, reflect conflicts among persons and groups. Like most political solutions, the curriculum comes about through compromise, bargaining, and other forms of accommodation. School organizations are not equal in their ability to balance conflicting pressures. Those schools which conduct more community meetings about curriculum issues have to satisfy fewer demands of special interest groups. Public meetings offer opportunity for citizen defense of challenged school policies. The formulation of curriculum policy does not follow a tidy rational procedure resting on the evidence from research. Curriculum, it seems, will continue to be developed by those who have little idea of its effect in the classroom.

QUESTIONS

1. Would you choose a "moral, principled, legal" model of curriculum making, in which curriculum decisions are made by authorities on the basis of logic and with the guidance of experts? Or would you prefer a model that depends on agreement between different political interests and that seeks no more than an imperfect justice because there is no other kind?

2. Should professional curriculum workers, supervisors, teachers, and principals exert more influence in the control of curriculum? Why? Why not? Consider in your answer such matters as whether educators have the unity as well as the necessary intellectual and moral authority.
3. What evidence can you supply that the discretionary power of local boards of education is being diminished?
4. The efforts of singleminded groups and individuals operating at local, state, and national levels have been able to gain support for special interests such as retarded children and health and consumer education. What has been the effect of these efforts on the total curriculum plan?
5. Some people feel threatened by national efforts to influence the curriculum; others see federal influence as desirable. What evidence do you have that one or more of the following consequences are associated with federal actions?
   a. Stifling inventiveness.
   b. Increasing range of local options.
   c. Stimulating local effort.
   d. Denying local needs and interests.
6. What new political alliances do you envision in state efforts to shape curriculum policy through competency-based examinations and academic graduation requirements? Who should determine the skills and knowledge to be measured and who should set the standards that determine passing?
7. What forces appear to have the greatest effect on what is taught in a situation familiar to you?

SELECTED REFERENCES

Boyd, William Lowe. "The Changing Politics of Curriculum Policy Making for American Schools." *Review of Educational Research* 48, no. 4 (Fall 1978): 577–629.

Koerner, J. *Who Controls American Education?* Boston: Beacon Press, 1968.

McLaughlin, M. W. and Lieberman, A., eds. *Policymaking in Education,* NSSE Yearbook. Chicago: University of Chicago Press, 1981.

Schaffarzick, Jon and Sykes, Gary, eds. *Value Conflict and Curriculum Issues.* Berkeley: McCutchan, 1982.

Scribner, Jay. *The Politics of Education,* Part II, NSSE Yearbook. Chicago: University of Chicago Press, 1977.

Wirt, Frederick M. and Kirst, Michael W. *Schools in Conflict: The Politics of Education.* Berkeley: McCutchan, 1982.

IV / ISSUES AND TRENDS

In the next two chapters we will examine curriculum in a wider context. Chapter 12 deals with some of the most pressing issues confronting those who would develop programs for American schools: multicultural education, moral education, vocational education, the hidden curriculum, and mainstreaming.

Chapter 13 describes changes in the school's presentation of academic subject matters. These subject matter trends reflect the culture of the moment. They also stand as early-warnings of developments that have not been generally recognized. Underlying the issues and trends is the tension between furthering the ideals of social justice and equal opportunity through the curriculum and maintaining the pursuit of excellence.

12 / CURRENT ISSUES DEMANDING RESPONSES

Six crucial curriculum issues—competition in education with other nations, vocational education, the hidden curriculum, moral education, cultural pluralism, and mainstreaming—are examined in this chapter. These matters are crucial because the resolution of any of these issues will alter the curriculum in very different ways. The chapter, though, will give no definite set of solutions to the issues. Instead, it offers a range of views on each problem, so that the readers can discover for themselves the grounds for choosing one position over another. The purpose is not to argue for one view but to consider all the factors that apply to each situation and each potential resolution.

Although each issue is important in its own right, you may regard those discussed here as just a sample from the many issues demanding curriculum responses. It is recommended, therefore, that the descriptions of these issues are used as opportunities to apply the curriculum orientations acquired thus far. In this way you will not only be thinking about the particular issues, but also developing ability to think about these and other issues as a curriculum specialist would. You may wish to examine the issues from the perspective of different curriculum conceptions or note how traditional curriculum questions are being answered by the proponents involved, for example. Using a knowledge of curriculum conceptions, you might try to analyze vocational education critically from the academic conception, the hidden curriculum from the perspective of a social reconstructionist, or criticize different views of moral education from the humanistic perspective. You may wish to treat the issue of cultural pluralism by comparing the likely responses of those with academic, technological, and social reconstructionist views of curriculum. If you choose to use traditional questions for examining the issues, you might ask: "Does mainstreaming advance the idea of a common curriculum for all? How is the subject matter of moral education related to method? Are principles of sequence applicable to the hidden curriculum?"

CURRICULUM COMPETITION: AN INTERNATIONAL COMPARISON

Is the curriculum in United States schools lagging behind those in other countries? If so, why is it, and what should be done about it? These questions are controversial. There are those who view Japanese, Soviet, and Chinese increases in educational productivity—particularly in science and mathematics—in contrast to declining test scores in the United States as a grave national concern. Others say that the data on the comparisons are questionable and that illustrations of the weaknesses of the American educational system create the false impression that American education should imitate the practices of competing nations.

Invidious Comparisons

Herbert Walberg has summarized the case for those who see America falling behind educationally and who believe that educational decline will have severe consequences on the nation's ability to compete in the world market.[1]

Walberg cites four examples that evidence the decline. First, H. W. Stevenson shows that American students fall further behind Asian students in mathematics the longer they stay in school, and that by the fifth grade, the worst Japanese classes exceed the best American classes. Second, Isaak Wirszup claims that in contrast to the approximately half million students who take a year of calculus in the United States, five million Soviet secondary students complete a two-year course in the subject. According to Wirszup, all Soviet youth are required to complete five years of physics, four of chemistry, and up to four years of biology by the end of secondary school. Third, Paul Hurd reports that during a visit by the United States science delegation to the People's Republic of China, he observed a massive effort by China to upgrade the science curriculum. In China, local curricula have been replaced with a uniform program emphasizing application and experiments. The academically talented are sought and encouraged to attend key schools. If one measures scientific literacy by an index of the number of years students must study science and mathematics multiplied by the number of students,

[1]Herbert J. Walberg, "Scientific Literacy and Economic Productivity in International Perspective," *Daedalus* 112, no. 2 (Spring 1983): 1–29.

the People's Republic probably ranks first in the world.[2] Lastly, Walberg refers to test data from the International Association for the Evaluation of Educational Achievement that permit reliable international comparisons of achievement. These data showed that Japanese students excelled the grand mean when compared with students in 14 other industrialized countries, while American students scored near the grand mean. Japanese students scored higher than students in other countries both on items that require functional information as well as items that test understanding, application, and higher scientific thought, such as hypothesis formulation. Walberg attributes the high Japanese scores to the requirement of the Japanese Ministry of Education that 25 percent of classroom time in lower secondary schools be devoted to science and mathematics. (Nearly all students are exposed to this much science and mathematics through the ninth grade.) In their three years of high school, nearly all college-bound Japanese students (about a third of the total) take three natural sciences courses and four mathematics courses through differential calculus.

The decline of science and mathematics achievement in the United States is also mentioned by Walberg. Both the science and mathematics scores on Scholastic Aptitude Tests from 1965 to 1980 and the science and mathematics achievement measured by the National Assessment of Educational Progress have fallen. The negative attitudes of American youth toward science are also considered. National survey data revealed that youth named science least often in comparison with other subjects as their favorite subject. Further, the number of Americans taking advanced science courses declined: about 50 percent of high school students took no science courses after the tenth grade, while the percentage of seniors intending to major in science declined from 39 percent in 1965 to 19 percent in 1975.[3]

Those who think that the United States is lagging in curriculum generally attribute the lag to such factors as:

Disruptive state and federal regulations that contradict each other and interfere with the operations of schools
The proliferation of minor subjects and nonacademic activities

[2]H. W. Stevenson. *Achievement in Mathematics* (Palo Alto: Stanford Center for Advanced Studies in Behavioral Sciences, 1983); Izaak Wirszup, "The Soviet Challenge," *Educational Leadership* 38, no. 5 (February 1981): 358–66; Paul de Hurd, *Science Education in the People's Republic of China* (Washington, D.C.: National Science Foundation, 1981).

[3]National Science Foundation, *Science Education Databank* (Washington, D.C.: National Science Foundation, 1980).

The reduction in required courses in the liberal arts and sciences
Inadequately prepared teachers
Inadequate materials, facilities, equipment, and supplies

Other factors related to the lack of achievement are student ability and motivation, amount of instruction, psychological climate of the classroom group, parental support, and characteristics of the student's peer group outside school.

Validity of Invidious Comparisons

Walberg himself raises doubts about the magnitude of the gap between American educational standards and those of other nations. He points out that the general ability of United States high school seniors intending to major in science and mathematics in college rose from 1960 to 1972. Moreover, as the ranking in the International Mathematics Olympics shows, the best American mathematics students stand up to any in the world.[4] Scholars who have directly observed Soviet classes have found that many Soviet schools do not have the textbooks and science materials required by the curriculum, that the preparation of teachers is inadequate, that students are not exposed to computers and programming, and that students lack motivation and often do not understand the lesson.

Iris Rotberg of the National Institute of Education has questions about Isaak Wirzup, one of Walberg's sources.[5] She charges that the comparisons between Russian and American schools are exaggerated, that Wirzup failed to compare the actual hours spent in instruction so that a report of a year of study in the USSR may actually represent less study than a semester depending upon how many hours are given to the task during the year.

As for the data from the Evaluation of Educational Achievement (IEA), Torsten Husen, the chairman of these cross-national comparative studies has pointed out their limitations.[6] Meaningful comparisons between countries in terms of what students achieve by standardized tests are difficult to make. Countries where the government dictates the curriculum with clear-cut expectations and accompanying examination

[4]Thomas Romberg and Charles L. Lambert, "Soviet Mathematics Education: A Response," *Educational Leadership* 38, no. 5 (February 1981): 365–67.

[5]Iris C. Rotberg, "Some Observations on the Reported Gap Between American and Soviet Educational Standards," *American Education* 19, no. 1 (January/February 1983): 3.

[6]Torsten Husen, "Are Standards in United States Schools Really Lagging Behind Those in Other Countries?" *Phi Delta Kappan* 64, no. 7 (March 1983): 455–61.

exercises for practice should do well on the corresponding achievement tests. One might expect an unfair comparison between the United States, which has a comprehensive curriculum (programs ranging from highly academic to vocational ones), with countries such as France, England, Germany, where the curriculum focuses upon college preparation. However, the IEA surveys showed that in both mathematics and science, the top 10% of all students at the end of secondary education (the elite) performed at nearly the same level regardless of whether they attended comprehensive or selective systems of secondary education. Opportunity to learn is the single most important factor accounting for differences in achievement. For example, in looking at the results of achievement in French as a foreign language, the United States, where only two years of high school French is required, recorded a dismal score; whereas Rumania, which requires six years of French, was at the top. Husen concludes that low standards are not the most serious problem in schooling. The most serious problem for all industrialized nations is the rise of a new educational underclass—those who from the very beginning tend to be failures in school. The key question is how to give an advanced education, one formerly available only to a small social and intellectual elite, to the educationally underprivileged—those who do not have the advantage of a background which stresses education.

Christopher Hurn also believes that most of the implications of American inferiority drawn from the comparisons are inappropriate.[7] He criticizes studies that compare systems having profound differences in objectives, values, and organization. Such studies lead to the false implication that effective reform lies in borrowing practices from abroad. Instead, Americans must realize that their weaknesses are bound up with their strengths. To expect single-minded concentration in one area—achievement in mathematics, science, or languages—is inconsistent with American values of egalitarianism, utilitarianism, and individualism. These values create a lack of selectivity, a suspicion of the liberal arts, and a desire for educational choices. The American utilitarian emphasis on the needs of students and society has influenced both how traditional subject matter is taught and even whether it is taught. The Council for Basic Education also recognizes utilitarianism as an American passion which has competed with the liberal arts education. For thirty years, the Council advocated unsuccessfully that all students should have a liberal arts education not a vocational education, and that there be other ways to provide for the different needs of different students. Furthermore,

[7]Christopher J. Hurn, "The Problem with Comparisons," *Educational Leadership* 41, no. 2 (October 1983): 7–12.

the decentralization of education in America does not create incentives for vigorous concentration on mathematics, science, and language. Finally, the imposition of narrow national standards for academic excellence runs counter to competing curriculum goals which attempt to foster informed citizens, a diversity of useful skills, self-actualization, and moral values.

VOCATIONAL EDUCATION

Four issues face curriculum planners in vocational education. The first issue is one of *purpose*. Should vocational education aim at broad intellectual development and guidance, helping individuals make decisions about careers, or should it aim at preparing students with marketable skills? The second issue is *access*. Should vocational education be open to all, to the slow, as well as to the gifted? Is the notion of courses limited to either male or female (home economics for the girls and auto shop for the boys) obsolete? The third issue is one of *content*. How well does the content of vocational educational programs match the present and future needs of the economy? The fourth issue is one of *organization*. Should vocational education be restructured in order to close the gap between the vocational programs of the school and the requirements of work?

Contrasting Purposes for Vocational Education

Americans have long been divided on the relative value of the liberal arts, which seem to have little practical value, and vocational studies, which promise to be immediately useful. During the first 100 years of American secondary education, for example, an elite group attended the Latin Grammar School which featured the classics, while commoners chose "adventure schools" which, for a fee, taught a directly useful skill of a technical or applied variety—bookkeeping, navigation, surveying.

Many who oppose vocational education reflect a traditional European view of education for different classes of students in which the most prestigious subjects are nonutilitarian.

The nonutilitarian view continues to resurface. A. Graham Down of the Council for Basic Education, for example, expresses this viewpoint with new arguments: "The idea that a school should prepare students for an entry level job is dear to many hearts, particularly if the vocational training is for somebody else's children. But in today's world, the rudimentary skills needed for success in a first job soon become inadequate. Both change and technology demand highly intellectual skills and adaptability. As Cardinal Newman once put it, 'a liberal education is the only practical form of vocational education.'"[8]

Early Rationale. The justification for vocational education does not rest on usefulness alone. The leading advocate for the comprehensive high school in the late 1950s, James B. Conant, regarded vocational education as an incentive ensuring student participation in the general educational program. He believed that for certain kinds of people vocational education provided the only motivation to keep them in school where they would benefit from education for citizenship.[9]

Early advocates of vocational education offered manual training as complementary to academic studies and as necessary for the balanced education for all students. Manual training was a more meaningful way of learning by doing. Similarly, proponents of modern career education are less interested in teaching specific skills than in erasing the differences between vocational and academic education, relating English, reading, writing, and mathematics to practical applications in careers.

Current Thinking. The current rationale for vocational education rests on three arguments—national interest, equity, and human development. Federal aid to vocational education began with the desire to conserve and develop resources, to promote a more productive agriculture, to prevent waste of human labor, and to meet an increasing demand for trained workers.[10] Presently, the government is interested in the shortages of scientists and engineers that could threaten the ability of United States to compete in the international marketplace. Thus, we can expect the national concern for scientific literacy and technical competence to become a priority in vocational education.

Equity in vocational education suggests that it should help the young, refugees, and the hard-to-employ to find a place in the economy. This goal includes training students in specific skills, in general occupational skills, in the ways of the working world. Students enrolling in specialized programs do so to increase their chances of obtaining and keeping a job. In their view of vocational preparation, employers have conflicting ideas. Some feel that the school should prepare students with the vocational skills for entry-level employment. Others think that the

[8]A. Graham Down, "Inequality, Testing, Utilitarianism: The Three Killers of Excellence," *Education Week* 3, no. 6 (October 1983): 20, 21.

[9]Robert L. Hampel, *American High Schools Since 1940* (Boston: Houghton Mifflin, 1984).

[10]U.S. Congress, House, Committee on National Aid to Vocational Education, 63rd Congress, Second Session, 1914, pp. 410–493.

school should emphasize reading, writing, computation, and social skills, leaving specific skill preparation to the employers.

Equity in vocational education suggests that it should help the young, refugees, and the hard-to-employ to find a place in the economy. This goal includes training students in specific skills, in general occupational skills, in the ways of the working world. Students enrolling in specialized programs do so to increase their chances of obtaining and keeping a job. In their view of vocational preparation, employers have conflicting ideas. Some feel that the school should prepare students with the vocational skills for entry-level employment. Others think that the school should emphasize reading, writing, computation, and social skills, leaving specific skill preparation to the employers.

Human development in vocational education underscores the intrinsic value of work. Students gain a sense of how things work—televisions, cars, businesses. Thus, the social environment is made more understandable and the learner acquires a feeling of control. Aesthetic values—the satisfaction of creative expression through the construction of a product— is another dimension in human development through work. Vocational education as exploration of different occupational areas—arts, industry, business—is a means for both creating interest and expanding it. Vocational exploration helps learners discover a broad range of possible careers and find which one might suit them. Experiential vocational education, where students engage in projects such as constructing a house, raising live stock, conducting community service, and programming a computer, points to the highest of educational ideals—knowledge of the relation between effort and consequences, team work, and sensitivity to community needs.

Access to Vocational Education

Vocational education has been accused of maintaining class divisions; in other words, working-class children are kept in school but do not receive an academic education. While the poor learn the attitudes and skills for work, middle and upper-class children have access to the more prestigious academic curriculum. Jennie Oakes in her study of the relation between race and vocational education found restrictions in access to such education for certain students, not only to academic programs, but even to higher status vocational programs.[11] Oaks ana-

[11]Jennie Oaks, "Limiting Opportunity: Student Race and Curricular Differences in Secondary Vocational Education," *American Journal of Education* 91, no. 3 (May 1983): 328–55.

lyzed vocational programs in twenty-five secondary schools. She found that on the average white schools and those with a substantial nonwhite population give about equal emphasis to vocational education. However, the characteristics of the program vary according to racial and ethnic composition. Students at the white schools have more extensive business and industrial arts programs than those attending nonwhite or mixed schools, while students in the latter schools have greater access to military training and home economics.

Within categories of programs, there are also differences in opportunity. In business programs, for example, courses in management and finance are offered predominately at white schools. Only in the white schools are students offered courses in banking, taxation, the stock market, data processing, and business law; typing, shorthand, bookkeeping, and office procedures are available in both nonwhite and white schools. Students at white schools could attend courses in marine technology, aviation, and power mechanics; students in nonwhite schools were offered cosmetology, building construction, institutional cooking and sewing, printing, commercial photography. Nonwhite students were more likely to be enrolled in courses teaching basic skills. The courses were long and often conducted off campus.

Clearly the curriculum planners play a part in restricting the access certain students have to future opportunity. Less clear is whether the restriction is a conspiracy or results from well-intentioned efforts to offer "realistic" career choices in a stratified culture.

Discrimination appears also in vocational education according to ability. The new focus in vocational education is upon the gifted. Whether existing programs will be redirected or new ones created for these students is not known. Some schools are offering new courses stressing high technology and carrying academic prerequisites. Others are grouping gifted students within traditional courses but modifying the content. The course in automechanics may, for instance, feature the teaching of mechanical engineering principles.

In addition, schools have discouraged members of both sexes from entering programs that traditionally are the realms of the opposite sex. Courses for skills traditionally thought to be male prepare students for jobs that pay more. The vocational preparation of girls in rural areas presents a particular challenge. As a group, rural women tend to focus their attention on the family, yet they have strong career goals. The rural labor market offers very few choices to most women. Those girls who depart from "sex appropriate" programs such as consumer and homemaking education may experience conflicts in the community and uncertain employment. One answer is a curriculum composed of courses which are sexually neutral—programs in food service, graphics, commercial horticulture and data processing—programs which attract both males and females. These fields lessen the conflict between community approval and self-esteem.

Content of Vocational Education

A central question in vocational education is determining the best response to the needs of students who will go directly into the job market. For a substantial number, the preparation they receive in high school is all they get. For those who think the best preparation is training in the basic skills of reading, writing, mathematics, and science, the problem is already solved. Others, however, urge substituting the familiar automotive, wood, and metal shops with new and broader courses on communication, construction, transportation, and manufacturing. These new programs will feature the processes and systems of each area and allow for the application of mathematics and science. The programs are designed to train students in general skills and knowledge about tools and materials.

The advocacy of increased mathematics and science in vocational education rests on the belief that future job opportunities will be in high technology. In California, for instance, the number of technically related jobs is expanding at twice the rate of total job growth. Many predict that 90 percent of the jobs that exist today will be obsolete in the year 2000. The demand for technical personnel in the military services is a long-standing problem.

Daniel Hull and Leno Pedrotti have suggested a means of designing a curriculum for high-tech occupations.[12] They recommend (a) a common core consisting of basic units in mathematics, the physical sciences, communication, and human relations; (b) a technical core of units in electricity, electronics, mechanics, thermics, computers, fluids; and (c) a sequence on specialization in lasers/electro optics, instrumentation and control, robotics, and microelectronics. Obviously, industry must play a part in assisting schools with the personnel and expensive equipment required for such a program.

Curriculum developers in industrial arts, one of the many different vocational fields in schools, are responding to the newer demands by starting curriculum with such goals as relating industrial arts to science and technology. In the curriculum pupils design models using principles from these disciplines. Again, a broad base of knowledge and an understanding of basic processes is required.

[12]Daniel M. Hull and Leno S. Pedrotti, "Meeting the High-Tech Challenge," *Vocational Education* 58, no. 4 (May 1983): 28–31.

Not everyone believes that vocational education must focus on high technology. Some studies indicate that only 7 percent of the new jobs created between now and 1990 will be in high technology.[13] The major demand for workers in the next decade will not be for computer scientists and engineers but for janitors, nurses' aides, sales clerks, cashiers, nurses, fast-food preparers, secretaries, truck drivers, and kitchen helpers. However, an unpredictable economy means that vocational education will have to adapt to a diversity of skills rather than to train students for a career in a single field. Students will require a broad base of technical knowledge and the ability to communicate. Specific training should follow high school and at regular intervals throughout one's career.

Although employment nationwide is likely to be in service industries— health care, trade, education—rather than in manufacturing, farming, mining, and construction, curriculum developers must balance the demand for response to national needs with the requirements of the local communities which many vocational programs are designed to serve.

Restructuring Vocational Education

Reorganization represents an effort to close the gap between the vocational programs of schools and the requirements of work. For example, there is the "cluster of skills" approach where students are trained in several occupational areas. A course in automechanics might be replaced by one in industrial mechanics which would include hydraulics, electronics, and internal combustion engineering. Similarly, day care programs might be renamed human service programs with courses in caring for children, the handicapped, and the elderly.

A second kind of reorganization is to add programs to meet expanding industries. "Quick start" programs, programs which offer customized training for a growing industry, are popular in states that desire to strengthen school ties with the private sector and influence local economic development.

Partnerships between industry and the public schools represent a third type of reorganization. Usually partnerships concentrate on a particular problem or population. For example, a group of Texas business executives have launched a program to do something about the disproportionately small number of minority students in engineering. About

---

[13]Henry M. Levin and Russell W. Rumberger, *The Educational Implications of High Technology* (Stanford University: Stanford Institute for Research on Educational Finance and Governance, 1983).

70 mathematicians and scientists from business and industry serve as tutors and role models, lecturing and conducting tours for students. About 6000 students have been enrolled in the program, and there has been an 80 percent increase in minority students going to engineering colleges.

Internships, without pay, that give students on-the-job experience are a form of partnership popular for talented students. In one executive internship, students spend one semester working a four-day week for a sponsoring organization in their field of interest. Each student functions as a special assistant to the sponsor, attending meetings and conferences and becoming involved in everything from answering telephones and typing to devising computer programs and preparing reports and studies.

The responsibility of business and industry to provide its own training and development is increasing. American firms allocate more than 30 billion dollars a year to education and training, nearly as much as the annual expenditures on the nation's publicly financed colleges and universities. The American Telephone and Telegraph Company, for instance, estimates that on any given day, 30,000 of the company's 1,040,000 employees are in its classes. Also, recent federal legislation for job training raises the possibility that schools will have a reduced role in training, and be replaced by private employer programs.

Trends in Vocational Education

Vocational education in schools is focusing on the development of attitudes toward work, basic communication skills, and knowledge of mathematics and science. National and local interests influence decisions about the particular occupations or fields vocational education should serve. Increasingly, vocational education is viewed as instrumental—a means by which students from underprivileged classes are able to have success in learning the content formerly available only to those in academic programs. Specialization in a specific occupation tends to be seen as the responsibility of employers and the more than 8,000 private technical and modern adventure schools.

THE HIDDEN CURRICULUM

The term *hidden curriculum* indicates that some of the outcomes of schooling are not formally recognized; these are unofficial instructional influences, which may either support or weaken the attainment of manifest goals. (Some curriculum specialists consider unintentional,

frequently negative outcomes, an aspect of the hidden curriculum.)
With a few exceptions, the hidden curriculum is portrayed as a powerful
detrimental force that undermines the professed commitment of schools
to intellectual development and a democratic community. The hidden
curriculum gives rise to several important questions. Does it educate
students properly? Whose interests are served by it? Should curriculum
workers control the hidden curriculum so that it is either harmless or a
tool for formally stated ends? Should we leave it unstudied, hidden, a
natural aspect of school experiences? These questions need to be
addressed, but first we should understand what is meant by the hidden
curriculum.

Sociological Views of the Hidden Curriculum

Sociologists are interested in social structures and systems. They
study positions, roles, and the interactional patterns among different
people. They study the uses of power and authority, and the norms and
sanctions that guide behavior. Sociologists are also interested in goals
and processes. They think of the schools as having functions, such as the
socialization of children and the preparation of the young for adulthood.
They distinguish between *manifest* and *latent* functions; the latter serve
ends not publicly recognized or approved.

Gordon's Study. C. Wayne Gordon was one of the first to reveal an
informal system that affected what was learned—a hidden curriculum.
In *The Social System of the High School,* Gordon advanced the idea that the
individual behavior of high school students is related to their status and
their roles in the school.[14] Further, the informal system is a subsystem
within the community and the still larger complex of American society.
In Gordon's study, students were involved in three subsystems: (1) a
formal system of curriculum, textbooks, classrooms; (2) a semiformal
system of clubs and activities; and (3) an informal one of unrecognized
cliques, factions, and other groups. Unrecognized groups controlled
much of adolescent behavior both in school achievement and in social
conduct such as dating. There was, in fact, a network of personal and
social relations. Status in this adolescent system ranged from the "big
wheel" at the top to the "isolate" at the bottom. It was a powerful
system, which presented a constant source of conflict to the teachers.
Teachers sometimes indicated the conflict by such comments as, "Jones
and his gang terrify me."

[14]C. Wayne Gordon, *The Social System of the High School* (Glencoe, Ill: Free Press, 1957).

Teachers and School Society. Teachers must recognize the expectations set by the informal system, which determines the prestige of the students, and integrate them with the formal system and its demands that students learn specific kinds of subject matter. However, any teacher's ability to adapt to this conflict is determined in part by the extent to which the principal will support the formal expectations of the system. The principal must back up the teacher when there are disturbances or disorders, for example. Also, in order to deal with the hidden curriculum of the informal system, teachers require insight into the informal system. They should be able to identify the roles in the informal groups (boss, brain, clown), the motivations of different cliques, and the individuals within these cliques. Armed with this knowledge, the teacher can make different responses in relation to that system. The teacher may decide, for example, to advance goals that are not part of the formal system by showing more interest in students whose values are not those of the formal system. Or the teacher can consciously decide to maintain objective or fair relations with all students and thereby run the risk of having conflicts with potent informal student groups. The teacher may also decide to bestow affective and other rewards selectively.

There are new trends in adolescent society today. Whereas the earlier social structure was an elaborate status system built around school activities, contemporary youths are influenced by popular figures in music, art, and television; they are concerned with self-identity, not just with status and conformity. Unlike former youths, they are now more likely to break with established values and beliefs, and not merely to rebel against authority. These characteristics have the following implications for curriculum: (1) allow for cooperative methods and choice of content, (2) encourage student examination of the values being promoted by popular figures, and (3) give attention to ways in which to evolve a value system and to judge the relative strengths of systems.

If the context of adolescent society is an important source in determining what is to be taught as well as how it is to be taught, then a major curriculum task is to analyze the context of adolescent society in order to develop programs. This does not mean that the curriculum must reinforce what is present in the adolescent society. It may attempt to weaken the power of that society. In any event, curriculum planners must keep closely in touch with out-of-school experiences of students in order to focus on the ethical situations students are facing and to offer courses for coping with these situations.

Robert Dreeben, too, has written about the social setting of the school, indicating that there is more to school than experiences derived from formal structural arrangements.[15] He believes that the school has produced different outcomes than expected because of the strategies learners discover in dealing with the school's regime. Different atmospheres may produce cheats, conformists, rebels, and recluses. Pupils derive their principles of conduct from their experiences in school. The principles acquired vary with the particular setting. Hence, a school staff should concern itself with socialization and other effects that follow from particular elements of their hidden curriculum. The staff should ask, "What kind of character is being produced by our practices of grading, grouping, eligibility, promotion, and detention?"

The Sociology of Knowledge

A quite different sociological view of the hidden curriculum comes from those who study the sociology of knowledge. The sociology of knowledge refers to the notion that the school is not an open marketplace for ideas but that particular kinds of knowledge are selected and incorporated into the curriculum.

M.F.D. Young in England and Michael Apple in the United States are prominent for their contention that specific social groups are unduly generating and distributing particular content and that this content affects the thinking and feelings of students in support of existing social institutions. Accordingly, curriculum materials bear ideological messages to which most of us are unconscious. Jean Anyon, for example, examined the knowledge in history textbooks and inferred that after reading these books students would be led to believe that governmental reform and labor-management cooperation are successful methods of social recourse, whereas confrontation and strikes are failures; that the poor are responsible for their own poverty, and poverty is a consequence of the failure of individuals rather than of the failure of society to distribute economic resources universally; and that there is no working class in the United States—workers are middle class. The author argues that just as the school curriculum has hitherto supported patterns of power and domination, so can it be used to foster autonomy and social change.[16]

The sociology of knowledge extends our definitions of the hidden curriculum by the assumption that there are hidden messages in curriculum materials—messages that influence by showing the world as certain social groups want the world to be seen by students.

[15]Robert Dreeben, "Schooling and Authority: Comments on the Unstudied Curriculum," in *The Unstudied Curriculum*, ed. Norman Overly (Washington, D.C.: ASCD, 1970).
[16]Jean Anyon, "Ideology and United States History Textbooks," *Harvard Educational Review* 49, no. 3 (August 1979): 361–86.

Other Views of the Hidden Curriculum

The hidden curriculum can be a vehicle for moral growth. The hidden curriculum can reflect an atmosphere of justice, giving all a chance to share in planning and executing activities, and in gaining the rewards of what they have accomplished as part of fair play. This curriculum, more than the formal curriculum, determines to a significant degree the participants' sense of worth and self-esteem.

The hidden curriculum is a determining factor in integration. In order that white and black children feel a part of the mainstream, curriculum developers must attend to the hidden curriculum by manipulating both formal and informal systems through conscious and well-intentioned guidance of pupil interactions. The staff must create specific programs and strategies for interactions across race, not leaving friendships, communications, and cultural understanding to chance. One effective way to encourage interracial relations, for example, is to provide situations in which children can discover similarities of interests and attitudes in other students or work together for a common good.

There is one final and quite different view of the hidden curriculum. Many school offerings have latent functions that serve special interest groups outside the school more than they serve the pupils themselves. Some courses, for example, may have the hidden or unrecognized purpose of creating student demand for commercial products. It is likely that driver training programs, which use late model cars, increase learners' desire to purchase cars, especially cars of a recent vintage. Similarly, many high school home economics courses may be kept well equipped with the latest appliances in order that young persons will purchase such items when establishing their own homes.

Suggestions for making the hidden curriculum more consistent with the ideals of the formal curriculum have been proposed. Henry Giroux recommends such actions as doing away with those properties of the hidden curriculum that are associated with alienation—rigid time schedule, tracking, testing, content fragmentation, and competition.[17]

In a like manner, Catherine Cornbleth notes that formal curriculum fosters conformity to national ideals and social conventions, while the implicit curriculum maintains social, economic, and cultural inequalities.[18] In order to make hidden curriculum consistent with these ideals, curric-

[17]Henry A. Giroux, "Developing Educational Programs: Overcoming the Hidden Curriculum," *The Clearing House* 52, no. 4 (December 1978): 148–52.

[18]Catherine Cornbleth, "Beyond Hidden Curriculum," *Journal of Curriculum Studies* 16, no. 16 (1984): 29–36.

ulum developers must examine the consequences of specific properties within these three categories:

organizational—time, facilities, materials

interpersonal—teacher-student, teacher-administrator, teacher-parent, student-students

institutional—policies, routine procedures, rituals, social structure, extracurricular activities available to the student and the community.

Curriculum specialists are expected to find out whether or not these structures and other practices in schools are consistent with the ideals of human potentiality and social justice. Moreover, they must not only make the hidden curriculum visible, they must try to alter it to enhance the satisfaction of human needs and spirit.

MORAL EDUCATION

Americans are questioning issues of right and wrong, are examining their values. Conflicts of conscience arise in such issues as sex, race, drugs, and politics. People are increasingly aware that without a moral base, no governmental, technological, or material approach to these issues will suffice. Hence, curriculum developers, too, are animated by moral concern. The question, however, of how best to take advantage of this moment is not a simple one. A number of possible approaches can be used to guide our conceptions of a moral curriculum.

Philip Phenix has defined the basic question in moral education as one about the values, standards, or norms and the sources and justification for these norms.[19] He sees four approaches that one can take: the *nihilistic* position (morality is meaningless), *automatic* position (each must create his or her own values), *heteronomic* position (the laws of God should rule human conduct), and the *telenomic* position (morality must continually be discovered).

The Nihilistic Position. This position is a denial that there are any standards of right or wrong. Nihilists hold that all human endeavor is meaningless and without purpose. This position contradicts the notion of education as a purposeful improving activity.

[19]Philip H. Phenix, "The Moral Imperative in Contemporary American Education," *Perspectives on Education* 11, no. 2 (Winter 1969): 6–14.

The Autonomic Position. The view that norms or values are defined by each person is the cornerstone of this position. It is the individual who invests existence with meaning. Advocates of this view believe that values are manmade and that all standards are relative to the persons and societies that make them. The implications of this position for curriculum are many. Inasmuch as human beings make their own values, their schools should *not* teach people how they *ought* to behave. All one can teach is how a particular person or group has decided to behave. Students then learn to adjust to a variety of values to maintain a harmonious society. As Phenix says, "It is not a question of learning what is right or wrong, but what is socially expedient." This position transforms ethical issues into political ones without reference to moral ends. It is not a question of what is good or right but of who has the power to prevail. Also, it causes the curriculum to be judged in terms of its effectiveness in promoting autonomous interests and demands.

The Heteronomic Position. This position asserts that there are known standards and values that can be taught and that provide clear norms of judgment for human conduct. People do not make values, they discover them. These moral laws are sometimes seen as originating from a divine source. Sometimes they are regarded as rationally and intuitively deduced demands apprehended by moral sensibility. Curriculum persons who hold the heteronomic position urge the adoption of strong religious or ethical programs in order to restore lost values to the young. They also have a pedagogical commitment to transmit established standards of belief and conduct.

Phenix himself believes that each of the above positions fails to provide a basis for moral education. The nihilistic position cuts the nerve of moral inquiry and negates moral conscience. The autonomic position substitutes political strategy for morality and allows no objective basis for judging the worth of human creations. The heteronomic position is characterized by ethnocentrism and is untenable in light of the staggering multiplicity of norms by which people have lived.

The Telenomic Position. This theory holds that morality is grounded on a comprehensive purpose or "telos" that is objective and normative, but that forever transcends concrete institutional embodiment or ideology. It rests on the belief that persons should engage in a progressive discovery of what they ought to do—a dedication to an objective order of values. The moral enterprise is seen as a venture of faith, but not a blind adherence to a set of precepts that cannot be rationally justified.

People preserve what is right through the imperfect institutions of society. They know, however, that these institutions will be subject to criticism and held up to an ideal order that can never be attained. A curriculum in accordance with the telenomic outlook would foster moral inquiry as a life-long practice. One would want to do right, not merely be satisfied in getting one's own way. One would also see that what is right is a complicated matter, that personal judgments are made on the basis of one's own experience, and that these judgments are extremely partial and unreliable. Hence, a person needs to associate with others who can correct his or her misunderstandings and bring other perspectives to bear. The learner, too, would perceive that every value determination is subject to further scrutiny and revision in light of new understandings.

In the domain of moral education, the schools should develop skills in moral deliberation through focus on personal and social problems, bringing to bear relevant perspectives from a variety of specialized dimensions. Sex education, for example, would be considered with the knowledge of biologists, physicians (conception, abortion, pathologies), psychologists (affect, motivation, sublimation), social scientists (the family, patterns of sexual behavior in diverse cultures), humanists (the literary meaning of sex, historical perspectives), and philosophers and theologians (creation, nature, and the destiny of the person, the meaning of human relations, the sanctity of the person, the significance of loyalty). In the end, individuals would respond in conscience to the issue. What matters from an educational standpoint is that the decision emerges from a well-informed mind, not from haphazard impulses or personal history.

Kohlberg's Theory of Moral Development

Much of the current writing regarding moral education in schools features the work of two men, Lawrence Kohlberg and Sidney Simon, who are having an effect on practice. Their approaches, however, are not as comprehensive as Phenix's, which deals with all dimensions of moral behavior, not just the intellectual. As indicated in Chapter 7 Kohlberg has attempted to define stages of moral development ranging from the learner's response to cultural values of good and bad to the making of decisions on the basis of universal principles of justice.[20] He regards his stages as stages of moral reasoning. Thus, his assessment of the learner's status is made by analyzing the learner responses to

[20]Lawrence Kohlberg, *Hypothetical Dilemmas for Use in the Classroom* (Cambridge: Moral Education Research Foundation, Harvard University, 1978).

hypothetical problems or moral dilemmas. Kohlberg admits that one can reason in terms of principles and yet not live up to these principles. He defends his work by claiming that the narrow focus on moral judgment is the most important factor in moral behavior. Other factors, which admittedly bear upon moral behavior, are not distinctively moral because there can be no moral behavior without informed moral judgment.

In trying to stimulate moral development, Kohlberg and his followers expose the learner to the next higher stage of moral reasoning, present contradictions to the child's current moral structure, and allow a dialogue in which conflicting moral views are openly compared to develop. Further, their curriculum in English and social studies centers on moral discussions and communication, on relating the government and justice in the school to that of the American society and other societies.[21]

The chief criticism of Kohlberg's view of moral education is that he has omitted important dimensions of moral education. He does not allow for utilitarian ideas of morality in which principles of justice can be problematic. He does not give enough emphasis to the need for conventional morality among all citizens in order for a society to function. He fails to appreciate that moral rules often have to be learned in spite of the temptation to ignore them. He has not attended to the affective dimensions of morality such as guilt, remorse, and concern for others, and he offers no suggestions for developing other factors, such as will, which are necessary in moral conduct.

Value Clarification

Louis Raths and Sidney Simon have another approach to moral education called *value clarification*. In value clarification the teachers draw out the child's opinion about issues in which values conflict, rather than imposing their opinions.[22] Value clarificationists think that the exploration of personal preferences helps people: (1) be more purposeful because they must rank their priorities; (2) be more productive because they analyze where their activities are taking them; (3) be more critical because they learn to see through other people's foolishness; and (4) be better able to handle relations with others. The approach is limited, however; it does not go much beyond helping one become more aware of one's own values. Value clarification assumes there is no single correct answer. Learners discuss moral dilemmas to reveal different

---

[21]David Purpel and Kevin Ryan, eds., *Moral Education . . . It Comes with the Territory* (Berkeley: McCutchan, 1976).

[22]Louis E. Raths, Merrill Harmin, and Sidney B. Simon, *Values and Teaching*, 2nd ed. (Columbus: Merrill, 1978).

values. One criticism of value clarification centers on its reliance on peer pressure (the bias of many of the questions used in the process), its premature demand for public affirmation and action, and its moral relativism.

In response to these critics, both Kohlbergians and value clarificationists claim that there is moral content to their programs. Value clarificationists, for example, say they value rationality, creativity, justice, freedom, equality, and self-esteem. Kohlberg says he believes in "core moral precepts" and that the stage-by-stage progression and group resolution of moral conflicts are more effective in arriving at the precepts than direct instruction.

Andrew Oldenquist, however, has raised another serious criticism of both approaches.[23] Neither has been able to show that the values and morality they wish to teach are rationally justifiable. The value clarificationists do not believe in rational justification and Kohlberg does not actually show teachers how to do moral reasoning. Oldenquist says that both the value clarification and cognitive development approach lead to indoctrination, not moral neutrality. They indoctrinate by pretending to be neutral in moral discussions while subtly inculcating their own values and moral outlook without reasons or argument. Oldenquist wants students to acquire a morality composed of (1) personal virtues such as courage, temperance, and a willingness to work for what one wants but lacks, and (2) moral attitudes such as honesty and the abandonment of violence and theft that a safe and satisfying society requires. His justification for these moral qualities is straightforward and in order to accomplish these moral goals, he looks to teachers who are themselves morally earnest, self-confident about moral education, and capable of engaging in moral reasoning.

In short, although there is much agreement that programs of moral education would strengthen the curriculum, there is great division as to what such a program should be. People disagree on the relationship between a moral judgment and actual conduct. Some people are not satisfied with having pupils learn only to recognize the right thing to do; they want pupils to do the right thing. A number of different expectations can be held for a curriculum in moral education. Curriculum makers must decide whether they want learners to act for a reason, to respect other people's interests, to be logically consistent, to identify their own and others' feelings, or to act in accordance with the law. In developing

[23]Andrew Oldenquist, "Moral Education Without Moral Education," *Harvard Educational Review* 49, no. 2 (May 1979): 240–47.

moral curriculum, it is a good rule, however, to stress the principle of respecting persons and considering the harm or benefit that the adoption of particular moral rules might have.

CULTURAL PLURALISM

Boards of education historically have resisted a differentiated curriculum for Italians, Blacks, Chicanos, and other ethnic, racial, and religious groups. Indications of a reversal in the "melting pot" concept appeared in the early 1970s. At this time, ethnic minority studies appeared in many schools. These were usually studies established in response to black, Mexican-American, Puerto Rican, or Oriental demands for content sensitive to their cultural experiences. American history was updated and interpreted from different points of view, which revealed the mistreatment of minority groups by the dominant white culture, the contributions of the minority groups and their leaders, and the social problems they face. These studies were offered as supplementary units, and as enrichment within existing courses such as literature or history.

Such ethnic studies soon lost their popularity for various reasons: rivalry among minority group members regarding what the content should be, fear that the studies were increasing the minorities' isolation, and the failure of our institutions to recognize the studies as intellectually valid. Eventually, efforts were made to refocus the studies. The refocusing led to new content treating intricate cultural patterns of different minority groups and the factors that account for their cultural distinctiveness in order to help students learn how and why minorities think, behave, and perceive as they do. Curricula included plans to teach the black, Mexican-American, or Oriental student reading, social studies, mathematics, and other subjects in terms of each child's cultural perspective. Also, multicultural studies were seen as valuable for all students. Acquisition of different perspectives on personal and social problems was thought to be helpful in understanding the conflicts in values that paralyze our nation. It was recommended, too, that students become aware of the many ways in which all human groups are alike, both biologically and culturally.

Cultural pluralism now embraces many aims. Among them are mutual appreciation and understanding of various cultures in the society; cooperation of the diverse groups in the society's institutions; coexistence of different life styles, language, religious beliefs, and family structures; and the freedom for each subculture to work out its social future.

A Pluralism Continuum

Not all schools have moved in these directions, however. Individual schools can be placed at different points along a separatism-cultural pluralism continuum.[24]

1. *Separatism.* Schools voluntarily separate along ethnic racial lines. The staff emphasizes academic preparation, cultural identity, ethnic studies, studies of inequality, and a matching of the programs to the community's cultural style.
2. *Segregation.* Schools involuntarily separate students. School leaders tend to deny the problems of diversity and try to maintain a status quo. Persons in these schools devote attention to operational concerns, giving more attention to bus schedules and pupil placement than to modifications in the curriculum. Teachers may receive cultural sensitivity training.
3. *Desegregation.* Schools physically rearrange children and try to fit the child to the school environment. Some children are bused. In early stages of desegregation, much energy is spent on processes and little on the curriculum. Usually, when rearranging children, districts find that just putting children side by side does not do the job. There may be preliminary ethnic study activities.
4. *Post-desegregation.* Schools have new programs, such as social studies, that include content aimed at the prevailing minority group. Teachers acquire new skills. The Third World child takes part in either skill development programs or cultural awareness sessions. There is emphasis on diagnosing academic weaknesses.
5. *Integration.* Achievement problems of Third World children are attacked in the following ways: more appropriate evaluation techniques, in-service training of teachers, low-level community involvement, and alternative classroom organizational patterns. Curriculum content is revised to include ethnic studies, nontraditional content, affective concerns, and different kinds of teaching strategies.
6. *Cultural pluralism.* Schools have new instructional goals, including the acquisition of cooperative skills and social analysis techniques. There is less concern about achievement. Cultural differences are emphasized. Students conduct inquiry into human development. They ask, "What makes us ethnically unique?" There is heavy

[24]James Deslonde, "Distinctive Features of a Minority-Oriented Needs Assessment" (Paper delivered at Conference on Administrative Strategies for Pluralistic Education, Phoenix, Arizona, April 17, 1975).

focus on values and how they are formed. The traditional role of teachers is changed. There is much community and parent involvement. Structural impediments to learning, such as stereotyping and grouping, are removed. There are new organizational patterns to meet cultural and ethnic differences of students.

By studying the continuum, the curriculum person can see where a school lies and where it must move if the multicultural ideal is to be fulfilled. In treating the issue of cultural pluralism as applied to curriculum, it is well to think of alternatives. We can have some common ends and common means. Interpersonal skills and cross-group friendships are common ends. Activities for achieving these ends require the same experiences or learning opportunities for all. We can consider having common ends and different means. Students of all races, for example, should feel positive about the school, but the means for attaining this goal may differ. In order to reduce alienation and anxiety about the school, attention must be given to ethnic perceptions of what is taking place. A staff might want to modify traditional competitive ways of working to allow for newer cooperative patterns more consistent with minority expectations. It might also want to introduce new activities that are more rewarding to minority students to give them a better chance of reaching the common goal.

We can propose the controversial idea of having both different ends and different means. Ethnic groups that consider it desirable that children be silent in the presence of an elder might request the school to treat their children accordingly. Teachers might use culture-matching strategies such as the use of nonverbal acceptance. They might consider, for example, a greater use of touch with the Mexican-American child.

We can avoid trying to apply generalizations about ethnic and cultural groups and let each learner freely choose the ends and means he or she wants. In order to do this, we must recognize the danger of stereotyping individuals on the basis of group membership. We will need a range of goals and procedures for achieving them. We will need to ask how best to introduce the options so that the student can make a considered rather than a random choice.

Bilingual Education

The current overriding issue of cultural pluralism centers on bilingual education. Advocates of bilingual education claim that it (1) reduces academic retardation by allowing non-English-speaking students to learn in their native languages immediately; (2) reinforces the relationship of the school and the home; (3) offers the minority student an atmosphere conducive to the development of personal identification, self-worth, and achievement; (4) has a positive influence on children's cognitive and linguistic abilities; and (5) preserves and enriches the cultural and human resources of a people. Those who oppose bilingual education fear that encouraging the use of languages other than English and foreign cultural values will divide American society, furthering political separation along ethnic lines and hindering the assimilation of minority students into the mainstream of American life.

In the United States, bilingual education is most closely associated with the teaching of Hispanics although, of course, there are bilingual programs for Asians, Haitians, Iranians, and ninety other minorities in United States schools.

A much discussed question is whether bilingual programs should regard the use of another language as *transitional*—a temporary means of instruction in English—or whether the bilingual program should be *maintained*, extending the child's language development in the native language and the child's acquisition of the culture associated with it.

After the abortive attempt of the then Secretary of Education, Shirley Hufstedter, to institutionalize bilingual education in Department of Education regulations, maintenance objectives lost favor. A few schools offered advanced content in Spanish to older, educated students from Latin countries. More people began to feel that the development among Hispanics of their native language and culture should occur through the foreign language program which had been isolated from the bilingual movement.

From among the 3.6 million students judged in need of special linguistic assistance to cope with the school curriculum, only 315,000 participate in some kind of bilingual program. The most common curriculum responses are:

1. *Submersion*—When there are fewer than ten non-English-speaking students, students are placed within English-speaking classrooms to learn both English and the subject matter of the course through instruction in English with perhaps the assistance of an aide who speaks the first language of the student or taped lessons in the first language corresponding to the English lessons.
2. *Pull-out Programs*—Non- or limited-English speaking pupils are separated from English speakers for a time in order to receive either English as a second language (ESL) lessons or lessons teaching children to read in their first language.
3. *Transition Programs*—The non- and limited-English speakers receive

intensive lessons in reading in their first language and at the same time receive ESL lessons. In many transition programs, the first language is the medium of instruction for teaching the pupils to read English.

The matter of whether bilingual/bicultural education programs should be only for non-English-speaking students or those with limited English is also pressing. Some advocate that the monolingual English-speaking student should be included in such programs. The Commission on Multicultural Education of the ASCD has stated:

> Implementation of multicultural education is vital at this point in our history. All our aspirations toward improvement of education for *all* children are tied to the success of multicultural education. Multicultural education is a tool for elimination of diverse forms of discrimination in regard to race, class, age, physical size, and handicaps.[25]

Briefly, minority group pressure for equity in education was greatly accelerated by federal legislation in the 1970s for bilingual and ethnic studies. However, the prevailing political, cultural, and economic climate has placed bilingual education under attack. There are a variety of extant curriculum approaches to multicultural education—special programs for culturally different students, programs where all students learn about cultural differences, programs that try to preserve and extend cultural pluralism into American society, and programs that try to produce learners who can operate successfully in two different cultures. In general, the schooling among ethnic groups reflects the fact that the United States is a multicultural society of competing social groups vying for limited political and economic resources.

MAINSTREAMING

Mainstreaming is another kind of integration: it is the inclusion of handicapped children in the mainstream of child care and education. Mainstreaming is partly a response to legislative and judicial decisions, but many people believe that it can benefit both the handicapped and the so-called normal child. There are, however, ethical and practical issues related to successful mainstreaming.

In practical terms, mainstreaming means that many mildly handicapped

[25]Carl A. Grant, ed., *Multicultural Education: Commitment, Issues, and Applications* (Washington, D.C.: ASCD, 1977): p. 4.

children are integrated into regular classes on a part- or full-time basis. Each handicapped child is provided with an Individualized Education Program (IEP) consisting of (1) a description of the child's present level of functioning, (2) short- and long-term educational goals, (3) specific services to be provided, (4) starting time and expected duration of services, and (5) evaluative criteria to be used in determining whether objectives are being achieved. IEPs offer flexibility in programming. Children may remain in a regular program for those subjects in which they have strength, while at the same time receiving remedial assistance in a special setting. Parents, teachers, a learning specialist, and, if appropriate, the child together prepare the IEP.

Arguments for Mainstreaming

Equal opportunity for all is the major premise that courts use in ruling that physically and mentally different children have the right to share with others in education. Instead of being confined to special education classes and specialized institutions such as schools for the deaf, handicapped children can now be placed with normal children so that they can learn to make inevitable adjustments to the larger world, to play and work with all manner of people, and to gain self-confidence. Some think it is good, too, for the intellectually dull to learn about the weaknesses of the gifted and for the gifted to learn the humanity of the handicapped.

Mainstreaming is seen as a way to meet the special needs of the handicapped child within the integrated classroom. Some educators, too, see the placement of those with obvious special needs in conventional classrooms as a device to draw the teacher's attention to everyone's individual differences. They view mainstreaming as an innovation with the potential for changing the system to better serve all children.

Problems in Mainstreaming

Thus far, the benefits promoted by the early mainstreaming movement are uncertain. Discussion of the problem focuses on the fact that both the term *mainstreaming* and the term *least restricted environment,* which was actually used in the legislation on the education of all handicapped children (Public Law 94–142), do not provide specific enough mandates to provide a single course of action. The problem of implementing a least restrictive environment, or alternative environments, centers on the distinction between a model of instruction versus a mode of instruction. The former implies a method for delivering services; while the latter implies the method, techniques, tactics, and strategies used to effect change in the learner's behavior. Current models of the least restrictive environment serve more to identify administrative arrangements than to specify appropriate modes of instruction.

The majority of mainstreaming programs use a variation of (1) the learning disability group model (the student receives additional assistance in the regular classroom); (2) a combination class model (the student is placed in a regular small-group classroom where special materials are available); (3) a resource room model (the student leaves the regular classroom for special instruction for certain periods of the day); and (4) a partial integration model (the student spends part of the day in both regular and special classrooms).

Implementing the principle of placing handicapped individuals in the least restricted setting required and appropriate for the individual's needs is difficult because (1) there is little likelihood of creating least restrictive environments a priori without reference to the particular individual to be served, and (2) there is little agreement on the part of educators, parents, and children regarding what constitutes an acceptable standard for success in least restrictive settings.

Most opposition to mainstreaming centers on teacher concerns and the lack of a sufficient model for the delivery of services. Not all teachers are willing to mainstream handicapped children. The opposition of many of these teachers can be overcome by informing them about the limitations and assets of these children. Teachers need to be acquainted with the background of the specific disabilities involved and helped to see the strengths and weaknesses the child has as an individual. Teachers must be equipped to deal with such problems as caring for the handicapped without shortchanging others. They need to learn how to provide for safety and arrange learning situations so that all children have frequent opportunities to succeed. Most of all, they need help in establishing an attitude of acceptance among all of the children. There are, however, some teachers who should not receive handicapped children. These are teachers whose reactions make it difficult for the so-called normal children to be natural, understanding, and accepting.

The lack of a suitable service-delivery model could be remedied by better communication between teachers and special educators, who might assist in classrooms. Special educators could inform teachers of assistance available from outside agencies such as the United Cerebral Palsy Association and local therapists. A good service-delivery model might provide for itinerant teachers who could help the regular teacher acquire needed skills. The model should offer administrative options in terms of resource rooms and other partial day plans. The teachers should have opportunities to learn about placement and reintegration procedures, and they should have the help that parents can give regarding how best to work with their children.

Mainstreaming and the Curriculum

Frank Hewett at UCLA is an educator in special education who has spoken of the curriculum implications of integrating the mildly retarded child into regular classrooms. Hewett believes that we must broaden our conception of curriculum. Instead of emphasizing the skills of reading, writing, and arithmetic, he says, we should stress such important and general skills as learner participation—overt response and attention. Other goals of importance to Hewett are persistence and the arrangement of tasks; the learner should show improvement in finishing something and ordering parts into wholes. Priority should be given to teaching retarded children how to make independent decisions. They should acquire sócial competencies, learning, for example, when and when not to make certain kinds of comments to others. In short, Hewett's curriculum would upset many current and probably exaggerated notions about the characteristics of the academically handicapped (that they are rigid, iterative, insensitive, and dependent). A practical way to enhance the teacher's respect for students of different abilities is the practice of having teachers meet with slow learners in adjunct sessions, preparing them for the next day's lesson. With preparation, the slow learners often match or excel the performance of others, gaining acceptance.

A new curriculum would attempt to show the strengths of the handicapped and the peaks and valleys that all of us have. Teachers must carefully arrange the classroom situation to attain such a goal. The classroom would offer multisensory stimulation and movement, which are powerful reinforcers for the child's active participation. There would be order centers, in which puzzles, computers, and other activities would help pupils acquire basic concepts. Teachers would incorporate academic lessons into social studies projects and crafts activities. They would include schemes for forming friendship groups and situations in which retarded children work with peers who are socialization models. Too often, we let the handicapped see only what they should not do.

Robert Bogdan completed field studies in twenty-five mainstreaming schools.[26] He reported remarkable movement in the curriculum for disabled children. Children who were once sentenced to the back wards of huge institutions are side-by-side with bright youngsters in prestigious schools. Teachers understand disabled students as people who have rights. Nevertheless, Bogdan found that in most schools handicapped

[26]Robert Bogdan, "A Closer Look at Mainstreaming," *The Educational Forum* 47, no. 4 (Summer 1983): 425–35.

children were separate additions to existing arrangements. For example, in a school that honored academic achievement, students who did not achieve were marginal to the school, exempt from examinations and a rigorous curriculum.

Mainstreaming is a social experiment. The philosophical commitment is ahead of research and practice. In order to understand better the potential of all our learners we will need both fresh conceptions of what to teach and how to teach it. The evidence concerning the effects of mainstreaming has been reviewed by Nancy Madden and Robert Slavin.[27] These researchers conclude that placement of academically handicapped students in regular classes using individualized instruction or supplemented by well-designed resource programs is favorable to achievement, self-esteem, behavior, and emotional adjustment of the handicapped. These findings contrast with the consequences of placing handicapped students in special education. There are few consistent benefits from full-time special education.

CONCLUDING COMMENTS

The comparative study of the curriculum and issues in vocational education, bilingual education, and mainstreaming point out the serious problems schools everywhere face—how to design instruction that will enable underprivileged students to have success with content formerly available only to an elite. A related problem is how best to revise curriculum so that all students explore shared values, reaffirm goals, and confront common concerns.

The hidden curriculum offers the opportunity to strengthen the formal curriculum with the desirable aspects of youth, but also the possibility of fostering poor educational attitudes in our schools. The moral curriculum raises old curriculum questions: What is the meaning of morality? Should morality be taught? Can it be taught? Is it possible to teach in an amoral manner? Cultural pluralism is important because it fits in with a growing interest in the rights of children, and because it gives us a chance to redefine the purpose of schools.

Most curriculum issues are instances of two fundamental concerns. Dedicated persons have sensed that aspects of the curriculum are not consistent with the premise that every human being is important

[27]Nancy A. Madden and Robert E. Slavin, "Mainstreaming Students with Mild Handicaps: Academic and Social Outcomes," *Review of Educational Research* 53, no. 4 (Winter 1983): 519–569.

regardless of racial, national, social, economic, or mental status. Exploitation of learners by the hidden curriculum, the denial of minority values in the curriculum, and the failure to accommodate the retarded are a few examples. Also, more persons are aware that the opportunity for wide participation in the cultural resources of the society is a fundamental right. Hence, vocational education, mainstreaming, and multicultural education are offered as new resources for helping more persons acquire prestigious cultural content.

QUESTIONS

1. What are some of the differences among countries that make a comparison of their educational achievements incomparable?
2. What cultural values in the United States make it unlikely that the curriculum of the United States will follow the Japanese pattern?
3. Should trade, proprietory schools, or industry itself be responsible for specialized training rather than the public schools? Why or why not?
4. It is often assumed that vocational education can contribute to the learning of mathematics and science. How could vocational education be planned in order to enhance academic development?
5. Describe aspects of a hidden curriculum in a school familiar to you. How should the staff respond to this situation?
6. Describe the sources of values, norms, or standards that you think should be used in planning a moral education curriculum.
7. What are the likely consequences of using each of the following approaches to moral education:
   a. Cognitive—Students are encouraged to use moral reasoning.
   b. Commitment—Personal and social action projects help students put their values into practice.
   c. Inculcation—Students observe good models and are reinforced for certain desirable social human behavior.
   d. Clarification—Through such exercises as thinking about things in their lives they would like to celebrate, students are led to define their values.
8. Using the six stages of cultural pluralism (page 282), locate the stage that represents a school familiar to you.
9. The content of many multicultural programs has expanded from ethnic histories and heroes to a comprehensive view of cultures—value systems, communication patterns, socialization processes; that is, ethnic culture is treated as a dynamic phenomenon rather than a static artifact. Give illustrations of a dynamic interpretation of a culture.
10. State two working hypotheses, one a description of situations in which mainstreaming will be successful and the other a description of situations in which it will fail.

11. Identify one or more common elements among these issues: the hidden curriculum, moral education, cultural pluralism, and mainstreaming.

SELECTED REFERENCES

Comparative Curriculum

Bloom, Benjamin S. "Implication of the IEA Studies for Curriculum and Instruction." In *All Our Children Learning,* pp. 15–33. New York: McGraw-Hill, 1981.

Torsten, Husen. "Are Standards in U.S. Schools Really Lagging Behind Those in Other Countries?" *Phi Delta Kappan* 64, no. 7 (March 1983): 445–62.

Walberg, H. J. "Scientific Literacy and Economic Productivity." *Daedalus* 112, no. 2 (Spring 1983).

Vocational Education

Dillon, Linda S. "Vocational Training in Japan." *Journal of Industrial Teacher Education* 20, no. 4 (Summer 1983): 39–46.

Grubb, W. N. and Lazerson, M. "Education and the Labor Market: Recycling the Youth Problem." In *Work, Youth, and Schooling.* Eds. H. Kantor and D. B. Tyack. Stanford: Stanford University Press, 1982.

Kantor, H. and Tyack, D. B., eds. *Work, Youth, and Schooling.* Stanford: Stanford University Press, 1982.

Kelly, Eugene W., Jr. *Beyond Schooling: Education in a Broader Context.* Bloomington: Phi Delta Kappa, 1982.

Lazerson, Marvin and Grubb, W. Norton, eds. *American Education and Vocationalism.* New York: Teachers College Press, 1974.

Silberman, H. F. ed. *Education and Work,* NSSE Yearbook. Chicago: University of Chicago Press, 1982.

The Hidden Curriculum

Apple, M. W. "Power and School Knowledge." *Review of Education* 3 (1977).

Gordon, C. Wayne. *The Social System of the High School.* Glencoe, Ill: Free Press, 1957.

Jackson, Phillip B. *Life in the Classroom.* New York: Holt, Rinehart and Winston, 1968.

Taxel, Joel. "Justice and Cultural Conflict: Racism, Sexism, and Instructional Materials." *Interchange* 9, no. 1 (1978/1979): 56–84.

Vallance, Elizabeth. "Hiding the Hidden Curriculum." In *Curriculum and Evaluation.* Eds. Arno Bellack and Herbert Kliebard, pp. 590–607. Berkeley: McCutchan, 1977.

Moral Education

Arbuthnot, J. and Faust, O. *Teaching Moral Reasoning: Theory and Practice.* New York: Harper & Row, 1981.

Beck, Clive. *Moral Education in the Schools: Some Practical Suggestions.* Toronto: Ontario Institute for Studies in Education, 1971.

Enright, Robert D. et al. "Moral Development Interventions in Early Adolescence." *Theory Into Practice* 22, no. 2 (Spring 1983): 134–145.

Ervay, Stuart et al. "Values Clarification and the Middle School." *The Educational Forum* 47, no. 4 (Summer 1983): 411–425.

Frazier, Alexander. *Values, Curriculum and the Elementary School.* Boston: Houghton Mifflin, 1980.

Mosher, Ralph, ed. *Moral Education.* New York: Praeger, 1980.

Overvold, Mark C. and Konrad, A. Richard. "Moral Reasoning and the Public Schools." *The Educational Forum* 47, no. 4 (Summer 1983): 393–409.

Phenix, Philip. *Education and the Common Good: A Moral Philosophy of the Curriculum.* New York: Harper and Row, 1961.

Purpel, David and Ryan, Kevin. *Moral Education . . . It Comes with the Territory.* Berkeley: McCutchan, 1976.

Raths, Louis E., Harmin, Merrill, and Simon, Sidney B. *Values and Teaching* 2nd ed. Columbus: Merrill, 1978.

Cultural Pluralism

Banks, James A., ed. *Education in the 80s: Multicultural Education.* Washington, D.C.: NEA, 1981.

Chu-Chang, Mae. *Asian and Pacific American Perspectives on Bilingual Education.* New York: Teachers College Press, 1983.

Franklin, Vincent P. "Ethics and Education: The Impact of Educational Activities on Minority Ethnic Identity in the United States." In *Review of Research in Education,* ed. Edmund W. Gordon, pp. 3–22. Washington, D.C.: AERA, 1983.

Otheguy, Ricardo. "Thinking About Bilingual Education: A Critical Appraisal." *Harvard Educational Review* 52 (August 1982): 301–320.

Piper, Alan. *Bilingual Education and the Hispanic Challenge.* New York: Carnegie Corporation, 1980.

Schlossman, Steven. "Self Evident Remedy?" And Sanchez, George I. "Segregation and Enduring Dilemmas in Bilingual Education." *Teachers College Record* 84, no. 4 (Summer 1983): 871–907.

Mainstreaming

Hendrickson, Barbara. "Teachers Make Mainstreaming Work." *Learning* 7, no. 2 (October 1978): 104–20.

Lindsey, Jimmy D. "The Secondary Learning Disability Program: Least Restrictive Environment and Instructional Models." *The High School Journal* 66, no. 3 (February-March 1983): 181–95.

Reed, P. "Mainstreaming in Secondary Schools." *American Secondary Education* 12 (Special issue, 1982): 1–32.

Strain, P. S. and Kerr, M. M. *Mainstreaming of Children in Schools.* New York: Academic Press, 1981.

13 / DIRECTIONS IN THE SUBJECT FIELDS

The material in this chapter is arranged chronologically, although more in the sense of trends than as a detailed recital of events. The chapter is intended to reveal what various subject fields were like in the past, describe the directions they are now taking, and indicate the forces that may shape them in the future.

There are two approaches for keeping abreast of innovations in the subject fields. One of these has already been outlined in Chapter 4, in which common trends were interpreted by purpose, content, method, organization, and evaluation in each curriculum perspective. A second approach is to analyze recent developments associated with specific school subjects as revealed by lay and professional journals, yearbooks of national scholarly organizations, textbooks, and curriculum materials in the subject fields. The results of such an analysis are reported in this chapter.

Two starting conclusions are drawn from this analysis: (1) there is inequality of access to the academic curriculum and (2) the academic subjects as taught in the schools are deficient: teachers emphasize textbook information and vocabulary, with little attention to application or to the relationship of academic study to personal needs.

Despite recent political and legal actions intended to assure equal educational opportunities, it is clear that in each subject, the able and talented students are given one curriculum and those students who are judged less able are given a very different one. When tracking occurs through a differentiated curriculum, there is no school integration in practice even when school desegregation is the social policy. This differentiated curriculum tracks some children in the programs leading only to less desirable jobs and restricted opportunities for advanced education. This is not to say all students must have the same curriculum in order to ensure equality of opportunity. It is possible, for example, to have science programs that differ in their approach with regard to topic, degree of abstraction or concreteness; yet both can be effective in helping pupils acquire useful knowledge and outlooks on science. Both approaches, however, must be shown to lead to outcomes that are equal in educational value.

The flatness of the curriculum in subject fields is cause for concern. Learner passivity is typical—listening, reciting (answering is a primary task in academic classrooms), and working on text and workbook assignments. Lacking at all levels are the activities associated with inquiry, creating meaning, and applying knowledge to social and personal concerns. The absence of a curriculum that encourages understanding and higher level cognitive processes will have long-term consequences. Moreover, the subjects taught in elementary and secondary schools do not offer what is needed at advanced levels.

The chapter reveals that swings in emphasis within the subject fields reflect a difference of opinion about the nature of knowledge. Some view it as a tool for resolving problems, while others think of it as a series of disciplines for developing the intellect. Further, one will see how political compromises made by policymakers in the subject fields to accommodate those of different curriculum orientations have resulted in conflicting purposes and incoherent programs in the subject fields.

MATHEMATICS

Mathematics in Our Schools

Before the 1950s, schools commonly taught mathematics around one central theme: student mastery of basic computational skills. This practical yet simplistic approach to mathematics instruction did not suit the nation's increasing need for theoretical mathematicians and scientists. By the early 1960s, a new trend in mathematics instruction had emerged—student acquisition of mathematics as a discipline. Two influences helped set this trend in motion.

The first influence reflected the above-mentioned need for competent and creative scientists. The other influence on the mathematics curriculum was the belief that everyone could profit by acquiring knowledge of mathematics as a discipline. Briefly stated, the belief was that subject matter fields should introduce students to the general concepts, principles, and laws that members of a discipline use in problem solving.

The new math consisted of the fundamental assumptions and conceptual theories on which every scientific enterprise is based. Unfortunately, it was deprecated for being abstract, just as the old math was criticized for being boring. For the average student, sophisticated conceptual theories had little practical relevancy. Instruction in topics such as set theory and use of bases other than the generally used base 10 replaced practice in the basic skills needed for everyday problem solving. Developers of the new math paid too little attention to the practical uses of mathematics in the student's present and future life. Hence, many specialists in mathematics argued that the school should stress a knowledge of mathematics as an end in itself, as a satisfying intellectual task. On the other hand, in order for knowledge to be meaningful, it must be applied. The main question regarding the mathematics curriculum is whether it can be useful both for development of the intellect and for the necessities of a technological era and still avoid a meaningless idealism on the one hand and a strict vocationalism on the other.

Both modern and traditional mathematics are found in today's schools. The move toward traditional mathematics results from the emphasis on basics such as computational skills, while the move toward modern mathematics results from a concern for bright students. A survey of the status of mathematics in secondary schools indicates that traditional mathematics courses—courses that feature drill and practice, computation, and memorization—are taken by slower students and students not planning on college, not by students who tend to major in mathematics.[1] The latter still take modern mathematics, algebra, geometry, and optional fourth year courses which place strong emphasis on structure, definitions, properties, sets, proofs, and other abstract concepts.

Trends

In order to facilitate the application of knowledge, three new directions have been suggested for future trends in mathematics. The first trend is an integration of mathematics with other subject matter. Opponents of the new math from its inception have proposed that mathematics be studied not as a separate theoretical discipline, but rather as an integrated part of liberal education. Integration of subject matter facilitates the application of mathematical skills to a variety of situations. The importance of mathematical skills in all subjects from homemaking to physics should be stressed.

Increased use of educational technology is a second means by which mathematics can be made more relevant. The United States Office of Education has funded programs to develop a television series on mathematics designed to show how it may be applied to all occupations and problem-solving situations. The series supplements the teacher,

---

[1]I. Weiss, *Report of the National Survey of Science, Mathematics, and Social Science Education* (Research Triangle Park, N.C.: Center for Education Research and Development, 1978).

who continues with regular computational skills. The series is staged with characters using basic mathematical skills to solve problems relating to measurement, quantity, estimation, and so forth. Technology in the larger sense is also having an effect on the mathematics curriculum. The mathematics educators recommend that calculators and computers be introduced into the mathematics classroom as early as possible.[2] Young children are expected to understand negative numbers and exponents. The use of calculators in all classes requires emphasis on the language of calculators—on decimals, fractions, and algebraic symbols. Less emphasis should be placed on pencil and paper arithmetic and more opportunity be given for mental arithmetic, estimation, and approximation. The availability of calculators allows expansion of the traditional program to include numbers of greater magnitude. Teachers are able to spend more time on concrete representations of concepts since they can check instantly for student understanding. Patterns can be more easily detected.

Community participation in curriculum planning and implementation is a third way being taken to increase the relevancy of instruction in mathematics. In the elementary school, use of parents as tutors, teacher's aides, and resource persons not only helps to reduce cost, but also provides a balance between classroom and community perspectives. In the secondary school, visiting mathematics lecturers from industry and opportunities for work experience can narrow the gap between classroom theory and practical application.

Concerns about curriculum content and about ways to develop ideas appropriate to the child's level persist. In their attempts to teach computation, some people ignore concepts and processes for developing proficiency, defining the curriculum as a series of isolated skills to be taught by drill. Also, the role of application and problem solving is far from clear. Incidentalists argue that systematic instruction in abstractions should be replaced with general problem-solving experiences from the real world. Mathematics, they believe, should be taught in relation to other areas such as cooking, building, and sewing. Others advocate experience in mathematical areas that closely resemble the physical world, such as measurement and geometry.

The immediate solution for these issues and concerns seems to be in the direction of a balanced curriculum. Content will be broadened beyond the teaching of whole number ideas in the primary grades. Ideas of symmetry and congruence will be explored. Shapes will be discussed and classified, and measurement and graphing will be popular. Metrics,

---

[2]Stephen S. Willoughby, "Curriculum Trends: Mathematics," *Educational Leadership* 41, no. 8 (September 1983): 76-7.

of course, will be necessary. Informal experiences with important mathematical ideas may contribute to greater success in future learning and to application in daily life. A balanced point of view also implies the use of different instructional procedures. No single mathematics program will fit all children. Briefly, the balanced curriculum means overcoming an undue focus on skills, mathematical content, or application. The National Assessment of Programs in Mathematics confirms that the "back to basics" movement produced improvement in precisely those mathematic abilities that are least important in a rapidly changing technological society. Computational facility improved, but children failed to solve problems in mathematics.[3] Teachers who follow the policies of the National Council of Teachers of Mathematics stress the interdependence of these three factors: First, techniques must be designed to help learners focus on specific elements and solve problems on their own. Second, a variety of strategies or ways to solve problems should be encouraged. Third, children should be given opportunities to relate events to mathematical models by estimating, applying estimated abilities in other situations, developing criteria for comparing lengths, noting the regularities of the coordinate system in the real world, and modifying or imposing order on a real situation and then summarizing it in mathematical form.[4]

In higher education, the supremacy of calculus in the freshman and sophomore mathematics curriculum is being challenged in part because the computer has changed the mathematical needs of students. Colleges and universities are initiating experimental courses in discrete mathematics which deal with individual values and quantities. Whether discrete mathematics courses will be offered as an alternative to the traditional curriculum or integrated with it remains to be seen.

SCIENCE

Evolution of Science Teaching

All branches of the scientific enterprise depend on the principles and laws of mathematics as a foundation for both theory and methodology. Because of this dependency, curriculum trends in the sciences often parallel those applied to mathematics. Science subject matter in the early

[3]Educational Commission of the States, *The Third National Mathematics Assessment* (Educational Commission of the States, Denver, Colorado, 1983).

[4]National Council of Teachers of Mathematics, *An Agenda for Action Recommendations for School Mathematics of the 1980s* (Reston, Virginia: National Council of Teachers of Mathematics, 1983).

1960s was shaped by the same forces that influenced mathematics, namely, the proposal to teach subjects as disciplines and the push towards specialization. These forces particularly affected the sciences because it was felt that advancements in a technological society required the training of highly skilled scientists and technicians.

Science subject matter at this time was conceptually and theoretically sophisticated. Students were introduced to the principles of science by the discovery process of simple experimentation. This instructional approach replaced the more traditional process of memorizing theorems and laws. It was hoped that this approach would endow students with the inquiry mode of thought used by specialists in the scientific disciplines. Science projects in the early 1960s were heavily funded and resulted in a number of new programs. Children were encouraged to participate in scientific research on a very theoretical level. Science fairs enabled more advanced students to gain recognition as practicing members of the science discipline.

During the late 1960s, the discipline approach to science instruction was criticized for dwelling too long on theory and ignoring the need for practical application. Science in schools had been too specialized to be successfully applied to anything other than scientific research. For students uninterested in pursuing science as a career, the new subject matter had little practical relevancy. The average student could not identify the role of science in the common affairs and problems of people. Also, Americans were becoming increasingly concerned about societal implications of the scientific enterprise. Prior demands for research relating to space exploration and national defense had distracted scientists' attention from the problems of air pollution, overpopulation, and depletion of natural resources. Scientists had neglected to study the relationship of research to the individual's place in the universe. As a result of this neglect, a new trend to humanize the sciences emerged in the 1970s. Accordingly, some multidisciplinary approaches to instruction appeared. Basic laws of science were applied to a variety of situations in subjects other than science. Science teachers sometimes worked in teams with teachers from other disciplines and helped students relate principles of science to current social, political, and economic problems. Students majoring in social science studied the relationship of scientific discoveries to industrial and technological revolutions. The role of the scientific enterprise in international policymaking was sometimes studied in political science courses. However, by the mid 1970s, significant numbers of citizens felt that support for curriculum in science was misdirected, if not in error. In the elementary school, the press for higher scores on tests and an emphasis upon isolated skills of reading and mathematics meant that science was seldom taught at all. Enrollment in high school science courses steadily decreased with more than half of high school students taking no science after the tenth grade. By the late 1970s, science courses had given way to rote learning with 90 percent of teachers using only a traditional textbook approach. By 1984 it was clear that there was a crisis in science education. The U.S. Government Printing Office reveals that the findings of several extensive surveys agreed on the following about the status of the science curriculum:

1. There is a mismatch between the science curriculum and that which ninety percent of the students want and need.
2. Nearly all science teachers have goals that are only directed toward preparing students for the next academic level. Science is viewed as specific content to be mastered.
3. Nearly all science teachers use a textbook ninety-five percent of the time. Science is virtually never being learned by direct experiences. Most students never experience a real experiment throughout their school program.
4. No attention is given to the development of a science curriculum; the textbook is the course outline, the framework, the testing, and the view of science.
5. The science program is ineffective in influencing interest in science or scientific literacy. Teaching by textbook summarizes the status of science education; to compound the problem, the textbooks in the early 1980s are inadequate.[5]

Terminology is the central feature in most science textbooks. The new vocabulary in typical science classrooms exceeds the vocabulary necessary for mastering a foreign language. There are too many terms, and words are introduced apart from their meaning. Paul Brandwein reported that the number of specialized terms in the typical chemistry course in high school exceeded 10,000.[6] Foreign language specialists suggest that in learning a foreign language vocabulary words should be limited to no more than 2,000 new words a year.

New Approaches

As indicated in Chapter 4, experts in science education in an undertaking called Project Synthesis predicted that the life science curriculum of

[5]Norris C. Harms and R. E. Yager, *What Research Says to the Science Teacher*, vol. 3 (Washington, D.C.: National Science Teachers Association, 1981); R. E. Stake and J. Easley, *Case Studies in Science Education* (Urbana: University of Illinois, 1978); I. R. Weiss, *Report to the 1977 National Survey of Science, Mathematics and Social Studies Education* (Research Triangle Park, N.C.: Center for Educational Research and Evaluation, 1978).

[6]Paul F. Brandwein, *Some Aspects of a Renewal in Schooling and Education in Science* (Proceedings of Annual Curriculum Update Conference, Iowa City, Iowa, 1982).

the future will be organized around the theme of human adaptation in both the scientific and social senses, and that the use of ethics and values as well as biological knowledge in making decisions will be an important goal of programs dealing with social problems. Scientific topics will be presented from the human point of view. Principles of science will be learned, not as ends in themselves, but as means of coping with personal and social concerns.

The multidisciplinary approach is frequently offered as a possible solution to the problem. In addition to drawing from several scientific disciplines, this approach involves inquiry and outreach to the community, thus serving two purposes. First, it brings new depth to all disciplines. Second, it reminds us of science's relation to the political, economic, and social affairs of humankind. A major goal of science teachers in the 1980s will be to provide students with the basic problem-solving skills they will need to cope with an often dehumanizing technological society. One effort in this direction is the Inquiry Training Project of Port Colborne, Ontario, Canada. This project hopes to improve students' ability to solve problems that a person might encounter now and in the future. To this end, instead of teaching students a single direct path between questions and answers, teachers in the inquiry project teach students to deal with questions that give rise to a number of plausible alternatives whose desirability must be thought out and ranked. The program attempts to teach children to analyze cause and effect relationships, a technique that has been profitable in the sciences. With respect to method, children are given simple scientific equipment and materials from the world around them and are encouraged to experiment. A typical activity is the raising of green plants under different conditions and observing and recording the results. Another favorite practice involves fermentation. In this project, pupils are given yeast, sugar, tubing, and a few other materials. They are asked to keep track of how the rate of fermentation is affected by changes in the amount of water used and the temperature, in order to learn about control of variables and effects of such controls. Ecological projects are also popular in science courses. As they progress, children using the discovery method are exposed to the basic concepts of many sciences, from botany and biology to physics, chemistry, and astronomy.

The broad recommendation is toward more inquiry in the science class. Two obstacles are economic and instrumental considerations. Initial investment in equipment for courses emphasizing experimentation can run as high as $500 per classroom. Also, teachers must know enough about the principles and teaching materials involved to be able to use them. One of the biggest problems in teaching science in the early grades is the teacher's insecurity with the subject matter.

Secondary schools are likely to continue to offer a few science courses of high quality for the most talented students. These courses will probably be organized around the traditional topics of biology, chemistry, and physics. Such programs are now designed for a minority of students. Indeed, data from the National Longitudinal Study of the High School Class show that entry into prestigious fields of biological science, business, engineering, physical sciences, and mathematics can be predicted by the science and mathematics courses taken in high school.[7]

The assumption that the best course for those with science aptitude is advanced placement is now questioned. J. Myron Atkin, for example, thinks that the high school years should be used for broad intellectual exploration rather than preparation for college level specialization. An opportunity to study topics of special interest in depth might be a better use of high school time than a course focused on examinations.[8]

Recommendations for the Future

There are several recommendations for improving the traditional courses. It is suggested that new materials be developed for use by the 70 percent of students now being inadequately served. These materials would deal with new areas of modern science. They also would contain less encyclopedic content and detail that have little bearing on students' present problems of living. Instructional activities would be tied to the ongoing scientific enterprises in the community. Science would be treated less as an end in itself than as a field that is related to other aspects of life. There would be more emphasis on the power, responsibilities, and limitations of science.

The idea of having the local community serve as a learning laboratory is another recommendation. Education Development Center in Newton, Massachusetts, for example, has developed science projects related to issues with social implications. In one such project, The Family and Community Health, students have health care experiences in schools, families, and agencies in the community. Units treat such topics as adolescent pregnancy, drinking, stress, environmental and consumer health. Such projects combine ideas and skills from the natural sciences, humanities, and social sciences.

In her agenda for the 1980s, Mary Budd Rowe recommends extending science as general education to more students over a large period of time

[7]Samuel S. Peng and Jay Jaffe, "Women Who Enter Male-Dominated Fields of Study in Higher Education," *American Educational Research Journal* 16, no. 3 (Summer 1979): 285–94.

[8]J. Myron Atkin, "The Improvement of Science Teaching," *Daedalus* 112, no. 2 (Spring 1983): 167–87.

and supporting science programs on television. "Three-Two-One Contact," for example, is a science program for eight to twelve year olds and produced by Children's Television Network. This program is unique in its goal to make children assert their curiosity about how things work and why and to discover the existence of science.

New curriculum efforts must avoid the failure of the science reform movement of the 1960s to distinguish between teaching and learning. While children can be taught to pass tests, they often do not really change their ideas of how and why they behave as they do as a consequence of science teaching. More time must be given to encouraging thinking about concepts in science, to searching out how pupils really think about how and why things behave as they do, and to comparing their own explanations with the explanations of others, learning the limitations of each. Emphasis must shift from what students are supposed to know to why students learn what they do.

The recommendations of the twenty-three science educators of Project Synthesis have set goals for a science curriculum—to satisfy personal needs, to deal with social issues, to prepare for further study of science, and to offer orientations to careers in science and technology. As with other curriculum fields, the central question for science educators is why certain content should be taught and to what purpose. Thus emphasis will be placed upon students (a) recognizing that scientific concepts are created, not discovered; (b) formulating ideas through direct experience before attempting to learn the technical terms for these ideas; (c) making analogies between modes of thought in science and in other disciplines such as art and history, and (d) knowing how scientific knowledge has influenced both intellectual history and one's own view of the nature of the universe.

PHYSICAL AND HEALTH EDUCATION

Its Place in the Curriculum

In the early 1960s, President John Kennedy proposed that a national standard of physical fitness be established. Shortly thereafter, most elementary and secondary students were required to participate in annual assessments of physical fitness. This period also saw the flourishing of international sports events. Participation of highly trained foreign athletes in these events aroused American interest in the development of physical education programs.

Unfortunately, physical competition as part of the 1960s sports ethic produced disappointment and humiliation for many children. Being good was often not good enough; excellence was the goal. Physical education offerings were limited to traditional team sports, and often aggression and competitiveness were the prerequisites of sportsmanship.

Throughout the 1960s, physical education offerings gradually expanded. Communities requested that more emphasis be placed on life-long sports. As a result, courses in scuba diving, bike riding, and golf were added to the curriculum. The direction was not away from strenuous exercise, but simply away from the harshness of competition. Competition as an American virtue was slowly being replaced by individualism.[9] Physical education has now established a new flexibility in course offerings. Less rigid views on sexual roles are also opening new opportunities for girls. Students, for the first time, may choose from a variety of programs best suited to their interests.

The role of physical education in the classroom has become a controversial issue nationwide in the face of budgetary cutbacks and the demand for renewed emphasis on basic educational forms. A 1979 New York State Education Department study, for example, found that most kindergarten through sixth-grade schools offered physical education only two days a week.

Guidelines for Future Programs

The American Alliance for Health, Physical Education and Recreation (a 50,000-member professional organization) has suggested five guidelines for future physical education programs:

1. Break down current mass education techniques.
2. Increase flexibility of offerings and teaching methods.
3. View sports as more than athletic competition.
4. Increase coeducational classes, sailing, camp counselor training, self-defense.
5. Promote physical activities that support the desire to maintain physical fitness throughout life.

The association recommends that teaching methods emphasize activities that can serve as vehicles for education of the whole person. Activities should be designed to introduce students to the subtle and often overlooked potentials of the human body. Here are some suggested activities:

Movement education. The objective is to develop an understanding of creative and expressive movement. Five-year-olds can be asked

[9]Stuart Miller, "Is Your School a Training Ground for Gladiators?" *Learning* 3, no. 3 (May/June 1975): 57–67.

to proceed down a marked line in any fashion they desire. Some
balance carefully, some run, some crawl, but all experience their
own style.

Centering oneself. Here the student develops a state of alert calm by
   becoming aware of physical energy in and outside of the body.

Structural patterning. Students become aware of variations in the way
   people move.

Relaxation techniques. By means of rhythmic breathing, the student
   learns how to gain control over habitual tensions.

Illustrative of newer curriculum in health is the Health Activities
Project (HAP) developed by the Lawrence Hall of Science, University of
California, Berkeley. This program offers an activity-centered health
curriculum for pupils in grades five through eight. The goal of the
project is to create a positive attitude toward health by giving pupils a
sense of control over their own bodies and by imparting understanding
about the body's potential for improvement. HAP activities, organized
into modules treating such topics as fitness, interaction, growth, decision
making, and skin, supplement existing programs in health, physical
education, and science.

New textbooks encourage students to evaluate their own food and
fitness habits and develop better ones. Texts are beginning to reveal the
role of the food industry in shaping the American diet and to feature the
future of women in sports and the effects of advertising on self-image.

Those planning the health curriculum confront concerns about drug
abuse, stress, and human sexuality. Social ambivalence toward drugs as
well as difficult home lives are factors in such problems. So, too, are the
images students have of themselves. The role of health curriculum has
been chiefly that of helping students learn how to deal with potential
problems posed by dangerous practices such as alcohol abuse. Peer
counseling projects in which students work with other students in
helpful relations have replaced the use of stern lectures and frightening
stories to discourage youths from abuse. Sex education sometimes
suffers from attacks by conservative political groups although a recent
study suggests that among conservative groups a majority supports sex
education.[10] Investigators are surprised at how badly youths in the
United States fare in their understanding of the various aspects of
sexuality. Although sex education is only one factor, some draw a
connection between it and the incidence of teenage marriage, divorce,

[10]Demythologizing Sex Education in Oklahoma: An Attitudinal Study," *Journal of
School Health* 53, no. 6 (August 1983): 360–64.

unwanted pregnancy, abortion, and venereal disease. Sweden with compulsory sex education has the lowest incidence of such problems, and the United States without a systematic program has the highest.[11] Trends in the development of a curriculum on sexuality in U.S. schools, including a sex education mandate in New Jersey, have been reported.[12]

ENGLISH

English as a Subject

English as a school subject is relatively young, hardly over 100 years old. In 1865, there was a variety of studies of English—rhetoric, oratory, spelling, literary history, and reading. In the following decades, these traditional offerings were united under the teaching of a single subject— English—with literature, language, and composition forming the major components of the subject.

Early in the twentieth century, there were efforts to emancipate the teaching of English in the high schools from the college program. These efforts took the form of rejecting a traditional body of literature as the sole purveyer of culture, giving up an analytic approach to literary studies in favor of studying types of literature. In the early 1920s, there was a functional emphasis on English; committees attempted to identify the skills learned in English classes that were most useful to people in a range of social positions. An experience curriculum in English was introduced. It featured an abandonment of formal grammar in favor of functional instruction through activities in creative expression, speaking, and writing.

The 1940s saw teachers of English trying to adapt their content to adolescent needs, the problems of family life, international relations, and other aspects of daily living. English became guidance. In the late 1950s, there was an academic resurgence, with attacks on such a conception of English. English as a discipline in the high schools followed the model of academic work in the college. There was a stress on intensive reading, the Great Books, and literary rather than personal pursuits. Language, literature, and composition remained the tripod of English. Teachers were expected to teach pupils how to give close analytic attention to what was read, asking questions about form, rhetoric, and meaning. Literary values once again prevailed over other considerations.

[11]Ronald Goldman and Juliette Goldman, *Sexual Theory: A Comparative Study of Children Aged 5 to 15 in Australia, North America, Britain, and Sweden* (Boston: Routledge & Kegan Paul, 1982).

[12]*The Siecus Report* (New York: Siecus Publications).

The middle 1960s saw the beginning of a counter movement with concern about making the English curriculum more relevant and meaningful to the disadvantaged. The emphasis again shifted to contemporary writing, including selections by black authors. In literature, there was a move away from the traditional historical and biographical approach that had focused on the social context, and toward topical units in the junior high school and thematic units in the senior high school. A theme like justice as treated by poets, playwrights, and novelists over the years often served as the basis for deeper study by the student. Reading literature was considered more important than reading what was said about it.

English teachers and curriculum workers still wonder whether courses should feature great works of literature or emphasize contemporary problems and modern psychological interpretations. The popular response is to try to include both the traditional and contemporary. One chooses important themes dealing with the human condition, such as guilt, and then selects material from traditional and modern American and British literature, folklore, and mythology that helps illuminate the theme. A danger in this approach is that it may induce a premature sophistication with respect to literary works. No single course can cover all centuries. Selectivity should govern both the scope and the details selected.

A conference on the teaching of English at Dartmouth College in 1966 brought American specialists in English in contact with British influences. The British offered the Americans a model for English that focused on the personal and linguistic growth of the child. Hence, many teachers of English began to copy the British practice of offering improvised drama, imaginative writing, personal response to literature, and informal classroom discussion. Like the Britishers, they gave less attention to textual analysis, to the study of genres, to literary periods, and to chronology. Parallel with the re-emphasis of English as a humanistic subject came technological influences. Behavioral objectives in English aroused much controversy. The skills thought necessary for speaking, listening, reading, and writing could be specified and taught. How these skills could be related to the goals of expression or response to literature is uncertain.

Trends in the Teaching of English

There are mounting concerns about the new English as graduating students find that they are not equipped with the basic reading and writing skills needed for employment. College entrance exam scores continue to decline, and many freshmen are required to take a basic grammar course before enrolling in college English. The failure of the new English to provide working skills has resulted in a return to teaching basic skills. This return has gained support among students, teachers, parents, and administrators. Some minority members are also supporting the movement. Courses for studying the contributions of minority groups to literature engendered racial pride but often did not prepare minority students for the demands of a society in which standard English is the criterion for social advancement.

The basic skills movement in English is seen in the demand for more history of classical literature, more traditional grammar, and a greater emphasis on formal rather than personal writing. There is a return to the workbook and hard cover anthology. Elective programs are being dismantled (they are accused of fragmenting and diminishing the goals of an integrated approach to English); the new linguistics is gone; "personal growth" and "creativity" are disparaged. Opponents of this movement urge English teachers not to succumb to pressures that would have them teach trivia because trivia can be easily measured, but to teach that reading and writing will help students find personal meaning in life. Some also urge including a critical study of the media, particularly television, because the media are so closely related to our quality of life.

As a compromise, The Center for Urban Education, in Amherst, Massachusetts, suggests that basic English skills be taught in conjunction with themes in literature that affect all humanity. The great theme approach focuses attention on the most profound and humane questions of all time, for example, people's response to nature, to beauty, to the relationship between fate and free will. Those who teach isolated skills often neglect to show how these skills relate to current social realities. Those supporting the basic skills movement will have to consider how skills may be applied in situations relevant to the students' lives. The acquisition of basic skills alone does not ensure communication of ideas. Communication of ideas requires both skill and interest. Indeed, some specialists in English believe that when subject matter is relevant to student interest, motivation to acquire skills is high. The late professor Mina Shaughnessy of the City University of New York, for example, believed that even if one is motivated to write and is equipped with the skills needed to write, there is still no way of learning how to write unless you write. She required students to write no less than 1,000 words a week. Writing activities included a journal, essays on topics of interest, timed class writings, and term papers. To keep up with the paperwork, Dr. Shaughnessy suggested the use of peer group teaching.

Students could exchange essays and help each other to recognize areas of weakness. There is a strong belief on the part of many language arts instructors that the focus in the teaching of writing should be on designing experiences that systematically develop the students' abilities, including their sense of audience and purpose. It has been shown, for example, that even young children can be taught to formulate their writing intentions—to amuse, to inform, to praise someone or something—and to differentiate their writing according to genres such as narrative, dialogue, exposition, and voice—to suit different audiences. Attaining knowledge of stylistic conventions—paragraphing, punctuation, and so forth—leads to writing in order to affect the reader. Once students start writing for others, they read their own writing, thereby improving it.

Recently there has also been a shift from "relevant" literature. There is a rising tide of criticism and displeasure about the reading material taught in schools. Book banning has risen remarkably in America during the last five years. Since the teaching of literature is a political act, the goals for this curriculum are likely to reflect one's prior assumptions about the nature and purpose of education.

An indication of the political nature of curriculum planning in the field of English is found in the policy statement of the National Council of Teachers of English.[13] This statement, entitled *Essentials of English,* concedes something to every special interest. The authors define English as *literature* (habits, classics, human experience); *communication skills* (using media); *reading* (search for meaning, judging literature, functions in life, skills); *writing* (personal development, techniques and processes of writing, mechanics); *speaking* (self-expression, group discussion, logical argument); *listening* (purposes, details, evaluation); *thinking* (creative, logical, critical). The definitions of the essentials are not consistent with each other and they are atheoretical (English as teaching isolated skills is incompatible with English as personally meaningful communication). The report is important for what it says about the status of English in the curriculum: English teachers are divided between utilitarian and humanistic purposes, and unsure about whether to teach performance skills or appreciation.

In brief, current trends in the teaching of English reflect three conflicting conceptions. Teachers who value an academic orientation base their instruction on what scholars are doing in the field. Those who think of education as personal growth concentrate on oral expression, projects, popular media, contemporary literature, and social commentary. Those who think of English as a set of mechanical skills focus directly on reading, spelling, and writing.

[13]National Council of Teachers of English, *Essentials of English* (Urbana: NCTE, 1983).

READING

The Curriculum for Reading

The curriculum for the teaching of reading in America from 1600 to the present has reflected different goals. The initial goal was religious. Children were expected to learn to read the word of God directly. With the forming of a new nation, reading was taught to help build national strength and unity—to instill patriotism. From 1840 to 1890, the teaching of reading as a means for obtaining information was the primary goal. This emphasis on enlightenment was an extension of nationalism—from patriotic sentiment to the ideal of an intelligent citizenry. To awaken a perennial interest in literary material was the overriding goal in the late 1890s and until about 1918. Thereafter, utility rather than aesthetics had priority. Reading selections were oriented more to the events of daily living than to literary appreciation.

Currently, there are three emphases in the teaching of reading. One emphasis focuses on word recognition and reading comprehension. These skills are taught without considering the purpose for which they will ultimately be used. A second emphasis focuses on the specific kinds of situations in which the student is to apply reading skills—reading want ads, Yellow Pages, job applications, and newspapers. The latter emphasis reflects a concern for those who are functionally illiterate—those who lack the reading competencies necessary to function successfully in contemporary society. Accordingly, there is increasing interest in the teaching of reading at the middle and senior high school levels. A third emphasis is to teach reading as conceptual development in which one's background of experience is brought to bear on the process so that the reader creates meaning from text.

Trends and Directions

Trends in the teaching of reading during the past decade followed those in the other language arts. Instruction in reading was influenced by scholarship, technology, and humanistic concerns. The influence of scholars in linguistics, for example, can be noted in more natural language in primers, controlled spelling patterns rather than a controlled vocabulary in texts designed for teaching word recognition skills, the use of language patterns to signal the meaning of what is written (for example, word order patterns), and greater acceptance of the learner's own articulation and substitution of words. On the other hand, the influence of the technologists is seen in today's instructional materials which feature task analyses, specific objectives with matching criterion-referenced tests, relevant practice, provision for feedback to the learner, and mastery of prerequisite tasks before proceeding.

Readiness to read is now conceived of as mastery of prerequisite skills rather than an assumed maturational level. Based on a diagnosis of the learner's skills, a reading program is prescribed which presumably meets the child's individual reading needs. Basal readers are now supplemented by a variety of self-paced reading materials, which enable students to advance along a continuum of competencies at their own rates. Greater emphasis is given to decoding skills, the relating of letters with sounds. Basal readers now feature phonic patterns to illustrate the sound and spelling regularities of English rather than emphasizing "sight words" and the irregular features of the language. More varied sentence structures are employed in beginning reading materials and some teachers use a language experience approach whereby children learn to read by reading what they themselves have spoken.

Future directions in the teaching of reading will respond to the following agenda of interest to researchers and policymakers:

1. Misuse of instruction based on hierarchical models. This reflects a concern that unfavorable consequences may arise from too much reliance on diagnostic and prescriptive approaches that rest on hierarchies that are not fully validated. Declining scores in reading comprehension are associated with reading instruction that is focused on specific decoding skills rather than the development of broad experiential backgrounds necessary for independent reading in the content fields.[14]
2. Relation of instructional tasks to developmentally determined abilities and cultural differences of children.
3. Ways to increase comprehension in reading. There will be greater emphasis on teaching the processes of reading comprehension instead of merely assessing comprehension. Students will be taught what to do *before* reading (set purposes, ask questions, make predictions), *while* reading (relate their own backgrounds to what they are reading, engage in mental imagery, revise predictions, check the text for its sensibleness), and *after* reading (write summaries, state conclusions in their own words, reconstruct the material, and do something with the content presented).
4. Ways to match reading materials to the cognitive development of adolescents and adults.

[14]Harry Singer, John D. McNeil and Lorry L. Furse, "Relationship Between Curriculum Scope and Reading Achievement," *The Reading Teacher* 37, no. 6 (1984): 602–612.

5. Stronger connections between reading in school and what students read on their own.

HISTORY AND SOCIAL STUDIES

History As A Subject

The "new" history of the 1960s, both in subject matter and methodology, evolved from the same forces that had affected other subject matter fields, that is, the discipline proposal and the push toward specialization. The subject matter of history was chosen in order to provide students with a conceptual foundation on which specialization could be based. Emphasis was placed in historians' methods of research, analysis, and interpretation. Students were no longer required to memorize sheer facts or chronology, but rather to express an understanding for general sociological theories. This conceptual approach encouraged students to doubt and openly criticize textbook interpretations of history. Students drew their own conclusions and often found previous perspectives biased and unreliable.

Campus demonstrations in the late 1960s reflected a general lack of confidence in politicians and governmental agencies. Students had been taught to examine, analyze, and interpret, and they freely applied these skills to national policymaking. The Vietnam War was history in the making, and students were determined to make known their interpretations of the facts.

Public concern about campus protests resulted in a demand that history be taught in a manner that would make it applicable to constructive resolution of community problems. To accommodate this demand, curriculum specialists suggested integrating the study of history with studies in other subjects. Emphasis is now being placed upon history with studies in other subjects and for building a basic understanding of the historical influences on community life. Suggested learning activities included studying the influence of science and technology on historical periods; identifying the relationship between historical movements and developments in the arts; and investigating the effects of business and industry on local history.

An Evaluation of History Curriculum

Current appraisals of the curriculum in history are negative. Teachers are accused of having an unintegrated interpretation of history, a limited range of teaching strategies, and a narrow conception of the

students' responsibilities.[15] Curriculum consists of a prescribed, fragmented body of material to be absorbed and repeated back to the
teacher. Whether the focus is the Federal Reserve Act, current events,
or World War II, the material is not related to the lives of students or to
larger historical process.

A current appraisal of elementary and secondary history textbooks is
also negative.[16] They are unrealistic; although they show the present as
a "tangle of problems," paradoxically, they are sanguine about the
future. Economic history is conspicuously absent; an analysis of ideological
conflict is missing from discussions of American wars; and the authors
do not attend to continuity. "Politics is one theory to them, economics
another, culture a third.... There is no link between the end of Reconstruction in the South and the Civil Rights movement of the sixties....
History is just one damn thing after another. It is, in fact, not history at
all."[17] Frances Fitzgerald attributes the lack of interest in academic
competence in history to the societal demand that the curriculum
promote good social behavior and learning for strictly practical purposes.

The 1970s demonstrated America's dependence on international
economy and policymaking. Interdependence among nations for natural
resources, economic stability, and environmental control is sure to
increase in the 1980s. History courses need to emphasize the importance
of economic, social, and political awareness in shaping the history of the
future as well as understanding historical periods of the past.

There is another way in which the history curriculum is likely to
change in the years ahead. Persons such as Bruce Burns are arguing that
curriculum design in the field of history must be based on cognitive
development rather than concentrating solely on the predefined meaning
of history as a field (the logic of the scholar) or on the concerns of the
students and how history can help them.[18] The meaning and function of
history change as children interact with each stage of their development.
Young children consider history to be a collection of stories and unrelated
events. As they grow older, they define history in concrete terms and
think it to be objective. As adolescents, they understand interpretations
and hypotheses in history. Although for the young child, history had to
happen as recorded, the adolescent can imagine alternatives and contemplate different outcomes. The future purpose of history in the

[15]Paula M. Evans, "Teaching History in Libertyville," *Daedalus* 112, no. 3 (Spring 1983): 199–229.

[16]Frances Fitzgerald, "Prizewinning Author Changes History Textbooks' Present Distorted Picture," *ASCD News Exchange* 21, no. 4 (Summer 1979): 1, 7.

[17]Frances Fitzgerald, p. 7.

[18]Bruce Burns, "History for the Elementary School Child," *The Social Studies* 74, no. 1 (January-February 1983): 16, 17.

school may be to encourage developmental transitions, helping adolescents to meet their need for identity, to recognize both a sense of continuity with their own lives and an assurance of significance within their community. An adolescent trying to be less egocentric and learning to relate to others might use history to reveal the basis for the cultural differences of others, for example.

Social Studies

Social studies is a broad term covering several subject matters including history and the social sciences. Originally, the purpose of the social studies curriculum was the "creation of rich and many-sided personalities, equipped with practical knowledge and inspired by ideals so that they can make their way and fulfill their mission in a changing society which is part of a world complex."[19] Today, there is disenchantment with the stated purpose. It is too vague, and there is doubt that those in the social sciences are able to furnish knowledge with which to resolve complex social issues like racial strife, war, and economic depressions. Indeed, social scientists have inflated hopes and made promises beyond the means of their knowledge and capacities.

In the 1950s, the curriculum of the social studies was varied. The authors of some programs aimed at social literacy. They wanted learners to understand social change as responses to the problems and needs of human beings throughout the world. Others said their mission was to help learners develop socially desirable behavior; social scientists felt they were demonstrating social processes, promoting understanding and skill in dealing with social problems. A common curriculum premise of that time was that the social studies program should combine both content and process. Students should have the opportunity to make decisions regarding personal and social problems using the generalizations from the social sciences.

In the 1960s, more than forty major social studies curriculum projects were financed by the federal government, foundations, and institutions of higher learning. Authors of these projects all emphasized an academic structure but did not share a common view as to what the structure was. They tended to define structure loosely as generalizations, concepts, or modes of inquiry. There was little agreement on which concepts or ways of working in the social sciences are most fruitful and representative of structure. Like most other curriculum programs of the 1960s, social studies projects stressed inductive teaching. Students were expected to

[19]Charles Beard, *The Nature of the Social Sciences* (New York: Scribner's Sons, 1938): p. 179.

make generalizations from data. Typical goals for the social studies during this period were to interpret problems of world citizenship using concepts from the behavioral sciences; to interpret social behavior using concepts from anthropology; to analyze problems of social change using concepts from a variety of disciplines; to analyze public controversies using the method of discussion and argument; and to recognize objective evidence using concepts from philosophy, psychology, law, and other social sciences.

Today, the social studies curriculum is in disarray. On the one hand, there are those who advocate drawing substantially from a wide range of social science disciplines in developing new social studies programs. On the other hand, others recommend studying non-Western societies and organizing curriculum content around the study of world cultures and international affairs.

The social studies curriculum in school is still more social studies than social science, with history, government, and geography the dominant subjects. In the elementary schools, the social studies receive little attention, serving primarily as another opportunity to teach reading and writing skills. At all levels the social studies curriculum is a textbook curriculum; the textbook is used to organize courses and students concentrate solely on the content of the text. Few teachers have ever heard of approaches oriented toward the social sciences, and fewer still use them. They also do not connect the course with anything in the student's life, with events familiar to them. The basic skills movement has weakened efforts to promote inquiry and problem analysis. There is little agreement among teachers, advocates, or analysts within the field as to what ends the social studies should serve or the most appropriate subject matter to teach.[20]

The Future of Social Studies

Problems concerning the social studies curriculum of the future center on the following observations. Rational discourse, critical inquiry, opportunity to exercise the skill of autonomous judgment, and other featured values in social studies programs seem to be no guarantee of behavioral change or even increased happiness of the individual or society. Inasmuch as human beings act irrationally on impulse, emotion, pride, and passion, we should not expect social studies programs that feature only facts and interpretations to contribute much to making students more reasonable about human and social behavior. Conse-

[20]Howard D. Mehlinger and O. L. Davis, Jr., eds., *The Status of Social Studies* (Chicago: University of Chicago Press, 1982).

quently, there will be a movement in the direction of the affective realm. Values and attitudes will become more important, and efforts will be made to involve students in ecological and political matters of personal interest. There will be a return to the project method, stressing ways to participate in acts of citizenship and to improve and perfect our governmental system, an emphasis that may overcome students' loss of confidence in the American political system.

The need to construct a better world will force those in the social studies to focus on social problems rather than on transmitting knowledge. These kinds of problems require that the student draw the best current thinking from both the natural and social sciences. Hence, we will see attempts at an integrative curriculum. The task will be difficult. Teachers, for example, are not always comfortable with the inquiry methods and concepts of a single social science. Now they will be asked to gain competency in several disciplines. Also, we know that scholars in a single social science have difficulty in agreeing on the objectives and content for course materials. Greater difficulty will be experienced in getting agreement from scholars in different fields about what should be taught.

In the short run, pressures will continue to make the social studies curriculum respond to the needs of special groups. Business interests will influence legislators to mandate instruction on the free enterprise system; Jewish groups will seek legislation to make mandatory detailed study of the Holocaust. Nuclear curricula, economic education, global education, and law related studies are examples of topics that have been included in the social studies curriculum in response to special interests. The social studies curriculum across the land might be just a hodgepodge of programs, but the topics should be regarded as vehicles for helping students acquire the common elements of citizenship—skills for participating in public affairs and understanding the premises of American liberty. Social studies could also be an opportunity for students to apply the concepts and generalizations acquired from concurrent study of history, geography, government, or other disciplines.

FOREIGN LANGUAGE

A Place in the Curriculum

Six years before Sputnik, the Modern Language Association of America expressed the conviction that we were not teaching enough people foreign languages. National concern for the advancement of scientific and technological research in the late fifties accentuated the need for international exchange of knowledge. Hence, the study of one or two foreign languages became a requirement of most secondary schools and universities. Over 8,000 elementary schools began to offer instruction in foreign languages.

An instructional method sometimes called the American method or the audiolingual approach for teaching foreign languages became popular at this time. This method was derived from the science of structural or descriptive linguistics that had proved useful in courses offered to the military during World War II. The basic principle of the method is that language must be learned as a system of communication by sound from mouth to ear. Student and teacher who used this method spoke the foreign language; they did not only talk about it. The first 300 to 400 hours of language learning were devoted to acquiring a skill rather than a body of facts. During this initial period, students began to comprehend the spoken word and to speak after listening; reading and writing were not emphasized. Students then practiced actively and aloud until they gained some control over the language patterns. The opportunity for such practice was generally provided by language laboratories in which the students heard recordings of a native speaker and tried to model their speech after the speaker's.

Interest in foreign languages began to decline in the mid-1960s as the national concern for space exploration subsided, and with it the push for communication with foreign scientists. Studies in language were criticized for being too specialized to be applicable. Foreign language requirements were eliminated in many colleges and secondary schools. By 1980, only 15 percent of high school students were enrolled in foreign language courses. Indeed, a presidential commission reported that only 4 percent of pupils graduating from high school had studied a foreign language for as long as two years. One-fifth of United States public high schools offered no courses in foreign language at all. Among those that did, Spanish, French, and German were most offered, in that order. A national sampling by the University of Michigan found that more than 52 percent of Americans questioned would like to study a foreign language in the future, but nearly 49 percent opposed making it a requirement in high schools.

Efforts to Revive Language Instruction

To counteract the loss of student enrollment, advocates of foreign language are attempting to concentrate on the human aspects of their discipline in hopes of regaining student interest. Language departments are expanding their course offerings in order to meet the needs and interests of students. In discussing ways to do this, teachers typically suggest integration of language study with other subject matter areas, early introduction of language arts, and student participation in curriculum development. Subject matter integration is accomplished by introducing students to the contributions of language to all subject areas. English classes study the contribution of foreign languages to the development of American English, music classes study lyrics of foreign folk songs, and art classes share their work with those in foreign countries.

In her study of the teaching of foreign language, Marlies Mueller found that students have few classroom opportunities to speak the new language in situations that involve genuine communication.[21] Instead the language is spoken only in dry grammar exercises as an abstract activity. Three quarters of the teachers visited by Mueller used the grammar-translation method whose origin dates back to the time when Latin and Greek were taught as means in forming the intellect. Accordingly, grammar is deductively presented—first the rule and then the example along with vocabulary lists to be memorized and later texts to be translated. Obviously, this method is inconsistent with the communication oriented purpose of language study. The latter goal is better served by (a) trying to approximate the manner in which children learn their first language (the natural language learning approach); (b) insisting on the conscious understanding and use of newly acquired phrases or structures in a meaningful context (the cognitive-code approach); and (c) thinking in the foreign language so that the student uses the language in direct association with classroom objects and pictorial representations or actions by teacher and students, and (d) teaching grammar rules inductively so that students derive linguistic generalizations after being confronted with many examples (the direct method).

The early introduction of foreign languages has gained general support from everyone concerned with the development of language skills. Young children between the ages of four and ten learn foreign languages easily. Children are usually flexible, uninhibited, and eager to explore different languages. Early introduction of languages also enhances cultural awareness among children. Languages may be used to explore the typical experiences in different cultures (cooking styles and names of foods, folk songs, games played in foreign countries). Among the innovations suggested for stimulating language learning are bilingual nursery schools, home visits by bilingual teachers, tutoring of younger children by trained school-age peers during play, and mobile classrooms to teach foreign languages.

Students are now being encouraged to participate in the planning of

[21]Marlies Mueller, "The Tower of Babel in Libertyville," *Daedalus* 112, no. 3 (Summer 1983): 229–249.

new language courses. This trend emerged from the need to make the language arts relevant to the needs of students. In addition, it is now realized that optimum learning takes place when the learner is meaningfully involved in determining what is to be learned and how it is to be learned. However, efforts to entice students toward second language learning through exposure to language and culture in games may backfire. If students are shielded from the serious mental effort required for learning a language, the subject may be trivialized and fail to gain student respect.

Language subject matter for the 1980s probably will include emphasis on basic speaking skills as well as those needed for reading and writing. Study activities will be designed to ensure relevancy and applicability. Speaking skills will be related to foreign cultural topics ranging from dating customs to urban problems. Use of current periodicals will also enhance relevancy of reading skills.

Resource persons can bring life to the languages. Non-English-speaking persons in the community may be invited to participate in classroom learning activities. Community businesses that employ bilingual persons may be encouraged to offer internship experiences. Field trips and opportunities for travel can be used to introduce students to the language in use, making language studies alive and vital.

Among the new methodologies is the *confluent approach* drawn from the humanistic orientation. Accordingly, students participate in group activities designed to elicit open interpersonal communication. Students in such classes explore and discuss various aspects of themselves, as well as less personal information, in the language. The most original of the new methods is *suggestopedia* which uses hypnotic and subliminal learning techniques, such as sleep learning.

Optimism for increased instruction in foreign language is found in such recent developments as the reinstatement of foreign language as a graduation requirement and as a college entrance requirement, language instruction beginning in the fifth and sixth grade, and the public's general awareness of the commercial and social value of learning another language.

THE ARTS

Fine Arts in the Curriculum

The broad direction of curriculum revision needed in the arts was set in 1958. At that time, the American Council of Learned Societies' panel on curriculum made two recommendations. First, that the basic approach be creative, allowing the student in studios and workshops to be personally involved. Second, that historical matter be incorporated to develop the student's sense of heritage in the arts. Instead of survey courses, an attempt should be made to involve the student in the study of art as it represents various epochs and cultures and as it might affect his or her own creativity. Critical judgment is to be developed by practice, seeing good examples, reading, and hearing about original works.[22]

Subsequently, some educators based their curriculum on aesthetic theory; others, mindful of learning theory's emphasis on conceptual structure, turned their efforts toward defining the structure of art in terms of concepts. The pronouncement that any subject could be effectively taught to any child at any stage of development had eventually influenced curriculum developments in art as it had in other subjects.

Art curriculum of the mid-1960s was designed to provide students with an appreciation for the basic aesthetic themes expressed in all art forms. Subject matter covered basic concepts such as rhythm, movement, harmony, and texture. These concepts were to be experienced through listening (music appreciation), performing (acting, playing traditional instruments), and composing (emphasizing classical techniques). The main weakness of this instructional approach was that it served the needs of only a small portion of the student population. Subject matter was too specialized for the average student's basic artistic needs. The narrow range of course offerings could not encompass growing interest in art forms of ethnic minorities, use of a wide variety of musical instruments, art forms of different countries, and use of new art media.

To help show the usefulness of art, curriculum specialists suggested integrating art with other subject matter fields. Examples of integration are when music instruction includes an examination of the cultural and historical influences and the development of lyrics is studied in English courses. Public schools in Columbus, Ohio, are known for their integration of the arts with other areas of the curriculum. Music in many of the schools, for example, is used in the teaching of poetry (rhythm), history (songs of people in history), mathematics (patterns and frequencies), and science (the physics of sound). Students studying future utopias might examine the authenticity of the proposed systems in science classes. Later, they could write a play in conjunction with a creative writing course. Finally, their play could be produced in a drama class.

Instruction in the arts should be related to actual experiences. Students will have increased interest and will be able to see how the arts can become an intrinsic part of life. Resident artists can help students plan a career in the arts. Local artists are participating in school art curriculum

[22]American Council of Learned Societies, "Secondary School Curriculum Problems," *Newsletter* 9, no. 9 (1959).

programs. Poets, musicians, sculptors, actors, craftspersons, designers, environmental planners, and filmmakers are a sample of the artists bringing the outside world to the classroom.

Use of peer group and cross-age teaching is also gaining support as a possible trend for the 1980s. Dr. Robert Pace, chairman of the piano department at Columbia University's Teacher College, has developed a system for music training which makes the most of peer teaching. Groups of eight to ten students of varying ages learn the techniques of music by participating in sight-reading games, ear-training musical drills, and exercises in musical improvisation. The program is cost effective, and children enjoy sharing their musical development with peers.

New methods are being developed for the teaching of music based on the interests and capacities of the average child. There are schools, for example, that offer programs, beginning in kindergarten, based on children's natural affinity for jazz. Other schools teach rock music and electronic music. Guitars have become major teaching tools. An art curriculum specialist faces only one fear for art in the 1980s: "Will art, music, dance, and drama be regarded as frills by an increasingly cost-conscious public?"

The basic skills movement is a threat to courses in arts although the Council for Basic Education thinks art is among the basics.

The best private or independent schools are as proud of their instruction in the arts as in science and mathematics. Such schools are concerned with the whole person, with creativity as well as performance on test scores. Instruction in the arts is viewed as an essential part of preparation for life.

The idea that the arts merit attention in all schools underlies the Rockefeller Brothers Fund which awards prizes to exemplary art programs in public schools. The variety of exemplary programs being offered is illustrated in arts essays produced by the American Academy of Arts and Sciences.[23]

In the Smokey Mountains, the Swain County High School arts program, for example, introduces students to the foundations of aesthetic awareness—line, form, color, and design—through the works of major artists and individual projects. The forms of arts and crafts include macrame, pottery, fibers, weaving, drawing, photography, silk screening, papermaking, batik, stitchery, quilting, lettering, and airbrushing. The program is strongly vocational—equipping students with the knowledge and skills for becoming commercial artists, artisans, and craftspeople.

[23]Stephen R. Graubard, "The Arts and Humanities in America's Schools," *Daedalus* 112, no. 3 (Special issue 1983): 29–35.

Nevertheless, it is the development of individual self-expression and personal aesthetic values that make the program successful.

The Fillmore Arts Center in Washington, D.C., is devoted to teaching the arts and offers a good education in the visual arts, music, dance, and drama. From kindergarten through eighth grade pupils rotate through all four basic arts during the year. Beginning at grade four, children take courses such as "discovery art," "music for voice, recorder, and xylophone," "puppet pizzary" and "video techniques." In grades five and six, there are such choices as painting and drawing, modern and jazz dance, calligraphy, poetry and fabric design. Students in grades seven and eight can take percussion, story dramatization, woodworking, filmmaking, cartooning or sculpture. The arts in this school are taught as a means for strengthening a person's growth in many ways—intellectual (solving problems), emotional (finding ways for self expression), and perceptual (experiencing the environment through the senses). Cognitive development corresponds to the development of oral and motor skills, reading and writing skills. It is a true curriculum in the sense of extending important elements. For example, in music, the physical expression of rhythmic patterns to body movement lays the foundation for reading notes; reading and writing music leads to sharper perception when listening to a symphony; listening for patterns in a symphony gives children ideas for expressing their own music.

Thus, the reasons for art in the curriculum are many—for self-expression, appreciation, a future career. Also, art is valued for its intellectual content, historical importance, and key role in culture. In an essay that is highly critical of the vague, lofty, and unexamined list of aims for teaching art, Jacques Barzun says we do not have to have eighteen reasons to justify it in the schools. One reason is enough: "Art is an important part of our culture. It corresponds to a deep instinct in man; hence it is enjoyable. We therefore teach its rudiments."[24] Harry S. Broudy, on the other hand, believes that the schools should cultivate the aesthetic mode of experience, not because it is a delight, but because it is necessary for the development of the intellect. He argues for teaching sensitivity to the appearance of things, the expressive properties of color, sound, texture, and movement organized into aesthetic objects, and the perception and construction of images that portray intimations of reality in forms of feeling.[25] Those who are giving the arts a firm place in the school program seem to say that both viewpoints are necessary.

[24]Jacques Barzun, "Art and Educational Inflation," *The Education Digest* 45, no. 1 (September 1979): 12–16.

[25]Harry S. Broudy, "A Common Curriculum in Aesthetics and Fine Arts," in *Individual Differences and the Common Curriculum,* NSSE Yearbook, eds. Gary Festermaker and John I. Goodland (Chicago: University of Chicago Press, 1983).

CONCLUDING COMMENTS

Most subjects are influenced by the same social, economic, political, and technological forces. Hence, it is no great surprise to see most of them moving in the same direction. We are in a period of great renewal in the academic curriculum. Policymakers have demanded that more students complete more work in the academic subjects—particularly mathematics, science, writing and the humanities. This renewal is accompanied by three problems—a crisis in purpose, a concern about student interest, and a desire for open access to knowledge.

There is a revival in all the academic subjects to find clear-cut goals and a body of essential content. In part, this activity is a response to the many incoherent programs developed at a period when individualization was prized. Thus far, there is little agreement on central purposes in any field. Curriculum policy statements in the respective fields reflect pluralistic interests—functional competency, intellectual development, traditional values, social relevancy, and self-actualization. There is a lack of agreement upon essential content and strong disagreement between those who would declare the traditional curriculum as the standard of excellence and those who want the academic content to reflect new conceptions of the fields. Even the new college board specialists for preparation for college reveal inconsistent expectations—more in keeping with political compromise (something for everybody) than an educational philosophy.

A new rationale for redefining goals in academic subjects is needed. It would be better to have separate curriculum programs reflecting particular philosophies, such as in some distinguished magnet, specialized, and private schools, than to create programs with conflicting purposes.

Student interest and access reflects the fact that most academic subjects are taught in a sterile manner—textbook information with corresponding emphasis on terminology and definitions. Also, only some students are given the opportunity to pursue subjects in an inspired way, asking new questions, thinking critically and imaginatively.

Studies of fields such as science reveal much student alienation from knowledge. Fewer than half of the high school graduates express interest in further study of science and there is little evidence that school science prepares them for either college or life. Fewer than 10 percent of secondary students are interested in the field. Should additional mandates for more work in the "hard" subjects, such as science, result in more of the same inferior curriculum, the alienation from knowledge is likely to be even greater.

A serious challenge is a curriculum design that will enable large numbers of students (particularly those from less academically privileged classes) to have success with content formerly available only to a small elite. Obviously, to define subjects in terms of the way experts view their subject is not enough. Neither is it adequate to offer a subject as a means for advancing up the academic ladder. Students expect to apply what they are learning to current issues and to their personal needs. Where in the new academic curriculum will there be opportunities for the students' active learning in exploring, drawing inferences, problem solving, collaborative learning, and creativity?

Curriculum makers in all fields are trying to relate subject matter to the development stages of different learners. This effort is putting curriculum makers ahead of academic specialists in the redefinition and integration of subject matter. The relation of vocational education to academic achievement in mathematics and science is one example.

It is clear that there must be closer attention to the relations among the ideal academic curriculum as stated by national and state policymakers, the perceptions of teachers about what they are teaching, as well as the perceptions of students about what they are learning. Course content, regardless of course title, is dependent upon the skills, interests, and preferences of individual teachers.

QUESTIONS

1. Sometimes academic trends attempt to bring about a desired future; others warn of practices that should be stopped. Identify some trends that you feel attempt to bring about a particular future and some that you see as warnings.
2. Try your hand at anticipating a likely future trend in a subject field by (a) identifying or analyzing political, economic, or other social factors that have the potential for shaping curriculum and (b) indicating how this force might affect the curriculum in this field.
3. Subject matter was never really viewed as an end in itself. The learning of a subject is always justified as useful for some social purpose. What social purpose or interests were fields such as history, science, English meant to serve at different times?
4. It is sometimes suggested that teachers offer varied courses like technology science, surgical science, science and pollution, health care science and the science of music so that students' interest and local needs are better served. What scientific themes might run through these courses?
5. What, if anything, should be done about the practice of offering a different academic content, pedagogy, and class climate to upper track students from that offered lower track students studying the same subject?

SELECTED REFERENCES

Benderson, Albert. "Foreign Languages in the Schools." Educational Testing
    Service Bulletin, *Focus 12,* 1983.
Boykin, Wilfred E. "The Next 10 Years' Trends for Mathematics Education."
    NASSP Bulletin 62, no. 422 (December 1978): 101–10.
Chapman, Laura H. *Instant Art, Instant Culture: The Unspoken Policy for American
    Schools.* New York: Teachers College Press, 1982.
Gardner, Howard. *Art, Mind and Brain.* New York: Basic Books, 1982.
Graubard, Stephen R. "The Arts and Humanities in America's Schools." *Dae-
    dalus* 112, no. 3 (Summer 1983): 29–35.
Harms, Norris C. and Yager, Robert E., eds. *What Research Says to the Science
    Teacher.* Vol. 3. Washington, D.C.: National Science Teachers Association,
    1981.
Judy, Stephen N. and England, David A., eds. "An Historical Primer on the
    Teaching of English." *The English Journal* 68, no. 4 (April 1979): 6–85.
McNeil, John D. *Reading Comprehension: New Directions for the Classroom.* Chicago:
    Foresman, 1984.
Mettlinger, Howard D. and Davis, O. L., Jr., eds. *The Social Studies,* NSSE
    Yearbook, Part II. Chicago: University of Chicago Press, 1981.
National Council of Teachers of Mathematics. *An Agenda for Action: Recommen-
    dations for School Mathematics of the 1980s.* Reston, Virginia: National Council
    of Teachers of Mathematics, 1983.
National Science Foundation. *Report to the National Science Board by Commission on
    Precollege Education in Mathematics, Science, and Technology.* Washington, D.C.:
    National Science Foundation, 1983.
———. *Science and Engineering Education for the 1980s and Beyond.* Washington,
    D.C.: National Science Foundation, 1980.
———. *Today's Problems, Tomorrow's Crises.* A Report to the National Science
    Board Commission on Precollege Education in Mathematics, Science, and
    Technology. Washington, D.C.: National Science Foundation, 1982.
Saber, Naama. "Science, Curriculum and Society Trends in Science Curricu-
    lum." *Science Education* 63, no. 2 (April 1979): 257–69.
Savignon, Sandra J. *Communicative Competence: Theory and Classroom Practice.* Read-
    ing, Mass.: Addison-Wesley, 1983.
Social Science Education Consortium. *The Future of Social Studies: A Report and
    Summary of Project SPAN.* Boulder: Social Science Education Consortium,
    1983.
Stake, Robert E. and Easley, Jack A. *Case Studies in Science Education.* Washing-
    ton, D.C.: U.S. Government Printing Office, 1978.
Walberg, H. J., "Scientific Literacy and Economic Productivity." *Daedalus* 112,
    no. 2 (Spring 1983).
Yager, Robert E. "The Importance of Terminology in Teaching K-12
    Science." *Journal of Research in Science Teaching* 20, no. 6 (1983): 577–88.

V / RESEARCH THEORY AND CURRICULUM

A popular publication recently carried the title *The Curriculum—Retrospect and Prospect.* The title would be a good one to apply to this part. The emergence of curriculum as a professional study is treated in a historical chapter. The views of a number of influential curriculum theorists and developers are examined to cast light on the nature of curriculum and the central concerns of curriculum specialists. A second chapter is devoted to appraising curriculum as a field of inquiry today, giving attention to future directions. The work of curriculum scholars is described, making it possible to see successes, gaps, and trends in curriculum research and development. The reader will find specific suggestions by which research in curriculum can be most fruitfully pursued.

14 / A HISTORICAL PERSPECTIVE OF CURRICULUM MAKING

There are at least two reasons for attending to the history of curriculum thought and practice. First, a review of the past can help us identify problems with which dedicated persons have struggled and are struggling.

Admittedly, we will still have to decide whether these problems are unsolvable, and therefore should be abandoned as unfruitful areas of inquiry, or whether their very persistence makes them worthy of our attention. The chapter also has a consideration of the issue of curriculum correlation. Correlation is the relating of ideas from different subject matters; for example, mathematics may be taught as a tool in science. As early as 1895, the issue of correlation was central. Some viewed correlation with suspicion and as a threat to the inviolability of the basic divisions of subject matter. Others saw it as an answer to the problem of an overcrowded program of studies and of value in helping the child's untrained mind relate an enormous number of topics.

Today, the issue of correlation is still important. The recent popularity of competency-based curriculum, in which pupils focus on a hierarchy of skills within a single subject rather than the relation of skills in different subjects, is not correlational. Also, the use of curriculum materials prepared by academic specialists—anthropologists, physicists, historians—tends to make the school's program of studies fragmental and piecemeal. Now, as in 1895, some people ask not so much whether there should be correlation of subject matter but how it should be accomplished. Should we group subjects around problems, using the facts from one discipline to illuminate another? Or should we put within a comprehensive course the important generalizations from many fields?

A second reason for studying the history of curriculum thought and practice is that we can gain a clearer understanding of the processes of curriculum making by examining the work of prominent exponents in the field. By examining what curriculum meant to those who developed the field during this century, we can see more clearly what curriculum means. Few issues are more important to current theorists than the formulation of an adequate concept of curriculum. Theorists believe that its clarification may contribute to the improvement of curriculum and that it will increase our understanding of curricular phenomena. Some concepts of curriculum are:

1. A set of guidelines for developing products, books, and materials for the curriculum.
2. A program of activities. A listing of course offerings, units, topics, and content.
3. All learning guided by the school.
4. The process by which one decides what to teach.
5. The study of the processes used in curriculum making.
6. What learners actually learn at school.
7. What one plans for students to learn.
8. A design for learning.

In 1890, there was no extensive professional preparation for curriculum making, and there were no curriculum experts in the United States. Yet less than fifty years later, curriculum was a recognized field of specialization. One way to illustrate this development and at the same time illuminate the nature of the specialization is to look at the work of the individuals who have been most associated with curriculum making. The persons chosen for review span a period from 1890 until the present, and represent a much larger group of equally important specialists. One basis for their selection is that they studied the theory of curriculum and engaged in making curriculum.

HERBARTISM AND THE McMURRYS

Charles A. McMurry (1857–1929) and his brother, Frank W. McMurry (1862–1936), taught for several years in elementary schools before going abroad to study at the University of Jena in Germany, a mecca for educators in the late 1890s. There they became profoundly influenced by the pedagogical theory of Johann Herbart whose *Outlines of Educational Doctrine* was the basis for many of the ideas and practices at Jena.[1]

Basic Tenets of Herbartism

Essentially, Herbartism was a rationalized set of philosophical and psychological ideas applied to instructional method. It rested on the assumption that only large, connected units of subject matter are able to arouse and keep alive the child's deep interest. Hence, it stressed "the

[1]Johann F. Herbart, *Outlines of Educational Doctrine*, trans. Alex F. Lange (New York: Macmillan, 1904).

doctrine of concentration," which occurs when the mind is wholly immersed in one interest to the exclusion of everything else. This doctrine was supplemented with "the doctrine of correlation," which makes one subject the focus of attention but sees to it that connections are made with related subjects.

Instructional Procedure. Specifically, Herbartians recognized five steps as essential in the procedure of instruction:

1. *Preparation.* To revive in the student's consciousness the related ideas from past experience that will arouse interest in the new material and prepare the pupil for its rapid understanding.
2. *Presentation.* To present the new material in concrete form, unless there is already ample sensory experience, and to relate it to the students' past experiences, such as reading, conversing, experimenting, lecturing, and so forth.
3. *Association.* To analyze and to compare the new and the old, thus evolving a new idea.
4. *Generalization.* To form general rules, laws, or principles from the analyzed experience, developing general concepts as well as sensations and perceptions.
5. *Application.* To put the generalized idea to work in other situations, sometimes to test it, sometimes to use it as a practical tool.

The Goal of Education. Herbart's followers believed that moral action was the highest educational goal and that education should prepare one for life with the highest ideals of the culture. Further, they believed that some subjects, such as history and literature, were superior for the development of moral ideas. They thought that if learners were guided by correct ideas and motivated by good interests, they would be prepared to discharge life's duties properly. Among the interests or motives to be advanced were sympathetic interest (a kindly disposition toward people), social interest (participation in public affairs), and religious interest (contemplation of human destiny).

The McMurrys' Thinking

The McMurrys recognized in Herbartian pedagogy a systematic method of selecting, arranging, and organizing the curriculum, something that had been missing in American schooling. On their return from

Germany, they joined with others to apply the Herbartian methods and ideals in American schools. During his career, Charles McMurry wrote thirty books and prepared a course of study for the eight elementary grades describing how to select and arrange ideas for instruction. Principally, he addressed himself to teachers. His own teaching in the schools of Illinois and at George Peabody College for Teachers centered on the making of lesson plans according to the Herbartian five formal steps. He also concerned himself with the special instructional methods required for the teaching of specific subject fields.

Frank McMurry taught and wrote at Teachers College, Columbia University. His students were chiefly teachers who would train and supervise other teachers. His course in general methods reflected the Herbartian concern about the ends of education, the means for their attainment, the relative worth of studies, and the doctrines of concentration and correlation. Both brothers participated in national organizations devoted to the study and improvement of school programs. The effect of their efforts was great. Charles's course of study provided an overall framework for teachers, giving details for conducting lessons, the types of studies, and the special methods thought best for organizing the content in each subject. Their influence on lesson planning was especially noteworthy. In the period between 1900 and 1910, "every good teacher was supposed to have a lesson plan for each class period, and the five formal steps were much in evidence."[2] Even today military instructors are expected to design their lessons according to the formal steps outlined by the McMurrys. Analysis of the McMurrys' work shows the questions and answers which define the nature of curriculum thought in this early period.

Basic Questions. Implicit in the McMurrys' thinking were five basic questions:

1. *What Is the Aim of Education?* The McMurrys broadened Herbartian concerns for the moral development of the child to include the desire to lead children into the ways of good citizenship and into a wise physical, social, and moral adjustment to the world.
2. *What Subject Matter Has the Greatest Pedagogical Value?* Initially the McMurrys regarded literature as most useful in bringing the aesthetic and the intellectual into helpful

[2]William H. Kilpatrick, "Dewey's Influence on Education," in *The Philosophy of John Dewey,* ed. Paul A. Schilpp (Evanston, Ill.: Northwestern University, 1939): p. 465.

association: they saw geography as the most universal, concrete correlating study. When the development of good character was the primary aim, they saw literature and history as the most important subjects. Later, the McMurrys differentiated between subjects that primarily helped the learner to express thought and those which primarily helped the learner receive or furnish thought. They noted that about one-half of schoolwork (that is, beginning reading, writing, spelling, grammar, music, numbers, modeling, drawing, and painting), depends on the other half for its motive and force. In their latter years, the McMurrys came to see that new subjects would claim favor. These new studies were nature study, science, industrial arts, health, agriculture, civics, and modern languages. Indeed, the introduction of new branches of knowledge and activity was seen by them as one of the greatest achievements of the age.

3. *How Is Subject Matter Related to Instructional Method?* The McMurrys believed there were formal elements of method and concepts for each subject, whether it be geology, arithmetic, or literature. They insisted that the child learn to think with these elements just as the specialists did in these fields and that the learner develop a consciousness of the right method of thinking in each subject. They saw that teachers at that time were not equipped with the fundamental concepts of each subject and, therefore, found it difficult to order instruction to clarify concepts in the respective fields. They were disturbed when curriculum workers ignored the fact that each subject matter makes particular demands on the organization of the curriculum.

4. *What Is the Best Sequence of Studies?* The McMurrys thought that suitable subject matter varies according to age and stage of development. Initially, they believed in the *theory of the culture epochs.* This theory holds that the child passes through the same general stages of development through which the race or culture has passed. Hence, what interested humanity at a certain historical stage would appeal most to a child at the corresponding stage of development. It was thought, for example, that teachers should present the stories of Ulysses to younger children. *The Odyssey* was seen as a means by which the heroic impulses of childhood could be related to an ideal person who achieved what the child would like to achieve. This work was deemed of pedagogical value, because it portrayed the primitive human struggle and at the same time revealed a higher plane of reason. Similarly, *Robinson Crusoe* was viewed as a good source

for showing humankind's struggle with nature and at the same time helping the learner see that myths were attempts to interpret nature. Myths, legends, and heroic tales were followed by biography and formal history.

By 1923, Charles McMurry, at least, saw the theory of culture epochs as vague in its implications and admitted he knew of no sound basis for the placement of studies. For him, any particular scheme for placement of subject matter had come to be no better than the broad plan for organization that ordered it. The importance of organizing studies in relation to the child's mode of thought was seen as the more pressing problem.

5. *How Can the Curriculum Best Be Organized?* Faced with new school studies and activities, the imposition of scholarly works on children, and the isolation of each study, Charles McMurry gave highest priority to organization of the curriculum. His first answer was to organize the school studies on a life basis. Knowledge from different subject fields was coordinated into a single project or unit of study. Pupils were to become absorbed in pragmatic life problems or centers of interest. There was, for instance, applied science, like "the problem of securing a pure milk supply"; there were geographic projects like "the Salt River Irrigation project in Arizona"; and there were historic projects like "Hamilton's project for funding the national debt." Most of these projects drew on history, geography, science, mathematics, and language. Also, each project or series of projects was to reveal the scope and meaning of a larger idea, which "like a view from the mountain top, at one glance brings into simple perspective and arrangement a whole vast grouping of minor facts."[3] The idea of evolution, for example, derived from a series of animal studies, becomes a principle of interpretation for use in other studies of animals and plants. A well-devised continuity of thoughts was kept steadily developing from grade to grade. The growth of institutions in history, for example, was one element chosen to ensure continuity over the span of several years of study.

Central Problem of Curriculum. Charles McMurry saw that the central problem of curriculum was to select the right centers of organization. These centers were to be points where older forms of knowledge and

[3]Charles A. McMurry, *How To Organize the Curriculum* (New York: Macmillan, 1923): p. 76.

new studies could be combined. The relation of centers of organization to the aim of education was most important. Further, he was concerned about who would develop the big topics or themes or organize them into effective instructional plans and materials. It seemed that experienced teachers were too absorbed with their teaching duties; scholarly specialists were too involved in the academic instruction of university students; and the pedagogical specialists were identified as members of an educational cult dealing solely in generalities and verbal distinctions.

JOHN DEWEY'S VIEW OF KNOWLEDGE

Dewey's School

In his own laboratory school at the University of Chicago, John Dewey introduced manual training, shopwork, sewing, and cooking on the ground that the traditional curriculum no longer met the needs of the new society created by the forces of industrialism. He wanted the school to take on the character of an embryonic community life, active with occupations that reflect the life of the larger society.

Younger children in the school played at actual occupations, simplifying but not distorting adult roles. Older children followed the Herbartian idea of recapitulating primitive life, but in a childhood social setting as they reconstructed the social life of other times and places. These children were expected to relate their own activities to the consequences of those activities. Primitive human life was supposed to reveal to the child the social effects of introducing tools into a culture. Still older children reflected on the meaning of social forces and processes found in occupations. They were to sense questions, doubts, and problems and to find a means of resolving them.

Dewey used his experiences in the laboratory school in formulating philosophical views that were different than those of the Herbartians. He insisted that the Herbartian interpretations of morality were too narrow and too formal. He protested the teaching of particular virtues without regard for the motives of children. Instead, he proposed that moral motives would develop when children learned to observe and note relationships between the means and the ends in social situations. It was not enough for the teacher to be the model of moral behavior for the children to emulate. Children should be asked to judge and respond morally to their present situations, which are real to them. Indeed, Dewey wanted life in the school to offer opportunities for children to act morally and to learn how to judge their own behavior in terms of the social ideas of cooperation, participation, and positive service. Thus, Dewey challenged the view that morality was an individual matter between oneself and God.

Dewey attacked the view that one's social duty should be done within a traditional framework of values, proposing instead that the method of social intelligence be a critical and creative force. The method of social intelligence means deciding what is right through experimental procedures and the judgment of participants. It requires recognition of different points of view and accommodations of one's own perspective. Whereas the Herbartians relied on ideas as the basic guide to conduct and conceived of knowledge as something to be acquired, Dewey thought more in terms of the child's discovery and evaluation of knowledge than of mere acquisition. He recommended that the learner become the link between knowledge and conduct. His was a relative view of knowledge, not a fixed one. In contrast to the Herbartians' assumption that there was a body of known knowledge, which was indispensable and which could be made interesting to pupils, Dewey argued that subject matter was interesting only when it served the purposes of the learners. Hence, he emphasized learners' participation in formulating the purposes which were the basis for the selection of subject matter.

Dewey's Curriculum

By setting purposes, Dewey meant, however, not only expressing desires but studying means by which those desires can best be realized. Desire was not the end, but only the occasion for the formulation of a plan and method of activity. Thus, Dewey would not have the curriculum start with facts and truth that are outside the range of experience of those taught. Rather, he would start with materials for learning that are consistent with the experience learners already have and then introduce new objects and events that would stimulate new ways to observe and to judge. Subject matter was not to be selected on the basis of what adults thought would be useful for the learner at some future time. Instead the present experience of the learners was to become the primary focus. The achievements of the past (organized knowledge) were to serve as a resource for helping learners both to understand their present condition and to deal with present problems.

In short, Dewey did not believe that the goal of the curriculum should merely be the acquisition of subject matter. Instead he believed in a new goal for curriculum, namely, that organized subject matter become a tool for understanding and intelligently ordering experience. He generated many of the fundamental questions that guide current inquiries. What is the best way to relate the natural view of the child and the scientific view of those with specialized knowledge? How can knowledge become a method for enriching social life? How can we help learners act morally rather than merely have ideas about morality? How can the curriculum best bring order, power, initiative, and intelligence into the child's experience? How can the teacher be helped to follow the individual internal authority of truth about a learner's growth when curriculum decisions are made by external authority above the teacher?

SCIENTIFIC CURRICULUM MAKING

Scientific curriculum making is the attempt to use empirical methods (surveys and analysis of human conduct) in deciding *what* to teach. The history of the scientific movement in curriculum making shows very well that curriculum cannot be separated from the general history of American education or divorced from the broader stream of cultural and intellectual history. Both Franklin Bobbitt and Warrett Charters were greatly influenced by these developments in their lifetimes.

Societal Influences

Industrialism. Large numbers of persons began engaging in manufacturing instead of agriculture. The technological revolution wrought many changes, including a concern for efficiency and economy. For the first time, there was a societal interest in the systematic study of jobs, practices, and working conditions as related to objectives. There was also a concern about how to set standards for both products and processes.

Changing Concepts of School. From an institution with fixed subject matter and concerned primarily with improving intellectual ability by disciplining the mind, the school was increasingly conceived as an agency with no less a goal than satisfying individual and social needs.

Scientific Methods and Techniques. The nineteenth century was characterized by great developments in the pure sciences such as biology, physics, and chemistry and in the application of science to agriculture, manufacture, and almost every other phase of practical life. Yet it wasn't until early in the twentieth century that the spirit of scientific experimentation began to push its way into the thinking of educators. Bobbitt and

Charters brought a scientific way of thinking into the emerging field of curriculum making.

Much of what was called scientific at the time is now labeled scientism, mere technology, or nose counting. Modern critics like to say pejoratively that educational scientists of those days equated efficiency with science. It is true that these early educational scientists were attempting to solve educational problems by means of experimental and statistical techniques. They particularly emphasized the measurement of ability and achievement with their development of intelligence and achievement tests. The zeal for measurement brought forth an abundance of facts about school buildings, school finance, pupil achievement and pupil traits, and learners' physical, emotional, intellectual, and social growth. The field of curriculum also caught this zeal for measurement. Data were collected about the content of textbooks, courses of study, school subjects, and appraisal of results. Studies were undertaken to find out how pupils learn and to design new methods for overcoming pupil difficulties.

Key Ideas

Two ideals were frequently associated with the scientific movement in education. One was the idea of an open attitude, the expectation that the school staff would be willing to consider new proposals and be alert to new methods and devices. Teachers, for example, were expected to join their pupils in asking questions. Second, there was an assumption that natural laws govern not only things and their forces, but also humans and their ways. Hence, it was the duty of education to shape the will into a desire to move in harmony with these laws. Science was seen as a guarantor of social progress.

Bobbitt's Contribution

Franklin Bobbitt articulated for the first time the importance of studying the processes for making a curriculum. He realized that it was not enough to develop new curricula; there was also a need to learn more about how new curricula can best be developed. This insight came through long experience in curriculum matters.

In his book, *The Curriculum*, Bobbitt tells of a personal experience that caused him to look at curriculum from the point of view of social needs rather than mere academic study.[4] He had gone to the Philippines early in the American occupation as a member of a committee sent to draw up

[4]Franklin Bobbitt, *The Curriculum* (Boston: Houghton Mifflin, 1918), p. 35.

an elementary school curriculum for the islands. Free to recommend almost anything to meet the needs of the population, the committee had the opportunity to create an original, constructive curriculum.

And what happened? The members assembled American textbooks for reading, arithmetic, geography, United States history, and other subjects with which they had been familiar in American schools. Without being conscious of it, they had organized a course of study for the traditional eight elementary school grades, on the basis of their American prejudices and preconceptions about what an elementary course ought to be.

Bobbitt was lucky. A director of education in the Philippines helped him and the committee to look at the social realities, and they then unceremoniously threw out time-hallowed content. Instead, they brought into the course a number of things to help the people gain health, make a living, and enjoy self-realization. The activities they introduced came from the culture of the Philippines and were quite different from those found in the American textbooks.

From this experience, Bobbitt saw his difficulty: his complete adherence to traditional curriculum beliefs had kept him from realizing the possibility of more useful solutions. He had needed something to shatter his complacency. As Bobbitt himself said,

> We needed principles of curriculum making. We did not know that we should first determine objectives from a study of social needs. We supposed education consisted only of teaching the familiar subjects. We had not come to see that it is essentially a process of unfolding the potential abilities of a population and in particularized relation to the social conditions. We had not learned that studies are means, not ends. We did not realize that any instrument or experience which is effective in such unfoldment is the right instrument and right experience; and that anything which is not effective is wrong, however time-honored and widely used it may be.[5]

Bobbitt was little different from most people who are entering the field of curriculum for the first time today. They are unaware that what they have personally experienced in school may not be the final answer. They have difficulty creating something different and more appropriate.

After his experience in the Philippines, Bobbitt stimulated other workers in the field. His book, *How To Make a Curriculum*, was the forerunner of others in the subject and had great influence on school practice.[6] Students of curriculum now see Bobbitt as the first to recognize

[5]Bobbitt, *The Curriculum*, p. 283.
[6]Franklin Bobbitt, *How To Make a Curriculum* (Boston: Houghton Mifflin, 1924).

the need for a new specialization, the study of curriculum making. It was Bobbitt who saw that professional agreement on a *method* of discovery is more important than agreement on the details of curriculum content. He offered the profession his method with the intention that others would try it, improve it, or suggest a better one. Bobbitt's method helps to define what is meant by curriculum making.

His method was guided by a fundamental assumption that would not be accepted by all curriculum makers today—namely, that education is to prepare us for the activities that ought to make up a well-rounded adult life. It is primarily for adult life, not childhood.

Steps in Making Curriculum. Bobbitt envisions five steps in curriculum making:

1. *Analysis of Human Experience.* The first step in curriculum making, according to Bobbitt, is to separate the broad range of human experience into major fields. One such classification includes language, health, citizenship, social, recreation, religious, home, vocation. The whole field of human experience should be reviewed in order that the portions belonging to the schools may be seen in relation to the whole.

2. *Job Analysis.* The second step is to break down the fields into their more specific activities. In this step, Bobbitt had to compromise with his ideal. He recognized the desirability of using a scientific method of analysis, yet knew that thus far there was not adequate technique for the work. Hence, he tended to fall back on practical and personal experiences to prove that a given activity was crucial to one or more of the categories of human experience.

   Bobbitt knew that only a few activity analyses had ever been made and that most of them were in the fields of spelling, language, arithmetic, history, geography, and vocation. He did, however, believe that activity analysis was a promising technique and turned to his colleague, W. W. Charters, for examples of how best to determine specific activities from larger units. Charters, in turn, drew from the idea of job analysis already common in industry. Business and industry at that time made an analysis for each job and prepared training programs for the tasks identified. For the position of application clerk the analysis would include these tasks: meets people who want to open accounts, asks them to fill out blanks, looks up rating in Dun's. A course of study was prepared to teach future clerks each of the identified duties.

   It should be clear, however, that job analysis could result in either a list of duties or a list of methods for performing duties.

The procedures for the analysis included introspection, interview, and investigation. In introspection, an expert related his or her duties and methods. Then, in an interview, a number of experts reviewed a list of duties to verify the tasks. Lastly, the investigator actually carried out the operations on the job. A problem in making a complete analysis occurred in trying to describe the mental operations necessary for the task when one cannot see the steps carried out with the material. The analyses only indicated what the activities were if one were to learn the duties of a position.

3. *Deriving Objectives.* The third step is to derive the objectives of education from statements of the abilities required to perform the activities. In *How To Make a Curriculum,* Bobbitt presented more than 800 major objectives in ten fields of human experience. Here, for example, is a partial list of the general objectives within a language field: (1) ability to pronounce words properly; (2) ability to use voice in agreeable ways; (3) use grammatically correct language; (4) effectively organize and express thoughts; (5) express thought to others in conversation, in recounting experiences, in serious or formal discussion, in an oral report, in giving directions, and before an audience; (6) command an adequate reading, speaking, and writing vocabulary; (7) ability to write legibly with ease and speed; (8) ability to spell the words of one's writing vocabulary; (9) ability to use good form and order in all written work (margins, spacing, alignment, paragraphing, capitalization, punctuation, syllabification, abbreviation). These objectives illustrate the level of generality needed to help curriculum makers decide what specific educational results were to be produced. Bobbitt also realized that each of the objectives could be broken down further into its component parts; indeed, he illustrated such detailed analysis.

4. *Selecting Objectives.* The fourth step is to select from the list of objectives those which are to serve as the basis for planning pupil activities. Guidelines for making this final selection of objectives include:

> Eliminate objectives that can be accomplished through the normal process of living. Only the abilities that are not sufficiently developed by chance should be included among the objectives of systematic education. Possibly the more important portions of education are not accomplished in schools but through nonscholastic agencies.
>
> Emphasize objectives that will overcome deficiencies in the adult

world. Avoid objectives opposed by the community. Specific
objectives in religion, economics, and health are especially likely to be opposed.

Eliminate objectives when there are practical constraints hindering their achievement. Involve the community in the selection
of objectives. Consult community members who are proficient
in practical affairs and experts in their fields.

Differentiate between objectives that are for all learners and
those which are practical for only a part of the population.
Sequence the objectives, indicating how far pupils should go
each year in attaining the general goals.

5. *Planning in Detail.* The fifth step is to lay out the kinds of activities,
experiences, and opportunities involved in attaining the objectives.
Details for the day-to-day activities of children at each age or
grade level must be laid out. These detailed activities make up the
curriculum. As project activity and part-time work at home and in
the community are introduced, there must be cooperative planning. Teachers, nurses, play activity directors, and parents together should plan the detailed procedures of the courses. Their plans
should then be approved by the principal, superintendent, and
school board.

Charters's Contribution

Although Charters enunciated a method of curriculum formulation
that was very similar to Bobbitt's, he differed in the emphasis on ideals
and systematized knowledge in determining the content of the curriculum. Charters saw ideals as objectives with observable consequences.
He believed that honesty, loyalty, and generosity contributed to satisfaction. Ideals did not necessarily lead to one's immediate satisfaction but
to satisfaction in the long run or to satisfaction as defined by social
consensus. However, he knew of no scientific measurement that would
determine which ideals should operate in a school. There was no scientific
way to determine whether open-mindedness or artistic taste should be
the ideal of the school or student. Hence, Charters thought it defensible
for a faculty to vote on the ideals it believed to be most valuable. Faculty
selection of ideals was not to be arbitrary, however. The opinion of
thoughtful men and women in public and private life needed to be
carefully weighed and the needs of the student investigated.

Once ideals were selected they had to serve as standards for actions.
They were not to be abstracted from activities. The teacher who wished

to inculcate ideals in the lives of pupils needed to analyze activities to which an ideal applied and to see that the selected ideal was applied in the pupils' activities. For Charters, the curriculum consisted of both ideals and activities. Unlike Bobbitt, Charters gave explicit attention to knowledge in his method for making the curriculum.[7] He wanted subject matter useful for living and of motivational import to the learner. But he also wanted to reassure those who feared that organized information in such fields as chemistry, history, physics, and mathematics would have no place in a curriculum built around objectives derived from studies of life in the social setting. His answer showed how job analyses revealed the importance of both primary subjects (mathematics and English in application) and derived subjects (subjects necessary for understanding the activity or the reason for the activity). Psychology, for example, was needed in order to explain methods of supervision.

On the one hand, Charters would determine subject material from analysis of life projects in order that one would know which elements of the subjects are most important and require the most attention. On the other hand, he would select school projects that would give instruction in the subject items and allow the pupil to use the knowledge in a broader range of activities.

As representatives of the scientific movement in curriculum making, Bobbitt and Charters brought forth the following conceptions and dimensions of curriculum: It is a process which, if followed, will result in an evolving curriculum. The process of curriculum making is itself a field of study. The relation of goals (ideals), objectives, and activities is a curriculum concern. The selection of goals is a normative process. The selection of objectives and activities is empirical and scientific. Objectives and activities are subject to scientific analysis and verification. The relation of organized systematic fields of knowledge to the practical requirements of daily living is a central question for students of the curriculum.

IMPROVEMENT OF INSTRUCTION

Local Development of Curriculum

Until the end of World War I, major influences on curriculum came from outside the local school system. Academic scholars set the direction for purposes and content through national committees and textbook writing. Usually, local schools participated only to the extent of deciding

[7]W. W. Charters, *Curriculum Construction* (New York: Macmillan, 1923): pp. 103–06.

what subjects to add and what textbooks to use. The high school curriculum was standardized on the basis of what college presidents thought students needed for college. After 1920, the scientific movement directly influenced the curriculum through new types of school textbooks stressing skills related to the everyday needs of adults and children. College scholars found their power to determine the curriculum challenged by the scientific method of curriculum formulation. The first local systematic curriculum making also began around 1920 when several school systems tried to develop courses of study in single subjects and the study of particular problems, such as learning difficulties in spelling and how to overcome them through instruction.

A course of study was a guide to the teaching of a particular subject or subjects. The course of study included a philosophy, suggested content (topics and their ordering for study), a structure (discipline-centered or interdisciplinary), and the relation of the content of the life of the learner and the larger society. Major themes and other abstractions were outlined for relating activities and suggested activities and resources were given.

The Course of Study Movement

By 1926, practically all schools were revising their curricula. They attacked the problem of curriculum development in a comprehensive way by defining the general objectives on which the entire curriculum was based and by which all subjects were correlated. It is true, however, that members of state education departments often chose the objectives and left the selection of activities to the teachers. Sometimes, the principals or representatives of teachers selected the objectives according to local needs. In these schools teachers worked in committees in order to list activities to be tested. A director was provided to supervise the preparation of the course of study for an individual school district or an entire state, and a curriculum specialist served as general consultant. Not all professional educators viewed the movement with favor:

> Too much of the present-day curriculum is amateurish, trifling, and a sheer waste of time—worse than that, an injection of pernicious confusion into what should be orderly progress. The let-everybody-pitch-in-and-help method is ludicrous when applied to curriculum building. It is too much like inviting a group of practical electricians to redesign a modern power plant.[8]

[8]Guy M. Whipple, "What Price Curriculum Making," *School and Society* 31 (March 15, 1930): 368.

Caswell's Influence

Hollis Leland Caswell extended our view of the curriculum field through his concern about the relationships between the course of study, teaching, and the learner's role. Caswell was one of the first to see the making of a course of study as too limiting in purpose. He shifted the emphasis from production of a course of study to the actual improvement of instruction. He saw curriculum development as a means of helping teachers apply in their daily tasks of instruction the best information on subject matter, the interests of children, and contemporary social needs. He involved 16,000 Virginia teachers and administrators in making a course of study for that state, for instance.[9] His involvement of all teachers instead of just a few selected representatives was a new thrust. Caswell considered the course of study as only one of several aids to the teacher and believed that when teachers made the course of study together they would learn the limits of its usefulness. He looked on the course of study as a means of providing source materials for teachers to use in planning their work rather than a prescription to be followed in detail.

Help for the Teacher in Curriculum Making. Caswell attempted to help teachers improve curricula by providing them with a syllabus of carefully chosen readings under seven topics. These topics or questions are important for what they tell us about the nature of curriculum and the tasks involved in making a curriculum.[10]

1. What is curriculum?
2. What are the developments that resulted in a need for curriculum revision?
3. What is the function of subject matter?
4. How do we determine educational objectives?
5. What is the best way to organize instruction?
6. How should we select subject matter?
7. How should we measure the outcomes of instruction?

The readings Caswell suggested to help teachers answer these questions included a range of sources, some of which gave conflicting opinions. Caswell himself believed that the curriculum is more than the experiences made available to the child. It consists of the experiences the

[9]Mary Louise Seguel, *The Curriculum Field: Its Formative Years* (New York: Teachers College Press, Teachers College, Columbia University, 1966): p. 148.
[10]Sidney B. Hall, D. W. Peters, and Hollis L. Caswell, "Study Course for Virginia State Curriculum," *State Board of Education Bulletin* 14, no. 2 (January 1932): 363.

child actually undergoes. Hence, the teacher's interaction with the pupil is a vital aspect of curriculum. Preparing a course of study is only the starting point for curriculum improvement.

Curriculum Revision. Caswell also believed in curriculum revision. He said that curriculum revision is necessary in order for the school to meet more social and personal needs. Curriculum should help sensitize people to social problems and give pupils experience in social action. Caswell wanted the school to be an avenue of opportunity for all the people, contributing to interracial understanding and relations, strengthening home life, stressing democratic ideals, and contributing to the conservation of resources.

Evaluating Demands. Caswell thought that the demands for curriculum change must be evaluated. He recommended that any proposed change be screened, and that changes be accepted only if they are (1) consistent with democratic values, (2) consistent with the development needs of the learner, (3) something that other agencies cannot accomplish, (4) something that has or will gain the support of leaders in the community, (5) something that does not replace other existing curriculum areas of relatively higher value.

Curriculum Design. Caswell agreed that a curriculum design should synthesize the three basic elements of the curriculum—children's interests, social functions, and organized knowledge. In the tentative course of study for Virginia elementary schools, for example, he helped developers provide scope and sequence. Social functions served as the scope. Some of these functions were protection and conservation of life, property, and natural resources; recreation; expression of aesthetic impulses; and distribution of rewards of production. These functions were worked on in some form in every grade. Sequenced experiences were arranged according to centers of interest; for example, home and school life were studied in the first grade, the effects of the machine on learning in the sixth. Specific activities were suggested to match both the social functions and the centers of interest using the most relevant subject matter.

Caswell saw the central task of curriculum development to be a synthesis of materials from subject matter fields, philosophy, psychology, and sociology. "Materials must be so selected and arranged as to become vital in the experience of the learner."[11] Thus, he saw curriculum as a

---

[11]Hollis L. Caswell and Doak S. Campbell, *Curriculum Development* (New York: American Book Company, 1935): p. 81.

field of study that represents no structurally limited body of content; rather, it represents a process or procedure.

RATIONAL CURRICULUM MAKING

In 1949, Ralph Tyler sent to the University of Chicago Press a manuscript, *Basic Principles of Curriculum and Instruction,* a rationale for examining problems of curriculum and instruction.[12] The rationale was based on his experiences as a teacher of curriculum and as a curriculum maker and evaluator. He had been especially active in designing ways to measure changes in learners brought about by schools' new efforts to help learners develop interests and perform more appropriately in society. Since then, nearly 90,000 copies of Tyler's rationale have been sold, and it is regarded as the culmination of one epoch of curriculum making.

Tyler's Curriculum Inquiry

Tyler assumed that anyone engaging in curriculum inquiry must try to answer these questions:

1. What educational purposes should the school seek to attain?
2. What educational experiences can be provided that are likely to attain these purposes?
3. How can these educational experiences be effectively organized?
4. How can we determine whether these purposes are being attained?

By purposes, Tyler meant educational objectives, and he proposed that school goals would have greater validity if they are selected in light of information about learners' psychological needs and interests, contemporary life, and aspects of subject matter that would be useful to everyone, not just specialists in disciplines. In order to select from the many objectives that would be inferred from such information, Tyler recommended that a school staff "screen" them according to the school's philosophy of education and beliefs about the psychology of learning.

Tyler realized that having purposes was only the first step. He used the phrase *learning experiences* to include a plan for providing learning situations that take into account both the previous experience and

[12]Ralph W. Tyler, *Basic Principles of Curriculum and Instruction* (Chicago: University of Chicago Press, 1949).

perceptions that the learner brings to the situation, and whether or not the learner is likely to respond to it mentally and emotionally and in action.

Tyler then turned his attention to ordering the learning situations so that they would be focused on the same outcomes. He was preoccupied with how the curriculum could produce a maximum cumulative effect. He wanted a cumulative plan for organization that would help students learn more and learn more effectively.

His answer drew heavily from the early Herbartians' ideas of organization. Like Charles McMurry, he thought organizing elements or controlling ideas, concepts, values, and skills should be the threads, the warp and woof of the fabric of curriculum organization. Tyler approved using the concept of a place value numeration system, for example, which can be enlarged on from kindergarten through the twelfth grade. Such concepts were seen as useful elements for relating different learning experiences in science, social studies, and other fields. He described optional ways of structuring learning experiences both within schools and in the classroom. They could, for instance, be structured within special subject courses, like English and mathematics, or as broad fields, like the language arts. Experience could also be structured within the format of lessons. He showed his own organization and curriculum preference by listing the advantages of relating content to real life through projects that allow for broader grouping of learning opportunities. He also saw merit in organizing courses that span several years rather than a single term.

Finally, Tyler regarded evaluation as an important operation in curriculum development. He saw it as a process for finding out whether the learning experiences actually produced the desired results and for discovering the strengths and weaknesses of the plans. He made a real contribution by enlarging our concept of evaluation. Rather than focusing on only a few aspects of growth, tests should, he believed, indicate attainment of all the objectives of an educational program. Further, he did not believe that tests should mean only paper and pencil examinations. He thought that observations of pupils, products made by learners, records of student participation, and other methods should also be included.

Criticisms of Tyler's Rationale

Criticisms of Tyler's rationale generally stem from Tyler's statement that the selection of objectives is a prerequisite for curriculum development. The late James MacDonald, for instance, felt that statements of

expected behavioral outcomes violate the integrity of learners by fragmenting their behavior and manipulating them for an end that has no
present worth for them.[13]

In prescribing three sources from which objectives can be derived, the
student, the society, and the subject, Tyler attempted to reconcile the
conflict between those who favored one or another as the most important
factor and to formulate a consensus that would allow individuals with
divergent goals to work together in developing curricula. To effect a
consistency among the resultant goals, he relied on the staff to apply
their own philosophical and psychological criteria. On this point, critics
contend, Tyler does not realize that information collected from the
learner and society is biased and that, once that information has been
gathered, there is no scientific way to infer what *should* follow from the
facts reported. Further, Tyler's proposal for filtering educational objectives
through a philosophical screen is regarded as vacuous and trivial.[14] It
leaves to staff in individual schools the question of which objectives to
keep and which to throw out. Tyler gives no criterion to use in making a
choice among objectives.

Tyler's rationale for examining problems of curriculum and instruction
summed up the best thought regarding curriculum during its first
half-century as a field of study. His debt to the McMurrys, Dewey,
Bobbitt, and Charters is clear. The four questions he poses and the
suggestions he gives for answering the questions define the field of
curriculum as it was understood until very recently.

CONCLUDING COMMENTS

As indicated in Table 14.1, influential curriculum leaders have
addressed themselves to significant questions about what should be
taught and why. Their questions ranged from inquiries into purposes,
such as whether morality can and should be taught, to questions about
the selection of content, the relationship between content and method,
and the way in which organization can have a cumulative effect on
learning experiences.

Any new effort in curriculum thought and action must still treat the
persistent questions of purpose, activity, organization, and evaluation.

[13]James B. MacDonald, "The Person in the Curriculum," in *Precedents and Promise in the
Curriculum Field,* ed. Helen F. Robinson (New York: Columbia University Press, Teachers
College, 1966): p. 41.
[14]Herbert Kliebard, "The Tyler Rationale," in *Curriculum and Evaluation,* eds. Arno
Bellack and Herbert Kliebard (Berkeley: McCutchan, 1977): pp. 56–67.

TABLE 14.1 A Summary of Early Curriculum Theorists' Ideas

Theorists	Purpose, Aims, and Objectives	Content	Method of Instruction	Organization
Charles and Frank McMurray	Moral development Good citizenship	Literature for related aesthetics and the intellectual History and literature for citizenship Geography for correlating studies Later, acceptance of new branches of knowledge	Five formal steps in lesson plans Special methods in each subject field	Studies sequenced according to age and stage of learner development Information organized around problems and projects Activities related by topics and themes

TABLE 14.1 (continued)

Theorists	Purpose, Aims, and Objectives	Content	Method of Instruction	Organization
John Dewey	Intellectual control over the forces of man and nature	The intellectual method by which social life is enriched and improved	Survey of capacities and needs of learners	Life experiences learner used to carry learner on to more refined and better organized facts and ideas
	Social intelligence	Knowledge from organized fields as it functions in the life of the child	Arrangement of conditions that provide the content to satisfy needs	Curriculum organized around two concepts: that knowing is experimental and that knowledge is instrumental to individual and social purposes
	Trained capacities in the service of social interest		The plan for meeting needs involves the participation of all group members	
	Development as an aim		Intelligent activity, not aimless activity	

Franklin Bobbitt	Meeting social needs Preparation of learner for adult life	Subject matter as a means, not an end	Deriving objectives from analysis of what is required in order to perform in broad categories of life Detailed activities to be planned by teachers, parents, and others	Specification of objectives to be attained each year Layout of activities involved in attaining objectives
Warren W. Charters	Satisfaction through fulfillment of ideals (e.g., honesty) that sway socially efficient individuals	Organized knowledge that can be applied in activities needed for a socially efficient life	Projects and activities that are consistent with ideals	Experimentation to find the best way to order ideals, activities, and ideas

TABLE 14.1 (continued)

Theorists	Purpose, Aims, and Objectives	Content	Method of Instruction	Organization
Hollis Caswell	Fulfillment of demo-cratic ideals (improved intergroup relations, home life, and the conservation of resources)	No limiting body of content Key concepts most helpful in the solution of social problems	Teacher in-teraction with pupil Teacher applying the best of what is known about sub-ject matter, children's interests, and social needs Key ideas to be woven in-to the child's performance of social functions	Selected social functions (e.g., the conserva-tion of life) to be worked on in some form in every grade Sequence of activities to be arranged according to centers of interest

Ralph Tyler	No stated purposes Each curriculum person to evolve own purposes through a rational process, involving consideration of learner, social conditions, knowledge, and philosophical position Objectives to be behaviorally stated, but specificity to depend on one's theory of learning	Subject matter from subject specialists that could contribute to the broad functions of daily living	Opportunity to practice what the objectives of instruction call for Each opportunity to contribute to several objectives Activities that are within the learner's capacity and are satisfying	Provisions for the reiteration of concepts, skills, or values Provision for the progressive development of the concept, skill, or attitude Correlation of concepts from one field to content in other fields

The emphases on these matters and the way they are addressed, however, are changing. The last decade saw special interest groups and governmental agencies taking over the leadership in program development—fragmentation was the result. Presently there are signs of another change in leadership in response to national interest in academic excellence and a growing concern for general education. Curriculum development at the local level is once more regaining importance because curriculum must be adapted to local interests and to the particular individuals to be served. How best to balance the demand for programs in response to national needs with the requirements of local communities is a current dilemma. The popularity of local curriculum development also rests on the desire for effective schools—schools that have a strong sense of community, shared goals, and high expectations for students and staff. Through collective decision making in the design of the curriculum, the preparation of instructional materials, and the evaluation of the program, school efficiency is achieved. A good curriculum making process requires deliberation—the coalescence of aims, data, and judgments.

A knowledge of curriculum history, including its theoretical and practical knowledge, is helpful in improving present reform efforts. For example, what better guidelines for the conduct of local curriculum development can be found than those based on Caswell's experiences? Similarly, the McMurrys' approach to correlation and the value of particular subjects in interrelating knowledge has value for current planners who want to strengthen general education. Also, Dewey's view of moral education is timely as planners consider the best response to public opinion that gives a high priority to education as a moral enterprise.

Contemporary scholars in curriculum need a manageable range of problems that can be investigated in depth. An examination of the problems undertaken by historically influential persons in the field suggests areas for research.

QUESTIONS

1. What are the continuing central concerns of curriculum specialists as revealed by the work of prominent historical figures in the field of curriculum?
2. What current curriculum doctrines and practices are carryovers from another historical period?
3. In what way is the present situation different from the past? How does this difference make some past ideas of curriculum irrelevant?

4. It is said that a history of curriculum thought and practice cannot be separated from the broader stream of cultural and intellectual history. What conditions, movements, or ideas had the greatest influence on curriculum making in the past century? What social and intellectual forces are likely to shape the curriculum field today?

5. What the McMurrys, Dewey, Charters, Bobbit, Caswell, and Tyler thought about curriculum is less important than what they make *you* think about curriculum. What do they have to say to you?

SELECTED REFERENCES

Bellack, Arno A. "History of Curriculum Thought and Practice." *Review of Educational Research* 39, no. 3 (1969): 283–92.

Bobbitt, Franklin. *The Curriculum.* New York: Houghton Mifflin, 1918.

———. *How To Make a Curriculum.* New York: Houghton Mifflin, 1924.

Caswell, Hollis L. and Campbell, Doak S. *Readings in Curriculum Development.* New York: American Book, 1937.

Charters, W. W. *Curriculum Construction.* New York: Macmillan, 1923.

Davis, O. L., Jr., ed. *Perspectives on Curriculum Development 1776-1976.* Washington, D.C.: ASCD, 1976.

Franklin, Barry M. "Curriculum History: Its Nature and Boundaries." *Curriculum Inquiry* 7, no. 1 (Spring 1977): 67–79.

Kliebard, Herbert M. "The Drive for Curriculum Change in the United States, 1890–1958—The Ideological Roots of Curriculum as a Field of Specialization." *Journal of Curriculum Studies* 11, no. 3 (September 1979): 191–202.

McMurry, Charles A. *How To Organize the Curriculum.* New York: Macmillan, 1923.

National Society for the Study of Education. *The First Yearbook of the Herbart Society for the Scientific Study of Teaching.* Chicago: University of Chicago Press, 1907.

———. *The Curriculum—Retrospect and Prospect.* NSSE Yearbook, Part I. Chicago: University of Chicago Press, 1971.

Schubert, William Henry. *Curriculum Books: The First Eighty Years.* Washington, D.C.: University Press of America, 1980.

Seguel, Mary Louise. *The Curriculum Field: Its Formative Years.* New York: Columbia University, Teachers College Press, 1966.

Tyler, Ralph. *Basic Principles of Curriculum and Instruction.* Chicago: University of Chicago Press, 1949.

15 / THE PROMISE OF THEORY AND RESEARCH IN CURRICULUM

Six crucial areas of curriculum research and development are appraised in this chapter, so the importance of each can be determined. Future directions in curriculum inquiry are also outlined by dividing the current work of the most prominent curriculum scholars into two camps, the soft curricularists and the hard curricularists. Finally, four frameworks for guiding curriculum research are presented. These frameworks and their specific questions should be of value to anyone wishing to engage in curriculum research.

Some curriculum workers do cognitive and empirical as well as practical research, adopting various methods for throwing light on what can and should be taught to whom. There are also theorists who attempt to stipulate what is meant by curriculum theory and how best to develop it. Many of these theorists are using forms of criticisms as a research strategy.

Ideally, theorists and researchers should aid practitioners by providing principles for formulating desirable outcomes and designing instructional means. At the very least, they should provide practitioners with intellectual tools for conceptualizing their situations and raising questions. At most, theorists should explain and predict relationships among a large number of variables such as life outcomes, school learning, and instructional plans. Attainment of the latter goal seems most unlikely, however.

It is the purpose of this chapter to examine representative samples of the work of curriculum researchers and theorists in order to illustrate curriculum as a field of inquiry and to suggest its future directions.

STATE OF THE FIELD

Both in 1960 and again in 1969, John Goodlad appraised the status of curriculum research and development.[1] These appraisals offer a good basis for measuring progress in the curriculum field. The appraisals were made with respect to six curriculum needs. They were the need for theoretical constructs, the need for concepts that identify the major questions in the curriculum field, the need to determine what subject matter can best be taught simultaneously, the need to arrange material for effective learning, the need for taxonomical analysis (classification) of objectives, and the need for studies indicating the relationships between specific instructional variables and the outcomes from instruction.

Let us look at each of Goodlad's 1960 concerns, and the status of research and development in each area in 1969 and in the present. We can then readily see where the field is progressing and where it is not.

The Need for Curriculum Theory

Status of Curriculum Theory in 1969. Between 1960 and 1969, little was added to our knowledge of how to derive educational objectives. Elizabeth and George Macia and others attempted to adopt theories from outside the field of education to conceptualize phenomena related to curriculum.[2] One consequence was the differentiation of four different kinds of curriculum theory. *Formal curriculum theory* involves theorizing about the structure of the disciplines that will constitute the curriculum. Elizabeth Macia would leave this theorizing to the philosophers and members of the disciplines. *Valuational curriculum theory* involves speculation about the appropriate means to attain the most valuable objectives and to present the best content in a curriculum. *Event theory* is very much like scientific theory in that it tries to predict what will occur under certain conditions. *Praxiological theory* is speculation about the appropriate means to attain what is judged to be valuable. Praxiological theory forms the theoretical base for determining curriculum policy, the decision to adopt certain objectives and practices. Using the perspective of science in theorizing (event theory), George Beauchamp described efforts to make theory in

[1]John Goodlad, "Curriculum: The State of the Field," *Review of Educational Research* 30, no. 3 (June 1960): 185–99; "Curriculum: The State of the Field," *Review of Educational Research* 39, no. 3 (June 1969): 367–75.

[2]Occasional papers by Elizabeth Macia, George Macia, Robert Jewett, and others treating educational theorizing through models (Columbus: Bureau of Educational Research and Service, Ohio State University, 1963–65).

the field of curriculum during this period and concluded that little theoretical research had been done. Today, Beauchamp finds theory making in curriculum a "shambles." Joseph Schwab said that theoretical pursuits were not appropriate in the field of curriculum. He urged instead direct study of the curriculum: what it is, how it gets that way, and how it affects the students and teachers.[3]

Status of Curriculum Theory in Mid-1980s. There have been several attempts to act on Schwab's recommendation. Decker Walker was one of the first to offer a model for guiding the study of deliberations, processes, and assumptions of curriculum developers. Walker faulted those in the curriculum field for being so busy prescribing curriculum making that they did not pay sufficient attention to discovering how it is done.[4] Although he has not changed in his opinion that curriculum theory should be applied in documenting what happens in actual important cases, Walker now writes of the value of curriculum theories in helping us to see curriculum in a different light and to interpret it in a way we would not have otherwise.[5] Walker conceives of families of theories with different purposes and forms bearing on the same problem—all trying to rationalize practice, to conceptualize it, to explain it. He observes that some curriculum theories accept the society as it is and that others work for a new and better society to come. Walker cites Paulo Freire and Benjamin Bloom as examples of those using theory for *program rationalization*; Franklin Bobbitt and Ralph Tyler as those who used theory in the *rationalization of procedures* for curriculum construction; John Dewey as one who used theory as a basis for thinking about *curriculum phenomena*; and Walter Ong as an example of those who use curriculum theory to explain fads, reforms, and curriculum changes.

There is, however, opposition to Schwab's call for attention to the practical rather than the theoretical. Some theorists are trying to develop a more comprehensive and realistic philosophy of society and the individual instead of merely engaging in the practical problems of curriculum maintenance and incremental reform. They view curriculum theorizing as a way to demythologize curriculum and to advance two concerns of

[3]George A. Beauchamp, *Curriculum Theory* (Wilmette, Ill: Kagg, 1968); George A. Beauchamp, "Curriculum Theory: Meaning, Development and Use," *Theory Into Practice* 21, no. 1 (Winter 1982): 23–28; Joseph J. Schwab, *The Practical: A Language for Curriculum* (Washington, D.C.: National Education Association, 1970).

[4]Decker Walker, "A Naturalistic Model for Curriculum Development," *School Review* 80, no. 1 (November 1971): 51–67.

[5]Decker F. Walker, "Curriculum Theory is Many Things to Many People," *Theory Into Practice* 21, no. 1 (Winter 1982): 62–5.

modern revolutionaries: heightened consciousness about the consequences of technology, capitalism and other institutional structures, and
exploration of the inner life to broaden our ways of knowing.

William Pinar and Madeline Grumet, for example, believe that curriculum theorists must constantly question curriculum practices, interrupt
the predictable in schooling with analyses that suggest alternatives.[6]

Another important theoretical development is the evaluators' usur-
pation of curriculum theory. As indicated in Chapter 10, theories of
evaluation have been broadened to include frameworks for determining
objectives, monitoring procedures for curriculum design and implementation, and guiding other curriculum decisions.

In her assessment of the status of curriculum theory, Gail McCutcheon
notes that much has been written about curriculum theory, but that
there are few examples of curriculum theories that integrate a cluster of
analyses, interpretations, and understandings of curriculum phenomena
—the sources of the curriculum.[7] McCutcheon sees a need for examples
that have a clear value and draw from multiple disciplines—psychology,
sociology. One such example is found in the work of Glenys Unruh who
tries to resolve competing claims about what to teach and how to teach it
by appealing to principles. Unruh sees democratic ideals as the theoretical
base for curriculum development. Her plea for a theory of responsive
curriculum development rests on John Dewey's concept of the democratic
person and the democratic school in which administrators, students,
parents, and community members cooperate and participate in curriculum planning and evaluation. She outlines seven propositions with
hypotheses to support such a theory:

1. If planning for the freedom of individuals occurs, the curriculum
   will be more responsive to social, ethical, and moral values. Illustrative hypothesis: Racial attitudes will improve as curriculum
   developers from different races study the concerns of each race
   about the cultures of others.
2. If planners draw on the local culture, the curriculum will be more
   responsive to the needs and concerns of those served by the
   school. Illustrative hypothesis: If people from the school and from
   the community cooperatively design work experiences in the

---

[6]William Pinar and Madeline R. Grumet, "Theory and Practice and the Reconceptualization of Curriculum Studies," in *Rethinking Curriculum Studies*, L. Barton and M. Lawer,
eds. (New York: Halsted Press, John Wiley & Sons, 1981).

[7]Gail McCutcheon, "What in the World is Curriculum Theory?" *Theory Into Practice* 21,
no. 1 (Winter 1982): 18–22.

community for students and learning experiences in the school for laypersons, there will be greater consensus on means.

3. If means are used to exemplify and strengthen the nation's founding goals, curriculum development will embody the purposes of American democracy. Illustrative hypothesis: Increased dialog on values by state and local school boards will result in greater curriculum emphasis on decision-making skills.

4. If there is a commitment to planned change, curriculum developers will consider new technological and social developments and respond to them in ways to enhance the freedom of individuals. Illustrative hypothesis: If students are given opportunities to confront value choices affecting the future, they will be able to judge whether legislative decisions harm or benefit the goals of a humanistic society.

5. If there is a more comprehensive assessment of needs, curriculum will be more responsive to both individual and group concerns. Illustrative hypothesis: Surveys of local needs as expressed by students, parents, teachers, and others will result in higher priority being given to humanistic and aesthetic developments.

6. If there is greater interaction and collaboration among groups, there will be more empathy for the needs of others. Illustrative hypothesis: If the purposes and needs of conflicting groups are presented in orderly discussion to all involved, then a mutually acceptable curriculum plan will be developed.

7. If there is a systems approach with procedures for setting goals, assessing needs, specifying objectives and priorities, and using evaluation to guide improvement, there will be more progress toward broad democratic goals. Illustrative hypothesis: The use of a systems approach will result in greater emphasis on formative evaluation, a wider variety of instructional methods, more positive expressions by teachers and students in the classrooms, and more positive attitudes toward school.[8]

There is great disenchantment with the notion that the curriculum field will amass empirical generalizations, put them into general laws, and form these laws into a coherent theory. The idea that theory will tell us the necessary and sufficient conditions for a particular result in curriculum has given way to the assessment of local events and to the development of concepts that will help people make their own decisions.

[8]Glenys G. Unruh, *Responsive Curriculum Development: Theory and Action* (Berkeley: McCutchan, 1975).

The Need for Curriculum Conceptions in Curriculum

Status of Curriculum Conception in 1969. General theory and conceptualizations in curriculum had advanced very little in the decade before 1969. John Goodlad tried to bridge theory and practice with a conceptual scheme for rational curriculum planning. His categories and suggested processes, which build on the Tyler rationale of 1949, were intended to stimulate research and organize thinking in the curriculum field. However, he later saw no evidence that the intent was fulfilled. Also, Dwayne Huebner elaborated on a conception of curriculum as a field of study. He criticized the means-ends conception of curriculum and argued that curriculum should be conceived as a political process for effecting a just environment. One of the major questions he would have the curriculum workers ask was, Does the present educational activity reflect the best that humans are capable of?[9]

Status of Curriculum Conceptions in Mid-1980s. In 1979, John Goodlad assessed his 1966 conceptual system for curriculum, a rational decision-making model for determining purposes and selecting and organizing learning opportunities. He found that the model or system provides a reasonably accurate identification of the elements of curriculum practice in complex settings such as the United States.[10] It does not, however, adequately reflect practices at different levels of decision making. Consequently, Goodlad and his associates suggest three modifications:

1. More attention be given to the personal and experiential as a decision-making level in the conceptual system. (This is partly in response to the work of the curriculum reconceptualists who see learners as potential generators and not mere passive recipients of curriculum.)
2. Values be recognized as playing a part in all curriculum decisions, not just stated as a guiding educational philosophy at the beginning of curriculum planning, as it was in the original conceptual scheme.
3. The sociopolitical interests of special groups—the political milieu—be recognized as bearing on each level of decision making.

[9]Dwayne Huebner, "Curriculum as a Field of Study," *Precedents and Promise in the Curriculum Field,* ed. Helen Robinson (New York: Teachers College Press, Teachers College, Columbia University, 1966): p. 107.

[10]John I. Goodlad and associates. *Curriculum Inquiry: The Study of Curriculum Practice* (New York: McGraw-Hill, 1979).

Incidentally, Goodlad sees a resurgence of interest in the classic curriculum questions, including organizational ones about scope, sequence, and integration.

Many theorists have lost faith in the ability of logical systems to solve curriculum problems. Some curriculum theorists are turning to aesthetic and personal dimensions. Dwayne Huebner would change curriculum language that now reveals a concern for effectiveness, objectives, and principles of learning (a language he thinks reflects a dated institution) to a language that will focus on different concerns. He wants a language that will illuminate economics and technical policies that affect education. For example: How much of the richness of the world is made available to the learner? He wants a language that will also direct attention to the learner's choice in subject matter. For example: How can we best allow the learner to draw on all the cultures of the world to create possibilities for the future? Note that Huebner's use of culture contrasts with the selection of curriculum content for its potential to serve the controlling social interests rather than the interests of the individual.[11]

Herbert Kliebard has proposed three possible ways of attacking the problem of conceptualization in the curriculum field. The first means of attack is the identification of critical and persistent questions that have characterized the field. Chapter 12 follows this suggestion. Second, Kliebard suggests regarding the field as a synoptic one in which the curriculum person brings perspectives from other fields to bear on school programs. This method means examining the more useful concepts of the economists, anthropologists, sociologists, and other specialists to see whether they can guide program development. Third, Kliebard suggests creating metaphors that might promise new directions and theoretical constructs. Instead of only using the metaphors that now dominate thinking in curriculum (for example, "production" with its technological implications and "growth" with its connotations of unfolding, readiness, and nurturing), we should experiment with alternative "root metaphors."

Kliebard points out how some social reconstructionists, such as Michael Apple and Jean Anyon, use the metaphors of culture as a form of capital.[12] Paulo Freire's use of the "banking" concept of education is another example. In the "banking" concept, education is an act of deposition in which the students are the depositories and the teacher is

[11]Dwayne Huebner, "Toward a Remaking of Curricular Language," in *Heightened Consciousness, Cultural Revolution, and Curriculum Theory,* ed. William Pinar (Berkeley: McCutchan, 1974), pp. 36-7.
[12]Herbert Kliebard, "Curriculum Theory as Metaphor," *Theory into Practice* 21, no. 1 (Winter 1982): 11-17.

the depositor. The teacher issues communiques and makes deposits, which the students passively receive, memorize, and repeat. These metaphors bring into focus what might otherwise be ignored—the unequal distribution of knowledge through the curriculum, the question of whose interests are served by an unequal distribution of cultural capital, and the static as opposed to the creative origin of knowledge.

Recently, Philip Taylor compared the kinds of metaphors in the educational texts of 1905, 1931, 1944, and 1968.[13] He found that in 1905 the *tabula rasa* or "blank slate" view of the child dominated; in 1931, the root metaphor emphasized curriculum as activity rather than facts to be stored; in 1944, the root metaphor "First the blade, and then the ear, then the full corn shall appear" stressed self motivation and the idea of stages in development; in 1968, children were characterized as "natural explorers," "agents of their own language." Further, the metaphors of 1905 tended to center on the teacher and have an explanatory, logical intent whereas the metaphors of 1968 were centered on the child and had a rhetorical and persuasive intent.

Currently, the field of curriculum is fragmented into several conceptual camps. In his 1978 map of the field, William Pinar discriminates among the following three groups, each holding a different view of what the field should be about.[14]

1. *Traditionalists.* Traditionalists, according to Pinar, value service to practitioners in the schools above all else. He names traditionalists such persons as Ralph Tyler, John McNeil, Daniel and Laurel Tanner, and Robert Zais. According to Pinar, service, defined as a response to the practical concern for curriculum matters, is more important to traditionalists than research or the development of theory. The close relationship between traditionalists and school teachers is said to prevent them from creating new ways of talking about curriculum which may in the future be far more fruitful than the present ways.
2. *Conceptual Empiricists.* These persons tend to be trained in social science and see service to practitioners as being subsequent to research. Their basic premise is that a scientific knowledge of human behavior, including curriculum, is possible. They argue that their research serves school practitioners and that by the

[13]Philip H. Taylor, "The Metaphor as a Source of Curriculum Knowledge," in *Conceptions of Curriculum Knowledge,* ed. Edmund Short (University Park: Pennsylvania State University, 1982).

[14]William Pinar, "Notes on the Curriculum Field 1978," *Educational Researcher* 7, no. 8 (September 1978): 5–12.

creation of a science of curriculum the traditional aspirations of the field can be realized. They differ from traditionalists by their allegiance to social science, rather than to practitioners and to "kids."

Decker Walker is named a conceptual empiricist and the following also seem to fit the category: George J. Posner, who explores the application of cognitive science to curriculum research and development; Richard E. Schutz, who applies programmatic research and development in the preparation of instructional materials; and Jerome Bruner, who uses theories of cognition and learning to select aspects of the world that are to be brought into classrooms. Pinar criticizes conceptual empiricists for producing only technical recommendations and principles based on static regularities that imply a subtle control of human behavior.

3. *Reconceptualists.* Their fundamental view is that an intellectual and cultural distance from curriculum practice is required for the present in order to develop more useful comprehensive critiques and theoretical programs. Currently, reconceptualists are preoccupied with a critique of the field—a field they believe is too immersed in practical, technical modes of understanding and action. The term *reconceptualist* is credited to the late James MacDonald, who sensed a need for reconceiving the fundamental concerns, questions, and priorities that give direction to curriculum as a field of inquiry. This task contrasts with both the prevailing intents of traditionalists, who view their task as giving guidance and prescriptive assistance to the practitioners, and the scientists, who pursue research on curriculum variables.

Reconceptualists include Michael Apple, who engages in ideological and social critique; Herbert Kliebard, who illuminates the shortcomings of curriculum as science through historical critique; and Dwayne Huebner, who exposes technological conception of curriculum through aesthetic critique. Pinar criticizes teaching by using a psychoanalytic method and devises means by which curriculum researchers can become conscious of their own participation in rigid social and psychological structures, and their complicity in the arrested intellectual development characteristic of American schooling. Pinar recommends a method of self-analysis, for example, by means of which learners can study their own responses to educational situations by (1) recalling and describing the past and then analyzing its psychic relation to the present; (2) describing one's imagined future and analyzing its relation to the present; and (3) placing this analytic understanding of one's education in its cultural and political context.

Daniel and Laurel Tanner have responded negatively to Pinar's map of the field.[15] They see the reconceptualists as radical critics rather than curriculum theorists. They also fault Pinar's notion of the need for an intellectual and cultural distance from school practitioners in order to develop a more comprehensive and theoretical program. Citing Dewey, the Tanners argue for "some kind of vital current between the field worker and the research worker." Without this flow, the latter is not able to judge the real scope of the problem being addressed. The Tanners also indicate how they think traditionalists and those representing empirical-analytical sciences have contributed to curriculum's body of concepts.

Replies to the Tanners, in turn, charge that they misunderstood what Pinar is saying. Reconstructionists, for example, are not repudiating research but do regard literary criticism, art history and criticism, philosophical inquiry, and historical analysis as research and as the forms from which reconceptualists' work is derived. Intellectual and cultural distancing only means "bracketing"—the suspension of judgments about things and events—a methodological tool to aid in judging the essence of the problem to be addressed.[16]

The Need for Studies of Curriculum

Status of Correlation Studies in 1969. Goodlad omitted any mention of studies during the review period that treated the effects of concurrent offerings. He did, however, call attention to the interest in problems of sequencing subject matters. Thus we can assume that curriculum knowledge increased very little in the areas of integration and correlation of subject matters. Instead, the period was marked by the separation of subjects and linear organizational plans within fields.

Status of Correlation Studies in Mid-1980s. The effect of correlating subject matter is currently of interest but there has been little research. This is true especially in connection with bilingual education. There is, for example, the issue of whether non-English-speaking children should be taught to read first in their native language before learning to read English. Practice is ahead of knowledge. Although bilingual programs are common, few studies have explored the effect of learning two languages simultaneously or the best ways to make transitions from

---

[15]Daniel Tanner and Laurel Tanner, "Emancipation from Research: The Reconceptualist Position," *Educational Research* 8, no. 6 (June 1977): 8–12.

[16]William F. Pinar, James H. Finkelstein, and C. Ray Williams, and Maxine Greene, "Letters to the Editor," *Educational Researcher* 8, no. 9 (October 1979): 6, 24–25.

one language to another. A notable exception is work in linguistics which suggests the importance of beginning initial instruction in a child's first language, switching at a later stage to instruction in the school language if the home language tends to be denigrated; but if the home language is highly valued, the second language is appropriate for use in initial instruction.[17] Similarly, research on the interrelationships of literature, language, composition, and popular culture lacks any unifying theory.

The growing concern for general education, for a more integrated view of knowledge, and a focus on larger social questions will create more efforts to correlate studies. Academic alliances are already being formed as sociologists, psychologists, biologists, and chemists seek answers to closely related questions. An emphasis on the interrelation of things through curriculum should invite inquiry about the effects of correlation. However, it is a false hope that curriculum developers can themselves effect an integration of knowledge.[18] Although curriculum scholars may encourage interdisciplinary approaches to a problem or area of interest, they are unlikely to integrate knowledge or synthesize concepts from various disciplines to create a set of new concepts.

With respect to administrative organizational planning, there is much discussion about the value of intensive or total immersion courses, which are taken one at a time, in place of traditional concurrent courses, which are taken three, four, or five at a time throughout the term. Some schools are experimenting with intensive courses during the one month of 4-1-4 plans. Yet, appallingly little research has been undertaken on the educational effects of either intensive or concurrent courses.

The Need for Studies of Sequence

Status of Studies Treating Sequence in 1969. The quest for the best arrangement of material in a field was very much alive in 1969. There were many experiments with different sequences in programmed and computer-based instruction. Robert Gagne's work stimulated several investigations to assess the effects of scrambled versus hierarchical orderings of learning tasks. The findings were mixed, indicating that increasing complexity is not always the best criterion for ordering material.

[17]Merrill Swain and James Cummins, "Bilingualism, Cognitive Functioning and Education," *Language Teaching and Linguistics* 12, no. 1 (January 1979): 4–18.
[18]Richard L. Derr, "A Note on Curriculum Integration," *Curriculum Inquiry* 11, no. 4 (1981): 387–392.

Status of Studies Treating Sequence in Mid-1980s. Current research is directed at methods for conducting inquiry into learning hierarchies. Richard White has proposed a rigorous model to overcome such shortcomings as small sample size, imprecise specification of component elements, improper placement of tests, and omission of instruction.[19] Models for sequential ordering are being expanded to take into account the cognitive capacities of learners.[20] The expanded models emphasize more the learner's point of view than a priori units based on subject matter analysis.

The Need for Analyzing Educational Objectives

Status of Taxonomical Analysis of Objectives in 1969. The pioneer taxonomy or classification of objectives in the cognitive domain was completed in 1956, and taxonomies in both psychomotor and affective realms were developed after 1969. Further, there was much research treating how best to refine educational objectives into precise behavioral objectives. Studies of the effects of behavioral objectives on learning were also common.

Status of Taxonomical Analysis of Objectives in Mid-1980s. The structural analysis of feelings, attitudes, and values has not kept up with similar research in the areas of mental abilities and personality. There is still interest in whether the levels of behavior given in taxonomies are cumulative or hierarchical. J. R. Calder and others, for example, found that in the *Taxonomy of Educational Objectives—Cognitive Domains,* the synthesis and evaluation of the categories did not depend on integration with lower-level behaviors.[21] In his critical review of taxonomies of educational objectives, Robert M. W. Travers faults the Bloom taxonomy for being chiefly an inventory of test items and not a taxonomy of cognitive processes.[22] He views Piaget's system, by which knowledge is classified in terms of formal properties, as a better potential basis for developing a taxonomy of cognitive processes. Piaget's framework has been used in a number of curriculum projects for analyzing learning activities in terms

[19]Richard T. White, "Research Into Learning Hierarchies," *Review of Educational Research* 43, no. 3 (Summer 1973): 361–75.

[20]Robbie Case, "Gearing the Demands of Instruction to the Development Capacities of the Learner," *Review of Educational Research* 45, no. 1 (Winter 1975): 59–87.

[21]J. R. Calder, "In the Cells of the 'Bloom Taxonomy'," *Journal of Curriculum Studies* 15, no. 3 (July-September 1983): 291–302.

[22]Robert M. W. Travers, "Taxonomies of Educational Objectives and Theories of Classification," *Educational Evaluation and Policy Analysis* 2, no. 2 (March-April 1980): 5–23.

of the logical operations they involve (Project SOAR at Xavier University of Louisiana, the STAR Program of Metropolitan State College at Denver, Project ADAPT at the University of Nebraska, and an elementary science program developed at the University of California, Berkeley).

Interest in instructional objectives has taken three directions. First, much attention is given to the rationale for such objectives. There are attempts to state their functions, such as to organize subject matter, to help learners organize their time, and to provide directions for learning. Second, there is much argument regarding the nature of behavioral objectives. Cognitive theorists believe that covert behavior can be stated in objectives and that overt behavior may be more important as an indicator of the covert behavior than as an important response in itself. Growing interest in the relations between subject matter and cognitive psychology has resulted in opposition to objectives that do not take into account changes in the student's cognitive processes as well as achievement in subject matter. Examples of cognitive processes are algorithms for division or problem-solving procedures.

Kenneth Strike and George Posner, for example, try to match cognitive states and processes with the logical and conceptual features which characterize organized subject matter. Posner has detailed a number of approaches specifying the cognitive structures and processes required to perform tasks.[23] Once these structures and processes are represented, curriculum planners can more adequately specify intended learning outcomes.

Third, proponents of behavioral objectives are attempting to overcome criticism about the triviality and proliferation of specific objectives. "Lists of objectives anatomize, not only subject matter, but teachers' thoughts about it, the patterns of instruction used to convey it, the organization of textbooks, and the analysis and construction of tests."[24] Proponents of objectives are trying to define domains of objectives and to find formats for stating domains that will be more useful for purposes such as test construction and classroom management than the narrow and numerous objectives found in classrooms today.

[23]Kenneth A. Strike and George J. Posner, "Epistemological Perspectives on Conceptions of Curriculum Organization and Learning," in *Review of Research in Education* 4, L. S. Schulman, ed. (Itasca, Ill.: F. E. Peacock, 1976): pp. 106–41; George J. Posner, "Tools for Curriculum Research and Development: Potential Contributions from Cognitive Science," *Curriculum Inquiry* 8, no. 4 (Winter 1978): 311–40.

[24]Joseph J. Schwab, "The Practical 4: Something for Curriculum Professors to Do," *Curriculum Inquiry* 13 (Fall 1983): 239–265.

The Need for Process-Product Research

Status of Process-Product Research in 1969. Process-product research attempts to relate instructional variables to learner achievement and the curriculum planning process to improved instruction and learning. Much process-product research between 1960 and 1969 dealt with instructional objectives. Most curriculum materials investigations dwelt on specific treatment variables associated with the materials (for example, organizers, relevant practice, knowledge of results, and prompts). Goodlad realized, however, that there were two problems with this research. The first was methodological. It was not always clear, for instance, what constituted the process or treatment, nor was it always established that the treatment had been carried out as stipulated. The second problem was theoretical. It was often difficult to know the significance of a small manageable process-product equation within some large frame of explanation.

Status of Process-Product Research in Mid-1980s. The methodological and theoretical problems of 1969 have not been resolved. They are, however, more widely recognized now. Research into instructional effectiveness by means of the input-output approach has not yielded consistent results. Background factors tend to dominate the findings. No single resource or variable is consistently shown to exert a powerful influence on learning. Perhaps one reason for this state of affairs is the emphasis on generalizations. Instead of making the search for generalizations the major priority, investigators should look for unique personal characteristics and uncontrolled events in situations. We should try to use generalizations only as working hypotheses and then look for clues to particular factors that might cause departures from the predicted effects. These factors might be *learner variables,* such as a learner's perceptions of the curriculum event, or a learner's cognitive style; *teacher variables,* such as a teacher's attitude toward the curriculum and the learners, or teacher pressure toward student conformity rather than toward independence; and *school* or *classroom ambient variables,* such as peer group interactions, morale, expectations, and consistency with home and community values.

As indicated in Chapter 8, work has expanded from concentration on isolated variables associated with effectiveness to include analyses of life in classrooms and from unambiguous tasks with certain answers to the study of tasks with several possible answers. This work has led to a recognition of the importance of (a) improving instructional materials which carry the major academic content and (b) attending to learning tasks which have the greatest consequences for the quality of academic work.

Two current models of the ways in which various features of schooling, including the curriculum, exert their effect are those proposed by the Swedish scholars Urban Dahllof and U.L.F. Lundgren, and by A. Harnischfeger and Dave Wiley.[25] Dahllof and Lundgren hypothesize that group achievement is a function of (1) general intelligence and initial achievement level; (2) the level of the objective; and (3) the time actually spent in learning. They draw attention to *frame factors*—the characteristics of the learning environment outside the control of the teacher and students. Frame factors include regulations of a legislative nature such as the duties of the teacher and the administrative apparatus and its policies, class size, the organization and objectives of the curriculum, the length of the school year, and the location of school buildings in the community. Harnischfeger and Wiley believe that all influences on pupil achievement must be mediated through a pupil's pursuits—seeing, looking, watching, hearing, listening, feeling, and touching. These pursuits control what and how one learns. The curriculum and the teacher both control and condition these pursuits but not the student's ultimate achievement.

FUTURE DIRECTIONS IN CURRICULUM THEORY

The best predictor of the future is present activity. We can predict at least two directions for curriculum theory because there are two kinds of theorists at work, the *soft* curricularists and *hard* curricularists. In the preface to *Curriculum Theorizing,* William Pinar says that 3 to 5 percent of curriculum workers are reconceptualists.[26] Their stated purpose is not to guide practitioners but to understand the internal and existential nature of the educational experience. They are called soft curricularists because they model themselves after those in the humanities, in history, religion, philosophy, and literary criticism, not the hard sciences. They include intuition and existence as sources of knowledge, not only the senses and reason. The hard curricularists follow a rational approach, relying on empirical data to justify means and a consistent philosophical position for validating ends proposed.

[25]U.L.F. Lundgren, "Frame Factors in Teaching," in *Curriculum and Instruction,* ed. Harry A. Giroux (Berkeley: McCutchan, 1981): pp. 197–209; A. Harnischfeger and David Wiley, "Teaching Learning Processes in Elementary Schools: A Synoptic View," *Curriculum Inquiry* 6, no. 1 (Fall 1976): 5–43.

[26]William Pinar, ed., *Curriculum Theorizing* (Berkeley: McCutchan, 1975).

The Soft Curricularists

The reconceptualists, or soft curricularists, do not study change in behavior or decision making in the classroom, but the meaning of temporality, transcendence, consciousness, and politics. Dwayne Huebner, for example, writes of temporality—existence in time—and the need for an awareness of history. He would mesh an individual's biography with the history of the individual's society so that the individual could realize his or her own potentiality for being.[27] Huebner challenges curriculum workers, for example, to present historical wisdom in a way that will be useful to particular individuals at different age levels.

For another example, we can look at Philip Phenix and his regard for transcendence as surpassing any certain state. As described in Chapter 1, transcendence suggests a curriculum that has regard for the uniqueness of the human personality and that is characterized by an atmosphere of freedom. Politics is very much in the minds of the soft curricularists. They are concerned about the political implications that might follow reconceptualization of curriculum theory and, in turn, curriculum development. They realize that the political climate does not now favor radical activities as it did in the 1960s, and they are divided about the best means for effecting social reconstruction. One group thinks it best to present what is known about the content of curriculum, stressing its racism, sexism, and classism. Another shifts from harsh criticism to ways of working. Advocacy groups such as the Children's Defense Fund are influencing legislation for children, improving organizations for the government of institutions, and becoming better acquainted with the knowledge from which new alternatives for schooling can come.[28]

The Hard Curricularists

The study of curricular phenomena by hard curricularists is undertaken for the immediate purpose of accurate description and for future prediction and control. Decker Walker, for example, a member of this group, has prepared a naturalistic model for curriculum development in order to illuminate facets of the curriculum development process.[29] The model is meant to be descriptive rather than prescriptive. Walker's naturalistic model assumes that the curriculum is developed in accordance with an

---

[27]Dwayne Huebner, "Curriculum as Concern for Man's Temporality," in *Curriculum Theorizing*, ed. William Pinar (Berkeley: McCutchan, 1975): pp. 237–50).

[28]*The Networker* 5, no. 1 (Fall 1983).

[29]Walker, "A Naturalistic Model."

idea or vision of what ought to be (a platform), and that a curriculum design consists of a number of decisions made in producing curriculum materials. The process by which beliefs and information are used to make these design decisions is called *deliberation*. The heart of the deliberation process is the justification of choices. Walker, as a hard curricularist, defines deliberation by logical, not social or psychological criteria. Empirical confirmations (data) are seen as a most persuasive basis for justification. Good decisions are those consistent with given platforms and available information, although a platform may be changed by the curriculum designer as the work progresses. A defensible set of objectives is the result of deliberations based on a platform. The purposes of the hard curricularist can be inferred from the five intended uses of the naturalistic model:

1. *To test propositions.* For example: Do curriculum-making groups with similar platforms conduct similar deliberations and produce similar designs and objectives?
2. *To make descriptive studies.* For example: How do the platforms of those in one subject field differ from those in other fields?
3. *To establish connections between design elements (curriculum variables) and learning outcomes.* For example: What is the effect of a specific design element on a given outcome?
4. *To formulate new curriculum questions.* For example: What kinds of grounds should be given greater weight in justifying decisions during deliberation?
5. *To identify questions in curriculum making that will be of interest to colleagues in other fields.* For example: Just as the curriculum practitioners' treatment of discovery learning led to renewed interest in this topic by psychologists, might not other matters of importance to noncurricularists come to light through study of platforms and deliberations?

Another hard curricularist is Mauritz Johnson.[30] Johnson sees the definition of curriculum and instruction as a directive force for the theorist. He distinguishes among curriculum, the source of curriculum, and the relation of curriculum to instruction. According to Johnson, a curriculum is the result of a curriculum development system—a structured series of intended outcomes. A curriculum is the result of curriculum development which occurs as cultural content is selected and ordered. Johnson is interested in the best way of selecting cultural content within particular realms or domains (such as vocational and general education),

[30]Mauritz Johnson, Jr., "Definitions and Models of Curriculum Theory," in *Curriculum and Instruction,* ed. Henry A. Girout (Berkeley: McCutchan, 1981), 69–86.

but has not been very successful in clarifying the criteria or in devising procedures for using them.

Johnson's position on the issue of whether objectives should follow or precede instruction is clear. He believes that curriculum should guide instruction. The restrictions of curriculum should be minimal, however, in order to allow flexibility in instructional sequencing. Johnson believes that a definition of instruction must encompass all training and instructional situations and all domains of outcomes for all kinds of learners. He views learning experiences as the instructional route to intended outcomes and holds that such experiences must have both active (what the learner is to do) and substantive components (what content is to be involved).

For Johnson, the curriculum restricts but does not prescribe the content and form of instructional activity. It influences instruction primarily through the mediation of an instructional plan. A curriculum does not guide all aspects of instruction or control for the spontaneity and effectiveness of discourse in the instructional act. Although curriculum does not specify the means of evaluation, it furnishes the criteria for evaluating instructional outcomes.

Presumably the purpose of Johnson's conceptualization is the clarification of the different components in a system. Improvement can then be enhanced by focusing on the components that are deficient, whether instructional techniques, materials, instructional plans, curriculum ordering, or curriculum selection. A soft curricularist might look at the language Johnson uses: "system," "detailed control tactics," "well-established rules," "review by experts," "results." The critic would assume that this technological and military-like talk with its means-ends, cause-effect structure is unlikely to answer a people's need for liberating activities.

DIRECTIONS IN CURRICULUM RESEARCH

General frameworks and specific questions for guiding inquiry in the field of curriculum have been given in prior paragraphs describing the state of the field and the trends in theoretical curriculum research. There are, however, five specific kinds of inquiry likely to be pursued by productive scholars and practitioners.

Comprehensive Curriculum Inquiry

Decker Walker believes there are only five questions to be addressed by curricularists:

1. What are the significant features of a given curriculum?
2. What are the personal and social consequences of a given curriculum feature?
3. What accounts for stability and change in curriculum features?
4. What accounts for people's judgments of the merit or worth of various curriculum features?
5. What sorts of curriculum features ought to be included in a curriculum intended for a certain purpose in a situation?

The last question requires a normative rather than an empirical answer.

Walker's questions reflect his assumption that the curriculum is a practical field of study. It is expected to make a difference in someone's learning. Also, the meaning of "curriculum feature" is vague in recognition of the field's lack of consensus on conceptions of curriculum. Hence, curriculum workers of different persuasions may define curriculum features according to their own purposes.[31]

Barry Franklin, for example, studied the social efficiency movement as a significant feature in curriculum.[32] He examined the social efficiency movement in the Minneapolis school systems from 1917 to 1950. The evidence Franklin obtained supported the claim that ideas of efficiency dominated policymaking in the system. However, he failed to find that efficiency-minded educators used the curriculum to achieve inequalitarian aims. In fact, in terms of actual impact on the practice in the schools, the curriculum ideas of those in the social efficiency movement was slight. The curriculum differentiations were minor and the changes in course content minimal.

Synoptic Activity as Curriculum Inquiry

As we mentioned previously, Herbert Kliebard has speculated that one direction for the curriculum field is to bring together widely separated fields into a larger common area. The curriculum person's competence may lie, not in unearthing new knowledge, but in putting together many of the findings from other disciplines. The curriculum expert can take a number of narrow perspectives and unite them by applying them in the development of school programs that will help students learn things that will be helpful to them and to society. The kinds of research borrowing that are useful in curriculum synoptic activity are:

---

[31]Decker Walker, "What are the Problems Curricularists Ought to Study?" *Curriculum Theory Network* 4, nos. 2–3 (1974): 217–18.
[32]Barry M. Franklin, "The Social Efficiency Movement Reconsidered: Curriculum Change in Minneapolis, 1917–50," *Curriculum Inquiry* 12, no. 1 (Spring 1982): 9–34.

1. *Concepts.* There are more concepts, such as concepts of motivation (locus of control), and concepts of learning (learned helplessness), than anything else that can be used. Developers of new courses should use such concepts in their developmental efforts.
2. *Generalizations.* There is growing concern that few generalizations have broad applicability. Generalizations depend on conditions that may not be present in particular school settings.
3. *Facts.* General facts are often less useful than generalizations. Particular facts have to be collected for each situation.
4. *Methods.* Problem-solving procedures can be borrowed from disciplines and applied to curriculum problems. For example, the anthropologist's use of naturalistic observation is currently applied in studies of classrooms.
5. *Values and Attitudes.* A commitment to truth, to the facts and an active skepticism are needed to solve our real dilemmas.

Examples of synoptic activity in curriculum, illustrating the contributions of different subject matter fields to curriculum development are seen in: *borrowings from linguistics* with its ideas of linguistic confluence (the concept of social linguistic confluence, the ability to use language appropriate to a context, was used as content in a bilingual program); *borrowings from social psychology* with its concepts about peer group learning in the selection of learning opportunities; *borrowings from personality psychology* with its notion of human needs and the self, particularly in designing curriculum for moral development; *borrowings from sociology* with its concepts of social class and social mobility; and *borrowings from the psychology of learning* with its concepts and findings about the learning process and their implications for curriculum and instruction. Synoptic activity is predicated on our willingness to question what our curriculum is doing and what we know about the changes we propose. It means using research from many sources, including historical research, in guiding our efforts.

Conceptualization as Curriculum Inquiry

As indicated previously, there is much interest in conceptualization in the curriculum field. Louise Tyler, for instance, adds another level to the societal, institutional, and classroom levels of curriculum decision by specifying a *personal* level and detailing the nature of personal decision making. She has, for example, contrasted an aspect of curriculum decision making at the four levels in terms of psychoanalytic constructs, such as *transference* (projecting upon another person the attitudes and responses attached to an emotionally significant person), indicating and explaining the dimensions of thought and feeling a student might experience in responding to learning situations and to the problem of revealing what has been learned.[33]

The opportunities for inquiry at the level of the personal domain are great. There is a need to know, for instance, about the meaning of various subjects for students at different developmental levels, the meaning of school itself for students, the nature of students' fear in the school setting, the function of their jokes and humor, and the meaning of their play.

Other curriculum researchers are trying to conceptualize curriculum to take into account the *inward* experience of students reacting to their educational environment. George Willis, for example, is grappling with speculative, analytic, and empirical studies in an effort to discover how students develop meaning from their educational environment and how these environments can enhance the quality of experience for the individual.[34]

Signs indicate that research in curriculum will center on new approaches to curriculum development for the teaching of nonprocedural tasks.[35] The need for a curriculum that attempts to teach intellectual tasks involving understanding and higher level cognitive processes has been mentioned previously. Most curriculum development approaches—especially competency-based models—assume that tasks are basically procedural and that the tasks can be broken down into elements which, when practiced, will yield mastery.

Alternative approaches have been suggested. James Martin and Margaret Uguroglu, for example, address the problem of teaching bodies of knowledge which do not have certain answers or specified educational results.[36] They offer a design approach by which groups of learners generate solutions to a problem. Students define the problem by determining the purposes to be achieved and proposing a unique solution—often one that may not be within the framework of the school as a social organization. There must be criteria for the solution, however. The solution must be cost effective and maintain human values.

[33]Louise L. Tyler and John Goodlad, "The Personal Domain: Curricular Meaning," in *Curricular Inquiry* (New York: McGraw-Hill, 1979): pp. 191–209.

[34]George Willis, "Creating Curriculum Knowledge From Students' Phenomenologies," in *Conceptions of Curriculum Knowledge*, ed. Edmund Short (University Park: Penn State University, 1982): pp. 45–49.

[35]Gary A. Klein, "Curriculum Development versus Education," *Teachers College Record* 84, no. 4 (Summer 1983): 821–36.

[36]James L. Martin and Margaret E. Uguroglu, "Building Curricula When You Don't Have the Answer" (Paper presented at the annual meeting of the American Educational Research Association, New York City, 1982).

Peter Lemish also has addressed curriculum development in response to uncertainty.[37] His "praxis process" for curriculum development involves posing problems which challenge the apparent order in the school and classroom. Teachers reflect upon the assumptions, values, and meanings of the activities found in their educational setting. The process involves teachers in critical inquiry; they question, seek contradictions and assess the consequences of their situation, leading to better understanding of themselves, students, subject matter, and potentials for change.

Qualitative Inquiry in School Settings

In the past few years, curriculum inquirers have placed themselves in direct and continuous contact with the objects of curriculum investigation—instructional materials, classroom interactions, and their meanings for learners. Often these investigators use ethnographic methods. Basic to this kind of inquiry is the nature of the interpretations given to classroom observations. Gail McCutcheon has illustrated how researchers construct meaning by relating their knowledge to the observations made.[38] McCutcheon recognizes that many qualitative researchers use a phenomenological approach. They interpret events in light of the meanings participants make of those events. Others use critical science—such as a Marxist orientation—and interpret events in light of wider considerations. McCutcheon offers the example of the influence of a researcher's orientation on inquiry by examining three approaches to the study of the 42-minute period. A technologist concerned with achievement and teaching effectiveness might approach the situation by considering the time spent on tasks within the 42 minutes; a phenomenologist might wonder what meaning 42-minute periods have for participants; a critical scientist might ask about the origin of 42-minute periods and how such time affects what students learn or how the time allocation denies some students access to knowledge, thereby producing social injustice.

McCutcheon refers to three ways in which interpretations are made. The researcher may look for patterns in the observations. There may be

[37]Peter Lemish, "The Technical Approach and the Praxis Orientation to Curriculum Development" (Paper presented at the annual meeting of the American Educational Research Association, New York City, 1982).

[38]Michael V. Belok and Nelson Hagerson, eds., "Naturalistic Research Paradigms," *Review Journal of Philosophy and Social Science* 7, nos. 1 and 2 (1982); Gail McCutcheon, "On the Interpretation of Classroom Observations," *Educational Researcher* 10, no. 5 (May 1981): 5–10.

an unconscious order in classroom practices (raising hands, asking questions, assigning projects, grading responses). Observations may also be interpreted for their social meanings. What, for instance, does the students' movement of their heads mean? Boredom? Agreement? Trying to please the teacher? Fatigue? Social meanings may be interpreted by asking the teacher or students to justify an action or to describe what a particular statement *really* meant. In a third type of interpretation, the facts of a classroom are related to a theory. For example, they might be related to psychological theories of learning, to a historical movement or theme, to a particular educational philosophy, or to a theory of social classes.

The validity of interpretations depends on the reasoning used in arriving at the interpretation, the amount of evidence that supports the interpretation, and the extent to which the interpretation seems to fit with other knowledge of the real world. How far can one generalize from a single case study? The answer is similar to how far one can accept truths in great literature. It rests on the assumption that others can apply the findings to their own situation.

Action Research as Curriculum Inquiry

In action research practitioners put the findings of research into effect in order to resolve their own areas of need. Practitioners use action research in attempting to study their problems systematically. The value of such research is not determined by the discovery of scientific laws or generalizations but by whether or not the application leads to improvement in practice.

In the mid-1950s, teachers began using action research to improve their curricula. Gordon MacKenzie, Stephen Corey, and Hilda Taba were among those curriculum specialists who involved teachers in the research process. Teachers under their direction accumulated evidence to define their problems, drew on experience and knowledge to form action hypotheses to improve the situation of their daily work, tested promising procedures, and accumulated evidence of their effectiveness. The rationale and technical procedures for conducting such research is still available from several sources.[39]

Three forces aborted the growth of action research. First, the academic

[39]ASCD, *Research for Curriculum Development* (Washington, D.C.: ASCD, 1957); Stephen M. Corey, *Action Research to Improve School Practice* (New York: Teachers College, Columbia University, 1953).

curriculum reform of the 1960s put little emphasis on local development of curriculum. Standardization was prized over uniqueness. Second, educational researchers in universities, who in the 1950s might have been willing to work with teachers in curriculum inquiry, found themselves in the 1960s attending instead to the interests of government agencies that were funding certain kinds of research. Third, many persons in the 1960s believed that problems of curriculum and instruction would best be resolved by the discovery and application of generalizations and laws of learning, not by individual teachers in unique situations.

Currently, there is a return to the recognition that teachers (as well as students and persons who are not directly involved in the school) are theorists and researchers in their own right. There are signs of a shift of responsibility for curriculum development from colleges and laboratories to classrooms and communities. We can expect again to see scholarly efforts aimed at helping teachers rather than at the production of research for fellow scholars.

The curriculum worker who is interested in trying to coordinate the learner, subject matter, teacher, and total environment would find action research literature of the 1950s useful. Important, too, is John Dewey's advice about how knowledge can enter the heart, head, and hands of educators. In *Sources of a Science of Education,* Dewey made these points.[40]

1. An inquirer can repeat the research of another, to confirm or discredit it. Moreover, by using this technique the inquirer discovers new problems and new investigations that refine old procedures and lead to new and better ones.
2. No conclusion of scientific research can be converted into an immediate rule for educators. Educational practice contains many conditions and factors that are not included in the scientific finding.
3. Although scientific findings should not be used as a rule of action, they can help teachers be alert to discover certain factors that would otherwise be unnoticed and to interpret something that would otherwise be misunderstood.
4. The practitioner who knows a science (a system) can see more possibilities and opportunities, and has a wide range of alternatives to select from in dealing with individual situations.
5. In education, practice should form the problems of inquiry. The

[40]John Dewey, *The Sources of a Science of Education* (New York: Horace Liveright, 1929).

worth of a scientific finding is only shown when it serves an educational purpose, and whether it really serves or not can only be
found in practice.

6. Research persons connected with school systems may be too close
to the practical problems and the university professor too far
away from them to secure the best results.

7. Problems that require treatment arise in relations with students.
Consequently, it is impossible to see how there can be an adequate investigation unless teachers actively participate.

Perhaps the most eloquent argument for action research as a form of
curriculum inquiry is found in John Dewey's answer to the question of
how educational objectives are to be determined. He thought it false to
say that social conditions, science, or the subject matter of any field could
determine objectives. He conceived education as a process of discovering
what values are worthwhile and to be pursued as objectives.

> To see what is going on and to observe the results of what goes on so as to
> see their future consequences in the process of growth, and so on
> indefinitely, is the only way in which the value of what takes place can be
> judged. To look at some outside source to provide aims is to fail to know
> what education is as an ongoing process....
> Knowledge of the objectives which society actually strives for and the
> consequences actually attained may be had in some measure through a
> study of the social sciences. This knowledge may render educators more
> circumspect, more critical, as to what they are doing. It may inspire better
> insight into what is going on here and now in the home or school; it may
> enable teachers and parents to look farther ahead and judge on the basis
> of consequences in a longer course of development. But it must operate
> through their own ideas, plannings, observations, judgments. Otherwise
> it is not *educational* science at all, but merely so much sociological informa-
> tion.[41]

CONCLUDING COMMENTS

In this chapter, the state of the curriculum field was appraised by
reviewing the status of curriculum research in six crucial areas. Curriculum theory is divided among traditionalists, scientists, and reconceptualists. There is concern about a lack of common ground of professional
action and responsibility. The status of conceptual systems for identifying

[41]Dewey, *The Sources of a Science of Education*, pp. 74–76.

major curriculum questions is giving more attention to the role of the learner as a decision maker in curriculum, the impact of social political forces in curriculum making, and curriculum criticism as a mode of inquiry in its own right. Although there has been little research in correlated studies, much activity is attempting to show how best to arrange material for effective learning. Work in educational objectives, which has dominated much of curriculum thought and practice, is now being extended to how to construct tests that will reveal reasons for the learner's inability to utilize knowledge and the relation between the content objectives and the cognitive processes and structure that underlie competent performance.

With respect to the methodological and theoretical problems associated with process-product research, there are two apparently conflicting trends: (1) acceptance of opportunity to learn and time in instruction as the key variables in designing means to *minimal* ends and (2) recognition that no single variable will consistently exert a powerful or predictable influence on student outcomes.

Future directions in curriculum theory promise to be fruitful. The soft curricularists are drawing our attention to both the political and moral aspects of curriculum making. The hard curricularists have posed specific propositions to be tested that will greatly contribute to our understanding of curriculum making as a process. Anyone wishing to do research in the curriculum field should be greatly helped by the guidance of those advocating comprehensive curriculum inquiry, synoptic activity, conceptualization, and qualitative research, including action research. The evidence suggests that the curriculum field is an exciting one.

QUESTIONS

1. How are the categories of traditionalist, conceptual empiricist, and reconceptualist related to humanistic, academic, technological, and social reconstructionist conceptions of curriculum? Are reconceptualists contributing to both humanistic and social reconstructionist curriculum? In what way are conceptual empiricists influencing technological and academic curriculum?

2. In which of the six curriculum concerns used to appraise the status of curriculum research is there the least progress? What might account for the difference in progress? Do all the concerns or problems have solutions?

3. The classroom teacher in the mid 1980s is likely to feel pressure to help

design curriculum and instruction. Which of the research directions in this chapter do you think will be of greatest help to the teacher in responding to this pressure?

4. Give examples of the language (metaphors) used in your discussions of curriculum. Characterize this language by its style, imagery, and what it implies about the learners, knowledge, or other educational views. What consequences might the use of this language have in your treatment of problems in curriculum inquiry?

5. Do you regard synoptic activity, qualitative research, and conceptualization as mutually exclusive areas of research? Why or why not?

6. Donald Chipley at Pennsylvania State University has identified three basic reasons for undertaking curriculum research. One of these purposes is to make an inventory of the content that is offered and the resources that are invested in particular educational developments. Another purpose is personal curiosity. An investigator has an interest in exploring new ideas and extending generalizable knowledge about curriculum relationships. The third purpose is decision making. One assesses various curriculum alternatives in order to make more rational decision in particular situations. Which of these motives is closest to your own?

SELECTED REFERENCES

Belak, Michael V. and Hagerson, Nelson, eds. "Naturalistic Research Paradigms." *Review Journal of Philosophy and Social Science* 7, nos. 1 and 2 (1982).

Goodlad, John I. and associates. *Curriculum Inquiry: The Study of Curriculum Practice.* New York: McGraw-Hill, 1979.

Pinar, William. "Notes on the Curriculum Field 1978." *Educational Researcher* 7, no. 8 (September 1978): 5–12.

Reid, William A. *Thinking About the Curriculum.* Boston: Routledge & Kegan Paul, 1978.

Index